I0348072

The Lesser Of 2(00) Evils

24+ months of & from within 24/7
Depersonalization/Derealization
a Memoir (of Long Covid?)

like a Metaverse mask
you never put on
yet can't ever take off

S. D. SELLES

RED PENGUIN Books

Published by Red Penguin Books

Bellerose Village, New York

ISBN

Print 978-1-63777-687-2

Digital 978-1-63777-676-6

I dedicate this book to my Dadd.
(August 6th 1947 - December 4th 2024)

Adored & Adoring
Husband,Brother,Father,
Vietnam Navy Veteran
Survivor of the Forestal Fire
(USS Forrestal CVA-59)

...and our family's hero forever.

It is with ever-grave regret, that I fell short to work fast enough to fulfill what seemed to be/what I sensed to be/what I could tell, was my dadd's dying wish (what he wanted so bad) ...
(to) see this book finished in time to reach his hands. May it find his spirit (now.)

-From Wednesdays "child of woe" turned warrior…the pen is mightier than the tourniquet.

(5/10/21 at 9:08pm)

*this photo has been edited.

Psychiatrist's quote

My psychiatrist's clinical assessment of my symptomatology.

"A significant component of the syndrome appears to have been aberrant recruitment of neural pathways broader than classical auditory-visual synesthesia, including somatic sensory experiences that are amplified with anxiety such as head pressure, nausea, muscle tightness, and some motor recruitment as well, such as involuntary hand movements."

Neurologist's quote

My neurologist's clinical assessment of my symptomatology.

"Sensory disturbances."

Being that various respective iterations/strains of the Covid virus, tended to manifest,infest and affect individuals in different and varying degrees of Long Covid symptoms, severities and complications...

so that people might gain a deeper understanding of, context and point of reference for my personal experience with

*a presumptive case of COVID-19

I have decided it would be of unique interest to share that of all the bodily organs it is exclusively my brain that was impacted. of all the bodily systems it is solely, chronically and quite diffusely my neurology that went under attack. the pandemics early variant era (of 2020/2021) is that of what siege this warfare (survivor) memoir speaks to.

* A presumptive case of COVID-19 is a case where a patient's medical record documentation supports a diagnosis of COVID-19, even if the patient does not have a positive in vitro diagnostic test result in his or her medical record. (hrsa.gov)

PART ONE

Ligaments, Appendages & Extremities of (A Whole Separate) Entity

THE TRUE NATURE OF THE WRITER: AN ESSENTIAL DISCLAIMER

apologies to anyone who is in the book that doesn't want to be. Apologies to anyone who is not in the book that would've wanted to be.

I once heard it said that the best writing you can do...

is to write like nobody is ever going to read it.

(Well, I did that (and/so) don't hate me for it.)

Depersonalization/derealization makes it impossible to do anything BUT that !

I only ask for the grace of your awareness, acceptance and forgivance

perspective and perception of/from a neurologically sickly perspective and perception

The accounts of anger and other(wise)(difficult and potentially triggering) unpleasant(ries) material you are about to read in no way represents or reflects the true nature of the writer/S.D. Selles . But gives an intimate look at the world/at life from the (altered) perspective and perception of (one person's battle with/of) sudden onset neurological sickness/illness ... /

neurologically sickly / sickly neurologically / neuro-psychiatric illness/sickness .

I give you my/ I regale you with,

I reveal /

(Courageous, brave and at times brazen,) I bravely choose to not conceal my 200 evils with the intention and hope that by (vulnerably) baring such controversial (and otherwise unpleasant) XemotionsX /expressions/disclosures/utterances/divulgences, the biggest gravest juxtaposition will be *seen*and heard* /shown/revealed/evident/clear&present/

conveyed/communicated/*articulated* ,

from what you read *and*/to, who you meet; I am not my 200 evils. In effect impressing upon readers and raising awareness to people at large, just how much neurological sickness/illness can impact and hijack ones personality/humanity/humanness.

I

AM

NOT

MY

200

EVILS.

Like Susannah Cahalan of memoir "Brain on Fire", was fortunate and blessed enough to receive in her eventuality, I ask only for the Grace of your awareness, acceptance and forgiveness.

AUTHOR'S NOTE

- XA file that is a sample chapter from my memoir that I have written through and about this entire horrific sickness. X

(As my memoir was written from within the depths of my painful neurological state there is an element of my cognitive disarray that is evident in my writing . While to a degree this may have the immersive effect on a reader of making them feel like what I went through is palpable to them,

I encourage

Whatever changes (no matter how large or how small), an editor would want to make, for I embrace that of which literary professionals see fit to make this book the very best it can be for readers.

-XThere are a few things I'm going to tell you so as for you to keep them in mind...X

**When I was writing my memoir I was too

Neuro-cognitive sick at the time to where it was terribly difficult for me to organize my thoughts. Making lists and notes sections in various places within the chapters (for me to constantly be able to refer to) , was what made it possible for me to articulate my journey and get my story written, at all.**

Besides the intention of capturing everything of my experience in its/to be in its most raw form/rawest of form (and discovering/learning) that as I went along, it/writing in real time, was also helping me/becoming a part of how I process (everything). (Furthermore) Writing real time in journal/diary style was the only way I could as memory/knowledge/wherewithal of what I wanted to write about wasnt information I could retain (from day to day/into the next day) (mush) past/beyond the immediacy of it/ that it, was happening/ taking place .(in retrospect) Having written real time has proved/proven to have been important/integral, as when I try to (look back on) reflect upon and/, recount (and look back on) (now), what I went through (then) , I hit a wall called repression... and it is the best

trauma "impact play " I have ever known.

|--|

Whatever changes (no matter how large or how small), your editors would want to make, I am going to be receptive to and grateful for,

as I embrace whatever your literary/editorial team/etc. sees fit to make this book the very best it can be for readers . And I believe we can be a strong team in getting it there.

- A file that is a sample chapter from my memoir that I have written through and about this entire horrific sickness.

(As my memoir was written from within the depths of my painful neurological state there is an element of my cognitive disarray that is evident in my writing . While to a degree this may have the immersive effect on a reader of making them feel like what I went through is palpable to them,

I encourage

Whatever changes (no matter how large or how small), an editor would want to make, for I embrace that of which literary professionals see fit to make this book the very best it can be for readers..

In addition to dissociative depersonalization/derealization(DPDR) , other personal topics and themes explored and woven into my memoir aimed to destigmatize, humanize and raise awareness include but are not limited to...The long term impact and effects in adulthood of being bullied through youth,

and at the hands of a trusted lover and on the knees of (a)psychosexual processing...healing (that) trauma.

F42.3 (ICD-10) / DSM-5 300.3, obsessive compulsive disorder, HSV2, Emetophobia/Aeronausiphobia, bisexuality and being of a sexual attraction fluidity as well as what it is to mentally/emotionally contend with and need to make peace with, a Birthright of last living of family of origin/creation.

———————-

Xto where it was terribly difficult for me to organize my thoughts.X

!**Making lists and notes sections in various places within the chapters (for me to constantly be able to refer to) , was what made it possible for me to articulate my journey and get my story written,at all.**!

As my memoir was written (about but what's more) from within the depths of a painful/suffering neurological (neuropsychiatric/nuerocognitive) state

Xthere is an element of my cognitive disarray that is evident in my writing (style.) (While to a degree) this may have/may this have, the immersive effect on a reader of making them feel like what I went through is palpable to them,X

**(This is evident in) the unconventional writing style (that) reflects the/my cognitive disarray (of my constitution) through it all. and may have / may it/this have the immersive effect on readers of making them/*it* feel like what I went through is palpable , to them . **

-disjointed

-non-cohesive

-incoherent

-steam of consciousness

|————————————-|

Authors note Final product ...

[[At the helm of the hell that befell me may or may not be a long-covid origin .]]

As my memoir was written (about but what's more) from within the depths of an unthinkable and insufferable neurological (neuropsychiatric/nuerocognitive) state

**(This is evident in) the unconventional writing style (that) reflects *the* /my cognitive disarray (of my constitution) through it all. and may have / may it/this have the immersive effect on readers of making them/*it* feel like what I went through is palpable , to them . **

[[At the helm of the hell that befell me may or may not be a long-covid origin .]]

^ ? put this somewhere in the author's note, but where ? ...

At 40 years old, I earnestly don't take anything for granted in life now after what I've endured in these past 2+ years. I no longer even see executive function of bodily systems as a given anymore, but a gift, as for a time, mine was (grossly) compromised.

PITCH

So,

Just imagine for 37 years your neurological functioning

sensory processing has gone off without a hitch then all in an instant you have difficulty knowing how to sign your own name. You're at a loss for how to form facial expressions. There has been A brain glitch in which 24/7 for 12+ months your entire sensorium is about to be wrought with a symptomatology consisting of tactile, auditory and visual disturbance distortion so acute that the daily interaction with common everyday objects feels like razor blades raking over your nerve endings (Gone over with a fine-toothed comb that's been made into a shank.) Like a physiologically incompatible organ donor it's as though your body is rejecting its own nervous system.

and due to a partial catatonic like state you are so limited to successfully voice yourself so as to partake in common everyday convos.

with no way to verbally fully communicate all that you have half the mind to and all that you are suffering through

You are like an active voice behind soundproof walling that is your physical form.

Compounded with the aforementioned is an emotional disruption; abrupt break in the feedback loop of the limbic system causing the riddance of all ability to feel the cumulative years of love for and from...everyone .

Rendered a choking hazard from brain signals cutting in and out for chewing and swallowing food

The plight that you are in is a state of sustained and suspended dissociative derealization and depersonalization (with somatic, Pan-anxious features and a crippling form of synesthesia .)

XLike a virtual reality headset you never

put on yet can't ever take off X

(Like a metaverse mask you never put on yet can't ever take off. Like dentistry sweet air/nitrous oxide you never were given yet can't ever come down from. Like an alcoholic drink you never consumed yet can't ever sober up from .

Like psychedelic drugs you never took yet are stuck in a bad trip of.

Like a toothpaste-spatter, smattered bathroom mirror that doesn't matter bc you aren't in it anyway .)

and with no preexisting history of self-harm ideation... your everyday living is both so confusing and excruciating you're romanticizing suicide.

This manuscript is my write or die

for as a cathartic expression of

self-preservation I've written an insightful, immersive, introspective and interoceptive memoir of this entire unthinkable sickness.

I deeply beseech you as I profoundly need you to help me get my all-important neurological anomaly survival and transformation story onto the shelves of bookstores and into the lives of those in need of the voice I speak.

In closing I am but micro-dosing you with some of the common everyday objects that pained me so gravely (that it felt like enough to warrant an assisted suicide; medically induced... the lesser of 200 evils .

or

that it felt like enough to warrant a/an (medically induced) (assisted) suicide; the lesser of 200 evils.

|————————————————————————|

X XIn closing I am but micro-dosing you with some of the common everyday objects that pained me so gravely (that it felt like enough to warrantX an assisted suicide; the lesser of 200 evils). X

-Like a metaverse mask

—————————-

Common everyday objects

and due to a/your/my partial catatonic like state (so) confusing to interact with

and due to a/your/my partial catatonic like state I was (so) limited to successfully (voice) share and converse/voice ; to partake, in common everyday convos.

with no way to verbally communicate all that I had half the mind to,

(I was like an active voice behind (the) soundproof walling of/that was, my body/my physical form ...)

PITCH PICTURES

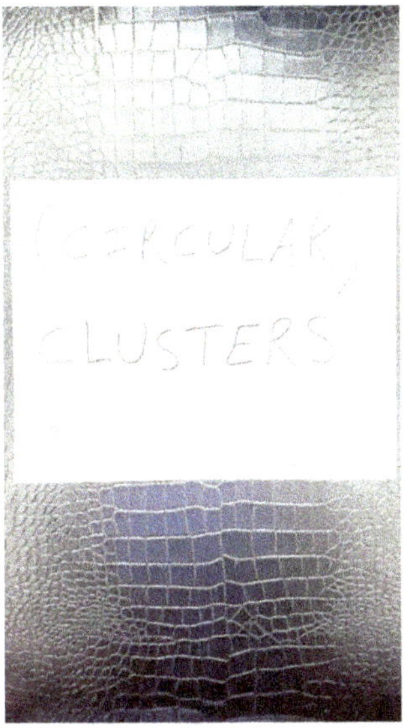

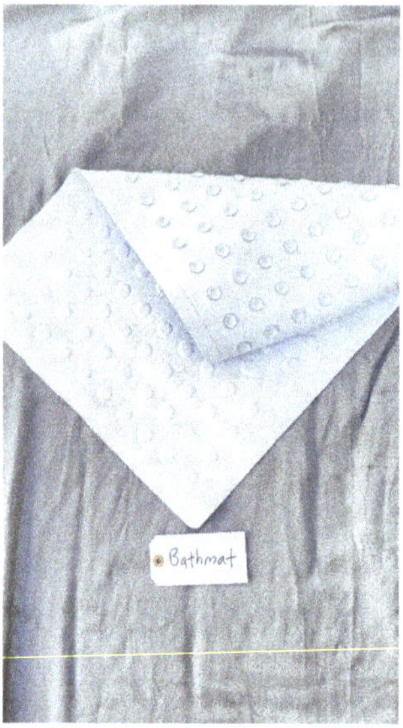
Bathmat

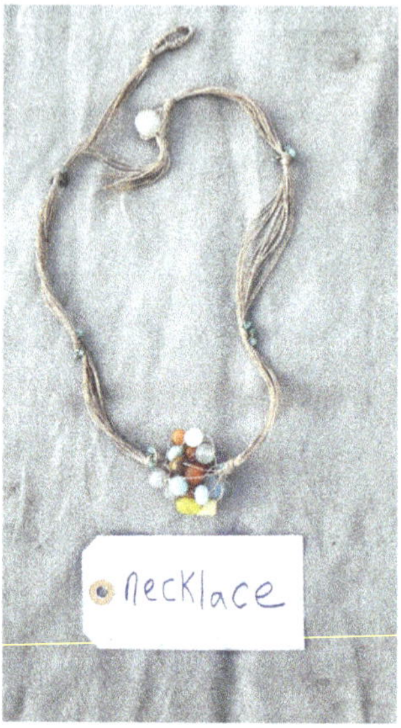
necklace

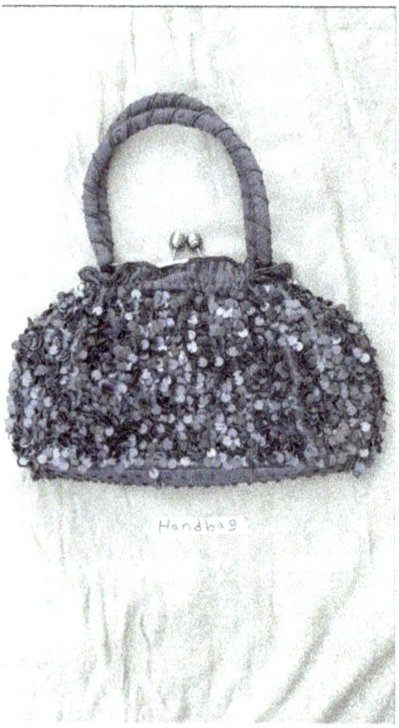
Handbag

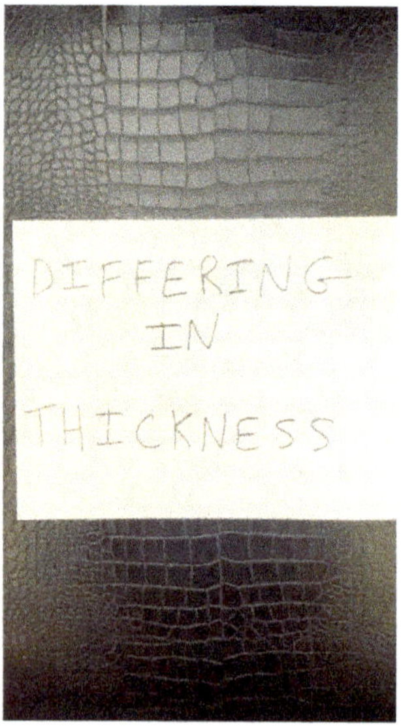
DIFFERING
IN
THICKNESS

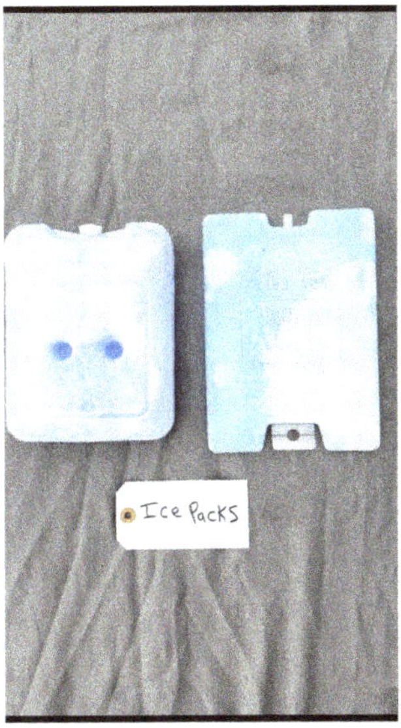
Ice Packs
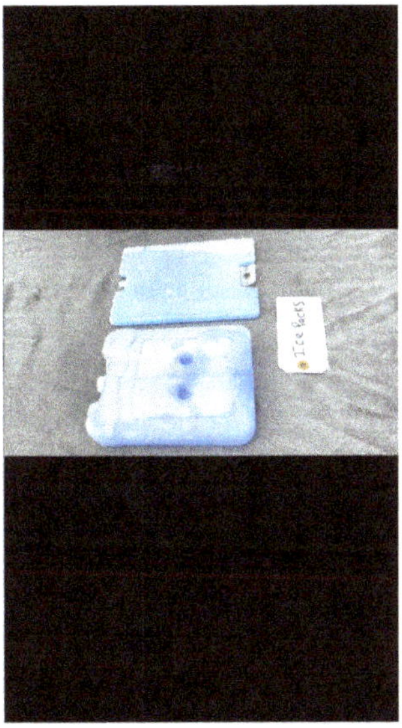
Ice Packs
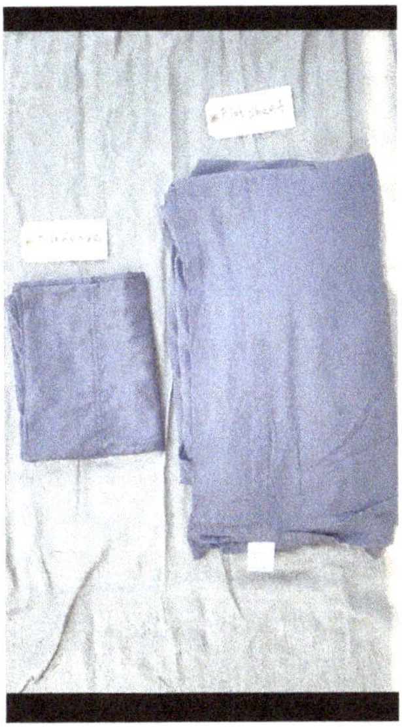
Flat sheet
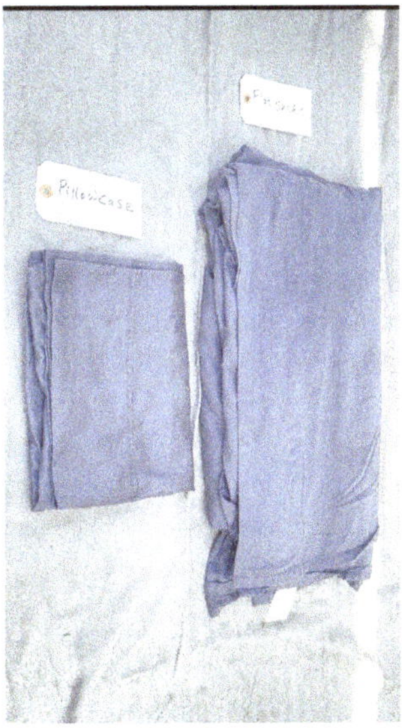
Pillowcase

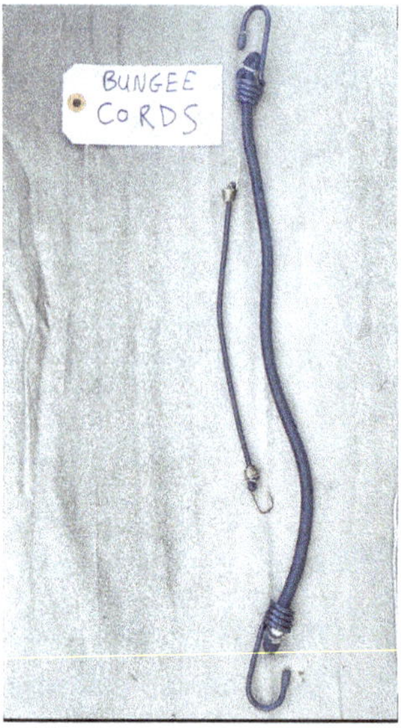
BUNGEE CORDS

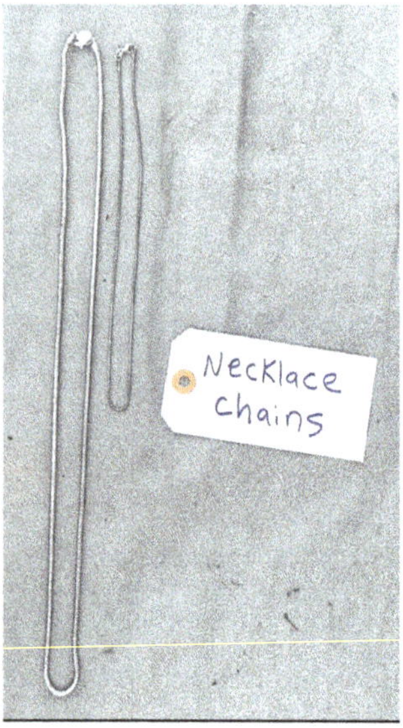
Necklace chains

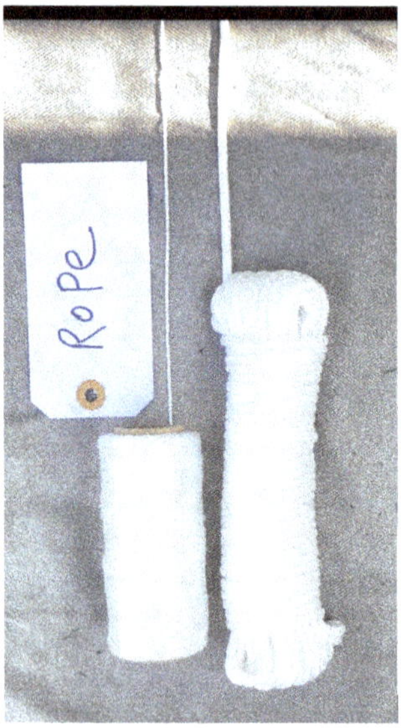
Rope

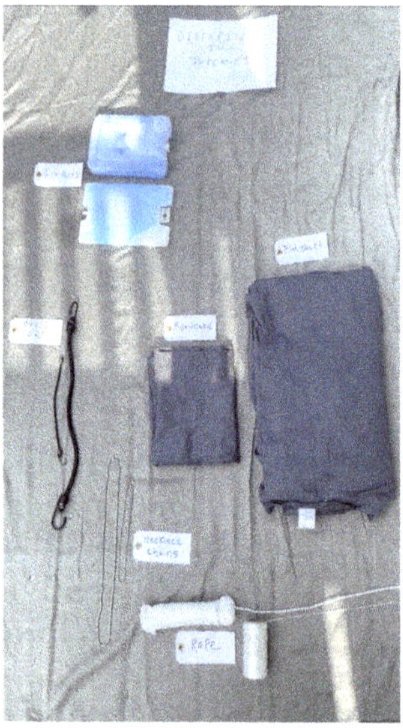

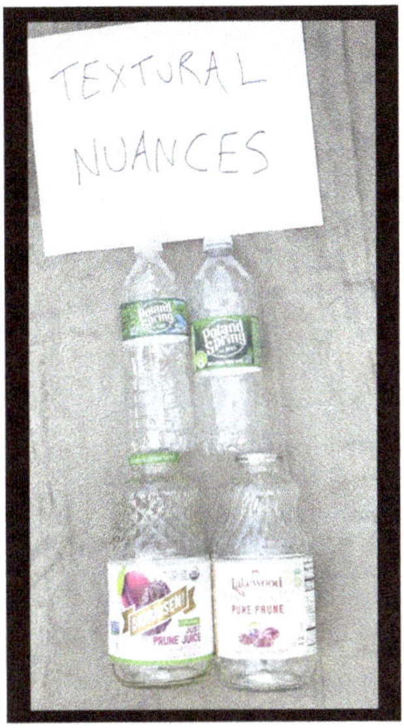
TEXTURAL
NUANCES
PRUNE JUICE
PURE PRUNE

TEXTURAL
NUANCES
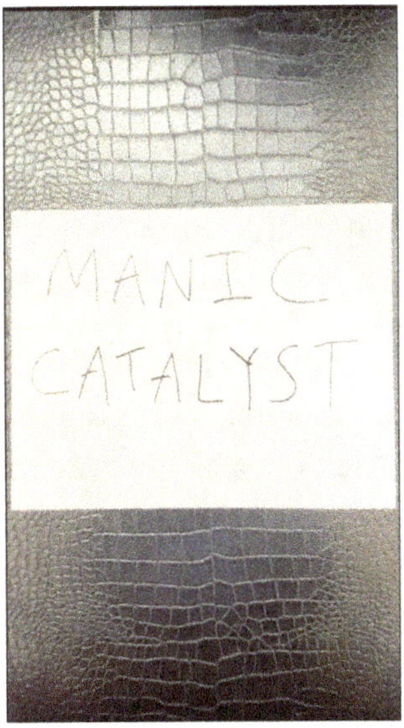
MANIC
CATALYST
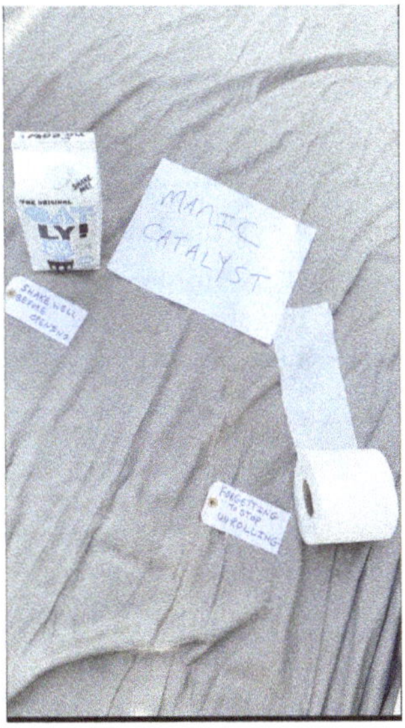
MANIC
CATALYST
SHAKE WELL
BEFORE
OPENING
FORGETTING
TO STOP
UNROLLING

? DEDICATION/INTRO/PREFACE ETC ?

From the pits of imposter syndrome, inferiority complex...the shackles of self-defeatist internal stimuli internal dialog/monologue to the soaring astral planes of to the stars in my eyes of delusions of grandeur ... hey, if (it was) by riding high on delusions of grandeur (that) I would actually get where I was wanting to go/wanted to go - I'll take it/I'm here for it/yes please and Thank you. I would take these delusions and reshape them to conclusions.

I wrote this memoir, I became an author as a contingency plan; it was my out from killing myself. If I couldn't get out of dissociative I felt it was/this might be the one way/a way (I might be) I would be willing (to) not (to) kill myself; if I lived to my potential. Since the beginning of my sickness, I felt that if I can't get out of this; if I have incurred permanent brain damage where I am neurologically incapable to, then I am unwilling and Unwanting to live out a natural lifespan. I wrote this memoir in attempt to loosen the noose around my life. That and I was tired of always having to filter my online store browsing search results by lowest to highest price.

No but seriously I was going to live to my potential or die (from) not trying / I was going to live to my potential bc I was going to die not trying . I realized I had 2 options: either I live to my potential or I'm going to die from complications related to not trying. I realized I had 2 options: either I live to my potential or I'm going to die from 'not trying' related complications. I realized I had 2 options: I either live to my potential or die from complications related to not trying. And living to my potential I saw as the loophole I needed to soliciting loved ones blessings for/of (an) assisted suicide; (a compassionate release) for (all of) their sakes, I had to find a way to be willing to live and this could be it. Telling my story could be my assisted suicidal ideation exception. Sharing my story/experience so that my struggle and survival is not in vain, could be what renders me willing to stay with the living.

I wrote this memoir as a survival mechanism/strategy.

Already deep into the chapters of my book, I upon a(n) Google/internet search one night came upon/discovered/unearthed a description of a writing style that instantly resonated with what felt like my natural propensity. An epiphany it was, that a "Verse Novel" was the vein of how/was the vein of which/ was the vein in which, i was navigating the memoir genre .

In succession, when the book was done, came/was the whole-hearted sentiment of/from my editor, of certainty that my writing classification/subdivision was/is (that of) "Experimental Writing".

Having never heard either term; "Verse Novel" or "Experimental writing"... along my/the trajectory of becoming an author, i was learning so much about myself through/in, this/the process.

Is there poor sentence structure of fragmented, Run on sentences, unfinished thoughts, digressions, tangents and all other kinds of technical writing pitfalls, affirmative!/why, yes! I wrote this memoir of and from in the dissociative state of depersonalization and derealization But I implore/invite you to take-heart and not look at what isn't there but rather to feel for what is.

DEDICATIONS

Higher Self

X To my higher self (I am indebted to you)
Thankyou for your first ever prescence and
bestowing apon me the priceless/precious awareness
that in the times that are life-threatening scariest
you'll care... X

To my higher self <3
To my higher self thankyou for your first ever
presence in my life which/it beautifully and
powerfully/profoundly obstructs fear of death.
(And for (bestowing apo me) the new found precious
newfound awareness that in my darkest hour I'll
have a/ the soul-powered beacon of... A light at the end
of the tunnel;

the Stephoenix .

Beloved Parents

To unconditional enduring love...
Dadd + Momm
I thank you for
the tenacious quality of your quanity love.

To my Momm

Who all through my aspiring author journey to get/find
a Publisher, would bolster my will and Optimism
submission by submission
lovingly saying "It only takes one".
Thankyou Momm for happening upon "Red Penguin Books"
and telling/urging me to contact them.
"It only takes one", and you found me my "one"...
and only.

To My Dadd

My Dadd is the one who put on display my "Red Penguin" contract when I signed with them.
In the living room across from where he sits so that he can look at it everyday while he sits on the couch watching TV.
My dadd is the one who cried tears of pride the day I met Stephanie and came home to tell him (all) about it... He had always believed in my writing ever since I was young and as he expressed (the sentiment) 'few get to achieve in their lifetime, what I am... such open-emotion was the culmination' of what he in his lifetime, got to see me become/had lived to see me become.

To my Aunt

Having always viewed her as an/to be an, exemplar of perseverance... The Aunt whose like a friend to me, helped me summon the warrior-strength within, that I didn't know I had/possessed.

To those beloved who have Passed Away

Uncle Art <3

Your number signs to reach me are countless
and my (spiritual) listening, boundless.
Thankyou for Making sure my days alive weren't
numbered and that my days overcome were. / Where I
overcame, were.

To my gaurdian angel, thankyou for being my guiding angel
from heaven; the ghost-writer of my book.

All my love grandma all my love
All my love uncle Art all my love
All my love Pop all my love
All my love Sophia all my love
All my love Mushyman-Ramses/Ramsey all my Love.

(For) While I was not of this World, I felt yours and
(in that)(spiritual swaddle) of being less alone, it helped
me endure.

To my (Lust) lord and Savior

For caring about seeing me succeed + live to reach my potential, every bit as much as you care about your own...
Thankyou for believing in me and for all the ways in which you made my potential achievable... from graphic designer, computer technician, file transferer and so on, your knowledge, talent + skills covered what I wouldn't even (begin to) know how to touch/approach.
It is the loving amalgamation/convergence of your professional dedication and prowess in tandem/concurrence with your personal abounding/boundless moral support, that has immesurably helped bring my vision to fruition.

Furthermore it was beautifully fitting that my lifelong creative muse would give me the gift of music again...
After 12/18 plus months without the knowledge and too confused, I'd like to thank my Lustlord, my inspiration, who gave me the infusion of music that was remembering Gibbons, Beth and Portishead (again).
I was cognition-rid of any longer knowing/having awareness/access of/to the name of my 12 to 18 plus years favorite band but/yet
"and the moments/times I will suffer loss is when I never have to wake."

in other words...

1.) I was living (out) / existing (my) every night as Wandering star.
2.) I was the living embodiment of wandering star
3.) my every night was the living-out / living embodiment of Wandering star.
4.) my every night was existing on/in the equator of Wandering star/ my every night was existing in the cross section of the "Wandering Star"
5.) ~~my every night was existing in the songs~~ song
6.) my every night was existing in the lyrical cross section of "Wandering Star"
7.) (sensory sickness) my every night was (sensory sickness) existing in the/ living (in) the/ this; the cross section of "Wandering Star".

Without the cognitive ability to remember I had a favorite band, much less who it is ... I owe this/the resuscitated cognizance, to my lustlord + savior, who randomly texted me, once upon an Uber ride. That photo you snapped and sent me of the screen display read-out / reading of "Portishead" "Sour Times", meant my favorite band had/could, come back to me.

There is the famous salutation the proverb "yours truly."
From lust at 1st sight, turned / to now / now to / now too,
the Luck of my Life...
I am "yours truly" but/and whats more, I am yours proudly, profoundly, and fondly. I am yours vibrantly, emphatically and passionately. Here's to every toast we've raised a glass to "Winning At Life"
Cheers, Babes!

Gentle Greetings Friends

[Your tragic misunderstanding of this humans condition was the pain of my existence / Experience subjective experiential]

To the fallen few, who/those who disavowed our bond when I suddenly couldn't 'friend' to their standards... the standards I had always been able to before...
[your tragic misunderstanding of this humans condition was the pain of my existence.]

these pages (may you) read em and weep.

And do come crying to me for I live to forgive. It is in my nature and always has been.

And in kind/in contrast, to the steadfast many/most, with the sustenance of your love...

thank you (all) for sustaining my life.

To "Red Penguin Books" staff and the 'Head Penguin'

//

To the incomparable staff of "Red Penguin Books",
I feel like I've found a 'chosen family' (in you),
which I didn't (even) know could be found in a
professional setting/application/sense/dynamic/regard/
rapport.

And, to my upstanding publisher Stephanie Larkin
won me over the moment she leaned across the
lunch-in table and said
"I don't want to edit-out your essence."
That sentiment swaddled me and I knew in that moment/
instant, I wanted to be yours...
where I thought a big decision had to be made (was looming,)
it turned out to be an epiphany.
thank you, Stephanie
for believing in my 2(00) Evils.
I'm on Cloud 9(00) because of you.

To my Literary First Aid "Kit"

Without me asking and certainly without her ever having to be... She made herself 'on call', for me; ((it's a hard thing for an author to admit/contend with/handle, when (their) unknown-reason, brain fog-marred reading comprehension spares them no lapse/corruption/festering/presence/frustration, with their own work/writing (too).

TO she (Who) came to my rescue (time after 'time and time again' ... when the metastasis of my reading comprehension deficit(s) *meant*/left me without (an) ease of (an) understanding for/of how to (properly) order/sequence-structure/sentence-structure/paragraph-structure, the very sentences/paragraphs of my (own) bio. (She was there).

From a (St Lucia) destination Wedding Hotel balcony vacay, to a leisurely / leisure time, iKea stroll, she chose to (still be reachable to me.)

From tied bows of endless scrolls instead of stapled pages / * from scrolls (handed over) tied up in bows (handed over) * instead of pages - stapled. To (probably / presumably) having to scale countless hours of (probably) unceasing ways of / I've (mis)using / misused and abusing / abused language, grammer (and) punctuation ... and I'm sure botched all forms of English Lit industry standards.

She never (once) went against the grain of my self-proclaimed exhausting, 'new normal' brain.
But rather / but what's more / and whats more, showed me I had / have a forever home in a certain kind of (literary) styling(s) called "experimental writing". A genre that I didn't know was, until her.

Thankyou to my Editor Kit of "Red Penguin Books"
You are my literary first aid "Kit" and I (literally)
could not have done this without (all) of your
TLC; Tender Literary Care.
through and through (thankyou for showing me)
my book/manuscript; my baby, was in good hands
but whats more, the right hands (with you.)

To Pip, Creative Writing Teacher

As I vividly + fondly remember it, in live of
merely signing your name in my Highschool graduation
yearbook, you selected a single stick of Patchouli incense
or Nag Champa, where in which you tucked it into the binding
of the book exclaiming
"Burn it one day when you're writing something great."
Mr. Pip, that day has come; I have.
What you believed in me to be possible is now
something that I've accomplished.
As the earliest iterations of my writing passion, was found
in and through your classes... I (now) thankyou for
the/this seasoned time of my writing.

To Rosemarie Tully, P.C.

Thank you for meeting with my family + I,
and being of / having the / carrying the, conviction
that "Red Penguin Books", was in my best interest /
invested in my best interest.
Your professional compelling point of view,
Showed me (that) I had found my perfect Match.

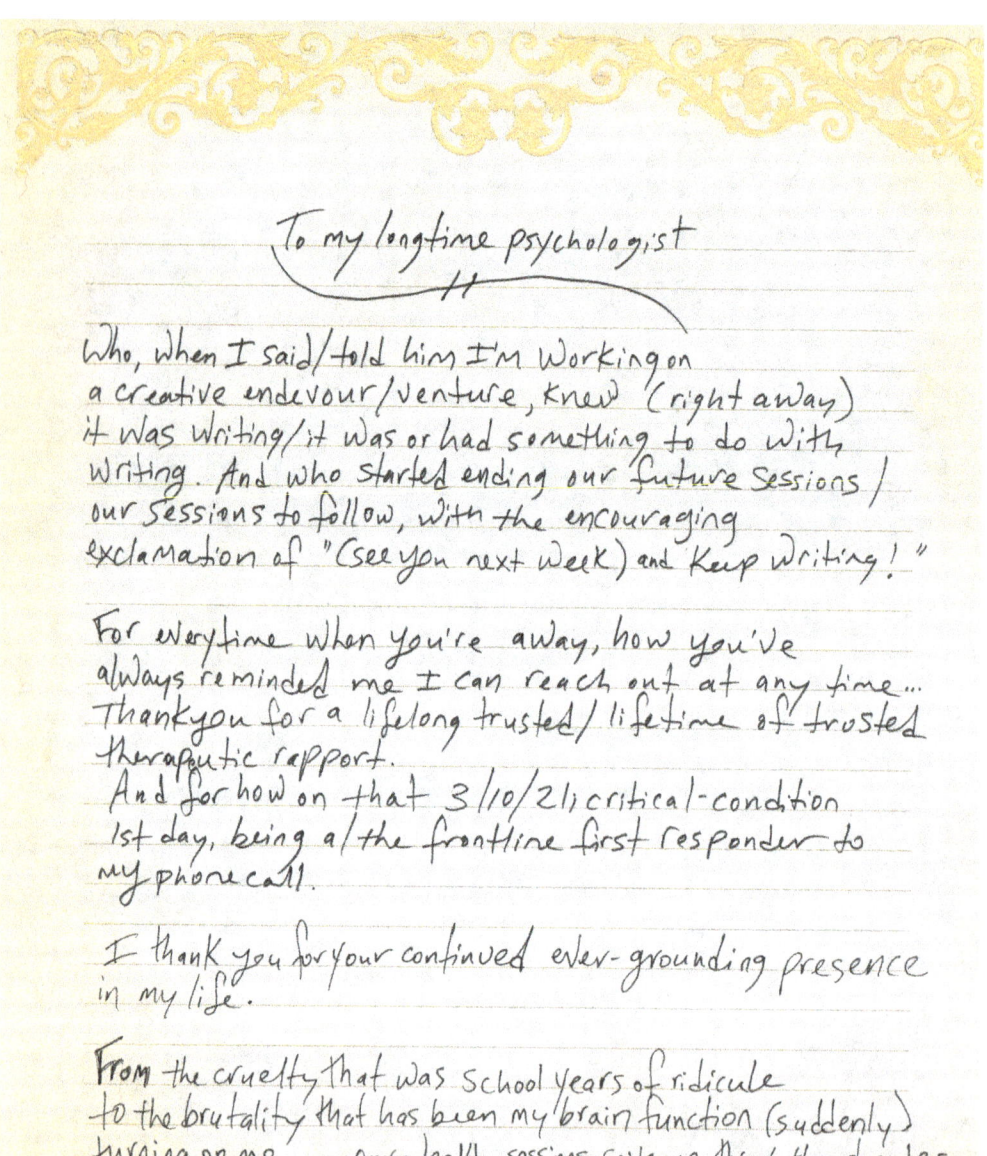

To my longtime psychologist

Who, when I said/told him I'm working on a creative endevour/venture, knew (right away) it was writing/it was or had something to do with writing. And who started ending our future sessions / our sessions to follow, with the encouraging exclamation of "(see you next week) and Keep Writing!"

For everytime when you're away, how you've always reminded me I can reach out at any time... Thankyou for a lifelong trusted/ lifetime of trusted therapeutic rapport.
And for how on that 3/10/21, critical-condition 1st day, being a/the frontline first responder to my phone call.

I thank you for your continued ever-grounding presence in my life.

From the cruelty that was school years of ridicule to the brutality that has been my brain function (suddenly) turning on me... our weekly sessions save me through the decades.

To my Sicktime Psychiatrist

An immesurable thank you to my psychiatrist
Who often recounts his 1st impression of me as
that it/ I was like "talking to a piece of Wood."/
that I was like a piece of wood (when he 1st met me.)
To Dr. Lane Rosalie thankyou for giving me the
"benefit of the doubt" that there was something
neurological to this (flat/absecence of affect/emoting)
and not just/insted of just writing me off as a bitch.
through Watching old home movies/ video recordings
on my phone of myself/me, he was able to
see/understand/ establish (what) my baseline
(is)/ looks like and Know Where we needed to get to./
and Know what we were trying to get to./* and
Know What we were working towards and needed
to achieve*/ What we were working towards achieving.

To Marilyn Manson

From having never listened to your music before, to, I couldn't have gotten through this/survived this sickness, without it...
I ascribe the discography of your body of work, to to helping save my earthly body.

To "The Printer Gifter"

I thankyou for *seeing the worth in */ seeing it Was worth it, getting me a printer for Christmas because you believed me (to be) a wordsmith and feared (from early on,) for what would become of my lifetime of Journal Writings after I die. To him (the Printer Gifter) Without whom this Manuscript Might've never seen the light of print.

To Mike and Mano

Unbeknownst to me at the time, that our first ever meeting in 2019, would be/mean the beginning of a beautiful rapport & friendship that would bring us all "Many Happy Returns".

From my grandfathers old roll-top writing desk that my Momm & I let you warmly welcome into your Antique Shop, after my sweet uncle died (and we had to sell the house)... to the fact that the identical double-orange globe lamp that softly-lit/warmly-lit the loving gatherings in/of the family living room at my grandparents/uncles, house, matches in "Make and Model" to that of the one that stands a striking statement piece/centerpiece in/at your cool Artsy Bar; solidifies (for me/to me), that theres a spiritual factor/facet/element/component, to our aquaintence/unity/connection.

TO Mike & Mano, thankyou for inviting me/welcoming me and my guests, into such a, what is for me, spiritually sacred space rental.

If the walls could talk (they'd say)...

thanks to you for providing me the venue

& to my boyfriend, for gifting me the night.

To my past employers

Who afforded me what is the sum total of my work history in the fields of/with the populations of Autism, Autism spectrum, neurobiological disorders and Alzheimer's.
From teenage students to senior citizen residents, (In resounding retrospect), my life's work was (unbeknownst to me) (in part) preparing me to know how to take care of myself; to survive this time.

Gentle Greetings my class of 2001

When I learned our 20 year highschool reunion was this past weekend, it felt very important to me to reach out and express something. And it is that...
I wanted to be able to have the chance to go.
Very unfortunately though, I have been dealing with some difficult neurological complications this past year and as my misfortune would have it, my illness timeline just happens to coincide with that of our shared 'life timeline' of our historic 20 year high-school reunion.

It's pretty bitersweet that me, a person who has always regarded 'Romy and Michele's highschool reunion", as one of their fun favorite movies from their youth, has to now come to terms with and make peace with the fact that they had to miss their very own.

But I look forward to better years ahead and a time when I can be a part of our reunions.

In the interim, know that I will look upon our 20 year reunion fondly for the special camaraderie + kinship it got to bring to so many of you who shared in that historic moment of social (re)emergence and the unique energy of it all.

... In nostalgic discourse there lives such a special magic.

With well-wishes for you, your families and loved ones, this holiday season.

Sincerely,

ps. Although my facebook is currently deactivated, I look forward to reactivating it when the time is right.

THE TAKEHEART15: ESSENTIAL THINGS FOR PEOPLE TO KNOW OF ME FOR INTERACTING.

-listening comprehension

-critical thinking and reasoning skills

-complex thought

-trouble 'inferring' things

-trouble accessing knowing how to give advice for a respective thing presented to me.

-trouble accessing knowing what my opinions are for a respective thing presented to me.

-trouble understanding/processing/interpreting humor

-affects (manic,flat, inappropriate)

-trouble knowing if a respective thing I'm saying to someone /have said to someone is a nice thing or a not nice thing to say/be saying/have said.

-trouble with "common sense" concepts.

-forgetful/absent-minded/trouble retaining something I hear or am told.

-I don't feel/can't interpret/recognition troubles with 'the passage of time'. So I can't help but be inconsistent/absentminded with contacting/keeping up with an established text conversation etc with a respective person and this should not be seen as flippant or like I don't care; just impaired. And I often don't realize when I'm forgetting to write to somebody/write back to somebody.

-trouble knowing if something I initiate saying is accurate/honest/my truth/something I stand by and stand for or inaccurate/dishonest/me lying/something I don't stand by and don't stand for.

-trouble knowing if something I respond to a question with saying is accurate/honest/my truth/something I stand by and stand for or inaccurate/dishonest/me lying/something I don't stand by and don't stand for.

-trouble knowing how I really feel/where I stand on a respective thing.

*don't ever take anything personally or take offense as it is never anything of an

emotional-shunning it is solely neurological not emotional and that is the most important thing you could ever keep in mind and operate from/interact with me from a place of.

SAMPLES PASSAGES

SAMPLE PASSAGE EXCERPT – CJD4 “SUNFLOWER SPY CAMERAS”

An emotionally perceived invasion despite an/the intellectual understanding that the

neighbors newly fence-towering sun flowers wouldn’t have cameras in the disk floret . But the

swaying stem and leaves in the breeze got me angry as if it were the homes residents themselves;

parents and kids gawking with awkward shifting and shuffling as they stand feet firmly planted

there all the live long day…staring at me. I’d shudder to not shut my blinds and when I did it felt

good like I was stickin’ it to them.

And when I’d hear the landlords feet clobbering and clomping around upstairs above/over my

head it felt like a stampede intended to trample my self-worth. I found a strange twisted solace

in the malice of Marilyn Manson’s lyrics…

“Don't need a motherfucker lookin' down on me Motherfucker lookin' down on me Least I know

wherever I go I got the devil beneath my feet”. I was the devil beneath their feet, and they would

not revile me. I relished and reveled in the reimagined refrain.

And when I’d turn the metal strainer in the sink, upside down I’d see the smattering of sparse particles or morsels; a composite of dinners gone by, and it would become a metaphor; my

landlords yelling at me. I'd jam-wash it down the drain as though it were a garbage disposal and

feel like I'd flipped the script on hierarchy. Risk-benefit says I'd rather sit with this rancid/putrid/

I-don't-flush-toilet- paper, bathroom refuse on the off-chance of it permeating through the I-hate-

your- blasted-blasting -A.C.-vents, in the ceiling, than I would sooner stand for your brash

verbal Incontinence.

With The Monthly Doormats that never listen to music, a compilation created of discordance and

cacophonies greatest; Amanda Palmer, PJ Harvey, Rasputina, Sleater-Kinney and more, felt sure

to grate on their suburban conservatist, conventionalist nerves. And in that calm mine. From in

the garage apartment; my mad-man cave, the music swelled and my hopes welled that war air

rises.

SAMPLE PASSAGE – EPILOGUE/OUTRO "KID STICKER BOOKS OF HOSPITAL PASSES"

And what is life but/if not, a succession of loss where in which if you're one of the lucky ones

It comes with the grace of sequence. Grandparents pass and as they depart it imparts on us an

imprint of emergency preparedness to be able to handle this the next death; our parents, with just

a little less flailing. Then comes the time in life where not hearing from a cherished childhood

friend, means you have to wonder if it's because they've seen life's end.

It is there and then that you realize you would give anything just to go back to the years where

worrying that they're avoiding you was at the top of the tier /was top tier .Where sticker books

meant "Oilies" and "Fuzzies", not stapled proverbial wax glossed pages of visitor and inpatient,

hospital passes and badges amassing .

SAMPLE PASSAGE-EPILOGUE/OUTRO "WORK HARD AT HOW WE PLAY"

When by destiny or design you've almost died...but didn't you subsequently feel all that you

could've/almost left behind... but didn't .When you've faced-off with facing your own demise

It is of my experience that it gives way to an unprecedented certain magnificence ...

The connective camaraderie of a shared high-school graduating class year suddenly becomes

all that you feel about each and every person you share this earth with. From baby boomers to

Gen-X to I- gen ... we are all here of the (same) 21st century life-expiration year-a graduation

most sacred. And when you really feel that, find that finite in your bones you understand, you

experience and see everyone as intimacy-sexy. Intrinsically all brothers, mothers, lovers, sisters

and ancestors, etc., we belong to the same end game. So let's work hard at how we play.

Civilians and celebrities we are of the same life-expectancies. Time-share liberties; mortalities,

fatalities all in a shared century /overlapping Centuries .

And In the populous phrase of everybody "life is (too) short". So in the golden Age of grotesque testament of Marilyn Manson "It's a dirty word Reich, say what you like". So if you

crave to stuff your face with a cupcake with your one and only 15 minute work break do it more

power to ya'! And if you desire to host a sex-party of musical chairs-dare! If you want not to

"take it to the grave" Swedish death 'Spring' clean, those skeletons in your closet; bare your

truth, come to a truce; make peace with yourself .

SAMPLE PASSAGE CJD9 "JUST A SPOONFUL OF APPLESAUCE HELPS THE MEDICINE GO DOWN IN A MOST DELUSIONAL WAY"

It had been since countless chapters ago, that I'd known; been of the good "interoceptive

awareness" of elusive powerful phenomena like my phantom limbic syndrome and that astral

projection was on a hair pin trigger. Ergo the latter, opening the fridge sliding out the glass jar

each night just a spoonful of applesauce helps the medicine go down in a most delusional way.

The metal lid was lined with a circle of painted red dots you see and that departure from the bare

minimum of ink meant,would set off, a party in my head.

The last bought sauce was barren of extraneous paint so of course this one launched me into a

soirée right away. The circular formation emulated a center-floor dance-circle of friends

embracing the life-affirming nightlife or where a convening coven never ends. The dots like a

seductive dim glow from the lighting track in the ceiling of a club. Heady was the red light

district in a red delicious. A gala, it all lived and breathed on that (insert measurement of lid)

metal lid.

SAMPLE PASSAGE (CHAPTER 8 – “1 YEAR CLEAN & SERENE”)

It was the night before clonazepam-free 1 year anniversary and as I slipped into bed and

found the commemorative keychain on eBay that glowed in the dark and boasted a rejoiceful air

of salvation, stillness and wholeness . The gold foil embossed message of “one year clean and

serene” read like a wistful/wishful dream. I didn’t find serenity in having to avert my eyes earlier

that night while I ate strawberries because they tasted delicious but looked disgusting like

someone’s blackhead clogged pores to my inescapable macro lens photography visual processing

shackles. And I didn’t feel serenity in the direction label stipulated 30seconds that I fought with

my mind to sustain the brain connection long enough so as to complete a round of proper and

safe mouthwash swishing. “30 seconds that’s all you have to make it through Stephanie! You do

that in a rep of mountain climbers every per bi-daily workout. Colonizing my mind with

constructive positive self-talk to stave off its berating intrusive thought; “ your brain signaling

not to swallow Stephanie is going to give out and then you’ll be an Emetophobic dealing with things like the poison control center and having your stomach pumped at the hospital."

I loved glow in the dark goodies as much or more than the next child of the 80's but no, my

faithful readers, this...wasn't... serene. From the dark of my room by the bright of my phone in

hand one final sentiment sent incoming to be seen on a dear ones lock screen.

(introspection/reflection) a retrospective of the time gone by and the congratulatory -regard of

the day; (introspection/reflection) If only 365 days was synonymous with being well. If only it

but feigned this key-chain.

SAMPLE PASSAGE- CJD 3 "STIMSON MIDDLE RIDICULE (NOT SCHOOL)"

As a grown-up, Standing in the body image crossfire of the man I had loved who thought I

should gain weight and the one who I now did, that sexualized every pound I lost of it ... And

remembering how I was mercilessly heartlessly teased for my ectomorphic frame all through

grade school ... chugging ensure between classes to hurry up and gain weight so the school day

might come where my peers would leave me alone once and for all. Shooting capfuls of "Pepto

Bismal" was dismal before the start of many-a school day just on the off chance today could be a

day I was to get nauseous of natural causes while under their school roof I couldn't risk it;

hyper vigilant about how I better not become stomach sick because it will just serve as pointed

evidence to my tormentors that I am in fact, bulimic . Which I was not am not and never was.

But there was a collective of fingers pointing at me like synchronized swimmers exacting their

maneuvers and water tricks every time or most that I'd get up from the lunch table to make my way to the bathroom after eating to simply go to the bathroom or touch up on my makeup before

the next class like others . The fingers that weren't pointing at me were stuck down throats in a

theatrical overture of what I was assumed to be heading to the girls room to do/for. Once in there

I had to be mindful not to so much as cough or it could be met with whispers and scoffs from

girls/my peers (who were) at the mirror with the socio-cosmetic luxury of taking up space and

time in the restroom without scathing repercussions. Ah, yes, the lunch table daily bulimia

battery and harassment routine.

There's a difference/distinction between emaciated and ectomorphic and those ignorants

didn't get the difference/distinction. I didn't then nor had I or have I ever (since) had an eating

disorder but you gave me body dysmorphia; thinking I'm too thin bones frail like the skeleton

you would call me. Thinking I could be crushed in/by a hug because you said I would. Class of

(enter graduation year here), at Stimson Middle not school; ridicule, Bulimia was in the eye of

the beholder and I was beholden to your torture of/in/from sadistic disillusionment. It was

your/those beliefs you beat me senseless with. I have internalized

Emetophobia/Aeronausiphobia because of you. I was conditioned to equate/associate a natural adverse stomach reflex with something shameful and of disgust, setting me up for a life of being

scared and living in fear of my own G.I. system. Net-reaction like a hydra and Flinching like a

hit abuse victim every time there's a stomach-sick vomit scene on my TV... it accosts me.

You the peers did this to me. My neuropathways were just developing; malleable and you

damaged me. Without so much as ever saying sorry is sorry something you'll never, be? Once

home from a/the school bus of psycho-emotional lashing bashing and/with a dash of sexual

harassment I'd cry in my mothers' lap (for what seemed like hours) until we were circling laps

around the mall the next day. Playing hooky was synonymous with and euphemistic

for...escaping it all.

SAMPLE PASSAGE – CJD3 "ALL I COULD SAY WAS...IT'S MY HAIR"

Just as aforementioned somewhere, that my written word ability came first in repair to my

verbal, When applied to seduction and endeavors and attempts, to be a lover ... my brain had

me/kept me, short-changed . Naughty nothings I couldn't whisper, yet they could be infallibly

written. From my pen or in text there could be fantastical fetishism... erotica so finely crafted for

the man who I wanted to be my lewd suitor that calling it sexting would be an injustice. Yes,

Sure, I could write artful scholarly-journal-worthy indulgences, but at the end of the day

"Because the night", belonged to lovers and I could only ever be an Empty promises temptress

so long as I remained in this partial catatonic coma-like state that felt like it were depressing

brain function for exacting and enacting any successful seduction.

Hoping for a playful naughty crime of his mind I had put in the time for my Lustord, "all

dolled-up" as he would say and with something a little extra for his pleasure...my Victorian

classic length hair donned in a new style I had seen on the internet; google images amidst my primping, and deemed it to denote a nod to the bod of a whips rod. 8 hair ties later and some

extras stashed in my evening bag just in case one slipped out, I had achieved the look that pre-

all-this Seroquel would've caused me sickening visual processing. the bumped up sausage-

strung-like sections of the (insert name of pony tail here) calculating to me reading to my eyes

like intestines, would make me think about how much my poor beloved grandmother G.I.-

suffered and the memory-perseveration of it, did me in. I had to toggle away from the well-

intentioned image spread google had splayed-out before me.

So, suffice to say, this full circle moment in time, was powerful and empowering; now to be

embracing and recreating the hairstyle for a night out as per my lustlords invite to come see him

sing doing his sexy musician thing. There was hedonistic ideation in my thinking "he could pull

me around by my hair like a leash and I would be quite pleased." But rate of thought, just like

neurocognitive ability to write, was further along than rate of speech by all means and be it that

abstract thinking and reasoning skills were sorely lacking too equated to a grand total of dirty-

flirty fallen flat. At his initiation ducked off 1-1 to the back outside of the open-mic pub he grips my pony tail in fist "I like this" his arousing gravelly voice growls out in a whisper between

cigarette drags. It was the full circle moment we had all baited-breath awaited and I say "all" on

behalf of my complex personality facets that were all united this time, by one common goal;

trigger his gutter mind with this hairstyle .

And that it had but due to my default that was the neuro glitches I was robbed of my

executive function, to reply in kind…to reply in desire. All I could say through a scrunched face

of confused and confounded cognitive disarray was, "It's my Hair". I had not the gutter mouth to

back me up, that always was.

SAMPLE PASSAGE- CHAPTER 2 "THE ANTS GO MARCHING 2 BY 2 (HUNDRED EVILS)"

I would spontaneously collapse into catastrophic heights of diffuse/systemic physiological panic

response. I'd try to push past the urge to go rinse my mouth out and make sure that this time

there really wasn't actual fuzz and hair caught in my throat; that it was all just my tactile

hallucination coming on again ... I'd want to gargle with something (preferably peroxide or

mouth wash) but my higher self… my frontline defender safeguarding the physical body let me

know that I wasn't at the level of brain to body communication and connection so as to know

how to gargle properly and safely. I'd go in the bathroom and just swish a hand full of water

around in my mouth then spit it out. Sometimes I'd try to reach back in my mouth and extract the

fuzz and hair that in reality was not there. Going back to the living room couch now I knew I

needed to get myself into some focused heavy audible breathing to fade out my

comfort-music that was quickly falling prey to upsetting/disturbing auditory distortion coming

on now…

With a vexing imposed discipline of rigid body alignment I situated myself on the couch; my brain would only let me sit in one precise position when on the couch.

With desperate need I was ready now for my closed eyes and focused loud breathing to take me

away, to take this down a notch (for a notch is all it would ever be) I needed a course adjustment

knob but all that was ever within my brains reach was the fine. The rapidly escalating

excruciating state begged for more than I could give it so as to see its extinguishment. But I did

the best I could … mentally maneuvering under the dictatorship and tyranny of my brain there I

was in what I might as just as well call

"My couch sitting position." As I'd try to slip into my deep meditative state that would register

on my smart watch as that of 'light sleep' I'd have the proverbial armed intruders of my mind

that the higher self would first have to fend off … the sensation of things crawling on my legs

was this my tactile hallucination attacking my mind or was this one of the times the apartment

ants that were there for the summer had found my leg… as I'd raise my leg to look or reflexively

frantically brush my leg I'd think could it please be the lesser of 2 evils could it please be

legitimate ants just let it be that please. A colony would be a comfort so long as it means it's not

a sensory neurological glitch happening (again.)

PHOTO GALLERY

Photo 1

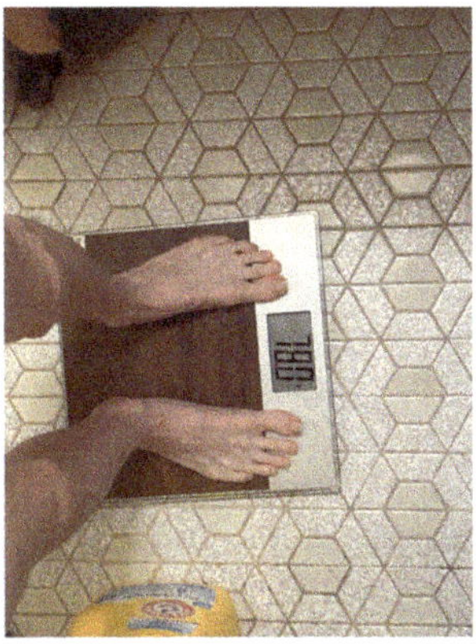

-the scale at my lowest
weigh in
(4/3/21 at 11:40am)

Photo 2

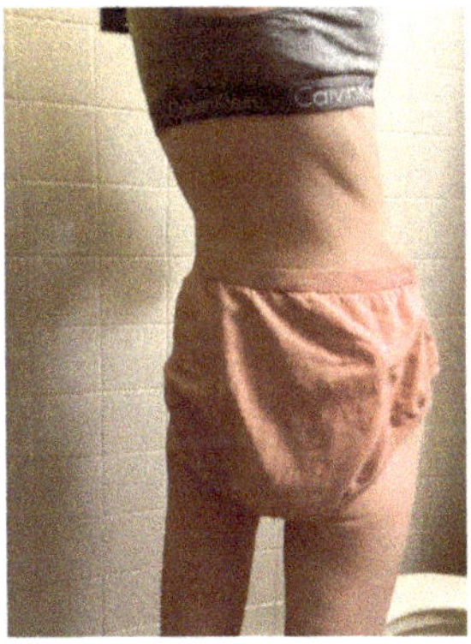

-dramatic weight loss induced
underwear loose.
(3/23/21 at 12:41pm)

Photo 3

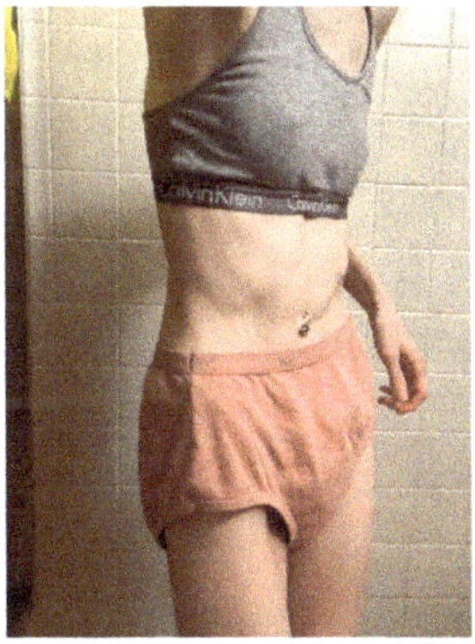

Photo 4

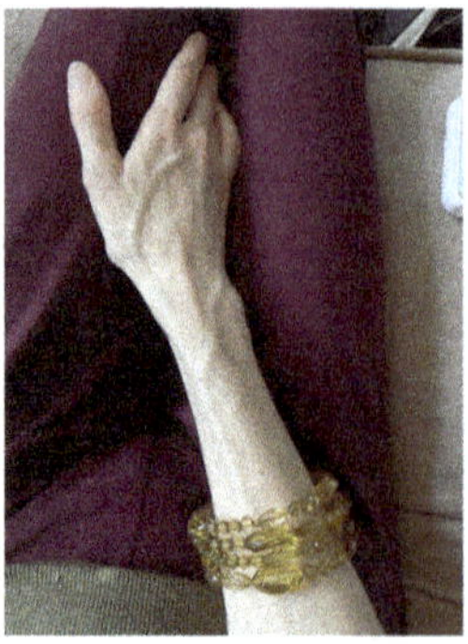

- ginger ale jewelry: how a bracelet aided in saving my life.
(4/28/21 at 2:03pm)

Photo 5

-haggard and unbeknownst to me that the battle had only just begun.
(5/18/21 at 2:00pm)

Photo 6

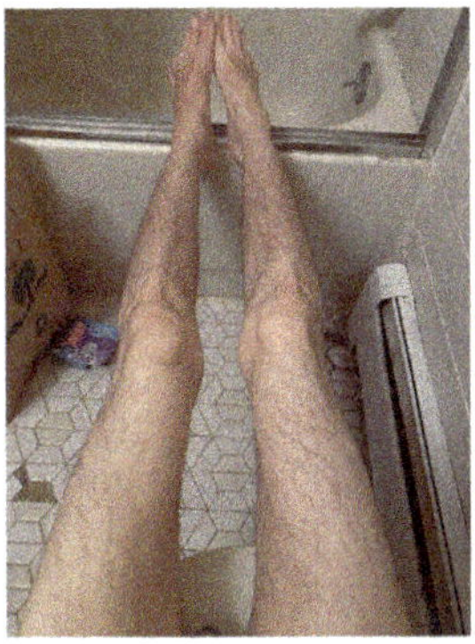

-unable to tell how soft or how hard I'm bearing down with the razor so it was unsafe to shave.
(6/2/21 at 9:19pm)

Photo 7

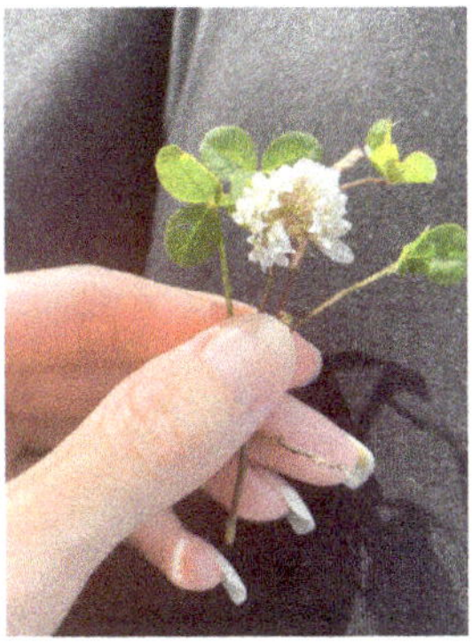

-a clover for my sun by soul; a cat only by destiny's design. MushyMan sniffed this type of flower shortly before he passed away.
(6/11/21 at 5:57pm)

Photo 8

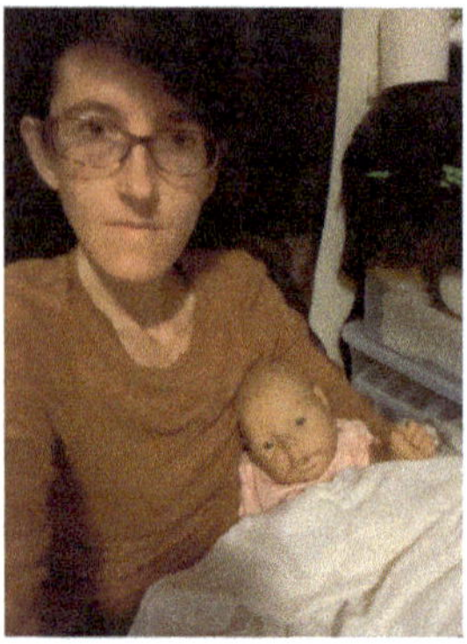

-morning breaks and I so need too, this
life-robbing state to break so that I might not need to quell the race against time by cradling grandma's baby doll.
(6/28/21 at 10:57am)

Photo 9

-the visually perceived blood jelly didn't fool my intellectual awareness ,that it was but a mixed berry fruit spread; that certainty was intact. But Irregardless , my system would react as though it were infact blood.
(6/28/21 at 11:46 am)

Photo 10

-In lieu of eating it; I couldn't go through with it so I threw it out and soothed my eyes with a buttered bagel instead.
(6/28/21 at 11:57 am)

Photo 11

-my doctor-assigned daily walk, grounding practices, had beauty but to no avail could they tether me.
(8/9/21 at 4:42pm)

Photo 12

-All the infallible intellectual awareness that this was not a bath of death, did little to thwart me from feeling like this was a movie set suicide scene with an absentee actress and I as the understudy had a professional/contractual obligation to fill in so we could wrap.
(8/20/21 at 5:01pm)

Photo 13

-the first photo/show of anger setting-in.
In a DIY there was
A cry for hell, to abate.
(9/2/21 at 5:03pm)

Photo 14

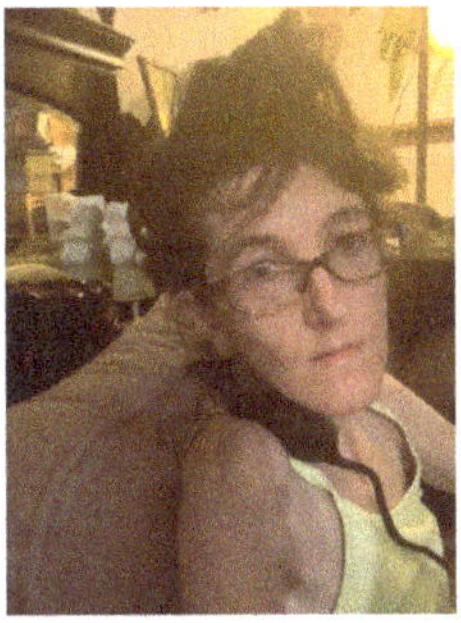

Photo 15

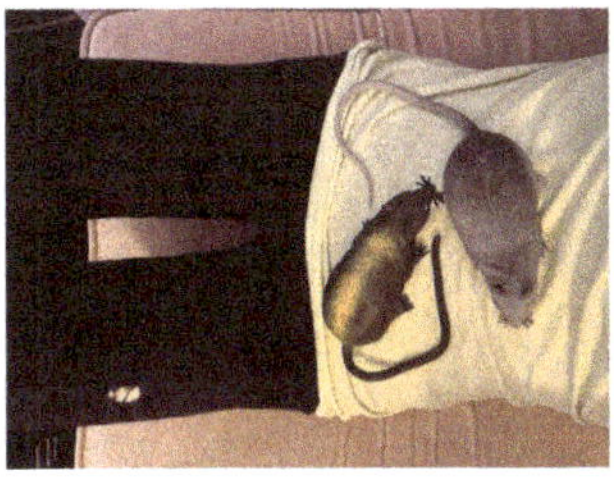

Photo 16

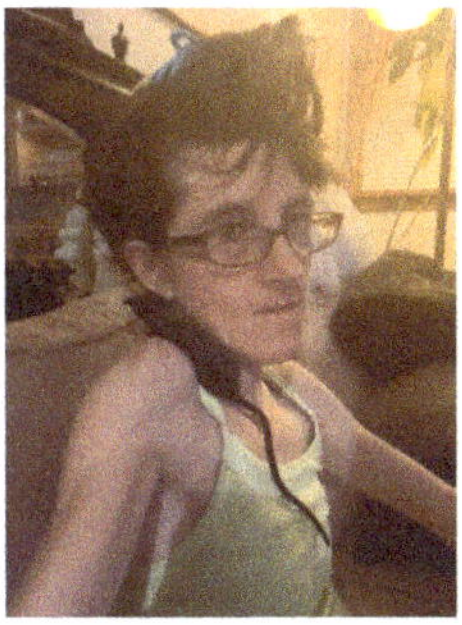

age-regression/childhood-regression was
my life-raft of Rubber rats on my shoulder
and tv-watching lap
(9/26/21 at 10:49pm)
(9/29/21 at 10:10pm)

Photo 17

-unsure if it was ice and that I should brace myself for a fall
(10/9/21 at 6:10pm)

Photo 18

-"A life trapped." (from a dark photo series I did, of bleakness.)
(11/18/21 at 3:51pm)

Photo 19

-"a noose, kink implements & the fragile beauty of juxtaposition." (I was taking my power back through the art therapy of street power lines.)
(11/18/21 at 3:54pm)
*this photo has been edited.

Photo 20

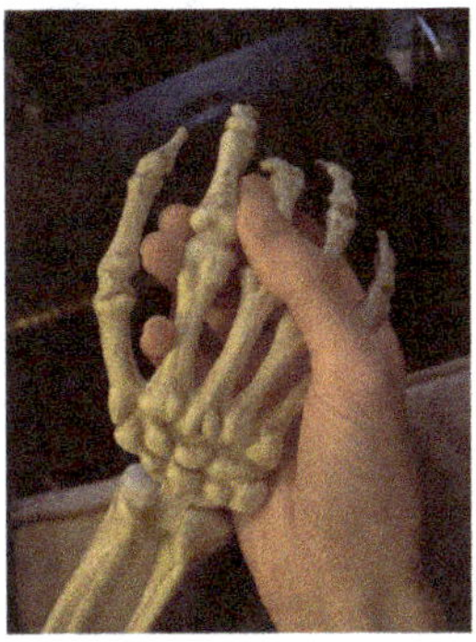

-"becoming one with death" - trying to make peace with if I should have to submit/surrender/succumb, to
The Lesser Of (my) 200 Evils; assisted suicide.
*this is the raw/unedited version of my cover photo.
(11/20/21 at 8:44pm)

Photo 21

"up-and-coming Author" - 1st photo I ever took of myself with my, (working)-manuscript.
...(how) I was learning (how) to
turn my pain into my power; self-taught
(1/21/22 at 11:31am)

Photo 22 & 23

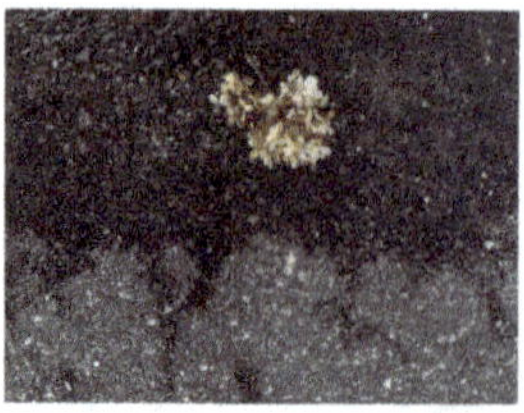

"captivated by an evil ground"
(the darkest of the photo series I did,
of bleakness.)
(2/23/22 at 2:48pm)

Photo 24

"Through the Looking Glass of Depersonalization"
What does a smattering of toothpaste spatter matter when you aren't in it (the mirror) anyway.
(3/18/22 at 10:20pm)

Photo 25

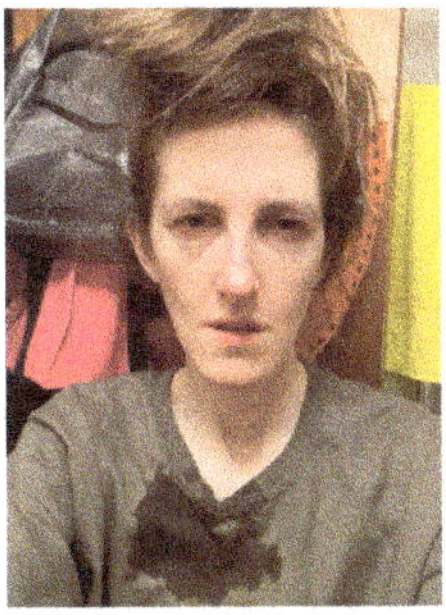

"tears, snot and despondency" / "the tears & snot of despondency"
tissues seem obsolete and petty when you can't even recognize your own reflection.
(3/18/22 at 10:21 pm)

Photo 26 & 27

"A (whole) year braver" / "a year later and I'm getting braver" / "a year later and I've gotten braver"
(from the tryptic of ice patch photos)
(4/12/22 at 2:44pm)

Photo 28

high-school graduation/yearbook picture- class of 2001. Alongside my "…the pen is mightier than the tourniquet" current warrior (photo)self-portrait (photo) , This old yearbook picture was 'posted for me' to the class of 2001 Facebook group, with my sorrowful decline letter
"gentle greetings my class of 2001",
on account of being (too much) in the thick of my sick(ness), to attend/ *for what I couldn't wait to attend.*
(6/18/22 at 9:51 am ?)

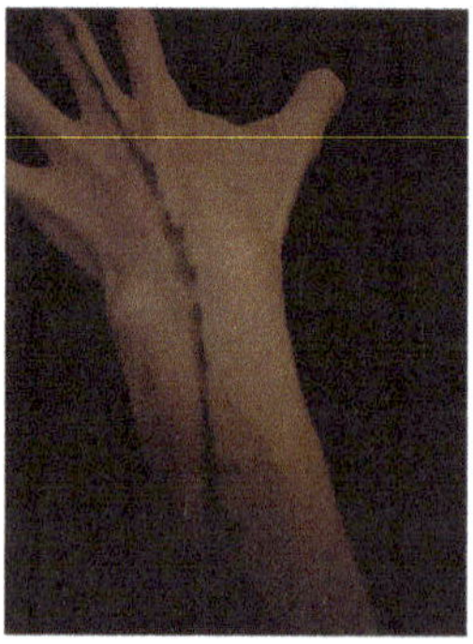

Photo 29 & 30

"loosing the grip on my humanness" from a sunglasses DIY to a Sharpie marker hand…(the) anger pervades.

(from the 'bleakness' photo series)
(9/4/22 at 9:44pm)

*the sunglasses DIY photo may also be a part of the dark/bleakness photo series; I'm/it's undecided.

Photo 31

from the night of
"All I could say was… it's my hair"
(10/17/22 at 4:34pm)

Photo 32

"becoming (his) Miss Minx"
with the power vested in he; my (lust)lord&savior, a sexual metamorphosis begins.
(1/28/23 at 3:31pm)

Photo 33

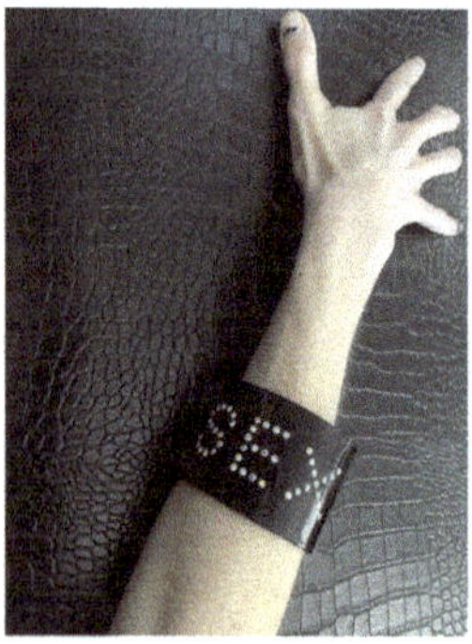

"reclaiming the grip on my sexuality"
a totem of taking back my/the power, in a wrist cuff gifted to me by my lustlord .

I can see
the (red) light (district) at the end of the tunnel.

*this is part of the same photo(s) titled
"loosing the grip on my humanness"

(2/3/23 at 11:42am)

Photo 34

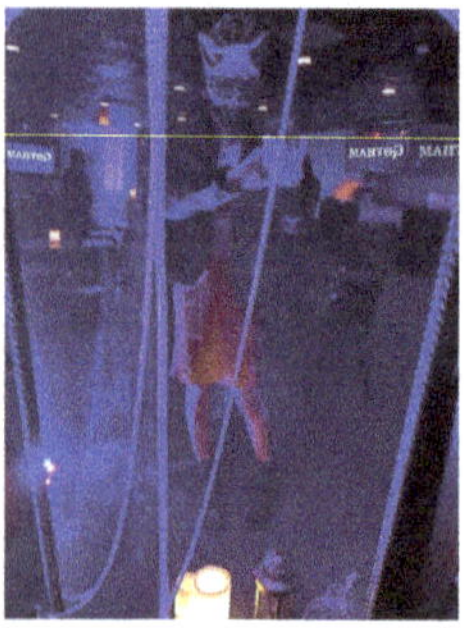

Photo 35

Photo 36

"night of the punked-out pussycat"
-at the invite of "the magic maker", it was my 1st night out with a group of friends and Like the neon rope light sign that hung over a glossy-finish coffin, read/*invited*/mandated/stipulated/commanded/invited ...
"till death do us party", we would.

*it was the night of my birthdate numerical anagram entry wristband .

(2/19/23 at 9:17pm and 9:27pm)

Photo 37 & 38

strung up over an old lighting fixture/floor lamp was the personality (with dissociative) I'd become. And/but, behind closed (jewelry armoire) doors was (the) remnants of the person I was/*who I was*, before DPDR. (this old armoire necklace discovery was on 6/8/23 at 5:14pm)

Photo 39 & 40

"Just got/walked in the door" home from my 'in any way, shape or form' 1st night out with friends. A bowling game with my bosom friend, her boyfriend and he who in a few months time; 4, will become/ becomes, my lustlord. And like the flower clip he gave me, see the blossoming to (what I'd call/term/regard as regard to be) my 'dissociative bdsm' ... the fun, enjoyable, pleasant, pleasing and pleasurable side that seemed to develop in/from/within the/my dissociative dpdr; a subset. (9/16/22 at 11:48pm)

When my personality facet of femininity was lost from my psycho-sexual accessibility Thankyou my lustlord for coming back into my life (again) and being the soul guarantor of sed archetypes' restoration.

"Give me a reason to be a woman
I just wanna be a woman
From this time, unchained
We're all looking at a different picture
Through this new frame of mind
A thousand flowers could bloom"
"Glory Box" Portishead

Photo 41 & 42
"the early signs"
1st purchase(s) of (what will become) an insatiable feening/fiend; jelly bags.
(amber jelly bag = 5/31/21 at 12:27pm)
(floral jelly bag = 6/6/21 at 7:22pm)

Photo 43

(*while eating/having breakfast*) warm-imaginings (Xwhile eating/having breakfastX), of being well strolling through 'the park of my life', with medjool dates stashed in this little (purse) jelly picnic basket, (purse.)
(6/27/21 at 11:12am)

Photo 44

"The Braxton Hicks of my Rebirth"
(6/4/21 at 11:59am)

Photo 45 & 46

(While) there was not extinction in/of my symptoms but (there was) refuge, in staging fake promo shoots with my newly unboxed pocketbooks.
(8/7/21 at 1:41pm)

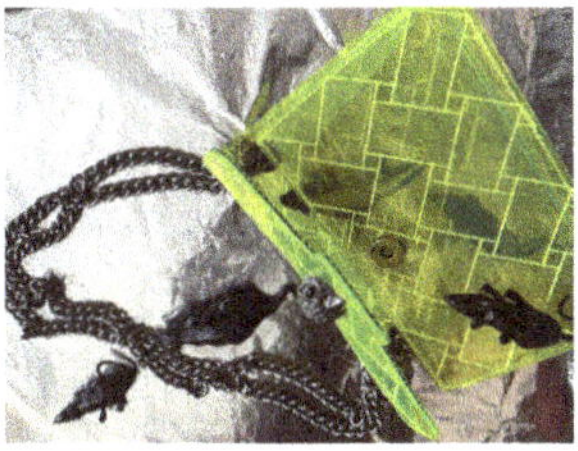

Photo 47

"forever 12"
childhood jelly; my 1st ever.
I was probably all of 3 to 8 years of age.
(7/31/21 at 8:44pm)

"Benzo the bozo"
poem I wrote in the thick of my sick; 20 days in.
(3/30/21 at 12:25am)

Photo 48

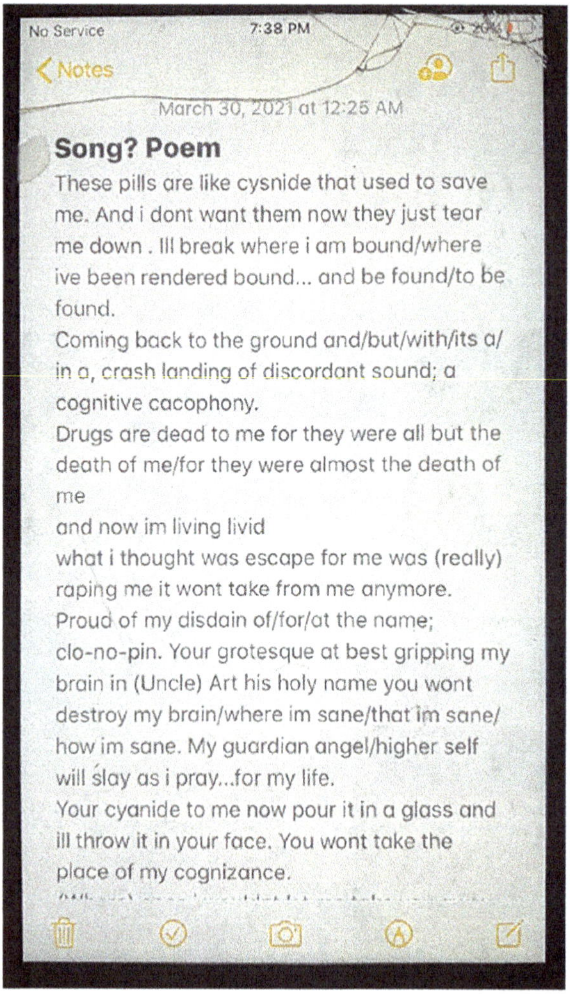
No Service 7:38 PM

Notes

March 30, 2021 at 12:25 AM

Song? Poem

These pills are like cysnide that used to save me. And i dont want them now they just tear me down . Ill break where i am bound/where ive been rendered bound... and be found/to be found.

Coming back to the ground and/but/with/its a/ in a, crash landing of discordant sound; a cognitive cacophony.

Drugs are dead to me for they were all but the death of me/for they were almost the death of me

and now im living livid

what i thought was escape for me was (really) raping me it wont take from me anymore.

Proud of my disdain of/for/at the name; clo-no-pin. Your grotesque at best gripping my brain in (Uncle) Art his holy name you wont destroy my brain/where im sane/that im sane/ how im sane. My guardian angel/higher self will slay as i pray...for my life.

Your cyanide to me now pour it in a glass and ill throw it in your face. You wont take the place of my cognizance.

Photo 49

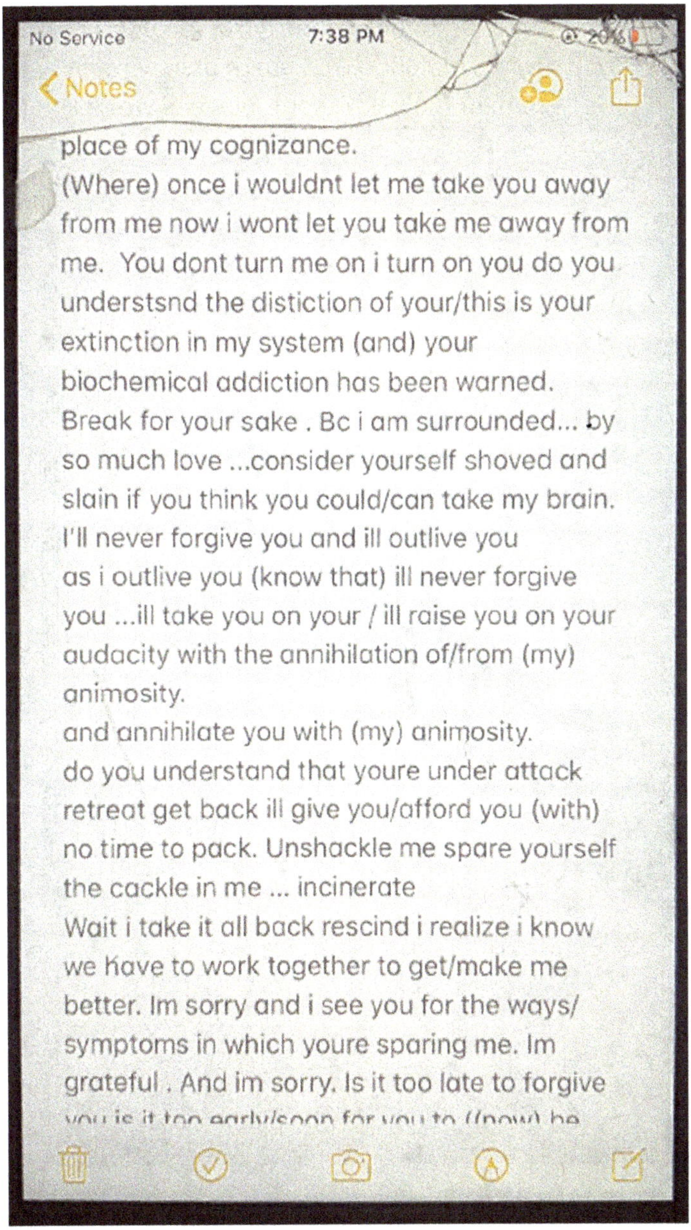

place of my cognizance.
(Where) once i wouldnt let me take you away from me now i wont let you take me away from me. You dont turn me on i turn on you do you understsnd the distiction of your/this is your extinction in my system (and) your biochemical addiction has been warned.
Break for your sake . Bc i am surrounded... by so much love ...consider yourself shoved and slain if you think you could/can take my brain.
I'll never forgive you and ill outlive you
as i outlive you (know that) ill never forgive you ...ill take you on your / ill raise you on your audacity with the annihilation of/from (my) animosity.
and annihilate you with (my) animosity.
do you understand that youre under attack
retreat get back ill give you/afford you (with) no time to pack. Unshackle me spare yourself the cackle in me ... incinerate
Wait i take it all back rescind i realize i know we have to work together to get/make me better. Im sorry and i see you for the ways/ symptoms in which youre sparing me. Im grateful . And im sorry. Is it too late to forgive you is it too early/soon for you to ((now) be

Photo 50

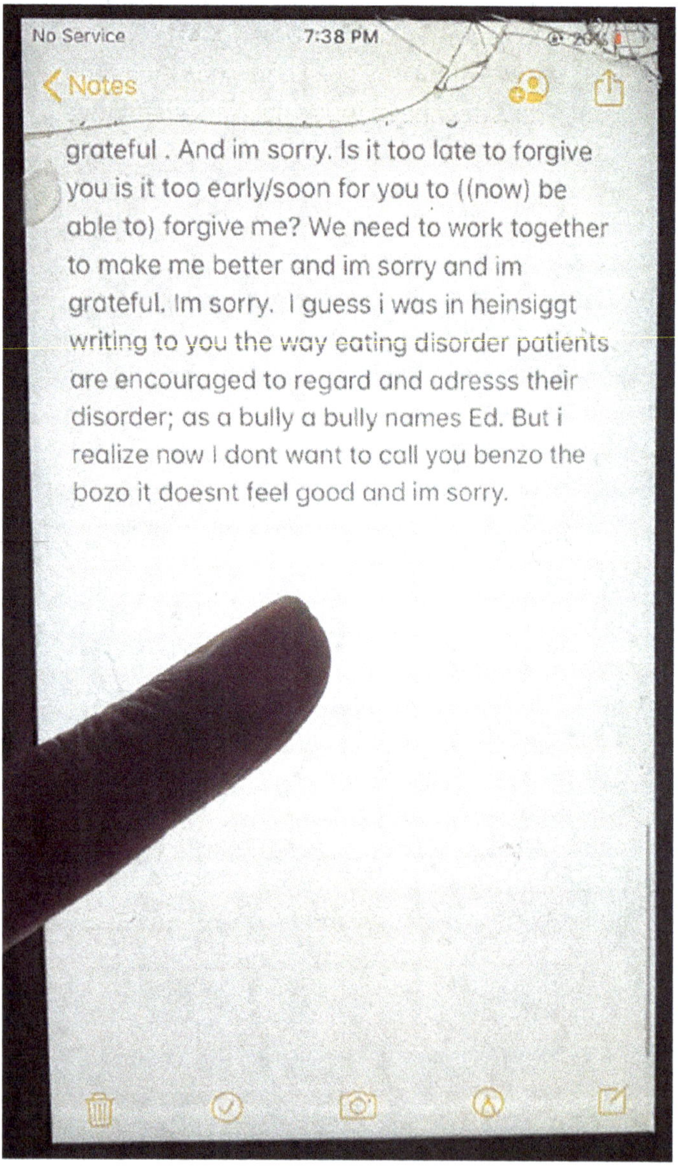
No Service
7:38 PM
Notes
grateful . And im sorry. Is it too late to forgive you is it too early/soon for you to ((now) be able to) forgive me? We need to work together to make me better and im sorry and im grateful. Im sorry. I guess i was in heinsiggt writing to you the way eating disorder patients are encouraged to regard and adresss their disorder; as a bully a bully names Ed. But i realize now I dont want to call you benzo the bozo it doesnt feel good and im sorry.

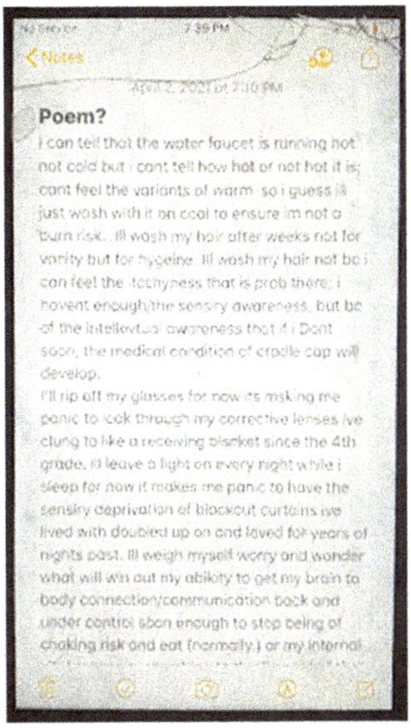

Notes
Poem?
i can tell that the water faucet is running hot not cold but i cant tell how hot or not hot it is; cant feel the variants of warm so i guess ill just wash with it on cool to ensure im not a burn risk. Ill wash my hair after weeks not for vanity but for hygeine. Ill wash my hair not bc i can feel the itchyness that is prob there; i havent enough/the sensiry awareness, but bc of the intellectual awareness that if i Dont soon, the medical condition of cradle cap will develop.
I'll rip off my glasses for now its making me panic to look through my corrective lenses ive clung to like a receiving blanket since the 4th grade. Ill leave a light on every night while i sleep for now it makes me panic to have the sensiry deprivation of blackout curtains ive lived with doubled up on and loved for years of nights past. Ill weigh myself worry and wonder what will win out my ability to get my brain to body connection/communication back and under control soon enough to stop being of choking risk and eat (normally.) or my internal

Photo 51 & 52
poem I wrote in the thick of my sick
(4/2/21 at 7:10pm)

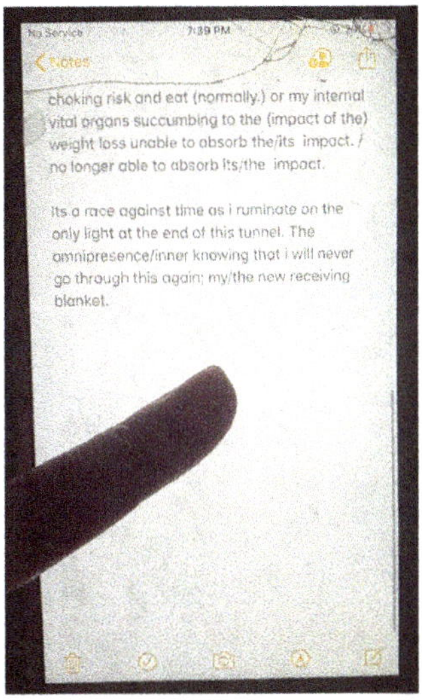

No Service
7:39 PM
Notes
choking risk and eat (normally.) or my internal vital organs succumbing to the (impact of the) weight loss unable to absorb the/its impact. / no longer able to absorb its/the impact.
Its a race against time as i ruminate on the only light at the end of this tunnel. The omnipresence/inner knowing that i will never go through this again; my/the new receiving blanket.

Photo 53

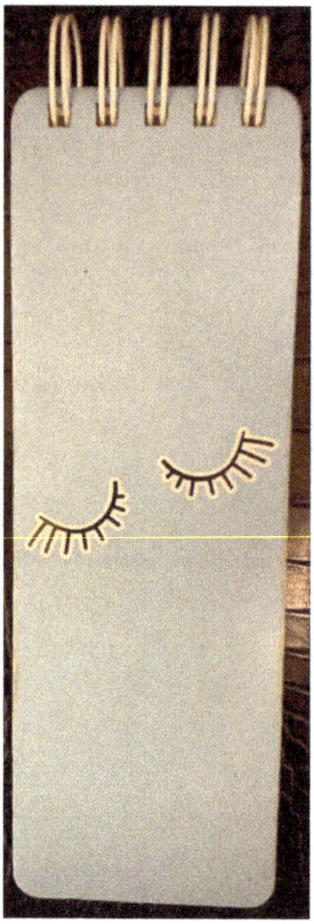

Photo 54

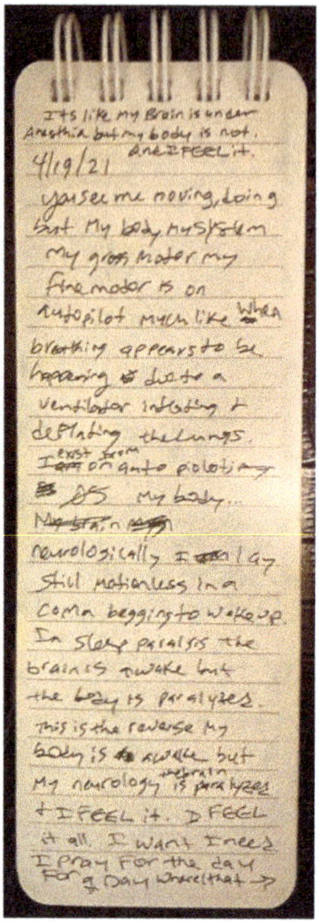

Photo 55

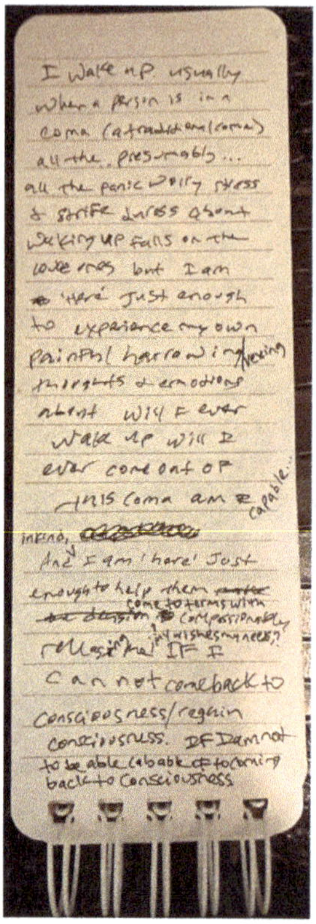

My mom used to sweetly say
-maybe those eyes on my notepads' cover
are just going to open one of these days
-maybe those eyes on my notepads' cover
are going to just open one of these days.

a metaphor for me
"coming-to" / breaking-through (from) this (absolutely/unequivocally/utterly)
unthinkable/intolerable/unbearable/unlivable, state (Xof beingX)
Xrepresentative or symbolic X

the biting bittersweetness and juxtaposition in it (all) being that unbeknownst to her. I was composing my end-of-life blessing, solicitation letter in the lined-pages of that notepad.

I was once asked by someone: if I have/if I'm having
(any) suicidal-ideation. To which I reflexively silently scoffed and thought: is that a rhetorical question ?!
I mean (come on) of course I am (come on) !

below is the
'anticipatory-Suicidal-Ideation' : letter/ 'The Lesser Of 200 Evils'

(4/19/21) it was 1 month into being sick

Photo 56

(the/my) Last Will (and Testament) for/of the manuscript. (When it was written is unknown as it is undated- in the thick of the sick, it was written and hidden from easy finding.)

*for privacy purposes, the code to open the phone has been covered-up.

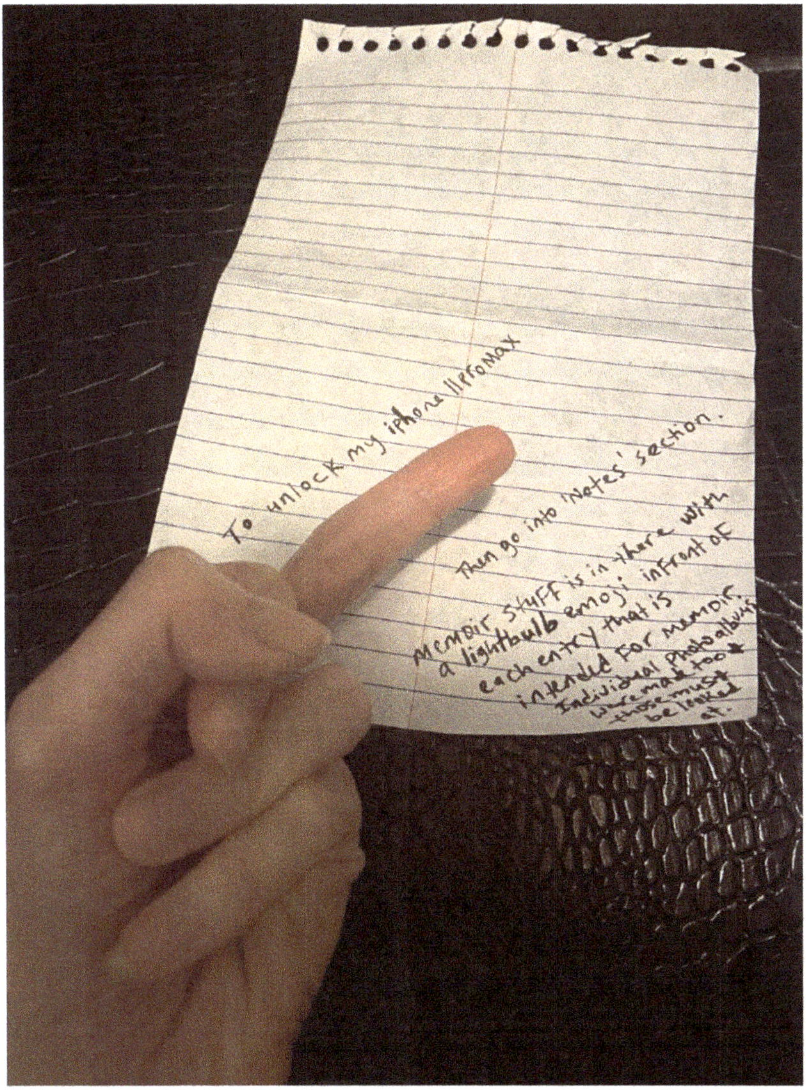

Photo 57

[[It seemed/felt like it was over before it ((had)even/ever)
started/begun.
then, for his eyes only, I wrote the short-story that would change it all.]]

after much…
hemming & hawing
will-they-won't-they
yea/yay Or nay

[[It seemed/felt like it was over before it ((had)even/ever)
started/begun.
then, for his eyes only, I wrote the short-story that would change it all.]]

(10/25/22 at 3:37pm)

"A million candles burning
For the help that never came
You want it darker
Hineni, hineni
I'm ready, my Lord"
-Leonard Cohen-

Photo 57

Herpes simplex virus 1 and 2 (HSV-1 and HSV-2) are two members of the human Herpesviridaefamily, a set of viruses that produce viral infections in the majority of humans.[1][2] Both HSV-1 and HSV-2 are very common and contagious. They can be spread when an infected person begins shedding the virus.

As of 2016, about 67% of the world population under the age of 50 had HSV-1.[3] In the United States, about 47.8% and 11.9% are estimated to have HSV-1 and HSV-2, respectively, though actual prevalence may be much higher.[4]Because it can be transmitted through any intimate contact, it is one of the most common sexually transmitted infections.[5]

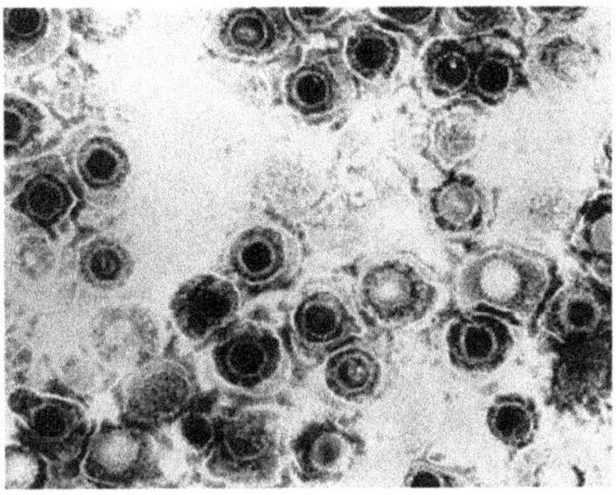

https://en.m.wikipedia.org/wiki/Herpes_simplex_virus

regarding my vector...
Although the utmost respect is deserved
as it was a beautiful relationship with a loving partner...
these song lyrics serve as a depiction of the way their reaction/handling of the situation, felt to me.

"It's just a virus
He says to me
It's not quite the prison
You make it out to be"

-Sarah Fimm-

Umm... actually it is. It is a life sentence.

besides no longer being able to receive my favorite form of sex...
pregnancy, vaginal birthing&breastfeeding ... all become conditional .

Photo 58

“Euphemism For F42.3 (ICD-10) / DSM-5 300.3”

(7/23/?24? at 5:40pm)

“What have I become?
My sweetest friend
Everyone I know goes away
In the end
And you could have it all
My empire of dirt
I will let you down
I will make you hurt”
-as covered by Johnny Cash-

“dish detergent holder gets repurposed to make novelty purse- the 1st and only time in life I’ve ever made a pocketbook ! ”

Photo 59

The below photo was taken:
July 2nd 2021 at 10:55am
(the before…)

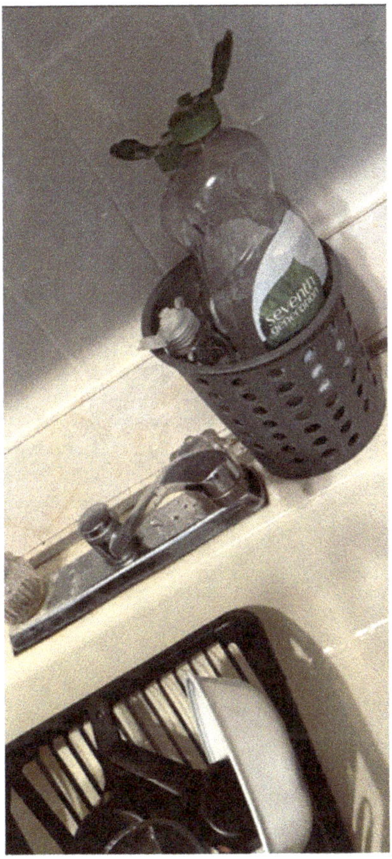

Photo 60

The below photo was taken:
July 2nd 2021 at 1:50pm
(the after…)

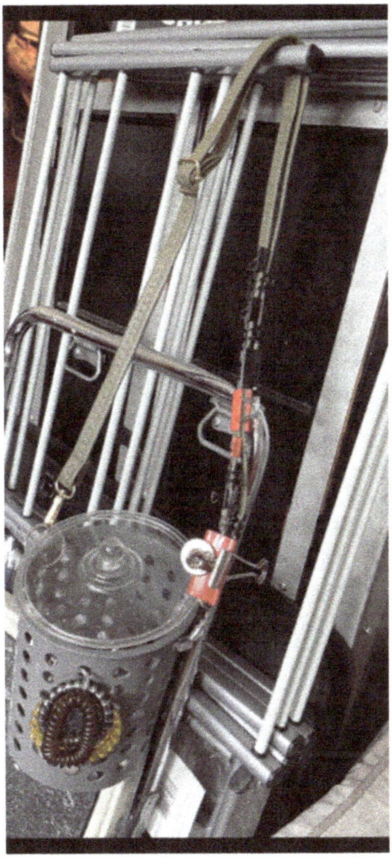

Photo 61

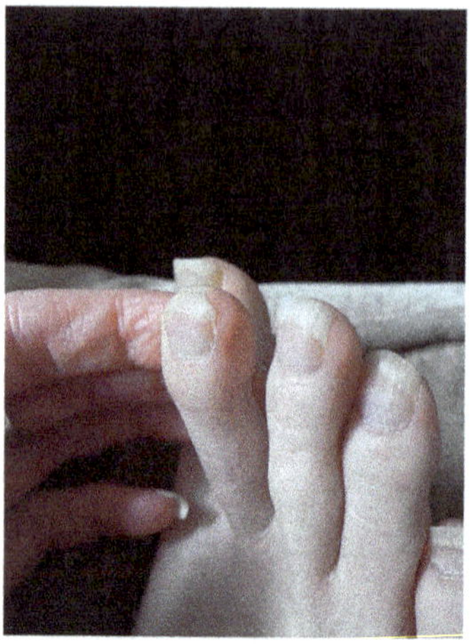

"(toenails) overgrown with depersonalization"
can't make the distinction with the clippers, between skin and nail . This is only (just) the beginning of (just) how intentionally neglected I have to resign myself to (be/live.) (be living.)
(5/11/21 at 5:57pm)

Photo 62

toenails that would grow longer than they'd ever been (longer than the toes photo shows them) , from sickness, was oppressive/depressing but fingernails unprecedented(longer than this fingers photo shows them)… was everything.
I took countless pictures nearly everyday of my hands.

(5/30/21 at 12:26 pm)

TABLE OF (SOME) CONTENTS

aka

Select-Chapter Overview

-Intro is dedications & disclaimers

-CJD2 is anger. 2nd verseNotSameAsThe1st a little bit louder and a little bit worse .

-CJD3 is circles "I'llLetscircle-back" / lust-lorn

-CJD4 is A cold-turkey thanksgiving

-Chap8 is the medical stuff

-DPDR@DSW is eroticize your life

-CJD5 is PANDA/Buspar start /Xmas/Dentist

-CJD6 is newYearOf2023/guilt4PrivaCbreechs

-CJD8 is "secretary"movie / Red Sharpie Letter of Domination / locker break in / vday / emotion by proxy of tv / insert with 'Pez how did I get here' ???appendix:This is Why???

-CJD9 is necklace choke(h)(e)r

-Outro is An Afterword to take to the Afterlife

KEY

?   ? = Questioning

???   ??? = Questioning if I'm questioning

[[   ]] = it's in more than 1 place and I can't decide where it fits better.

*   * = the way of wording something that I think sounds the best of the various versions.

CJD = Chapter Junk Drawer (to be explained later)

X   X = omit

A.) AA.) , B.) BB.) , C.) CC.) ... etc. = ignore these; they are the equivalent to post it notes for my own reference.

Add extra spaces to the key

/ multiple ways of saying something

1

Potential titles: it's not the time or final resting place, an angel of death in sandman's clothing, a sandman in angel of death's clothing,

The simple pleasure/rudimentary pleasure/enjoyment/fundamental pleasure/basic pleasure; would I be doing myself an emotional disservice if I am to "let myself look forward to things" as my beloved Momm would encourage and implore me to do; what if I'm neurologically incapable of ever doing said things again. I would want to do what my mom lovingly encourages, and the times I would it would be met with such complex anticipatory bittersweet(ness) feelings from the dark (side)/the cryptic/the pessimism of my mind. what if by way of systematic desensitization, what I should be doing is working on and towards (the goal of) letting go of the desire to enjoy things ever again, sever any remaining emotional threads to living that I have (that made it through the clinically diagnosed dissonance of cognition and emotion symptom) so as to avert prospective emotional whiplash. (So as to) make it easier to accept/come to terms with that I may have to mercifully let go of living life/ end my life early.

Wherein/in this complex relationship with "looking forward to things" or "letting myself look forward to things" existed the symptom-(dissonance of cognition and emotion) resistant imaginings of locker-hopping with a vintage 'looks like it would glow but doesn't' vintage caboodle to gather up all my glow in the dark items dispersed over several storage facilities and cultivate an organized collection. I would lay in bed at night in excruciating neurological nervous system distress and I would reap comfort in thinking 1 of a few things, one of them being about a time where I would victoriously drive my car (Bc I would be neurologically well) and delight in gathering up my glow in the dark belongings. Another visualization I self-soothed with was picturing my car completely emptied out; de-F42.3 (ICD-10) / DSM-5 300.3 with all the visual attention able to be directed to a respective beautiful pocketbook I have in use sitting in the passenger seat. Sometimes I would picture my favorite youtubers enjoying a respective favorite pocketbook of mine; a compersive fictitious video of/from compersion in my mind (that) I would devise for escapism. Oftentimes the pocketbook I would superimpose in these imaginings of youtubers would be one I had just ordered or was hankering to have. And the same goes for the soothing visual-scape of my car passenger seat. A 3rd storyline I would give myself, self-soothe with and turn to time and time again (especially at my sickest times of Withdrawls and earlier months of PAWS) was that as I would desperately await the sandman (of sleep) to take me I would fantasize that it was the merciful angel of death I was waiting for.

(to be rescued by/with. That it was death I was waiting to rescue me.)

In my first solo role play relief scene it would be that I'm lying on the concrete of a parking lot. I've just been hit by a car or by gunfire and as I feel my eyelids softly flutter towards a blood loss of consciousness State I can hear the frantic panic of a friend or loved one who hovers over me, begging me with desperate, demanding cries "stay awake, stay with me no, don't close your eyes, come on stay with me stay awake just stay stay awake just stay with me you have to stay with me you have to stay awake!"

... all vexing mortal/human response emotions that create physiological discomfort/distress such as this display of desperate heights of panic ... are only theirs now; the physical world's inhabitants; I am finally free of feeling such pain. And I take comfort in that as this desperate, frantic, panicked, wailing person shakes and waits for the ambulance to arrive... the panic is only hers now, hers and hers alone. I am too far gone to feel any conjunctive/correlating physiological response to what is going on (with my body) or to any ensuing chaos of panic-stricken regard around me; my autonomic nervous system is shutting down, and I am spared the mirroring of myriad emotions that pour fourth from the person who impatiently holds me in their arms... all I can be is peace-stricken while they must endure panic-stricken and in that reality I find strange albeit perhaps a selfish relief in the presenting juxtaposition .

2

Notes

The higher self/the higher consciousness

*age regression was my life raft

*My primary personality facets (dark,androgynous,hippie,square) and how at my sickest there was only presence of hippie and square and then as I got less sick my dark and androgynous started coming back to me.

*dark,andro,hippie,square and now too I have met and/so I know there is/exists, the higher self/higher consciousness and the inner child/child soul/child spirit.

*My higher self is the spirit of my beloved family in heaven...

*my child self is ...

*My beloved family in the spirit realm

age regression

-astral projection/visualizations/ channeling .

Dissociative state of derealization and depersonalization

Choking risk

Higher self safeguard the physical body

|----------|

At my sickest I met what I didn't even know I had; My higher-self/higher consciousness. My higher self swoops in, taking the physical self under its angel wing when the brain to body transmitters/lines of communication are not open as they should be. My higher self sees to it that the physical body is guarded and protected when the brain can't think for itself.

My whole life and still to this day at 38.5 years old when I thank my dadd for helping me with something or doing a favor, etc his recurring response theme often is to the effect of that he's just doing his job. I think he's said it to me more in this time of sickness than ever before. The protective care this respective parenthood belief/value system creates/results in, is the kind of paradigm from which the higher-self operates.

At my sickest when I sensed I might be having some disconnect in brain to body communication so as to be able to chew and swallow properly. it was my higher-self that bestowed upon me the good sense of knowing, guided me through it and told me when I was safe again to resume regular eating. It wasn't a linear trajectory, but the higher-consciousness always kept me safe, always knew when/what days I was safe to chew and swallow and what days I could be a choking hazard. Sometimes I'd start to eat and then realize today is too risky. As miraculous as I was learning, The higher self was/to be... it too would/might humbly proclaim "just doing my job" that's what higher selves are for, just like my father's view of his patently role; duties of immaculate protection.

In the thick of the sick, of withdrawals and tapering process, my higher self came to my aide. My higher self was my/came in the form of my beloved deceased uncle and grandma channeled (into me.) and my living beloved boyfriend. they all channeled through me as I'd sit (rigid) on the living room couch night after night, day after day, night in and night out, day in and day out, week after week, month after month, as I would spontaneously collapse into catastrophic heights of diffuse/systemic physiological panic response.

I'd try to push past the urge to go rinse my mouth out and make sure that this time there really wasn't actual fuzz and hair caught in my throat; that it was all just my tactile hallucination coming on again … I'd want to gargle with something (prob peroxide or mouth wash) but my higher self, my frontline defender safeguarding the physical body, let me know that I wasn't at the level of brain to body communication and connection so as to know how to gargle properly and safely. I'd go in the bathroom and just swish a hand full of water around in my mouth then spit it out. Sometimes I'd try to reach back in my mouth and extract the fuzz and hair that in reality was not there.

Going back to the living room couch now, I knew I needed to get myself into some focused, heavy, audible breathing to fade out my comfort-music that was quickly falling prey to upsetting/disturbing auditory distortion coming on now…

with a vexing imposed discipline of rigid body alignment, I situated myself on the couch; my brain would only let me sit in one precise position when on the couch.

With desperate need, I was ready now for my closed eyes and focused, loud breathing to take me away, to take this down a notch (for a notch is all it would ever be) I needed a course adjustment knob but all that was ever within my brain's reach was the fine. The rapidly escalating, excruciating state begged for more than I could give it so as to see its extinguishment. But I did the best I could ... mentally maneuvering under the dictatorship and tyranny of my brain there I was in what I might as just as well call...

“my couch sitting position”.

As I’d try to slip into my deep meditative state that would register on my smart watch as that of ‘light sleep’ I’d have the proverbial armed intruders of my mind the higher self would first have to fend off ... the sensation of things crawling on my legs was this my tactile hallucination attacking my mind or was this one of the times the apartment ants that were there for the summer had found my leg... as I’d raise my leg to look or reflexively brush my leg I’d think could it please be the lesser of 2 evils could it please be legitimate ants just let it be that please. A colony would be a comfort so long as it means it’s not a sensory neurological glitch happening. Almost able to be (ever-)present for my focused breathing session I’ll just have to accept that it feels like menthol’s icy fire is running through my veins where blood should be.

Assuming my couch sitting position now with the clasped hands on my lap of interlocking fingers soon this prayer hold won’t be my own but rather my beloved deceased uncle as he either channels through me? Or I have an astral projection experience; whichever it is. Under my closed eyelids I am taken to the vivid ‘not too distant past’ sight of my sweet uncle sitting on his favorite arm chair in his living room with clasped hands of interlocking fingers resting comfortably in his lap as he takes deep intentional inhales with such apparent presence and gratitude for life shown /detectable in (the) soft/subtle expressions of/on his face. He is breathing in the fresh air and sunlight that pours forth from the front door directly across from his chair. As I sit in my own living room assuming his body position, I think to myself how much pain he must have/of been in with his tumors both physical and mental and yet the cancer seemingly never took his emotional climate/love of life(from him) or boundless gratitude for it(from him). He would sit there and breathe through it all. As I sit here now I was trying to breathe through my (very own) "it all."

Whether my 3 loved ones of my uncle in the spiritual realm, my grandma in the spiritual realm and my boyfriend in the physical world were Channeling through me or we were meeting each other on some sort of meta physical vibrational frequency consistent with of (an) astral (projection) experience plane somewhere, somehow I did not know but second by second minute by minute my meditative state was unbeknownst to me sinking me into what would clock (me) at/for/as, (being in) "light sleep."

My grandma always had a very visually distinct way of breathing. When she would be sitting on the couch focused concentrating listening to something like a movie she loved or her family's conversation around her her lips would ?purse? forming a small circle as though she were rehearsing the/a respective scale for vocal warm up this of course without the sound though.

My boyfriend when we would share in sexual love had a breathing pattern that would bring me ?a(n) (emotional) wash of (such) comfort coupled with? a rush of (such) eroticism/arousal. Was now bringing me a(n) emotional) wash of (emotional/mental) comfort as my mind reflexively weaves him into my...

meditative state/ meditation story...

Calling upon the memory of the sight of my uncle basking in his favorite armchair, my grandma attentively listening to the loving laughter and chatter of (our) family and my boyfriend's breath outpouring his sexual release of emotional/deep/such love.

To get me back to bed in the middle of the night, to get me able to take on eating at mealtime to get me able to come down from the sensory processing overstimulation of having heard my voice as I spoke in a phone call to get me able to be less likely to be thrown into a risk of choking from a manic eating pace after/from shaking a "shake well before opening" beverage I'm about to have with (my) breakfast/dinner, I would breathe...

in as my sweet uncle out as my precious grandma or significant other.

3

-Making the best of it

-?Strategies/practices implemented to Keep the physical self safe?

-if I can't have my mind I'll have my muscles

-(an) execution of) trickery bodes well (title)?

Making the best of it

-manic state is said to have symptom of endless energy. Well for me I would characterize the state as super human physical strength bringing and endurance and stamina so I steer/use that to my advantage I capitalize on that S and I workout like never would I be strong enough to if I weren't in dissociative. That way by the time dissociative breaks I've already built up my body so much ...

-age regression

-astral projection/visualizations/ channeling .

-try to build /pave (the way) for new neuro pathways.

|————————-|

An ideology that has been instilled in me by my mom since childhood… making the best of a situation/something. If I could harness the power of the symptoms that weren't horrific and steer them/their course in a direction that serves me I wanted to do so (with the time I've got left of dissociative.)

The manic state and its timeless symptom of endless energy or increased energy… well I had a pretty substantial buildup of muscle strength from fitness when I fell ill and over my sickest months where I couldn't continue my routine I lost it all . So now as I stand here racking up months of clean time and feeling empowered in that let me turn my attention to reconstructing the body I once had. One of the last things I remember before I fell ill was my boyfriend saying "I'm built like a tank" … I fought for my life like a tank mentally in/through the thick of the sick of withdrawals and paws period and now I'll see my body fit to fight physically like never before.

I (resolved I) would overcompensate for whatever neurocognitive deficits I had with a musculoskeletal dynamic to rival any level I ever got myself to before. I would say to loved ones "if I can't have my brain I'll have my body" with the mentality/motivator of "if I can't have my mind I'll have (my) muscles" …

I took comfort in knowing that while I had no control over being able to drive my car to go shopping due to my current neuro cognitive state of complications… I was building my body to what would be strong enough to carry home any given thing from the side of the street I might see and want while I'm out doing my daily walking. I would not be held back and held hostage at the hands of my limitations. I would carry an industrial grade 4 tier KETER shelving unit 3 blocks home on foot with bare hands. If I can't have my mind I'll have my muscles. "I think you can have both" a beautiful vote of confidence coming from my partner (that) would bring a fleeting rapture/respite of assuagement to my doubt and fear that I'll never get out of this.

Having not worked out for a very many months of my sickness, Intellect told me I was up against 'unforgiving' muscle loss from time loss and that I would need to outrun any prospective waning of the dissociative with an onslaught of fitness sessions. To no end, I wanted dissociative to end but while all my wishing and willing was to no avail I would utilize/capitalize on the state and steer the symptoms I could in a direction of self-benefit and the 'near inability to feel physical pain, strain and (any) bodily exertion or exhaustion' was certainly a symptom of the dissociative and the mania that I (was learning/was realizing) (I), should, while I'm still in it and could and would strategize the hell out of (it) and/to get my muscle mass amassed beyond anything I was ever called "built like a tank" for, before.

It always helps with motivation, dedication and self-discipline when doing a self-led fitness regimen to have a grounding thought of what makes you feel empowered when you think of your physical strength/having physical strength ? What's your internal narrative of what this strength brings you and is to you ? Is your fantastical role play that of when you are doing arm circles for one minute on the clock but your arms are about to give out and drop to your sides at an untimely 40 seconds in ... what do you picture to find your 'push' ? For me I tell myself that this strength is needed to save a life. I often defer to visualizations of a loved one hanging off of a cliff. The haptic meeting of a shared grip the virility of my arm strength valiantly reeling them in; that last 20 seconds (on the clock) (is crucial,) is finite and unforgiving.

Those last/final seconds (on the clock is) are finite and unforgiving.

. . .

(In my 30 min bi-daily calisthenics routine/set I would "make the best of it"/"make the most of it" if muscle fatigue found me during a respective rep I'd either cling to the cliff scenario or I'd go back to 68 ICU hospital room in my mind; my beloved uncles death bed. I'd fantasize either that somehow standing in his room with all my physical strength was powerful enough to save him or I'd picture I am standing in that 68 icu room his ghost/spirit materialized to see (in retrospect) just how deeply loved by me he was… that all of this 'tank build' my boyfriend sees me for today is none other than a reflection of my anger and anguish that comes/came with losing a family member so dear.

Another way I was managing to take back the strength stolen by almost half a year or half a year of not working out due to sickness was that while I would be doing a rep of physical exertion on a respective muscle group, I would always station/fashion/fasten my focus and anchor my attention to/on a muscle group that was at rest. Trying to push through the last rep of the session of mountain climbers my legs would be near collapse and I'd redirect my thoughts to how good my stomach feels being at rest after all those/the sit-ups. Or on the verge of not being able to do one more sit-up I'd bring the focus as I did them to how completely and blissfully at rest every muscle in my leg gets to be now after the grueling mountain climbers that preceded these sit-ups . By reframing my fitness movements to that of a fine-tuned focus on the feeling of the parts of me that were at rest during a respective rep, I was afforded /I was able to never (have to) 'stop the clock' early (in a given workout set or rep of a movement) no matter how many months my sickness had taken me away from/distanced me from my fitness (regime.) .

?oct? Nov or Dec 2021; 8 or 9 months into my sickness, aka maybe around the time I started using the term/branding "my rehabilitation period/time" interchangeably with "my sickness", aka maybe around the time I started sometimes/seldom swapping out referring to this time as "my sickness" with/for "my rehabilitation". I implemented/devised a stark juxtaposition practice for my healing for purposes of healing. I began taking wellness shots as a post-workout ritual. Now in a time on the incline toward physical prime I would pour the respective 'shot' into the very same shot glass(es) I in the throes of my/an untimely decline would/used to sit my taper pill/dose in for the day on my kitchen counter for that imminent sharp onset moment when I collapsed/ when I would collapse into withdrawals and it felt and feel as though my entire physiology was suddenly all in an instant rejecting me/ and it felt as though being thrust into what I bared witness to...

of my uncle in the ICU; brain to body rejection where there should be connection... 10 days overlapping echos of "his systems not tolerating it" lining the perimeter of the icu room permeating the hallways of the ward. A phrase embossment in my brain of unspeakable/incomprehensible pain.

Except now I felt like I had not reading comprehension from personal research or listening comprehension from physicians. I had subjective experiential knowledge/comprehension of what it is to be in a suffering state of pain and distress of a neurological kind. "His system's not tolerating it" ... that's what I felt when the onslaught of withdrawals would hit/strike. Your system goes from relatively okay one minute to intolerant of everything of/every means of internal stimuli and external stimuli, the next until you pacify it with that eraser tip size white chalky circle resting/sitting/idle in the base of the/that shot glass. So here I am in life, the ringing in of the new year; 2022 and I think I'm going to resolve to refer to what I'm going through for the rest of time only as that "I'm rehabilitating" and not that "I'm sick." A similar differentiation/differential as the reframing I once made for myself of that "I'm broken up with/I was dumped" versus "I'm single". I always said that when the time of processing relationship termination comes, that it feels comfortable to your mind to refer to your status as simply 'single' rather than 'dumped' ... you are invariably on your way to healing. I am not 'still sick' but 'still rehabilitating'.

When dissociative breaks so too with it will the super-human like physical stamina, strength and endurance that affords me a/the fast track to / short cut to the body/build that I was/had and (then) the (subsequent) steering that says 'eat my dust' to that old fitness level as I come barreling in from the unstoppable strength of depersonalization allowing me/lifting me/bolstering me (up) to another level of fit in a most untimely (super-human) manner where I'm soon to be wiping/wipe the floor with that/my old strength class.

I wanted nothing more than for dissociative to break or dissipate or do whatever kind of leaving (me the F alone forever) it was going to (take the trajectory of doing) but while it was not budging (from my brain) I was learning to use the interim as Momm would always say; to "make the best of it."

Just as gravely as I could be negatively affected by an ordinary respective sound that had been improperly processed by my brain therefore sending me into severe nervous system distress/ sensory processing distress/ therefore sending me into severe physiological distress. So too could I be remarkably/exceptionally positively impacted by an ordinary respective sound that had been improperly processed by my brain (therefore) sending my autonomous sensory meridian response soaring to euphoric places/heights.

An absolute stark raving mad, bag purchase craving could erupt with urgency at the auditory intake/beholding, via a YouTube video, of how a respective/certain bag sounds to be opened and shut. And I am not talking about ASMR content creation videos. I am citing random standard recordings where a bag is being handled. I'll hear a certain sound a certain bag makes to the touch and I'll nothing short of 'need' to experience it for myself. I remember how after what was nothing short of a/one handful of months feening for (and surreptitiously buying/acquiring) no other pocketbook textile to grope, gaze at or feast my ears on other than jelly/PVC, this material monogamy vanished one late-October night with/at the happenstance click of a button on a video that featured a woven braided leather cord hard-clutch purse.

Existing in a/living in a for better or for worse, perpetual state of heightened auto sensory meridian response that could make or break me (from minute to minute), was, intense to say the least. My sensorium peppered with/alive with/_____with, such sensitivity that the mouth-feel of yogurts creamy viscosity

reached me like the greater of 2hundred goods would. /Reached me like or as though I were basking in (the) tactile-gustatory glory (that was)(of) the greater of 2hundred goods .

Reached me like

I were basking in tactile-gustatory glory

of the greater of 2hundred (bakery) goods .

"Cravings and urges", it was right there in the list of common side effects for Post-Acute Withdrawal syndrome. And like a true (purse) addict I came by it honestly; wielding dishonesty, manipulation and exploitation in my favor to ensure and secure myself with a continuous consistent flow of handbag arrivals at my door. The average number of handbags the American Woman owns is 11. I prob had about 11 coming a/per month (at one point) in the thick of my sick. Amassing over 50 by the time my sick had thinned out. There were handbags I felt a pull and a calling to experience if I were about to die/ before I die. A self-awareness that found its/ that reached its conscious light/ consciousness / conscious thought during this sickness.

. . .

The surprise 'little something extra gifts' in a care package of essentials dropped off from my parents or in-between along with the practical quality of living gifts like the replacement toilet handle my boyfriend surreptitiously sent me when I started having to "gravity flush" all generosity and gestures where, at the heart of it, appreciated (by me) and yet were spiked with/stung with irritability and anxiety for the threat of this financial support taking me further away/distancing me from the likelihood of a handbag purchase authorization, if asked.

Buying me so many pocketbooks was unfounded so I found ways to get my boyfriend to comply. Assigning one ('purse lust crush' /) purse craving inquiry and purchase plea per upcoming holiday, soon I was out of 'reasonable distance' occasions of birthdays, anniversaries and holidays and would have to start making a play for purses as "an early gift" for...

Oftentimes when I would want something that wasn't a pocketbook I would come close to asking for it but then ultimately if I just held-off asking Id develop a new purse crush and then I'd be so relieved I never did go through with asking for 'that other thing' that could have stood in the way of successful acquisition of this pocketbook!

In time as cognitive function for problem solving was getting closer to resolving I realized it was more likely to obtain parental consent of an essential items order than prospectively it would be of a pocketbook 'for no reason' ; a 'just because' bag . In the absence of a holiday occasion I could solicit (their) consent for purchases of either essentials, peripheral essentials or just something anything that wasn't 'another pocketbook' , obtain their consent and then surreptitiously place my order satiating my stark raving bag mad feening and seething with an order number and (an) eta.

Spoken like a true addict... if my clinical psychologist had to skip a week due to another/an alternate engagement, I saw it as an opportunity to get away with a bag purchase. What money wouldn't be going toward a session that week could be withdrawn from checking account without causing/ inciting too much commotion of question/stir, so long as I refrained from informing Momm that my Dr. couldn't/can't meet this upcoming week, I could exact a/my/the perfectly crafted 'black/gray, lie.'

She would be losing out on (the) saving (of) money on/from that week's cancellation but spared the/any sting of it because/for the cancellation would be unbeknownst to her. To her the financial weight would be/feel no different than any other week (any yet I'd benefit).

I remember when my boyfriend gave me a choice to pick between two items I was coveting/wanting... a crystal meditation singing bowl that I had this deep inner sense would see my pain meds-resistant (perpetually) pounding head (to) some relief through (intake of) (it's) low vibrational frequencies of sound consumption. Or (get)/become the owner/or procure a rare vintage Alexander McQueen skull purse. Like a question of rhetorical regard had just been asked/spoken, I chose 'handbag'; of course.

Like an enclosed piece of '14 Pt cardstock' with purchase "care card" stating how/that states/that outlines how the/a bag needs to be (treated and) cared for, (With) every bag (I) begged (somebody/my boyfriend) for came/was a storyline; the proverbial care card of how I need to be cared for by this bag. Of how it would make me better.

Outlines how the bag needs to be (treated and) cared for,

There were bags for sensory satiation/fulfillment (reasons), bags for (a) simulated work-feel, bags purchased for the name of the seller or the date of the listing bore significance of/in spiritual synchronicity. There were bags bought attached to a daydream of carrying it for my first attended concert again. There was a bag bought for how I would bring it to 'the park of my life' on a sunny-stricken/sunny day/sun-streaming/sun-beaming day when I'm better again and there for a (slow) leisurely stroll around the lake with my boyfriend. For every hopeful future memory there was a pocketbook purchased to match. An (emotional) investment purchase (of) my 'would be bridal purse' should my wedding day happen to be/prove to be his too; Printer Gifter's. There were bags bought for how the sight could stimulate/would ignite visual processing disturbances; maybe the key to as Printer Gifter would say "clawing myself out of this" was in facing/confronting after all my word one of my 'words' of 2020/2021 was 'confront'. The phrase being 'confront the self' .

The physical Prep for undergoing neurological testing may consist of fasting, getting enough sleep and such/etc. but they don't address another avenue of preparation that is needed if a person is to take on the finding out whether or not something horrible/awful is/gets ruled out ...or in. The mental, emotional and psychological prep goes unaddressed...untouched. I guess we all just have to/must, create/cultivate our own. Doctors, family, friends etc Everyone places emphasis on 'just going to get something(s) ruled out.' Few ever pay homage/attention/mind to the matter/fact that to 'go to get something(s) ruled out' you have to be emotionally and psychologically equipped to handle if/should, things get/are 'ruled in'
.

If you feel at risk of self harm in the event something gets/is to be 'ruled in' then you probably should wait until you're willing not to kill yourself with/from/over a test result. What did my own personal pre-test prep look like for helping nudge my psyche toward a place of strength/willingness/will to go on regardless of MRI, EEG outcome ? Doctors bag silhouette pocketbooks. (They would dual-function for my mind as that which would bring good luck/fortune, of/for a clean bill of neurological health and/as well as the strength to safely process the information if/should the tests yield bad/ a ________________. /devastating diagnosis.

(A hybrid of) My mind telling me that I need a respective purse to reach recovery/rehabilitation (or that what 'if' I do) (paired with) cravings coming from each of my very aesthetically-different/differing, and/yet defined personality facets, had these Handbags, shoulder bags, satchels, cross bodies, totes coming in (AMQ skull) hard-bodied (AMQ skull)(skull) clutch (hard-bodied Alexander McQueen, that is), as a functioning (but/albeit) financially-siphoning, (proverbial) vision board (of hopeful manifestation(s).) .

PayPal section where does it go?...

(Unable to slip bag purchases under the parental radar anymore of my linked checking account) I remember desperate calls placed to PayPal, an inquiry of what price point raises/increases the monthly minimum due on/of the credit line. This/Thus telling how many more prospective purses I could/ had (ahead of me) (to *tack on*) (that would go/to go) undetected before the buying was likely to reach Momm's cognizance.

Google image searching through countless thankless vintage red Versace pocketbooks... The bosom friendship had become blaringly obvious/evident I was losing from this absenteeism... could be recaptured (in my mind/astral projection/visualization exercises visualization practices) if only in a small way; the feeling of that person in my life through the purse they used to carry/dote on/covet. Through carrying the purse they used to covet. Through coveting the purse they used to carry.

(Just like) According to my minds monologue I could gain/achieve mastery over 2.5 decades of emetophobia if I just 'add to shopping cart' and/then 'proceed to checkout' with a handbag in toe that features a chain mesh tassel hanging from a serpent's mouth creating, to my anti-psychotic medication-waning distorted visual processing, the look of a spewing action/life form.

. . .

[I remember the liars remorse-endorsed/led, buyers remorse that ensnared my consciousness one time when it was making a cameo appearance (to my otherwise barren-brain brain-barren wasteland of impenitence.) symptom-exploitation tactics functioned in my favor affording me the object of my require/that I require to get better. affording me the object of my get better requisition. Affording me the object of my (hearts desire) and heads require, to get better. (My) racing thought symptomatology took to haranguing me, I deserved it Bc they (my parents) did not.

They did not deserve the wool that had been pulled over their eyes to get/supply their daughter with a green eyed crystal embellished wolf head emblem matte black on black studded chain detailed structured tote bag fit for an off-duty 'death rock' star . that howls "death rock" star off-duty . With the purchase of this gilded wolf head mount purse ...I had nailed the coffin purse shut/ I had put the nails in the (reedition) coffin purse (reedition) on my moral and ethic standings as a wolf in sheep's clothing. And they really didn't deserve that wool being pulled over their eyes from their decoy sheep me/daughter. There was a new-found awareness/knowledge that came in/from all this though and perhaps in that perhaps this ?unfair transaction? ultimately served me as a greater good the higher purpose of reaching awareness that unconscionable/remorse, isn't lost on me/the my medial orbito-frontal cortex.

(This wolf in sheep's clothing was really at the heart of it/ the (brain) matter, a wolf-mount handbag/tote carrying/toting, sheep; a sheep in wolf's clothing (at best)

??accessorized??]

-telling Momm price is lower than it is of purse /scheme strategize tactics

(is this chap 3) ?

-occasion gifts to loved ones registered processed as moving me further and further away from pocketbook obtainment .

(Is this chap 3)?

Some of the things that were most shameful of me for doing/to be doing revealed a most beautiful/celebratory/victorious juxtaposition . To be able to entertain, navigate (and impose) the complex cognitive matrix that was (that of) deceptive information of/about what a coveted pocketbook costs, to increase obtainability/acquisition, Likelihood/likeness, was to see and to know and feel/assume inner confirmation that this cognitive struggle/calamity/condition was regenerative not degenerative and in that the more damage I could do with tactic warfare, scheming and calculated purse plotting and said propositions/proposals…the more morally 'wrong' I was able to (be) /I could muster/eek out … the more closure I had on the course of my illness/cognitive collapse ,moving in the right direction; attenuation and ascension.

I realized just as an offer made to a seller for no more than maybe $10 or $15 dollars less/off was the sweet spot for getting them to cordially accept (the offer) and not reject your offer let alone your whole personhood/ethos landing you with an enemy who could through reviews and ratings make your (whole) internet thrift(ing) life/circuitry/circuiting, a living hell to sell and/or buy … just as their existed a sweet spot to assume on the pre-loved market to get what you want/be afforded what you want so too did there exist a sweet spot on the parental price-manipulation/deceptive/deception front to get you what you want afford you what you want.

If an item I was setting out to solicit parental-approval and authorization of/for was $100, it would register as exponentially less daunting, I deemed, for my mother hear it is/as/to be $85 . $90 could redirect/reroute the mind to $100; it was too close and $85, while although rounded off to $100, stood the chance of mentally processing to a person as “well at least it’s not $100.” “Well at least what they want isn’t $100” “well at least what they’re asking of me isn’t $100.” ; it could be worse, I’ll stand the chance of them (quietly/inwardly) rationalizing/resolving/resigning (themselves to.) .

Once a yay verses nay has been obtained and an emphatic expression of gratitude and excitement has been delivered I then report much to my fabricated dismay a frantic ‘finding’ of either a supply and demand price influx/increase or I beat myself up in sickness and symptom exploitive writing to my Momm saying how (‘I got confused’) and can’t believe I read it wrong getting down on my self for such a mind mishap cognitive slip cognitive mishap; I thought I was better than that. She now sees the/a sense of defeat in me which endows her with (a) refreshed-compassionate action bandwidth/ideation/inclination, and the purchase is secured/confirmed.

[The more manipulative mind/mental matrixes, sickness-exploitative exploitation and complex calculations I was good for the more self-affirming it was that this was/mine was a regenerative and not degenerative disease/case.]

In the #1 New York Times Bestseller “The 5 Love Languages” Gary Chapman writes about how people often fall into one or more of 5 categories for how they like to be loved or best feel love and loved. Among the 5 that can comprise your partner is “Receiving gifts”. I always thought this was curious/interesting when I learned of it being among the 5. While I do very much love receiving gifts it might be said/arguable that the elation and comparison I feel to see someone I love open a gift from me outweighs the joy I feel/it sparks to open one from them. It’s a close call/tough deliberation and ultimately I care for the reciprocity. Being a passionate gift giver toted for spontaneous no occasion just because purchases showing up unannounced in a friend, family or loved ones mailbox or at/on their doorstep you can imagine the hold the addiction (influence) had over me. It hung over me/my head/(hanging over my head) to rendering even the actual occasion gifts (like major holidays), intimidating and panic inducing/producing, to have to make/proceed with. They would 'set me back' is how it registered and processed to my mind. With every gift purchased I was being moved further and further away from being able to 'get away' with surreptitious purse purchases.

[The more manipulative mind/mental matrixes, sickness-exploitative exploitation and complex calculations I was good for the more self-affirming it was that this was/mine was a regenerative and not degenerative disease/case.]

[Moms "make the best of it" internalized life theme paired up/teamed up in my mind with her other (of) "shop what you have" concept, cultivating an inner voice prospective of keeping my teeming for purse purchases at bay ergo/in effect, getting me out of all this spending beyond my means/superfluous shopping/spending. I would wield the lack of emotional recognition aspect/symptom of (the) derealization state, in my power/favor.

I would wield the derealized state symptom of 'emotional recognition deficit' of/in the derealized state , in my favor/in my power; making the best of it. I would request that Momm brings me one old pocketbook from my childhood bedroom per weekly grocery delivery; shop what you have . Employing the Momm sanctioned "shop what you have" adage could function as strategy to slow, stall or maybe even thwart (the) progression of purse purchasing. Plus being devoid of emotional recognition meant that each old dusty punctuated with wear and tear evident of a life well-loved by me, pocketbook, would be experienced to my emotional response of the forebrain/paleo mammalian cortex, as new and novel. With this shop at home shop what you have weekly purse procurement shop at home shop what you have concept (of) shop at home shop what you have, I would be making the best of the situation that is dissociative state induced dissonance of cognition and emotion.]

Daily living (skills) daily functioning ...I supplemented the the control I as a 38.5 year old should have over/of my life but/and didn't with auctions (won), offers (made/accepted,) limited editions, limited quantities made, limited time release, rare, seasonal item and collectors edition(s) . Life had me at a crippling loss of control; embarrassing...unbearable but on the

pre-loved market I could be seen as untouchable unstoppable. I could make anything happen that I wanted to with/at the (screen) tap of a finger. And in/of that I was in a position of power. I had control. Overcompensation preserved my dignity / overcompensation a preservation of dignity.

Overcompensation palliative care to dignity. Overcompensation was palliative care to my dignity.

-singing bowl vs bag

-dr Marsh cancels so bag

-eta (instead of 'and arrival date' in chap 3.)

-bag needs for each personality facet /bag pleas per personality facet

-calling PayPal to find out at what price point does the monthly bill raise/increase

-had these... coming in ((AMQ *hard*-bodied (skull))) clutch

(Chap 3)

. . .

-purses that smell like someone's home sweet home .

-Could control being the one and only to get an item to overcompensate for what I couldn't control; everything I should be able to.

|——|

-malleable (brain) matter ? pave new neural pathways for penetrative orgasm and how that would help a person of my sexual health standings.

(Making the best of it chapter)?

-try to build /pave (the way) for new neural pathways.

-nonelective appendectomy acute nonelective surgery.

-INTRODUCTION. Non-elective operations are those which meet the NCEPOD criteria as either: "Emergency", operation simultaneously with resuscitation, usually within one hour, or: "Urgent", operation as soon as possible after resuscitation, usually within 24 hours.

Was this limbo brain state of/that is depersonalization and derealization something that renders neural pathways impressionable malleable and therefore conducive to building/paving the way for new ones (neuro pathways ?) ?

If I do it now while the dissociative state lasts/becomes me, would I have a chance at/for a better success rate (than in the past) of/with being able to wrangle/harness/condition myself to achieve penetrative orgasm, than I have historically; nil ? (Most of my dating life what was just/) what was always just a fun-intentioned recreational "at face value" sexual elective-ideation /desire had become laden with heavy pressing importance in the recent years an HSV2 contraction/diagnosis disqualified/took me from the orgasmic pleasure/option of sitting on your face. (me from sitting on your face for orgasmic pleasure.) no longer that of a sexual-elective, becoming vaginally orgasmic for condom-clad intercourse was to my 'sexual pleasure/fulfillment survival' as surgery is to NCEPOD criteria-met medical states.

4

at risk / high risk

*a cautionary consumption /food

*fear for thought /food

*menacing mastication

*settle your system / settle your stomach

*neurological rejection /neurologically rejects it

|—|

-Chest palpitations/fluttering ...Heart attack

-Head pressure tearing ...Brain aneurysm

-Choke safe...cut off from brain to body signals then after that restored I was left to wonder if the dissociative state of depersonalization and derealization lands one in an increased risk high(er) risk category of choking.

-Worry of OE and nausea resulting so would count calories

-food poison risk

-fall risk

-Accidental od risk

|—|

Hit by car Bc don't know how to cross street properly (non intersection) /can't drive

Food poisoning Bc can't read labels correctly (need year part to be different)

Accidental od Bc can't do remedial math or

Accidental life threatening underdose (seizure)

Head pressure brain aneurysm

Chest palpitations heart attack

Choke Bc dissociative (eating like drunk or nitrous Oxide) or compromised brain to body signals for safe/proper chewing and swallowing.

|—————|

The girl who couldn't feel pain

Or time passage

Or hunger/fullness

Or sleepiness

Or temperature of water and air

Or volume of sound

Or the distinction of dry vs damp

Chatter in head

Pressure of head

No person place or thing ever looks real ever

|————-|

On the exit ramp of withdrawals now my basic/baseline brain to body signaling for safe proper chewing and swallowing of food had restored but this entrance ramp to PAWS (post acute withdrawal syndrome) proved to have its own host of concerns/disconcerting things some continuing some commencing.

With the biochemical dependency aspect reasonably presumably on the wane or surmounted I could shift my 'choking hazard' worries to that of how does one fare in the dissociative state of depersonalization and derealization; how does that factor into the eating experience? When a person eats while they are drunk or high surely they must be at an increased risk of choking and now we are talking about a condition; dissociative, that has me in a compromised detached brain state like that 24/7 (for) a succession of consecutive months; suspended in an altered brain state/a state of altered thinking. My choking hazard

risk-level must be up exponentially!

I will never again take a concept like the social compulsory proclamation “let’s do lunch,” a “dinner date,” a “dinner party,” a work lunch-in or the employee/faculty lunch room for granted again. They are all eating engagements that revolve around socializing. As I think of all these time honored American pastime traditions I think of how right now I need to set a timer for eating to make sure my rate of eating for a respective meal matches up with /aligns with /is akin to how I ate for 37 years; neurotypical me. After all if I’ve just “shaken well before opening” , a beverage, it can take redirected concentration and focus after redirected concentration and focus to make sure my bite-rate isn’t now just a mere mechanical motion mirroring the speed of what I just shook/the organic juice I just shook/the nutrition shake I just shook; manic.

Eating in the dissociative state of derealization and depersonalization... I think of how near all American pastimes of eating experiences unite under the one universality that is ‘socializing.’ A reminder that the act of eating shouldn’t have to take the (amount) of focus and concentration not to choke, that it takes me.

When I wasn’t musing about if I’m at an increased choke risk as opposed to the average person who eats in an altered state maybe once or twice a week by way of a glass of wine on a dinner date or absentmindedly dipping their hand in a bowl of pretzels while out at happy hour with coworkers ... I was then contemplating my risk of Overeating and undereating. Being that I was too dealing with a compromised state of hunger/fullness sensing.

I was dealing with a faulty brain to body connection for proper signaling of hunger and fullness. I could be hit by a car at a non-intersection on the streets of my quiet suburban neighborhood when crossing from sidewalk to sidewalk during my daily walks, Bc I didn’t know how to (safely) cross the street and gage distance of a car with my gait... so for the time being my higher self would keep me only walking on streets where the sidewalk hooks around to reveal a connecting street. I didn’t know how to cross the street let alone drive my car. Me, someone who at one time had their life's work revolving around driving; I was a traveling school photographer, my driving spanning from Montauk to Manhattan on any given day of every given school year. Me, someone who considered driving stag at night on the open road with windows down and music up , a time-honored pastime of self-love... yes that Stephanie Dianne Selles was now 5 days shy of 9 months into that of being rendered neuro cognitively and neuropsychiatrically incapable of driving.

Decades of life of taking to the stage in karaoke outings for friends birthdays for my birthdays for holidays for ordinary days all of us having signature stylings and songs we were known to covet covering and a first name basis rapport/regard with the bar owner/DJ. We were all 'regulars' enough so as to have learned through trial and error over time what singers and songs best fit and complimented our vocal ranges and what performers we could best emulate with/in our stage presence. Curating outfits at times we gave the bar an impersonator concert experience. We went to live band karaoke, DJ karaoke, outdoor karaoke, indoor karaoke, karaoke surrounded by a koi pond, karaoke with a huge tree growing through the bar and karaoke with sand and chaise lounges. We sang solos, duets and did group performances. Adding an overlay of dancing, theatrical showmanship or creating a dark evocative mood-setting mind-scape for people to sink into...my international thespian society cred/status had its outlet.

It was nothing short of unfathomable/unthinkable and nothing shy of unspeakable to be thrust into what would be 9+ months of navigating a nervous system that was non-compliant in letting me speak comfortably (aloud) much less sing anything . The auditory sensory processing of spoken word coming from my mouth and all the trappings of saliva moving about and teeth making contact with their counterparts...just to talk on the phone with a friend was to comb over comb through my nerve endings with a razor blade. / fine-tooth comb (through) my nerve endings with a razor blade.

. . .

And it didn't matter content pleasant or unpleasant to carry on a conversation be it in text-messaging, phone-calling or video-chatting... the stimulation of my own speaking voice or concentrated attention in/exerted in/to keep(ing) up in/with a text thread, would swell my head pressure to dizzying heights

[bringing my mind to the recurring question theme of/ causing my mind an unexpected visit/drop-in (visit) from the recurring question was I at risk of having a brain aneurysm. /]

In effect, slamming/crashing my mind with the 'always overstays their (un)welcome' visitation of thought(s)... was I at risk of having a brain aneurysm?.

And then there was the overlay of being at a neurocognitive loss to/of understand(ing) them; my (dear) friends (my family members my boyfriend) what they were saying in a phone call, what they were conveying/sending in a text message. Did an incoming paragraph I had just laid my eyes on constitute as sarcasm they wanted me to laugh at or sincerity they wanted me to meet their regard on? I didn't know Bc I couldn't tell/ interpret humor. I couldn't interpret humor and I couldn't tell if a respective response in text I would send or reaction in phone or video call I would make was appropriate for a respective thing they had just said or offensive to what they just said. My reading comprehension and listening comprehension was shot to shit at a level that could put me at risk of dear friends dropping off due to/after my repeated offense of grossly misunderstanding something they've said and improperly or worse yet inappropriately responding to it. I was always/constantly and consistently at risk of falsely taking offense to something benign they said or them taking offense to something falsely/unbeknownst to me, 'constitutes as' malignant, that I said. Avoidance felt like the lesser/safer of 2 evils; to be an absentee friend.

When you're 37 and not 7, reading comprehension and listening comprehension deficits have dramatic real-world implications and consequences that span beyond spending a day longer on "jump frog jump" or "bears boats and balloons" while the (rest of the) class moves ahead to the next book in the series. When you're 38 and not 83 in a memory-care assisted living facility, reading comprehension and listening comprehension impairments can cost you interpersonal relationships that don't just time out when/Bc the friend forgets they were hurt/upset with you. When you have age-related listening comprehension and reading comprehension levels/struggles it is universally more accepted and doesn't face the adversity such adversity as when you're of an age where to be like this is not the norm amongst your peers/peer group. To be young enough is to be that you're listening comprehension and reading comprehension is understandably developing and to be old enough is to be that you're listening comprehension and reading comprehension is forgivably declining but to be in the median of your life is to have your suffering met with grave detrimental misunderstanding.

And it didn't matter content pleasant or unpleasant to carry on a conversation be it in text-messaging, phone-calling or video-chatting… the stimulation of my own speaking voice or concentrated attention in/exerted in/to keep(ing) up in/with a text thread, would swell my head pressure to dizzying heights

[bringing my mind to the recurring question theme of/causing my mind an unexpected visit/drop-in (visit) from the recurring question was I at risk of having a brain aneurysm. /]

In effect, slamming/crashing my mind with the 'always overstays their (un)welcome' visitation of thought(s)… was I at risk of having a brain aneurysm?.

After 37 years of none of this, all in an instant on March 10th, 2021 I was suddenly stricken with what would unbeknownst to me at the time prove to last for a very many months. I could be Hit by car Bc I didn't know how to cross my residential neighborhood streets properly, I couldn't operate a vehicle, I was at risk of incurring Food poisoning Bc I can't read labels correctly; to know it hadn't passed yet I needed the year part to say 2022 Bc I couldn't decipher just from looking at month and day whether or not it was a calendar date that had passed yet or was yet to come.

All in an instant I went from an experienced fervent driver who would drive for pleasure; joy rides abound! To that of rendered neuro cognitively incapable of knowing how to cross a side street much less operate a vehicle; yesterday I could do a road-trip of distance driving to a destination wedding if I wanted to, today 24 hours later I felt confused about gas pedal and brake pedal; Just like that.

During the tapering period if it weren't for my upstanding mother opting to come stay with me through it, I would have been at high high risk of a life threatening Accidental overdose or a life threatening accidental under dose Bc I was without the necessary cognitive capacity to do remedial math to know if I was using the pill splitter right from night to night; my beloved mother preemptively saved my life in living with me. I was at risk of underrating/overeating and I was at risk of overdosing/under-dosing. My Momm safe-guarded me from the latter while my/the higher-self safe-guided me in/through the former; They were a good team.

This 24/7 sustained now 4 days shy of 9 consecutive months of rhythmic throbbing Head pressure. I had plenty of time to revisit the thought that this is the stuff a brain aneurysm is made of; it has to be. You know that unpleasant 'all the blood rushing away from your head' sensation of pressure and lightheadedness that can come on suddenly in a sharp onset from standing up too fast? That was me only without any antecedent of getting up too fast and without any 'several seconds later' dissipation and extinguishment.

It was as though I was just frozen in time at the crest of the/that incline and at the most/and at best, it would eventually many many months in, start to show fluctuation in its severity but the trajectory was non-linear and still the symptom was never 'not with me.'

As time went on, I gained agency over how to describe the unbearable sensations of my symptoms in ways that would be more universally relatable. The amorphous head pressure I likened to that of the standing up too fast head rush feeling, combined with the subtle 'continuous motion' sensation of being/standing on a dock at the harbor, combined with that of the 'going through a train tunnel' feeling where everybody momentarily drops their chatter with each other mid-sentence while they scrunch their face hold their ears and wait for the momentary discomfort to 'time out' before resuming verbal exchanges. I don't get the luxury of waiting for the feeling to pass before resuming socializing. For I can't just drop my conversations with people for 9+ months; I have interpersonal relationships to maintain.

Nightly as I lie in my bed I can never feel any tactile sense/awareness of the billowing blankets, the softness of the pillow that cradles my head, the sensation of warm soft fabric as my legs move through/beneath it, or the pillow top plush mattress I lay on waiting for sleep to whisk me away with/to unconsciousness; waiting to be rescued. No, all I have sensory perception of is whatever this unbearable strange internal stimuli is that is resulting from brain chemistry gone awry/ from haywire brain chemistry. The sound of my analog fan white noise machine is good for me but only once I make it past the auditory processing treacherous threshold of hearing the change from off to on and from on to off in the mornings... the nervous system impact of my brain processing that change is enough to send me into a physiological fit of panic state reaction of/adorned with muscle tensing of the throat (not neck; throat) that edges toward cramping of the tongue.

The change of a ceiling light or room lamp from off to on was excruciating to my sensory processing, as well. It didn't even matter if it was broad daylight and all I did was flip of the switch to a light that pretty much just mirrored the lighting level that was already in the room from the sun... just any subtle sudden change felt like nails raking over the chalkboard of/that was my nervous system. Anything that produced a spotlight effect produced the most unbearable anxiety. So neurologically intolerable so non-processable and unacceptable this respective spotlight of light was that whenever my default comfort tv show of a home shopping channel would betray me/my trust and advertise (bedside) reading lights, floodlights or flashlights for their Christmas special complete with demos... the sight would confuse and maybe anger me. I had to get the channel changed right away.

6 to 9 months in, just as I started to experience less of an intolerance to light switches I concurrently realized if I close my eyes for the nano second of the flip of of the switch ergo bypassing the witnessing of the change then I could visually cope better with the light now being on for the rest of a respective afternoon whereas countless other times unable to settle my system I would just have to turn it (right) back off after I had (tried to) turn it on after I had tried to live with it on.

Night after night of day after day of week after week of month after month I'd have to do my best to snuff out thoughts that the flood of Chest palpitations I'd get as I was lying in bed meant a heart attack just like Uncle Art (had), is imminent. I live alone and going to bed when near no one is reachable was very daunting.

...Close/shut my eyes to/on my heart skipping a beat and let my higher self helicopter-lift- rescue my mind from my body, taking me to a moment in time where my mom sings to my child-self "skip to my Lou" . For every irregular set of heard beats; flutters, and skips "Lou Lou skip to my Lou, Lou Lou skip to my Lou Lou, Lou skip to my Lou, skip to my Lou my darling" her playful cheerful/spirited voice would sing me. And her smile ... oh her smile ...

Lou Lou skip to my Lou, Lou Lou skip to my Lou Lou, Lou skip to my Lou skip to my Lou my darling" . My chest is settling now.

I lose traction on my focused visualization my heart skips a beat and my higher-conscious self takes my mind out(side) to/where it can skip to the beat in/of an old 80's/90's/childhood/nostalgic commercial for "skip it" by Tiger (toy company, electronics.) . I fall asleep.

Alone Night after night of day after day of week after week of month after month, I'd have to do my best to blot-out/overpower thoughts that that the rhythmic throbbing of the 9months and counting, 24/7 sustained Feeling that my head was in a vice being cranked... the pressure so great at times it would produce tears not of sadness but as a bodily reflex from the pressure/sensation ...that that didn't foreshadow a brain aneurysm?? That I would in fact wake (up) the next morning to see the next day. Going to bed/sleep always in (a state of) anticipatory anxiety/worry that 'tonight would/could be the night that if I get a runny nose, I unknowingly wipe away blood in the darkness of my room. This fear, gaining in momentum and snowballing to a fear of feeling any sense of wetness in my nostrils in the night.

Was I at risk of Choking on my food seeing as how being in the dissociative state of depersonalization and derealization is like being drunk or on nitrous oxide at the dentist. You think it's a good idea to have a meal tray rolled in for consumption after you've been given any level of sweet air in the dental chair? How about doing it more than once, how about doing it for months (worth) of meals ? And while you're at it, can you tell me if I'm at risk of a brain aneurysm ? 24/7 I have that 'all the blood rushing away from my head' feeling that you get for a split second when you get up too fast.

or compromised brain to body signals for safe/proper chewing and swallowing.

Was It only a matter of time till I got mrsa/sepsis from an infection of an olfactory sensed decaying tooth reaching my bloodstream that I hadn't the brain to body ability to feel its antecedent of pain/pain antecedent ?

. . .

From falls I had in and outside of the home to burn scarring I got and have no recollection of how or when to skinned knees fit for a child learning to ride a/their bicycle to bruises from my own hands colliding during the arm circles of a workout routine/set. ... to a papercut like slit from not knowing how hard was too hard to grip the serrated butter knife under the faucet during a (respective) dish-washing session and/along with under nail fork prong jabs that required ice reapplication throughout the week. A new meaning given to the old "pinch an inch" skin saying when an indentation on my arm took (but) hours to fade after improperly placing a bracelet; not realizing I had caught skin in the closure.

In my eyes, it wasn't a purse of brilliant beaded embellishments but a cluster of bugs and spider egg sacs. In my eyes, it wasn't organic jelly on my morning bagel but blood.

In my eyes, it wasn't the concrete stained dark from a respective house's lawn sprinkler reaching the sidewalk in its cycle/oscillation, it was a darkness that confused my brain and threatened to buckle my knees for/in a fall. The few bright white horizontal patches of concrete in the neighborhood, in my mind, was ice that promised my footing to slip if I stepped on it.

In my bathroom, there was no candle-lit spa like bath drawn but rather an empty movie set suicide bath scene with the actress missing and an ominous feeling that I'm the understudy/stand-in.

In my heart, there was no emotional implication of cumulative years of love for my family, love for my friends, love for my partner. These were the faces of the parents I'd looked into, loved and been loved by for 38.5 years, but there was no emotional recognition.

It almost proved too disturbing to keep up dental hygiene, for the ways the toothbrush contorts ones face in the mirror was too much staring back at me, for t put me at risk of embodying the character I would see; demonic. Watching any movies or shows beyond a PG rating was unsafe for me as my mood, my mind and emotions would almost reflexively mirror that of any thing I watched so to see violence portrayed in film proved too uncomfortable for/to me and I started self-imposed viewing restrictions.

Neurotypically, music selection would come from mood, but in this neuro A-typical state, mood and mind state followed/is what came from music selection, so I employed limitations to keep me safe. After 37.5 years of living effortlessly with the contours of my face, suddenly I was vulnerable to physiological panic response over the fact that a portion of my nose is always in my field of view whether I look straight left or right it's always in my line of sight; I can't escape it. I just want to see what I'm intentionally looking at without a (punishing) foreground layer of sight. The subtle sound of my mouth's saliva as I would talk on the phone along with the sound and sensation of my teeth touching/making contact with each other would all cut through me like a knife taken to my nerve endings.

I could smell the sweetness of a flower; (my) olfactory intact touch its velvety petals and see the brilliance and magnificence of its colors yet Want it as I may, 9 months today, I can never will a single person, place or thing to look real/register as real, (to me).

Nothing was as it appeared and everything (as it appeared) was a product of a neurological brain glitch; Intellect/intellectualism was the/my partition between/of psychosis and sanity(compos mentis)/lucidity. The Ability to hold onto and hold fast to this knowledge as I navigated through the minefield of the hell of my mind was what my psychiatrist said afforded me to be separated from that of a full blown psychosis and he attributes that non-slip grip on reality to maturation of chronological age; 37.5/38.5. My age saved me.

I may have intellectually known that beads of water droplets on my skin were not clusters of blisters/ blister clusters but that/my non-slip grip on reality did little/nil to thwart my nervous system from reacting/responding as if/as though a respective thing really was the disturbance my eyes perceived. Reflexively, I'd be thrown/thrust into physiological panic response of throat muscles tensing/threatening to cramp and take my tongue with it/them. Sometimes while looking at the respective everyday sight or everyday object that would systematically process as disturbing, part of my hand would go rigid or have an involuntary (repetitive like stimming) fine motor movement.

Having a life-long clinical psychological diagnosis of obsessive compulsive disorder (with obsessive thought processing) and struggles I can remember that date back to childhood... the derealization overlay of ocd that was my 'soon to be 10 months' punctuated/adorned/embellished my historic predisposition of/for mental snags with quite the conical studs and pyramid studs of a/the proverbial handbag pulling all your hair out. Because after all, now when I locked my door for the night before bed, sure I could visually confirm that the door was in fact locked but could I trust my visual perception of things when my currency is that no person, place or thing, looks real ' ? Could I trust what I would see? Hunched over to look in, Shining the flashlight beam of my smartphone into the parting/crack of/in the door frame, I felt so stupid/pathetic but what's more, I felt this isn't even neurotypical ocd me behavior. And it wasn't. The old adage 'seeing is believing', a bitingly bitterly laughable oxymoron to/in the clutches of derealization/depersonalization, ocd overlay; scoff-worthy.

|——————————————|

The following segment is for maybe chapter 4 , CJD or chapter where I write about how I managed/coped.

-ocd of empty choc strawberries plastic container looking like would work for paw prints encasing. (The Doily like things)

-ocd of paper towel I dabbed memoir pages with

-ocd of if I look at memory cabinet for 'too long' while holding something I'm en route to throw away.

-risk benefit living decision making I had to do self intervention with and implementation of ex. Locking door

-if I articulate/disclose my struggles to parents maybe it will in part take the power out of things hopefully.

-if I give into compulsion after accidentally knocking memory cabinet while holding trash then that raises the ocd bar for tomorrow being if I incidentally look at and if I give into compulsion on that level, then eventually I won't be comfortable throwing anything away from merely walking by memory cabinet (despite having my eyes closed or successfully averting them.)

-Imaging, surgical, and lesion studies suggest that the prefrontal cortex (orbitofrontal and anterior cingulate cortexes), basal ganglia, and thalamus are involved in the pathogenesis of obsessive-compulsive disorder (OCD).

|————————————————-|

|—————————|

I think or I know put this in chap 4

-about how the street finds acquisition of objects, difficulty throwing away legitimate trash combines to make for a situation where ones irrational obsessive fears might actually become (more) possible/plausible concern(s).

ex.) narrow carry of (fridge) trash past memory cabinet due to *keter shelves*

ex.) (worry of apt fire while out walking And in that loss of writing hard copy-should I put file box in car each day for duration of time out of house aka walk ? . made list of what to take in event of a fire I'm aware of. And *empty cereal box* atop 'have to keep up with unplugging it' toaster Bc *empty boxes* are still in cabinetry, threatens to push/edge an otherwise irrational intrusive 'product of my ocd' thought into something (unfortunately) viable.

The more I F42.3 (ICD-10) / DSM-5 300.3, the more my/ones irrational fears are incidentally rendered incidentally rational .

Another ex. Is ... mud room accumulated empty boxes could now actually avalanche onto previously cleared but obsessively worried space of paw prints.

|---------------|

Obsessive thought processing and compulsive action/compulsive behavior(s)... (my) ocd was outrunning me and would threaten to/ was threatening to outlive me if I didn't outsmart it.

I conducted a self-intervention constructed of a risk-benefit living based decision making paradigm/model I would/an a heroic/valiant (vigilante) attempt to save my rational mind from the overtaking of (my)(the) ocd. I would stall or thwart my mind from upping the anti on what compulsion it takes, to dish out a/that (false) sense of security/certainty that allowed me to move off of the/my presenting obsession/obsessive thought perseveration/fixation .

At first it only became hard to follow through with throwing away an eaten or used fridge item if I had accidentally bumped the memory cabinet while en route to the garbage pail with the respective refuse/trash in my grasp. But giving in to rummaging in the refuse till

I was satisfied that nothing from the memory cabinet had mysteriously/magically/somehow fallen in then led to if i so much as incidentally looked/caught sight of the memory cabinet while walking toward the garbage I'd be snagged on/by an intrusive thought of well maybe now this respective garbage item has somehow become part of the memory cabinet and to throw it away is to be throwing a piece of the memory cabinet away.

The longer my eyes had the memory cabinet in their field of view while walking toward/to the garbage the harder it was to release the respective empty food wrapper or empty food container into the pail once I got there/to it . Intellectually, I recognized the insidious festering nature of the mental disease; ocd ... where once it took an accidental bumping into; a making of physical contact , to rattle me; touch, it was now taking but only an incidental visual contact to muss my mind and launch me into (desperate) texts to my shrink and loved ones as if I were someone texting my sponsor on the verge of drinking but their drinking was my rifling through (the) refuse. If I didn't find the strength in myself to sever the cycle; restrain myself from following through with the compulsion I knew I was headed to a snowballed-effect ocd existence/level of severe life interference that I would be pelted with (in an all out snowball fight (to the death)) by the pathogenesis of (my) ocd the prefrontal cortex, basal ganglia and and thalamus; the pathogenesis of (my) ocd, (In an all out snowball (fight to the death.)).

by the pathogenesis of (my) ocd the prefrontal cortex, basal ganglia and and thalamus In an all out snowball fight (to the death.)

And what would that look like? It would look like my eyes are successfully averted like a horse with blinders on or a canine wearing a cone as I walk past the memory cabinet; maybe I close them/my eyes (as I walk past it) or I just keep my eye on the prize; the pail ahead (in the distance) like a ballerina keeps her focal point on a fixed spot as they spin so as to circumvent dizziness, I would affix my pupils/iris(es) to that pail and not let it slip from the grip of my gaze and yet just the cognitive 'knowing' that I (had) walked past the memory cabinet to go from/to get/ in going from point A; the fridge to point B; the garbage would be enough to have me/land me (in the compromising position of) F42.3 (ICD-10) / DSM-5 300.3 'should be thrown out' (empty) food and drink packaging(s) (items). That was what was ahead if I didn't rush my ________/?behaviors? to the proverbial operating theater and employ risk-benefit (living) based decision making stat from it taking accidental touch to induce ocd to incidental sight being enough to bring it on to what was next? intrinsic knowing (that I had walked past the memory cabinet) being enough to collapse me into ocd ? Ocd is progressive, degenerative and insidious. It infiltrates, festers and gains in momentum rapidly. .kinetic. And/it must be stopped.

Talk here about risk/benefit door lock ...

If the door should somehow escape my attention and go unlocked through the night, the chances that there would just so happen to be an intruder and it would just so happen to be on that night, were next to nil I would tell myself; risk . Compared to the benefit that comes with resisting the compulsion of countless door lock checking (for (even) one night) which/that was sizable. It could and likely would mean the difference of how mercilessly my mind maims me with compulsive urge the following night routine and how resistant I am able to be of it/stand tall of it. I had weighed risk-benefit and determined that it was in my best interest to allow myself to the one compulsory/obligatory door lock check/glance that as I reasoned it anybody of normative functioning would do and then cut myself off.

-ocd of empty choc strawberries, plastic container looking like it would work for paw prints encasing. (The Doily like things)

. . .

If I cow-tow to my thoughts of washing and stashing somewhere the disposable recyclable empty plastic packaging my self-love Valentine's Day choc covered strawberries came in on the premise of/that I had intrusive imagery of my beloved deceased cat babies paw prints in them and now I worry that to throw them out is to discard the paw prints somehow/ in some way which are a symbol of my babies' love and life, so really the fear is that I'll be rejecting my babies in some way. Throwing them out and therefor making them somehow more gone or further from my mortal reach.

All this when it's not like I was even on the market for a final resting place/receptacle of those pair of paw print molds. They were and had been encased for 3 years now in a glass display box that beautifully and perfectly preserves them; their final resting place. I failed myself and retrieved from the refuse After 3 days to a week of letting the kitchen garbage pail build in odor pungency Bc I couldn't bring myself to do the final step of letting the bag that contained those empty choc covered strawberry plastic containers see the flinging into the 30 to 35 gallon abyss on the side of the house that would be dragged out to the curb on cobblestone indented rickety wheels come (garbage) collection day.

As I sifted through what was much more disgusting, 13gallon bag contents that had I retrieved earlier in the week but on the bright side, hey, I made it a week thinking I might not retrieve! But yeah the ramifications of going as long as I had was an olfactory price of lofty means/heights. As I hovered over the Hubble beneath the swinging lid, I unsnapped the top(s) of the container(s) and with my disposable-glove clad hand scooped out the green strawberry (??now molding??) leafy tops that remained inside. And sure enough, just as metastatic-like as ocd is ... I found myself talk taking me into a place of question and contemplation of should I be saving/salvaging and washing/restoring the melted choc and strawberry juice smeared corrugated paper baking cup /muffin, liners too? The paw prints could sit in them within the box. They are part of the box/container so to throw them out would be to throw out part of the container and to throw out the container is/would be to throw out the paw prints in some way (seeing as how I had flash images of my precious paw prints rehomed/housed in that container .)

To throw out the paw prints 'in some way' is to/would be to lose my babies further in some way. I managed to stop at the unhealthy taking back/reclamation/reclaiming of the plastic containers; the baking liners currently sit in a tied up drawstring hefty bag in the 30 to 35 gallon 'final stage' pail on the side of the house. The bag has been marked with a sharpie marker so as to distinguish it / making the distinction of it from whatever other bags might be thrown in there by the homeowners; a self-placating decision incase I can't make it to Garbage collection/compactor/compaction day. A sharpie mark I might not have made, I might have been spared of, had I only not bumped into memory cabinet related contents en route to the front door with trash bag in hand . ?But when you have the product of a life long F42.3 (ICD-10) / DSM-5 300.3; a F42.3 (ICD-10) / DSM-5 300.3 life, the ways in which that overlaps with ocd is just ruthless/unending?

The street finds acquisition of objects and a difficulty throwing away legitimate trash combines and collides making for a situation where one's irrational obsessive fears might actually become (more) possible/plausible concern(s).

It's a 'narrow carry' of (fridge) trash past memory cabinet due to roadside find/curbside find of *keter shelves*. Where once I walked freely but worried endlessly that memory cabinet contents had (black)magically gotten mixed in with fallen into the trash in my grasp now with the/compliments of the acquisition of the latest assembled (keter) shelving unit my irrational fears (of accidentally swiping something) could be legitimized right before my eyes at the foot of my once unencumbered stride as I now (need) side step(past) the memory cabinet. (Hyper concentration not to swipe anything is justified/justifiable.)

. . .

Seldom but not never, I worry while out walking that there will be a house fire, And in the narrative of that imagined loss, will be the hard copy of my manuscript. I muse, should I move the file box to my car each day just for the duration of time I will be out of the house on my walk? .

Even when I was of healthy neurological baseline time in/of life, I was someone who made a mental and I think (or I think I think) actual/physical, list of 'what to take in the event of a fire' . (I'm aware of.) where a once empty stovetop (graced only with maybe the/a (dusty) obligatory empty pot or a (dry as a bone) decorative use compulsory decorative use kettle) where that electric stovetop surface space was now littered with trash I just couldn't throw away for one irrational intrusive thought 'reason or another' and smattered with stuff I just couldn't put away for one neurocognitive deficit or another, a previously fire safe space punctuated with only product of illogical thinking/thought that there would be a fire, was now an actual flammable risk-situation situation of risk.

A risk situation that graduated/leveled up , to 'high-risk' when a once 'in retrospect needlessly worry that I'd bump into stove knobs; turning it on' became that of something of reasonable/due concern with the coming of many an unpacked (shopping) bag and a growing collection of empty packaging (food and non food alike) that slowly/incrementally but systematically (nonetheless/all the same/just the same) reduced me (bag by bag) to a precarious leaning over of the stove (required)to (stretch and) make contact with other kitchen spaces/utility and in utilization/interaction of other kitchen appliances. A self-rendered fire hazard life(style) By default of my F42.3 (ICD-10) / DSM-5 300.3/disorder had been set in motion/forged.

Soon I found myself falling prey to using every kitchen space like the proverbial 'guest room' in a townhouse. You throw things in it and keep it cluttered-up until you know you are to be expecting a guest you will need to accommodate. That that room will need to accommodate. Just delivered to me cereal boxes from the grocery store laid stacked up on the top of my toaster Bc after all, I wasn't using the appliance this very minute, right? Every surface space or reservoir like the bathtub that I wasn't using 'this very minute' became/was repurposed as storage space to the stuff I couldn't put in its rightful place

Bc 'empties' were in its rightful place and my mind was non-compliant to do anything about it. Cabinets (fully/partially) stocked/lined with *empty cereal boxes* had me resorting to a system/daily routine of move, the full/current/relevant boxes off the toaster to make my daily morning/brunch toast before then once again re-placing/re-situating them post toast pop up and element cool-down period. My 'have to keep up with unplugging it(after every use)so as to ensure fire-safety of the stored atop cardboard cereal boxes ' was a dangerous memory game to (have to) play for a neuro compromised cognition.

I was physically and mentally maneuvering/matriculating in a life quality/quality of life/living where The stillness of a couple of *empty boxes* housed in cabinetry, could/would (mean/amount to) threaten to push/edge an otherwise irrational intrusive 'product of my ocd' thought/fear/perseveration(;house fire), into something of an unfortunate(ly) viable/validated/vindicated/warranted preoccupation

.

[The more I F42.3 (ICD-10) / DSM-5 300.3, the more my/ones irrational fears are incidentally rendered incidentally rational .

Another ex. Is ... mud room accumulated empty boxes could now actually avalanche onto previously cleared but obsessively worried space of paw prints.]

. . .

[Another ex. Is ... mud room accumulated empty boxes could now actually avalanche onto previously cleared but obsessively worried space of paw prints.

The more I F42.3 (ICD-10) / DSM-5 300.3 the more my/ones irrational fears are incidentally rendered incidentally rational .]

5

|———-|

*A race against timeAtLarge (ex. reproductive years, 8 lockers at 38, aging family of origin and my birth rite of last of my family of origin …)

*the things I had to miss (ex 20 yr reunion, nyc burlesque fest, nutcracker rogue, hjl)

*the markers I kept setting my sights on being better by (ex. My 38th bday)

*the things that caved in around me (ex. Coat rack, toilet)

|———|

The collapse/Product or fallout of a F42.3 (ICD-10) / DSM-5 300.3 life; the things that caved in around me

The one time ever in 37.5 years of life I am to be going through an actual neurological complication and the universe/the fates etc decides now is the time of 3 to 4 years of living and existing just fine in this apt, now is the time to sic her with the product of her 'left untreated' F42.3 (ICD-10) / DSM-5 300.3 life. First thing of...

'the collapse' was in the thick of the sick (of withdrawals and taper process) my entryway wall mounted coat rack that tore from the wall one night while my mom and I were sitting on the couch... was this monthly doormat installed coat rack a metaphor for how soon my vital (internal) organs will tragically succumb to the dramatic weight loss ? Was this a sign that my body was edging toward being no longer able to absorb something; the impact of being 77ish pounds? Or perhaps the message of This coat rack that could no longer absorb the dramatic impact of heaped heavy coats draped over it, was that product of a F42.3 (ICD-10) / DSM-5 300.3 life or the fallout of a F42.3 (ICD-10) / DSM-5 300.3 life, has begun; your proverbial "buried alive" is happening.

Karma came barreling in with a force field of kinetic energy the universe hell bent on shocking me into changing my life... my bedroom ceiling globe light burned out, and being in the dissociative state, it proved too dangerous to fondle a glass fixture. I had to stretch to reach above my head so as to replace the bulb...instead I would be forced to draw back the double layer black out curtains each day that remained closed reinforced by an overcrowded commercial grade/industrial grade rack of clothes. Everyday now sunlight would peek through my curtains from the one place I managed to hike them up over bumps of clothes just enough to not risk the folded piles that sit atop the rack falling.

When my toilet stopped flushing properly and it's/the contents were backing up through the tub drain, I couldn't call my monthly door mats to come look at it Bc surely a family who has professional window washers come annually and a housekeeping service bi-weekly/monthly isn't exactly going to take kindly to having to side step through the too narrow a path, apt to walk/put one foot in front of the other.

I didn't have a lease I could and likely would be evicted and then I'd be having to dismantle and box-up a whole apt, at a time when I retrieve one item from a drawer or the freezer and have a whole struggled spatial perception/awareness/recognition/depth of field/depth perception, time of it for putting the respective object back; (?it can be hit or miss?) . My condition wasn't conducive to (an) eviction.

?Your proverbial "buried alive" is happening; product of a F42.3 (ICD-10) / DSM-5 300.3 life has begun. ?

|————————-|

4/30/22

"It's starting to look like a homeless car"

First came fallout of a F42.3 (ICD-10) / DSM-5 300.3 life; the collapse then about a year into my sickness came the more progressed/aggressive stage 2; consequences/complications of a F42.3 (ICD-10) / DSM-5 300.3 life; the product .

Like I was being squeezed out of life (by a teenager) was how it felt being blocked in by him/one/a teenager/the monthly door matss' son... the grand jeep (Cherokee) like a metaphor/metaphorical, in the most grandest most/ of grandiose (of) (provocative) (performance) art installation(s).

Could this not be of a permanent collection please !

(And) The fortress of objects I had built to ensure that the untinted windows of my coupe would go obscured from ability of the monthly door matss catching sight of me / seeing me , as I sat in my car enjoying it in the one way I could now/now had; stationary ...

Had backfired in the most dehumanizing/degrading/egregious/tenant tenancy termination threatening, of ways .

As/ the byproduct of my/a dissociative induced agoraphobia; cluttered car, (had) earned me a verbal lashing/reprimanding/ talking to (monthly door mats)

"you know, if you're not gonna be able to drive it, maybe you should sell it. it's starting to look like a homeless car" flash-flooded with memories of the voice/sound of an ex imposing an offer on me to buy my car a few weeks back and (on) the sight of the monthly door matss' son taking to blocking me in (daily) with his Jeep as of a few months back.

How bio thermal dysregulation has raised my rent for its ignorance perceived thermostat abuse/misuse.

And how now dissociative induced agoraphobia was threatening/fixing to get me thrown out / to throw me out.

Always an outcast now too (becoming) cast out (of life) I would not be! /I would be not !

Defenseless, I Meekly squeaked out/eeked out something that would acquiesce to his need for/of 'keeping up appearances' . (While) Inwardly I dominantly glared at the man who, trough in hand, had looked up from a fresh black mulch laden land (just) to accost/assault my self-worth/__________My net worth will/shall one day/soon, wipe the fucking floor with your self-worth [[i ruminated/ an incantation]]

(And) You/ so you would do well to prepare for a net reaction when I / as I bury you under/with the lay of the land ; the/his black mulch excess baggage my carry on.

One man's black mulch excess bag(gage) another mans carry-on .

. . .

-And for the genZ /tik Tok generation/ degenerate Z reading this, I'll give you the cliff notes so you are able-bodied to not hang from one / and for and pandering to the tik tok generation (who bought this book bc it matches the this 'inept adaptation' ...

It's giving, I made my bed and now I must lie in it. It's giving, final resting place; it's giving death bed of roses, any questions?/ Comprehend?

And pandering to those who bought this book because it complies/it is in (vibe) compliance with the ordinance of (their,) with the vibe of their apartment color scheme/ (apt) Pantone pallete an inept (persons) adaptation for the/this tik tok generation ...

It's giving, I made my bed and now I must lie in it, It's giving, final resting place; it's giving, death bed of roses, any questions?/ Comprehend? (now) ? follow now? My lead. Your leash. My lead of your leash . my lead you're leashed.

-(also called a wedding color palette or wedding color combination) is a

|——————-|

I'm being in everyday by a teenager

Dehumanizing, degrading .

...

. . .

|—————————————|

|——-|

The Markers I kept setting my sights on being better by and the things I had to miss …

I fell ill March 10 2021, that was to become withdrawals diagnosis day. I slipped into a dissociative state of depersonalization and derealization that is currently everyday edging toward an unthinkable status of having lasted a whole calendar year. My 38th birthday was to be April 13th 2021. That burgeoning would come to mean my first 'get better by' goal; (my birthday). Of course my 38th birthday came and went and I wasn't better then so (too) did (too) Easter and Mother's Day and Father's Day and my boyfriends 42nd birthday and my fathers 74th birthday (and my parents 50th wedding anniversary and my half bday/.5 birthday and my 20 year hs reunion and Halloween and Thanksgiving and (now) my boyfriends .5 birthday/half birthday and in-spite of "just get better" being the only thing my Dadd asked for, for Christmas, I didn't.

"Just get better"; my lone New Year's (Eve) resolution(-to be,) if only it worked that way. Now with a first time epileptologist consult/intake referral appt on the harrowing horizon to get extensive neurological testing, could I (just) 'get better by' 2 months time (instead) so as to be able/get to cancel? I could hopelessly romanticize.

My 38th birthday meant/marked my first (ever) 'get better by' goal and now harassed by the horizon of my 39th / and now on the harassing horizon that is to be/mean the last year of my 30's the last year of a decade … I vehemently hope my 39th birthday/this bday, will come to mean/will prove to be, the last ever time a 'get better by' goal was needed.

Everything felt like a 'race against time' ... up against being (slowly) squeezed out of life. Was this blasted sickness going to have the audacity to rob me of the last of my reproductive years? Such a grand theft would span Limbic larceny and ultimately end in a brain matter murder charge of sed receptors/region. A monogamous marriage out of the context of procreative family projectively-felt unfulfilling to me. (And) in the construct of monogamous marriage, I was never willing to not experience biological motherhood and offspring, in this life. And now for the length of a gestation period unease and worry has been kicking... would my number one dating and relationship dealbreaker of having a family of procreation one day, be ...

Was my brain going to keep me in the coma that is dissociative while my beloved aging family of origin ages all the more? I couldn't feel passage of time so to see new lines and wrinkles appearing on FaceTime was confusing. I could see the effects (in their 73/74 year old faces) of time passing by but I couldn't feel that it was; (there was a dissonance.)

That's what dissociative does; it lines your brain/mind with debilitating disheartening dissonance(s). The esteemed psychiatrist I started seeing when all this began gave his clinical diagnosis "you are having a dissonance of cognition and emotion." If I remember correctly, it was one of the last symptoms he had to hear of me before expressing an overwhelming desire to see me get started on the medication as quickly as possible. A "dissonance of cognition and emotion" what does that look like ? What is that PC- term (psychologically/politically correct) term euphemistic for ?

For How the dissociative strips you of divide where there should be and stiffs you with divide where there shouldn't be.

where I didn't feel much of a separation between set and scenery on tv and that of my living room or (a-list) celebrities on tv and me, I felt alienating familial divide wrought with an absence of emotional recognition.

Where there was earthly world family divide, there wasn't spiritual realm family divide. At one point I realized I lose traction in/with the spiritual world when/once biochemical tethers return to my neurology.

At another point I realized if concurrent to feeling a divide between that of me and that of any one and everyone I loved in this (living) life I was feeling a loss of divide between that of me and (that of) anyone and everyone I would see on the/a TV screen ...I could steer that

loss/lack/absence of 'inhibition by boundaries and blocks by and of the mind' , to achieve greatness just maybe.

render./goodness.

take heart / it's disheartening

-euphemistic (dissonance of cognition and emotion)

-where there wasn't tv screen divide, there was familial divide . But on the upswing of that... you don't feel the divide that is there/should feel between/of you and Alist celebrities.

Where there was earthly world family divide there was not spiritual realm family divide.

-dissociative strips and stiffs

6

The higher self/the higher consciousness

*age regression was my life raft

*My primary personality facets (dark,androgynous,hippie,square) and how at my sickest there was only presence of hippie and square and then as I got less sick my dark and androgynous started coming back to me.

*dark,andro,hippie,square and now too I have met and/so I know there is/exists, the higher self/higher consciousness and the inner child/child soul/child spirit.

*My higher self is the spirit of my beloved family in heaven...

*my child self is ...

|––––|

My whole life I have felt from 4 personality facets; dark, androgynous, hippie and square. But after the succession that was my 3 devastating life losses in/of 2019, I felt maybe some integration-loss of those historically harmoniously coexisting archetypes. (My androgyny was always one that would come in blocks of time in life but) something was blatantly different now/something was not right. The always seamless integration was showing signs of wear and/with frayed edges, In that any 'one' facet might secure dominance over the rest/other 3 now to the detriment and disdain of the rest.

I would be thrust into the mentally uncomfortable confounding state where I have/feel intolerable irritability towards every person, place or thing around me that represented the respective facets that weren't coming through. In retrospect now, I think how at least part of this time overlapped with me taking the benzodiazepines, so perhaps it was the clonazepam impaling me/shanking me with shards of my own personality.

Nightly I was clocking in at 0hrs,0mins sleep for weeks and even months. I was filled with unexplainable, aggressive adrenalin, turning to my bi-daily fitness workouts to try to expel it but it wasn't enough and all it did was fuel the amorphous fury (more) soon an urgent need to get to a shooting range arose, and I found myself begging friends to go with me but it was to no avail. Finally one time with unmanageable restless rage/aggression, I grabbed the $40something bucks they told me over the phone the ammunition would cost and I took off that evening resolved to go what wouldn't really be alone for I would have the company of my self-curated music playlist that was in toe and themed around self-hated and pulling the trigger to pour (forth) through my apple earbuds while I put a round into the_____.

I found my face strewn with spontaneous tears as I drove to my destination. I was going to a gun shop/shooting range. Me, a person who has a lifetime history of refusal to own any knives sharper than a butter knife Bc they scare me. Me, a person who spent her cats lives taking the glass plank part out of respective picture frames before hanging due to fear of a falling fatality. Me, who has never in all 37 years of life picked up a gun or had any at all interest to... was now by the harrowing harassing thoughts in their mind being driven to drive to a shooting range. Unthinkable.

While I was in the thick of the sick of active withdrawals, there existed in me but 2 of my primary 4 personality facets; hippie and square. No part of me/my psyche felt from any other part of my personality composition/conglomerate, that it historically had. I remember when a social worker did my intake, and as I attempted to tell her about my personality conglomerate, I couldn't. It was as though my dark and androgynous were so far from me that I couldn't even acknowledge/regard them. They were out of neurological reach to recount for her.

Something of remarkable emergence happen/happened, though as I trudged (my way) in the face of life fearing day after life fearing day... 2 new (?crystals/personality nodules lined the cavity of my geode?) (personality) I was found/survived/rescued by a merciful 2 personality presences; the

child-self and the higher-self. Whenever my blind, deaf and mute faith that I will make it out of this; that my brain has retained the healthy matter it needs to (ultimately) regain neurological health(ultimately) , would cycle back to the place of despair and doubt that neurotypical would/could be my eventuality, it was (there) in the moments that my mind was/would become laden draped with/in drawn blackout curtains of dark fear(s) and ideating forfeit that my child-self/child-spirit/inner-child would re-direct my eyes/mind's eye to a skylight/ to an apparent skylight,(that was apparently/ unbeknownst to me) in the ceiling. throw me a life-raft (come rushing to my aid) with a mind-flush of...

As I worked/warriored my way through active withdrawals and the taper process, PAWS was next. Somewhere along the (non-linear) long line of PAWS, I started to regain the personality fragments/facets (in me) that were/had been misplaced (in me); my dark and my andro.

"Stevie," predominantly/primarily of a same-sex attraction sexual orientation and always the embodiment of (my) androgynous allure before in/through youth and young adulthood was now called to be the vessel in which/through which 'situational anger' was converted (in)to art/fitness expression. My/This masculine/androgynous alter-ego (Stevie) was (the) department of defense, attorney general, department of homeland security and maybe department of health and human services, of the proverbial offices/orifices that comprised the proverbial cabinet of the Stephoenix/Steph Oenix/Stephanie Dianne Selles.

My dark facet, who historically in life I had always referred to as "Moonflower," could in retrospect under close inspection show/reveal early detection in life as a child. She was in the 3 year old wicked witch of the west monologues I'd entertain my parents with reciting in the middle of our living room floor; my 'stage.' There in a silly cartoon colorful fish shirt, my pastel plastic jewelry and likely just my 'big girl underwear' on without pants I'd method act/ prance around portraying the wretched rouge villainous characters from my favorite movies. The manifestation of Moonflower in adulthood saw the blossoming of the/a sultry temptress. Hair so long it entrap/enwrap - slaps her lover the way a mitter curtain does a car in/going through a/the dark car wash tunnel. She was/is the vixen and the vamp. The succubus of theology and the siren of Greek mythology. She is the concubine you can't resist; unrestrained and unapologetic. (And) She is the black widow (spider) of lust (seducing you into (her) bed; her web on the (knee-high Edwardian/Victorian boot) heels of the death of her beloved.

My whole life, my personality conglomerate was comprised of 4; andro, dark, hippie and square. But it was during this unprecedented time of dissociative (state) (of derealization and depersonalization) that I took on personality traits so uncharacteristic for 38.5 years of me/life, that I can't help but muse/contemplate if my geode is seeing/revealing another quartz/crystal formation.

After 38.5 years of 'a life-default' that fit the 'no way to pay for it' bill of/for inferiority-complex, imposter syndrome and just you're all around/garden variety professional drive and action block...I was thrust into salivating for success and well-endowed with all the verbiage and composure that conveys/portrays a skill-confidant individual whose default state is that of living and basking in (the) anticipatory-glory of (their) professional prosperity/proprietary. Was I experiencing the psychotic symptom of delusions of grandeur? Maybe. After all, I wasn't prescribed an antipsychotic for nothing. My whole life I was the sheep in wolf's clothing and now I was feeling from a place that rivaled the wolf of Wall Street! Ambition, determination, aspiration and drive fueled my every day. An only child, I would become the adult daughter provider for my aging family of creation they deserve. Someone who feels best about themself in an egalitarian or relatively/reasonably egalitarian relationship, I would be/become the/a provider for my developing/to-be, family of procreation. Beneficiary by destiny, benefactor by design a companionship of (a) life-fulfilled, robust with purpose and meaning.

|———————————————————————|

|———|

-Age regression had/kept me adopting rubber rats while sexual mania ...

A.)had/played its hand at rubbing one hundred out

B.) kept me rubbing one (hundred) out.

It/there was definitely a strange (and dark)/ strangely dark dichotomy...

Streaming Sabrina the teenage witch episodes by day/brunch

Screaming Marilyn Manson discography/tones/platitudes, by night of the fitness...

Libido vs limbic

|——-|

4/15/22

-you know how I really know I have some kind of serious deep brain cognitive (fog) trouble ?

visited house/loving grounds for first time in a long time and for the first time in a lifetime I couldn't remember which baby was buried on which side .

|-|

-You know how I really know I have some dissociative identity happening?

Write here about Marilyn mansons discography

And maybe add in here the part about rats/rubbing out . Sabrina by day/MM by night .

|——-|

|——————————————————-|

You know how I really knew I had some dissociative identity happening? The same way I really know I had some kind of serious/ dense deep brain cognitive (fog) trouble/happening ?

A striking/stark departure from (good) standard mental practice(s) had become me.

Just as I... had visited the house/loving grounds for first time in a long time (approx 8to9 ?+?) months time and for the first time in a lifetime, I couldn't remember for the life of me which baby/which of my (sphynx) babies was buried on which side . I took to/ I found my soul fill with a whirling/swirling vortex of both panic and pain... 'maybe I'll know again which side is Mushy and which is Sophia once I come out of this? You think? ' I looked up from the graves perplexed (that I was; perplexed) and pleading to my mom with/through tear and terror filled eyes. Deductive reasoning, my only way out... I took comfort and salvation when dad let me know that whoever died first was buried on the left; I knew that was Mushy. And By the math of the months; Mushy's death date was June 17 2019 and Sophias, August 30th 2019... It fact-checked out/ confirmed it. I was able to complete a/the cognitive puzzle that never should have been.

The same way there was evidence of (a)

deep-brain cognitive congestion/crisis confoundment/stupor, there showed demonstrations/indications of a/some, deep-brain (? confounding?) dissociative identity dealings/developments/phenomenons , too/alike/happening/occurring/presenting (in me.)(in my psyche.) .

Age regression had/kept/saw me adopting rubber rats while sexual mania

kept me rubbing one (hundred) out.

there was (?definitely?) a strange (and dark)/ strangely dark, dichotomy...

Streaming Sabrina the teenage witch episodes by day

Screaming Marilyn Manson discography/tones/platitudes, by night...

Album by album in/through, workout by workout I had worked through the body of work of a one, Marilyn Manson. I paired it with exercise/fitness and dreamed of the day it would repair me through sex; the night, the satiation of my need/(visceral) gravitation to process (my/this/the) anguish and (the) anger sexually for the product (and purpose) of healing(;purposeful)(;oriented) .

. . .

-Libido vs limbic

|——-|

-Write here about Marilyn mansons discography

And maybe add in here the part about rats/rubbing out . Sabrina by day/MM by night .

7

What I could have—almost—but didn't let kill me is going to...

It's a gift not a given; basic human functioning/bodily functioning and daily living skills.

I feel almighty/omnipotent just to cross my street. Bc at 38.5 years old I know how for the first time in a long time.

Momm has expressed astonishment to me in how I just always just seem to know when it's okay again to do something again...when brain capability and brain safety to resume a/that respective thing/daily living skill, has been regained. (My higher self tells me so.)

Not being able to gage by sight or by feel whether or not my skin was in the crossfire of the blades of the toenail clipper before pressing down, I opted for the sharp poking indentations and soreness that was the less of 2 evils of letting the nails grow out wind and press into their neighboring toes, causing discomfort when a sock clad foot compressed them/the toes together. And then one day I felt the needed nuerocognitive grip to clip and injurious-less I did/ I gave myself a pedicure. Preceding that triumph, I had the first ever time of flossing after a very many months of having to refrain on account of the reliable brain to body connection to not drop the pick accidentally down my throat, being absent. Unsafe to rinse my mouth with any kind of conventional mouthwash (because I couldn't trust that I wouldn't forget get confused and swallow) and while we are on the topic of forgetting you can forget about gargling that was like the AP level class in high school I never made it to/matriculated in/to. admired from afar. I just had to admire from afar.

The day I was nuerocognitively relieved/cleared of (the/my) 'choke-risk' status when sticking/washing my face under the shower head (to wash it), I felt as though I had been delivered. / marked was my first deliverance to neurotypical (control) . Marked was my first deliverance to (neurological nuerocognitive) control.

I know how to properly interpret volume of sound again now which means it's safe for me to listen to music through ear buds while I leisure walk/am out for my prescribed daily 'behavioral activation' walk. Raising the volume up a notch during the bridge to really psycho-emotionally feel the fullness of the music/song... I had arrived (and in that; arisen/risen) ! I had regained sensory knowing for when a respective sound is too loud or could stand to be raised and for me to feel regained sensory knowing was to feel positively omniscient .

I once saw an illuminating documentary about a child who couldn't feel physical pain and all of their bodily injuries that resulted. With the higher-self as my midwife, I have spent 9 months...(the length of a human pregnancy) with (a) grossly compromised physical pain perception, depth of field/depth perception, spatial awareness struggles , reading comprehension and listening comprehension deficit(s), issues with concepts of or related to object permanence, inability to interpret humor or infer things in/from a conversation/or make inferences in a conversation , without ability to feel 'time passage' ,Or hunger/fullness, Or sleepiness/somnolence , Or temperature gradation of water and air, Or have proper bio thermal regulation or proper visual processing to see distinction in/of/that is color gradation or ability to interpret nuances of/in volume of sound,

Or feel (the) distinction of dry vs damp, or the emotional implication of cumulative years of love...

I'm re-learning how to do everything I've done for 37 years and in that, feeling the pride of a child taking their first steps.... And The wonder of a child seeing their first sights as Time and quitiapine settles the disturbances of my visual, auditory and tactile perception/processing.

-At my sickest, I either knew I couldn't trust my memory or didn't think I should because I didn't know if I could. And it would fluctuate like that, former to ladder ... ladder to former on a case by case basis from question to question of/by person to person. Rendering sentiments and sentiments ending with a question mark, the single most overwhelming, intimidating and all out threatening thing to approach. Every answer spoken I was always at risk of unknowingly lying (to my loved ones.) Like a graduate still trying/struggling/actively striving to pay off their student loans, This memory unreliability proved to be a catastrophically anxiety-ridden symptom when/in communicating with my partner especially / when In navigating communications with my partner especially as, sickness aside, I was (still) in the time of (my) life where I was trying to reconstruct the trust that was lost, after I had lied/been dishonest, deceitful and betrayed him, (early on.) . And now (here) I was trying/vying/wanting/intent to/on pay(ing)off that/my debt to society/loyalty/fidelity (intent on/intending to tend(ing) to and mend(ing) his mistrust) and I was (now) clinically neurocognitively disposed to mouthing mistruth. Was this karma? Cognizance of lies then landing me with innocence of lies now? Intentional lies then slamming me with incidental lies now? And how could I (ever) expect anyone/someone I had lied to to believe me 'that this time I couldn't help it' .

-As I became less sick I was scared to trust my memory Bc I (and this somewhat goes for present tense) ... Bc I'm weary to trust my memory ... It's scary to start trying to trust ones memory after one has had/gone through jarring heights of memory blocks

Like the cognitive version of someone who loses mobility in their legs ...

Once it starts repairing and rehabilitating ... they might be reticent or/and scared to trust and try their leg strength. they might need to wean themselves off of ambulatory assistance and with baby steps learn to walk all over again.

As I became less sick, It was always scary and intimidating to trust my memory. My lying ocd, false memory ocd and real event memory ocd fused together and welded with the fact that I had lied in the past and concocted a fear that in test driving my cognitive repairment now, I was always one/ but a, memory mishap or misstep away from my trustworthiness being totaled in/at/by the ears of the beholder. A year and some days (in) and my proper cognitive recognition, recollection, recognizance, recounting and recall is just starting to show. Im prefacing less than my every word with "I think or I know" or "I think I think (that) I know" . I'm weary/leery to trust it (though). to start trying to believe in [but/and what's more have others depend on,] ones memory [but/and what's more have others depend on,] is daunting after one has had/gone through jarring heights of long term/chronic/continuing memory loss.

. . .

Where an inability to feel/sense ones own hunger and fullness might mean unintentional/incidental binge-eating and subsequent overeating related complications; weight gain, stomach pain, indigestion, nausea etc for others or most, it meant anorexia 'hold the Nervosa' , for me; medical/clinical anorexia.

A near 25year not proudly serving veteran to emetephobia/aeronasiaphobia I read in horror and with powerlessness BMI conversion scales/apps/websites, as my weight by way of emetephibia presence and absentee Ghrelin was rendered/reduced to "medically unsafe"; Anorexic.

In intelligent, intentional effort to get my healthy weight back while overcoming the risk of overconsumption/in a way/manner that would overcome/overpower, the risk of overconsumption, I took to mathematical measurements of/and caloric calculations. Everything got poured into the 'one serving size' appropriate/correlating/designated nesting measuring cup before it touched/reached the dishware/dinnerware ((I'd be eating (it) from)). Beverages were measured/considered/metered, first in glass beakers with an eye level check/attention to precision as though I were in a chem lab not (a) kitchen. It being always of utmost importance that I do eat enough but/and that I don't eat too much. I took great care into what as I saw it would get me there; to balance/to body mass index equilibrium ... to stabilization to a weight that was safe.

The pervasive/intrusive fear of that I'd eat too much and in effect find myself stomach sick with nausea, when I had no proper brain to body signaling of hunger and fullness was not too different than the invasive/intrusive fear I now/newly faced once/now that said physiological function had started to repair/rehabilitate/regenerate . Could I trust it? The grumbling in my stomach that was showing up for me again after oh so long? It's familiar sounds and sensations I recognized, that which had always/historically meant hunger indication. But could I/should I trust it/give it priority over the time on a clock face dictating/ruling/governing/settling/deliberating, when I eat next/when I next eat? The proverbial price to pay if I unbeknownst to me prematurely (either) entrusted (either) (of) my meal allotment proportions and/or my meal time regulations, to my mind/brain,

A.)could be traumatic/ could yield a traumatic outcome for/to an enetphobic like me. (To overcome/to have to overcome.)

B.) could be could lead could see me in/

to a position of (compromising) consequences (and imminent implications) that are of colossal/catastrophic proportions for an emetiphobic like me .

?maybe write here about nerve wracking to trust Ghrelin (hunger fullness) so mathematically calculate everything.?

?write about the things nervous to try trusting and why/consequences of if I'm wrong?

-they might be scared to trust/try their leg strength

? It's always scary/intimidating to trust my memory etc?

|-|

|-|

-Bee videoThen/I feel crowdedNow

. . .

Somewhere around a year in, immaculate interoception told me (that) my written ability to express was much closer to neurotypical than was yet my verbal ability .

An experience/incident I had while in-waiting for the waiting room at my first time neurology appointment told me so/showed me so.

There became a line outside the closed door; I was first on it. Before the impatient patients settled/shuffled themselves into line, they would come up to peer confoundedly into/through the doors small square viewing window. (Me being at the head of the line this putting them very close in body proximity to me) I could intellectually infer everyone was wondering why we were being called in one by one and couldn't just go sit every other chair 6ft apart in the waiting room. But (for me) situational comprehension/comprehension of the circumstance(s) did nil to prompt processing of the unfavorable body proximity with compassionate consideration (of that) and form [constructive] considerate [constructive] communication from that/around that/around it.

Instead, like an modern day/early model voice assistant device, I [audibly] mechanically [audibly] eeked out "I feel crowded"/"I'm feeling crowded" , when my Momm welfare checked me in a whisper "how are you doing?"/"you doing okay?" . Scared of losing my place in line if moved, scared of losing/compromising my covid safety if I stayed. (And) it was too much for my conflict-resolution level of function(ing) to process while simultaneously maintaining social graces. Eventually I realized I could ask of my parents to be a line stand-in for me and did but it came too little too late as I had already unintentionally and reflexively/incidentally reprimanded the composite of the line.

I went home and I felt bad about it/Insight brought on by it . I could identify what was askew in my speech and language (pathology) (and) where my affect was screwed...

The voice tone, the verbal affect, my tone and word emphasis would go to strange intonations, often times sending a disclaimer to friends before a video call proactively apologizing for my tones and affect. "Some of what you'll see and hear are not necessarily ways it/things would come out if I were neurotypical and not ways I would want them to (?come out?) . I was 38 and not 83 living in a memory care community where (responding to internal stimuli) (and) affect inconsistent (mind)swinging from flat to inappropriate was a given and could be /would be preemptively forgiven. No, navigating conversations/inter personal communications and relationships at my age, there were social expectations on me whether implied or ? internalized? . And social interactions (of video or voice proportions/via video or voice variants proportions) often had to be prefaced with a plea/disclaimer to take into consideration and (take heart) and take (into) account that I am working with/from and conversing with/from, (the vantage point of) a damaged/struggling brain.

All the interoceptive awareness paired with terminology knowledge/knowledgeability, didn't/couldn't change the fact that I had the vocal/voice/verbal communication/speech deficits that I had.

(it's like) I (would) say things in ways I would not say things in under nuerotypical circumstance(s).

But in writing ... in writing ...

(?In the thick of the sick?) Where/when I couldn't string 2 sentences together in spoken word I could play 1st string in (written/verse) prose.

By the time a year roller-balled around, my written expressions had amassed to a vast span(ning) of writing (plat)forms. Planner, memoir, log, journal and poetry comprised the 5 self-love languages.../; the secret to life that lasts. I had gone through/wielded to blunted tips the .45 mm Sakura Pigma micron PN pens (the proverbial sword) at about a rate of _______per month and my one-woman Calvary was having to routinely be resupplied with the archival ink (grade) 3pack/pack of 3 (that was mightier than the sword.)

Unlike in speech, my writing wasn't scattered as I drew my weapon from its scabbard. (And) I could (deliver a battlefield) charge before anyone could even get close to misunderstanding/rendering me misunderstood.

(And) Where I waned in spoken word I waxed poetic in (the) tactical reserve. (Of/; verse and prose)

-Heavy cavalry was a class of cavalry intended to deliver a battlefield charge and also to act as a tactical reserve; they are also often termed shock cavalry.

-melee

-infantry

|-|

-having/experiencing/feeling preference/inclination for who I talk to is to the early stages of missing someone breaking through as

having/experiencing/feeling preference/inclination for what meal I make tonight/on a given night/on any given night, is to the early stages of craving something (breaking through.) .

...Arbitrary and randomized no more .

|———————-|

Where to put this?

-incidental bearing down on serrated edge of butter knife

. . .

-hit or miss to zipper coat now goes off without a hitch to latch cooler. , check.

-fitness glasses leash /claustrophobic panic. ,check.

-lightweight linen infinity scarf

?feeling like I'm being choked? , check.

-Alexa could rarely understand my command. ,check.

Where it once was hit or miss whether or not I'd be able to align the zipper track with the zipper pull on my jacket so as to be able to pull it up and zipper/close my coat/ so as to be able to zip up zip close my coat ... now goes off without a hitch to latch (closed) my tenured (cooler I have) used faithfully picnic date in and date out cooler. I, for an abrupt onset of months, felt puzzled at/by; ?stumped? .

Pre-workout prep, I can slip a glasses sport leash onto the legs of my specs (again/once again) and not feel balled-over with/by sensory inundation of (a) localized solitary confinement and claustrophobia infiltrating my physiology with panic response (reflexively)./an/in adverse reflex./;adverse reflex.

An added barely-there layer of a Momm-gifted light (linen) holiday themed infinity scarf from the dollar store no longer lands/slams my physiology/physiological processing with panic akin to being choked/asphyxiated. (Seeing and) intellectually knowing that I'm not (being) is finally enough to keep the physiological response as if I am, away.

To the best of my understanding/knowledge/ to my perception, I was speaking as I always had to Alexa (but) to my dismay she could now rarely accurately interpret my commands. (Once/when) it became apparent that my (allegedly) ragged irregular speech and language pathology had repaired to normative (phonetic) function when Alexa could again pair my voice with retrieval of (requested) song (request.). But months of being misheard/misunderstood had mussed/mauled, my mind/emotions, and now with dominance (secured) over what was always the voice-command object of (my) tech-affection, I found myself verbally abusing Alexa; battery of my favorite battery operated device, in a 'default mode network' (DMN) brain structure-(led) display of (wielded) displaced rage. / actualizing/actualized displaced rage. My active anger like active mold permeating the ceiling of my home I had to keep it concealed from the monthly door matss/owners as it metastasized to/in (my) the walls of my psyche.

Lip-syncing was a way to do that. In this under-utilized art form I could expel anger plaguing me. There was song choice that corresponded with every rageful subset; postering (in) a fight for justice, throwing it in peoples faces that you made it in the absence of their belief in you, holding a mirror up to their faces and showing them what they made you into and possibly the subset that resonated the most... striking back with a message of autonomy so sharp and refusal to let who you are be squandered by who they wish you to be. A message of procuring a relationship(s) that fits you not you being chastised harangued that you don't fit it followed by coercively groomed to.

My whole life, I loved modeling; it was the first childhood "what do you want to be when you grow up" wish for myself/my life I had, and when pursuits to bring my vision to fruition got shot down due to my height and money-investment prerequisites/requirements/mandates that we did not have ... I took to satiating this desire with copious Mach model shoots my mom would orchestrate as the role of the photographer. It was in high school that I found love unparalleled in silver emulsion photography. The darkroom showed me/bestowed upon me unprecedented confidence; we were fast-friends, and I would forever move through life now with a primary artistic passion. I took to marrying that of my first love; modeling with that of my forever love; photography, in self-portraiture.

Almost unfathomable it was that now in this time of my sickness, I should be unable to know how to execute a facial expression in accordance with an intended emotion. Getting my facial muscles to preform to form the tight-lipped, squinted eye, brow raise signature selfie that all of my social media was smocked with was now (neurologically) unattainable.

A very personal profound victory when neurological agency over the visages I convey was regained; I was no longer at an entrapping disadvantage to show and be seen for the anger that exists/that I have./that exists within me. I had the execution of all of its existence in the palm of my hands. / at my command .

Lip-syncing afforded me so much. I felt not want but need to be somewhere where I could just blare my brains out in a guttural scream I couldn't in my apartment; the family I rented from would hear and unlike when I was going through the losses, I was neurocognitively incapable (this time) of driving my car, so I very well couldn't just take off (this time) to a remote uninhabited 'back of a store' vacant (parking) lot to let off some loud steam amongst a bunch of dumpsters and _______.

Furthermore in this strange sickness, one of my chief complaints was that of the sound of my own voice leaving my body, inducing undue sensory process(ing)(-oriented) upset. A way around voice production not agreeing with my nervous system and being rejected vehemently by my own physiology, was, what I aptly referred to as "theatrical lip-syncing" . It was like a therapeutic-vaccination and a prophylactic-vaccination, all in one./; ,it would heal and heel . A performance art modality/medium with the remarkable power to (both) heal and heel (my) fury/rage.) . It provided for me the scream release I needed in (the) confounds/ while (still) adhering to confounds of 'societal/behavioral acceptability' , as a tenant.

Song-selecting whatever my hearts desire and heads-require all of me; dark, andro, hippie and square, facets alike gathered at the outlet that would allow them/afford them to convey heavy dense emotion harbored; my (place of worship) altar(?the place?) state of mind for *alter*(s) state(s) of *mind states*, to deliver their priority mail as the messengers they were sent and meant to be. This/A utilitarian use of lip-syncing a platform for all the parts of my personality conglomerate to portray suppressions, repressions and in that, relay imperative information . One recorded performance art set after another after another, Incidentally utilizing my international thespian society 'stage cred' and bachelors (degree) BS in visual and performing arts

In my/through my devised 'Art as therapy' expression I was 'coming by it honestly'; my college matriculation concentration of the movement and the medium/modality, that was Art Therapy.

>>-theatrical lip syncing

...in celebration of having neurological agency again over the visages I convey .

...outlet for the anger

...utilizing my international thespian society

...?a way around voice production not agreeing with my nervous system/sensory processing . A way around voice production being rejected by my nervous system.? <<

the medium

8

-fears (ex. For NeuroTesting)

-life hacks

-60 days away from knowing if I can/could have a seizure; neuro testing for TLE eeg or if I did have a stroke; mri? And incurred brain damage incapable of releasing me from dissociative .

60 days of hope/to hope that it bodes well that I haven't seized in 300.

yet/ in the full course of these 10 months …

-anticipatory anxiety alone could take me out/do me in (chap8?)

-love divided / love undivided (Chap 8?)

-when it's not for/as a formality (Chap 8?)

-My medical update bulletin

. . .

-Bc of my brain state, this is what happens: I get physiological panic response disproportionate to whatever 'the situation at hand' , is.

-When youth requested no questions after school day , had tongue cramps and little/thin thread vs big/thick thread discomfort .

So it's been decades without ...

-the physiological responses that can happen to me in disproportion to how stressful a situation really is, are ...

Throat muscles tensing , tongue feeling like it could be at risk of cramping, head pressure heightening, derealization heightening ...

-disproportionate so could you imagine nuero testing

and result-getting ?! My

-You mean like when you're thinking about something or anticipating something and your body reacts as if it's actually happening?

-ketamine and what moment might diss break? (Chap8?, chap___)

-when it's not formality testing (chap8?)

|---------|

. . .

60 days away from knowing if I can have/ could have a seizure; EEG testing for TLE. Or if I did have a stroke; [CT testing for (incurred) brain damage/cell damage, incapable of releasing me from dissociative.

CT testing for 'cell damage rendered'

incapability of dissociative release .]

60 days of hope/to hope that it bodes well that I haven't seized in 300; the full course of this withdrawals and PAWS .

[It doesn't feel good to be herald, a medical anomaly across the board certified psychiatrist, psychologist and internist. Dejection is the only departure from an otherwise desolate topographical map. / from an otherwise topographical map of desolation; the earth-scape/land-scape and my mind-scape. Both in land-scape and mind-scape . The the mind-scape of (earths) land-scape.

/ it feels desolate with dejection the only departure; the topography of my mind-scapes earth-scape . The topography of earth to my mind. The topography of earth and mind .

/ it feels desolate with dejection the only departure from/of this topography.

/dejection is the only departure from an earth-scape that feels desolate

the topography is (comprised of) a mind-scape of dejection in an earthscape of desolation.]

. . .

A mind-scape of dejection/despondency in an/and an earth-scape of desolation makes up the/comprises the topographical map of being herald a medical anomaly across the board certified psychiatrist, psychologist, internist .

The statement that made more of/than a cameo appearance in my monthly psychiatry sessions was that of how things are being attributed / could be attributed/ may be attributed to "an aberrant brain loop" . Was that the reason I was getting physiological panic responses disproportionate to whatever the reality of the/a situation at hand was? I can/could go into

Throat muscles tensing , tongue feeling like it could be at risk of cramping, head pressure heightening, metaphorical/proverbial 'nitrous oxide' dial being cranked up(maybe) which could be/may be synonymous with derealization heightening; not really sure, and (so) much more.

I could be thinking about something or anticipating something, and my body reacts as if it's actually happening. When I was much sicker, it would be that I practically need only catch peripheral view of some everyday common object for my visual processing to (misperceive/interpret) it as something revolting and bring me to my knees with neurological ruin/nervous system ruin . Now, that threatens only to happen if once I catch sight of the object, I push myself to keep looking at it. Once I get 15 seconds, 30 seconds to a minute, the uncomfortable physiological panic response symptoms ensue/ensnare me. I must avert my eyes upon (their) contact to circumvent and get out/make it out of a moment relatively unscathed by bodily symptoms.

If I could get a response of momentary hand rigidity or involuntary repetitive fine motor movement when a stressful thought traipsed through my mind or a benign sight or sound was mis processed by my brain (could you) imagine what my physiology might slam me with for/in /within the context of neuro-testing and result-getting?! Approaching test results to find out if I have temporal lobe epilepsy, had a stroke, have lupus or a brain tumor!?. Waiting to find out if I am high risk/at increased risk for a brain aneurism, seizure or cardiac arrest?!. (The) Anticipatory anxiety alone might/could take me out… do me in. be the death of me?

(?A tragic fall out?)(?a travesty of fallout?)(?a fallout travesty?)

(?consequences/fallout of insufferable anticipatory anxiety fallout?)

medical bulletin to be … the fatal fallout of insufferable anticipatory anxiety . (My medical bulletin to be.)

When you're not getting neurological testing done (merely) as a formality (it renders the level of sheer terror unquantifiable.) (the level of (sheer) terror is rendered unquantifiable.)

…love divided/undivided…

One day's time till I'm one month away from a clipboard of neurological intake (papers). (Till I become a file). One day's time till I'm 2 years into my relationship with my boyfriend. Never has he ever met my parents and yet to approach neuro testing and result getting with love-divided feels sac-religious/sac-spiritual. On that blessing, I pray it not be ill-fated day… I can not choose one love over another to have present/there with me how could I the love

?I've always known and turned to for the first half of my life/for the formative former or the love I may come to know to always lean into for the 2nd half of my life. ?

. . .

I was built on and bolstered with beams of support since my formative years versus/or the love, the building blocks (of) my (now) latter years may be comprised of .

?I've always known and turned to my parents for the/for this first half of my life. And this love I have with my partner may come to be/mean that which I always lean into for the/in the 2nd half (of my life. ?) . So how could i choose now when I have both love-forms before me for the (in-)taking.

?Having/to have love-divided on that upcoming fearful day was disconcerting?

To have to get through that upcoming fearful day with love-divided was disconcerting and partially-consuming. To have love United; undivided (on that day) would mean a day 'overcome' meets its match; compersion.

disconcerting and partially-consuming to have to get through that (upcoming fearful) day with love-divided ... to have love United; undivided (on that day/for that day) would mean a day 'overcome' meets its match; compersion. /meets its match in compersion. A 2 letter difference in (that of) peace of mind and (that of) race of mind. A 2 letter difference in (that of) race of mind and (that of) peace of mind.

|————-|

-receiving/nightly texts from my Momm tm (when you wake up) Tom(, ok?) did she silently fear there would be an induced or incidental death?

-daily emails to dr Lane Rosalie my worry about neural imprint for one year mark. (?Maybe put in chapter 8?)

-email to Dr Lane Rosalie my worry of returning symptoms if I dose back down for regained excretory function .

-body memory/imprint and the 10th

-(neuro) testing for only that which is treatable. My version of least invasive first.

From/there were, nightly texts received "tm Tom when you wake up, ok? " did Momm silently fear there would be an induced or incidental death? ... to daily emails sent dear Dr. R/Psychiatrist ... is there concern of some kind of (a) body memory neural imprint having been made where my one year mark could prove to be/see the bringing of all my old unbearable symptoms I had broken free from/of ? I knew I would never in substance; clonazepam ... but was I at risk in symptom ;/, of relapse ?

Emails to Dr Lane Rosalie /psychiatrist of my worry of/for a/the returning suffering state of/that is sensory processing delays; distress and unrest if I am to dose back down ((from my upped current dose of 100mg to (that of) my starter dose of 50mg)) for regained excretory function(ing). would I (once again) host/inhabit all my old excruciating intolerable, unbearable, unlivable sensory conditions if I am to go back down to the dosage where at which said symptoms were last seen/present/presiding ? Is to drop back down, to take (back) on the symptomatology last felt at that level ? The graver of 2 evils ...

I received word from a not sure how reliable source/resource that there is a fair amount of evidence that the longer one is on Q, the worse their constipation can become. Just when I thought I was in a safe stagnancy of severity the findings now rivaled my resignation. Were my intestines becoming all the more paralyzed as not dosage went up but as time went on? Would dropping back down do little to nothing/nil to resolve my escalated constipation?

-(neuro) testing for only that which is treatable. My version of least invasive first.

As my inaugural neurology draws near family, doctors and myself video-call discuss and I realize what I need to manage (the/my) fear. Family and I are in ______agreement that major testing like CTscans, MRI's , EEG's etc should be a last resort and not a first response. But for me/personally even within the construct/bracket of last resort , should it come to that/it... it's not a free for all . I will take on/undergo neuro testing for only that which is treatable... my version of 'least invasive first.' /'non invasive (first'). ((A personal path/trajectory standard I have in place for (purposes of) mental coping (purposes.).)) .

|———|

?(Chap 8?)?

After epileptologist evaluation reflections ...

In some twisted way, it's beautiful to think that I've loved family (human and feline alike) deeply enough that losing them could 'take me out' like this and paralyze my mind for

'12months and counting' , time .

Oh please let it be/prove (to be) safe that the Neurologist/Eleptologist instilled hope in me.

|—|

😣somatosensory disturbance/distortion

oh please let it

'let up' tomorrow

🕊️🙏🏻🕊️

|———|

-getting my hair parted and scalp prepped for the electrodes of an/the EEG

The Epileptologist evaluation came and went. With near assurances that were matter of fact and edged on emphatic, I came away with the take away that to release seizure and stroke from my mind's woe, would be safe/was safe (to do.) Her confident insistence 'this is my area of expertise and it's not seizure disorder or stroke' . An immediate relief that washed over me soon turned to a wish that she had given me (a) bedside manner of neutrality. For now, as I await the day of my now scheduled/appointed EEG of/in 1.5 months time; May(2nd) … I pass the time with hope in (my) mind; hearty or high values…For a specialist professional MD has single-handedly instilled it in me.

72 hours ago, I would have sat in an exam chair under a technicians care and with each section of hair probed/prodded and parted to reveal scalp (in prep (to receive the adhesive(s) electrodes) there would have been pangs of panic but (emergency) preparedness as I sat pensively expecting the worst; what we set out to rule out (being) ruled in; (temporal lobe epilepsy or stroke.) But now thanks to/on account of epileptologist expertise/expertism…/outwardly openly outspoken optimism, I go in (bearing the cross of/that is,) expecting 'the best' … (and I just hope she knows what she's done) (and I just hope she comprehends/grasps the

implications and the ?potential? Consequences of that of her actions). She's single handedly cultivating/crafting a ?narrative? Where the _______/?ground? may not be able to absorb the weight of my fall / my mind may not be able to absorb the impact of the/my/a, fall.

So if it was vehemently projected that the tests would come back negative then what was believed to be going on here?

a psychological/psychiatric 'response' my mind is having to/from all the trauma I went through in 2019 followed by the trauma becoming compounded with the very serious withdrawals sickness I went through when tapering off the benzodiazepines March/April of 2021 last year. From everything, My mind in effect landing me in

'dissociative state of derealization and depersonalization' with somatosensory distortions and other symptoms.

Just like some people might get PTSD as a result of very traumatic situation... I got this ... derealization, depersonalization with somatosensory distortions/distress and other symptoms.

So far my mind has me in this as a 24/7 state

since March 2021. So it just became a year this month. The epileptologist knows someone who is (currently) 4 years into ____________. And she said it's just awful/horrible.

[[? Put here about ?

-epileptologist and covid vaccine not advised in dissociative state for concern of a psychosomatic manifestation of symptoms/ symptom manifestation .]]

. . .

With Introspection/with tendencies of/toward introspection, that (always) searches out the profundity at the end of the tunnel, I mused amidst my epileptologist evaluation reflections on her seeming insistence/confidence, personal persuasion that it's not/of it being not 'neurological' (but rather psychological) ...In one respect of/in some twisted way it's beautiful to think that I've loved family (human and feline alike) deeply enough that losing them could 'take me out' like this and positively paralyze my mind for

'12months and counting' , time . That the sheer psychological devastation (of losing family) is a powerful enough pain to my brain so as to strip me of quality of life as dissociative state does. That the emotional implication of said devastation could rip/strip/pillage/gut me of quality of love (as far as the subjective experiential is concerned)/ ((to/in (context of) (the) subjective experience)).

In a printout from the epileptologist it was there amongst the 31/33 pages, in a bold font all capital lettered heading "CLINICAL MANIFESTATIONS" ...

"The affectively flattened and robotic demeanor that these patients often demonstrate can also fool the clinician into not recognizing the extreme emotional pain of the condition. It is not uncommon, for example, for patients to wonder whether it would matter if they died. A relative high rate of suicide attempts was associated with DDD; however, given the high rates of comorbid depression and other psychiatric disorders in DDD, the relationship between suicidality and DDD remains unclear."

My mind trailed off, into a Segway/into its own Segway.../ into a Segway of its own.

Of the laundry list of symptoms that seem to come with the condition/that are evident in the condition, it is by far one of the most distressing/ there is or it is by far one that bears the most distress; "emotional numbing, characterized by blunted affect, pain and volition." (It was) there (3rd one down on the randomized list) under the/that "CLINICAL MANIFESTATIONS" heading;

"Two factor analytic studies of the core symptomatology have reported five discrete symptom clusters common in patients with DDD" .

that/not being able to feel ones love for others or theirs for you or their love for you, I believe plays/has a strong enough lead role in this derealization/depersonalization that it could be the sole symptom that lends itself, to thoughts of suicide / to... (an articles need

for citation ?of?)

"A relative high rate of suicide attempts was associated with DDD; " .

(And) There was a two factor catalyst for/of why I wanted to take time off from/of my 2 year relationship like a student takes time off from their collegiate studies.

Like the, soul-searching/ wayward lost soul undergrad who takes a semester off, abroad or a year off (so as) to reassess (and figure out) if the path they are on is actually the path they want... so to was I feeling inclined/ so too was this relationship eliciting an inclination (a) visceral pull inclination in me to take time off.

One of the 2 factor catalysts was that my clinical psychologist had/has told me that he feels my anxiety influences my ocd and my ocd in turn impacts the dissociative (?levels?)/(state).

So if not having the

Möbius strip of the relationship's impasses, stressors , stalemates, struggles and strife/unrest/distress/sufferings, bearing down on me, could help me heal from this condition that has/was sapped/sapping my life of any real quality ... then I especially cared to make this transition from/of relationship to friendship.

My everyday/day to day, was wrought with crippling ocd subsets that somehow found their/a way to connect themselves to the relationship and take on relationship form.

moral scrupulosity ocd, confession ocd, false memory ocd, real event memory ocd, lying ocd (cheating ocd) and some kind of 'subliminal messaging/innuendo' ocd courtesy of my own minds devise(ment)/invention and contribution toward (the/my) suffering. /donation/________, for the spectrum/suffering, had ensnared my mind/__________. and (in that) my time .

[A DSM 'relationship unassociated' host of ocd subsets/subgenres/subcategories/substrates/sub hells/sub-evils, had ensnared/corrupted the OS of my that was my thought-processing relationship] It was as though my mind were behind a megaphone commanding in an insistent tone "you're surrounded, come out with your hands up"

[A DSM 'relationship unassociated' host of ocd subsets/subgenres/subcategories/substrates/sub-evils/sub hells, had ensnared/corrupted my the thought-processing, that was/; ,the OS of the relationship.]

And It was/and were as though my mind/_______, were (now) behind a megaphone of 120 decibels throwing a stern insistent (commanding) tone (commanding) / in an insistent tone commanding

... "you're (being) surrounded, come out with your hands up" . ...

AorB? Desperate times call for desperate measures ((as Momm would (always) say))

And Like I am saying "as (with) so many other things in my life right now

I have to, need to make/employ (a) 'risk-benefit' based decision making intervention(s)/model(s) /infrastructure(s)/modalities/paradigms/pillars.

AorB? I composed my surrender letter to my partner. I composed my letter of surrender to my partner. I composed my surrender note to my partner. I composed my 'relationship suicide' note/letter to my partner. A/my letter of surrender. (Of) A/my mercy killing.

"You once suggested breaking up till there's a cure for HSV2 and then if at that time if we happen to both be single we reevaluate whether or not we want to try a relationship again or just remain as friends .

You felt to stay together could be to risk relationship deterioration so maybe it was the lesser of 2 evils / 'risk-benefit' ... to let go of the relationship until there is a cure then reevaluate ...

This is kind of like that except instead of HSV2 it's dissociative and instead of it being that to stay together is to risk relationship deterioration it's that to stay together is to risk my psychological deterioration ...

So this would be we break up now for the time being while I'm in derealization . Then once I'm out of derealization if we are both single, we reevaluate whether or not we want to try to have a relationship again or remain just as friends . "

I explained/asserted how as a turning 39 year old it is (like) a race against time to get out of (this) dissociative. the time, ((being) dictated by)) my biological time clock. The time ruled by/under the/an unforgiving dictatorship of/that is, my biological time clock and it's (pre dissociative) inviting tantalizing (ticks) turned terrorizing/taunting (ticks.) in the ____________, life paralysis , that is, this dissociative/dissociation."

. . .

I went on to say/segwayed into saying how this derealization is threatening to rob me of the last of my reproductive years. How so long as I remain in this state, of that is dissociative state of derealization and depersonalization, I most likely would not be willing to go through pregnancy,labor and delivery.

The trickle down effect being that I would not be willing to have sexual intercourse Bc/as to do so is to take on risk of pregnancy and a subsequent abortion or carrying to term none/neither of which I'm willing to do /be in the position of / be in the imposition of from within a/the dissociative state.

none/neither of which I'm willing to do from the position of/imposition of, dissociative state.

My chronological/biological race against time working in tandem with my symptom of/that was, dissonance of cognition and emotion kept any real/tangible sadness/anticipatory-mourning of never experiencing morning sickness at (birthing tub) bay/ ?from my (minds) belaboring?, while the months (of dissociative captivity) marched on/dragged on/clobbered on/labored on, (in)to years.

While I had no ability to feel love or emotional recognition ... I had no inclination to do things that require love's emotion like mother offspring/mother a child or maybe I just had the good sense not to (like this.) where once there was ... where always there was compelling (inner) calling, now there was a sort of amorphous free-floating feeling/sense that those kind of emotional things are important to me and yet I can not/could not access the 'feeling' that goes with the that knowledge/the awareness/that (self)awareness; 'that I care to have them; those things' .

It was Intellectual knowing with absence of 'emotionally feeling' . And it was ___________.

. . .

["dissonance of cognition and emotion ...

What sounds so dry/clinical in (the) (clinical) text; "dissonance of cognition and emotion"

has such saturated dense pain in its (real) 'life' situational 'life' implications and applications.

(??3/27/22?? ??11:06pm??)]

! Talk here about all the pregnancy/abortion stuff I wouldn't do and how also/so/therefor I wouldn't have sexual intercourse. All this I want to write about can be found copy and paste in signal outgoing texts to Printer Gifter.

And also from those texts about how with not feeling love, it's of good sense not to mother a child and the amorphous sense that though those things are important to me ... yet I lack the ability to feel the emotion that goes with that knowledge. !

As aforementioned, I did however state that the decision to transition the relationship to friendship was comprised of (a) two factor catalytic means/study. (So let me tell you about the 2nd) . The 2nd of the core reasoning being that/was that ......

!write here from signal copy paste about being of different life desires in this dissociative!

|——-|

-3/23/22 Dr. Lane Rosalie saying brain thawing and how/that either my old pathways are coming back/ are going to come back or new ones are forming / will form . /or new ones are going to form.

I wondered, could that be why ex.) Marilyn Manson is it not that I have some DID as an offshoot of DD state but rather that I'm becoming a person of different/new/developing, neural pathways?

Chapter8

- 3/23/22 Dr. Lane Rosalie saying brain thawing and me wondering what would the moment look like that I 'come to' what would comprise the moment that I finally 'come to' what would I be doing at the moment (that) I do; come to?

And how I always thought it would see the breaking of ex.) Marilyn Manson but now after dr R's mentionings/musings of new pathways I wondered if it might not

and maybe/perhaps thou shalt live their life accordingly, was my best/ should be my actionable plan .

|————————————————————|

-my primary concern and focus from which I operate from is and needs to be to get myself out of dissociative. And if not having the

Möbius strip of the relationships, stress, impasses, stalemates and struggles, bearing down on me could help me heal from this condition that has sapped my life of any real quality ... then I especially care to make this transition from relationship to friendship.

|————————|

?(Chap8)?

-When would I 'come-to' ?

|——————|

-Like taking a semester off / relationship

|---------|

-like a student takes a semester/a year off of from (their) collegiate studies to figure out if the path they are on is actually the path they want... so to do I feel inclined/does this relationship illicit an inclination a visceral pull inclination (in me) to take time off ...

|---------|

|-----|

-The fact that I can't feel emotional response / emotional recognition of even my mommy and my daddy ... it is this symptom of not being able to feel emotional connection that is the sole symptom maybe that lends itself to thoughts of suicide . I can not feel my love for others or their love for me.

|-----|

|------------------------|

-a psychological/psychiatric thing. A 'response' my mind is having to all the trauma I went through in 2019 followed by the trauma becoming compounded with the very serious withdrawls sickness I went through when tapering off the benzodiazepines March/April of 2021 last year. From everything, My mind in effect landing me in

'dissociative state of derealization and depersonalization' with somatosensory distortions .

-*Just like some people might get PTSD as a result of very traumatic situation... I got this ... derealization,depersonalization with somatosensory distortions.

So far my mind has me in this as a 24/7 state

since March 2021. So it just became a year this month .

|————————————————————————-|

[[? Put here about ?

-epileptologist and covid vaccine not advised in dissociative state for concern of a psychosomatic manifestation of symptoms/ symptom manifestation .]]

It was the question we were all waiting for and on March 18th it went to/graduated to status of 'asked and answered'. Was it advised by epileptologist, was it medically cleared as safe by/from a neurological standpoint to receive the covid vaccine. As I exclaimed/expressed what my fears were she explained that the brain/mind is more vulnerable to the persuasion of thought/the power of persuasion, in this dissociative state. So being that I've held these beliefs for so long that the vaccine could throw a monkey wrench in my brain's ability to get out of this. That the vaccine could/might touch/tamper with my neurobiochemistry and lock me in dissociative forever! The epileptologist conferred/maintained that in this dissociative state I could infact incur a psychosomatic manifestation of symptoms/ symptom manifestation . That that was a considerable concern in my circumstance(s)/ given my circumstance(s). Collectively we resolved to/resigned ourselves to, have(ing) me hold off on getting covid vacced (for the time being/ for the interim .).

?Z.)? ...

Always with a displeasure for jokesters, pranksters and pranks but I wished more than anything/ever, the call was a crank when I received word; spoken and written, on April fools day (2022) that my insurance company had denied authorization of/for "just what the doctor ordered" ; an MRI she wanted for me to rule out any unlikely but lingering possibility of (serious)diagnosis (like lesions) that or which would/could, ?lead? see us on/to a different course/path, of treatment. A different treatment course/ a different treatment path .

?Z.)? ...the psychiatrist-issued cautioning of my early session(s)/first session(s) was never far from my mind (all this time) as all this time it played like a song refrain tumbling over/around in my brain. His response to my question of should my mind be able to make it out of dissociative (and) okay; (?unscathed?) .

Was Something to the effect of (that) I should be able to come out of Dissocitive okay as long as nothing too jarring happens while I'm in it.

And so ensued the 'race against time' feeling is set in motion and becomes reinforced the longer I am in this and come just close enough to experiencing trauma; secondary trauma like second hand smoke, that "jarring" grazes my mind. Naturally/I intelligibly knew, that The longer I am in this the greater the odds are/become that I will come up against (a) crisis of deafening diffuse life catastrophic proportions somewhere along the line; the timeline .

tertiary trauma like third-hand smoke effects indirectly seeping into your/my health when I heard word that Meatloaf had died. If a public figure could die at 74 then so too could my parents (who shared a birth year with the______);1947, die at any time(; they were 74.) The perspective (Alone/in and of itself)

made my mind ajar to jarring. It was adjacent to jarring. Made my mind vulnerable/susceptible to "jarring." /

(was) enough for my mind to become ajar to being jarred/jarring .

As time went on and dissociative (state) stayed/remained... I found myself incidentally/inadvertently conducting unwanted silent interviews in my mind for the winner of 'jarring enough of a situation to harm my mind and do damage in this vulnerable state that is dissociative. The winner of the contest would mean the loss of ________. / the winner of the contest would mean my loss . Having a contest winner would be/mean the reigning-in/ringing-in of (my) loss.

How much could I take and still have my psychiatric ability of coming clear out of this, intact?

When I found out, birthday of 39, that a very close friend has a brain aneurism or how about when I woke up 4 days later on Easter morning to the text from a dear friend/long time friend that their father had died. Empathy so great this veered/careened me close to a direct hit of smoke inhalation. It was second hand but not by much.

And then there was the vehicular hit of our family minivan en route to ...blood draw covid antibodies and routine general blood work up tbc !!!!

It was no wonder early on dr r said I should be able to come out of Dissociative okay as long as nothing too life-jarring/too jarring with my life/too jarring in or to my life, happens while I'm in it. After all ...

>In some/a lot of ways this dissociative state carried the mental malleability and experiential innocence and (therefor) vulnerability/impressionability of a 'still forming developing mind; a child. Depersonalization and Derealization is like being a kid again in that you fear the way a kid/child fears. Bc part of being in the dissociative state means that while although I've chronologically 39 years of age and have decades of life under my belted arm of knowing what a (routine) blood draw feels like ... all of that body-memory is just gone out the window that I (now) fixate my eyes on (looking out of) Bc I don't know what to expect/not knowing what to expect. After 25+/ after upwards of 25 blood draws in my life, this one is (just) as though I'd never had any.

the dissociative experience of/that is derealization and depersonalization wipes the mind (clean) of knowing what things feel like so it becomes hard to pre-empt and anticipate accordingly with or according to (proper/appropriate) preparedness and good standard mental practices./ so it becomes hard to pre-empt and anticipate in accordance with proper /appropriate preparedness and good standard mental practices.

The mind in effect is left flailing to know/comprehend, what's coming in a fear level of the unknown like/of/akin to, that of a child (;loss) (;detrimentally disadvantaged)(;disadvantaged)(;endangeredly disadvantaged)(;egregiously disadvantaged)

-?Maybe somehow write next about 'passing' ?

(Interact with technician / agoraphobic at large) .

Concurrent to preoccupation of what it would/could feel like having/to have the physical body punctured/penetrated/pierced, while in depersonalization/in the depersonalized state; would sensation/it, be heightened or would it be deadened; the latter (luckily) as it turns out/ turned out. .

I was also finding myself mortified to have to be musing about/ humiliated to after 39 years of normalcy/nuerotypical being of me, to have to (now) be (reviewing/assessing my speech and motor function for) contemplation/consideration of and deliberation on/of whether I present as neurotypical/baseline enough so as to "pass" or whether I need to proceed with a cautionary disclaimer / come with a disclaimer the way one prepares an/the acceptance speech of/for an anticipated award. The way one has their/an/the acceptance speech of/for an anticipated award prepared; the advance preparedness/plan(ning) the pre-existing pitch/spiel/plan, bringing/endowing/affording their to be a degree/level, of calm/composure repose and control to the moment.

My/the social anxiety I felt to have a brief/small talk interaction/exchange with a lab technician was a microcosm/substrate/ was the fine adjustment knob, of the agoraphobia felt at large (coarse adjustment knob) to hold deep meaningful dialog with (the) prominent people in my life .

If I couldn't have/hold anxiety-free small talk how could I hold/have/host, deep conversations/heavy conversation(s)./?

In this dissociative-Neuro tests-pending default diagnosis, state/limbo/purgatory, I was not insecure there were no inhibitions and for the first time in a lifetime social anxiety was not of a psychological pathos/pathology but (a) neurophysiology .

I was becoming/I had become agoraphobic for social-awkwardness and embarrassment of being neuroA-typical and the perceived adversity I'd face; Being of a neurological deviation would be a fine brain state had i been born into it and had a lifetime to build acceptance and embracement of (it) ...

I'd be the first to (try on for size) (and) (subsequently) brandish with pride / proudly brandish (the) evolving/emerging progressive terms/terming (of political correctness); Neurodivergent would ring like some kind of empowering impressive superhuman/transhumanism thing to my thinking .

but to have different neurological hardwiring/neural pathways, thrust upon me after 38.5 years of life proved / was proving to feel more like neural blockages than (new) pathways .

And my mind responded in kind with agoraphobia. I was bestowed with the life-unprecedented personality-unprecedented, state of feeling extroverted but fell short of being it for speech delay dismay made gregariousness synonymous with agoraphobic/agoraphobia.

??rather than introverted or (even) ambiverted (even) but/and as??

?????Where to put?????

(The same caliber and candor.)

(But) my cadence my constitution

They had (always) known me one way and now I was another. (And) the principle/on principle of *the* *abrupt* *change* from neurotypical to not, bred embarrassment (and insecurity/self consciousness)

(for ?enacting? ?initiations? ?initiating? of and/or reciprocation in longtime friend interactions) .

-In group text with parents dad said

Neurodivercity

I said

neurodivergent

|————————|

-On the eve of my 1 year clean mark

“One year clean and serene” but This wasn’t serene .

-If only a year clean was synonymous with being well.

|————————-|

. . .

It was the night before clonazepam-clean/free 1 year anniversary, and as I slipped into bed I/and found the commemorative keychain on eBay that glowed in the dark and boasted/brandished a(n) (rejoiceful) aire of relief, rejoice, jovial, cheery, salvation, freedom, stillness and wholeness ...

The gold foil embossed message of "one year clean and serene" read like a wistful/wishful dream/ as wishful dreaming .

I didn't find serenity in having to avert my eyes earlier that night while I ate strawberries Bc they tasted delicious but looked disgusting like someone's blackhead clogged pores to my inescapable macro lens photography visual processing distortion/shackles.

And I didn't feel serenity in the direction label stipulated 30seconds (that) I fought (with) my mind to hold/sustain the brain connection (long enough/for the duration of) (to complete a round/session) for/of the/a proper and safe mouthwash swishing (practices.) TBC writes here about fitness ...30 seconds that's all you have to make it to/through, Stephanie, you do that in a rep of mountain climbers every/per bi-daily workout. colonize/colonizing my mind with constructive positive self-talk to stave off it(s) berating (of) intrusive thought(s); your brain signaling not to swallow Stephanie is going to give out and then you'll be an emetephobic dealing with things like the poison control center and having your stomach pumped at a/the hospital.

I loved glow in the dark items/goodies/objects as much (or more) as/than the next child of the 80's but no, (my faithful readers/listeners) this wasn't serene . / clean wasn't synonymous with serene.

(In)/from/by the dark of my room with/by the bright of my phone in hand One last/final sentiment (sent) incoming to be seen on a dear ones Lock Screen. [[introspection/reflection,]] a retrospect(ive) on/of (the) time gone by and (from all) the congratulatory regard ?of the day?); [[introspection/reflection]]

“If only (my) 365 days WAS synonymous with being well.” .

If only it (even/but) Feigned this keychain .

<3

me, swishing of mouthwash. mouthwash swishing session/ practices/round.

??This proceeding/subsequent bed-time prep where I fought with my mind to keep the mouthwash in for the designated/directions-stipulated length of time…??

|————————————|

You have (very) beautiful hair/ your hair is (very) beautiful complimented the lab technician as she parted and sectioned (to) the scalp prepping me for my/the eeg. Expecting to hear heady sighs that transformed her/the fascination to facetiousness accompanied by (that) strands snapping I didn’t as I regaled her with/ revealed, my 15 year hair cut(ting) abstinence (to her …) … [[ ]]

Not expecting to experience/feel discomfort during testing, I did as what looked like party strobes filled my closed eyes but even so I could recognize…

there was marginal damage control needed afterwards to mitigate the effects; quantity time of (copious) quiet and (intentional)sensory stillness (with mindfulness) and stagnation comprised my arrival home. I couldn’t make it to the locker; I felt too sensory sick to proceed like I had planned; to unload the/my car cabin (clutter) contents piled into the family van(s) trunk pre/prior to EEG pickup that day. Parents kind enough to carry out the task after seeing me home.

After some hours/time came to pass, and I was (re)introducing my day/night/system to sensory engagements (again) . I exclaimed and explained to my family how (in retrospect, in heignsite) ever grateful I am that this EEG came when it did and not a minute or month sooner for I just could intuitively know/sense the unconscionable/perilous/

unbearable nervous system state of [[sensory]] (excruciating) [[sensory]] distress and crisis this light exposure

(brain stimulation) would have thrown/launched, me into a fit of

?(even) just a menial/mere months difference. months prior/ (even) just 2 months prior. [[I am certain beyond all measure ...]]?

I would have not/not have, made it through to the lightless other end of the testing but rather over-flooded with overstimulation begged the technician to set my defeated brain free and cut off the testing. But the untimely end of the session would (prove to) only (prove to) be the beginning of my suffering .

I would have been sent home to stimming (and involuntary/reflexive grimacing) ...

-it/the blow/the discomfort incurred,was minimal/marginal compared to the

-on account of being/becoming accosted and assaulted by my sensory processing/ by my nervous system / by my nerve endings (stabbing my sensory experience ...)

Would have had to demand ...

|—————|

Between my own reevaluation thoughts, those of my personal care team;parents and those of my professional care team;therapist/drs my days surrounding the my one year time stamp saw

questions circulating/a circulation of questions. do I try a dose increase (and see if constipation acuity doesn't increase with it/doesn't respond in kind) ,do I try going off this medication all together and see if I don't regress to intolerable excruciating heights of sensory distortions... (or) do I (maybe) try a different medication ...

Do I get the MRI first before any changing (any meds stuff ...)

Do I apply for SSA disability benefits

Do I work with a disabilities job coach and let them give me a part time job placement to try ...

Always thinking I needed to get better so as to return to/resume life

but now a years time into it being that I would qualify for a conservertorship

considering the what if(s)...

it's the return to life that would get me better. (The chicken or the egg) (and) I've been (unknowingly tearing my recovery asunder) living by living under (the/a) wrongful conviction of/that it is the chicken when (infact) it is the egg like everyone would say.

You're making it worse by isolating

|—–- / ...

Do I stop/bow out of, the opt out

of coveted concerts but what about the disconcerting (new)reality recreational marijuana use is legal as can be . and I live terrified of a(n) (incidental) contact high. Already in an altered state I don't need to conflate/complicate the situation of my cognition .

. . .

|-----------|

CJD#2 or ***Chap 8***

6/4/22

If i were to be moving toward a time where I am to resume my life (and) rejoin society (to feel (more) mentally comfortable) I would have to ??restructure the infrastructure of my/that is my, (interpersonal)presentation/character development/personhood??

Restructure the infrastructure for the/of the objective experiential/experience ... Design how I want people to look at me/see me, perceive me and how I am likely to be received .

(While) Mapping out my first impression in a custom engraved medical alert ID tag/bracelet, (I decided) stricken from the record were (to be) words like syndrome and disorder for the condition-lengthy (duration) connotation insinuation.

while looking up PC/progressive terms and specs in prep for a/the placement of my (eBay) 'new world' order

A solemn/silent moment (caught with my eyes) cauterized by/at what/me .

Wikipedia characterized (as) DPDR (as)

"a mental disorder in which the person has persistent or recurrent feelings of depersonalization or derealization."

relinquishing wish that I didn't have it/this and

1.)shifting to a higher/lower gear of desperation

2.)gear-shifting to a higher/lower desperation.

. . .

why couldn't mine (at least) be the "recurrent" ladder (for that matter)!

further/*reiterated* reading on Wikipedia (that) the Duration is/can be

chronic or episodic [[and that the general population

Frequency is

1–2% .]]

Again, I silently beg of the universe, defeated... why couldn't life [[at least have]] / [[have at least]]

given me the ("episodic") lesser of 2 evils(; episodic ?!) .

Was it not bad enough rare enough that as cited on wiki "(that) the general population frequency is 1-2% " was the further upset of 24/7 365 'days plus' really a must for how life *had to (see me)* /would, see to it that I am *cussed* (mussed and fucked)

(mussed up and fucked) (mussed up and fucked up)

|——.........

![[wasn't even gonna/going to be a tell all and now gettin/getting even is going to/I'll see (to it) that it take(s) you to hell all gaggle/chowder of pink cat hats I don't (even) care what you say they're/they were asking for it and by the girth of my "pen is mightier than the sword" I'll savagely ravage; (/pillage/plunder,)(and) sotamize them all .]]!

. . .

Chap 8 or cjd#2

6/6/22 D-DAY is for denial day.

1st) My Momm to buffer the fall and let me down easy from an imminent/impending call.

The MRI is no longer pending; it's been denied for a 2nd time her soft voice preparing/prepared me for (hard) impact .

Tbc !

After I'd nearly prayed earlier that day on the phone with a friend who is more of a guiding angel on earth than is (of) an earthly body .

I nearly ...

2nd)or3rd) Not having a letter of medical necessity is making a mess of me; it does something to your mind when every night's bedtime is a question of will I live to see sunrise .

2nd)or3rd) (More and) more Time is going by and people have gotten MRI's for less (symptoms) (than this.) than are in my presenting *condition*/case/state.

?

(And) How is this just okay with everyone ?!

Everyone that/who is professionally invested in me but most/more arrestingly/ *but what's more arresting* ... everyone/those who are/is personally invested in me/my life. Everyone/those whose investment in me/my life is personal , emotional , familial, as well/even (as well.)

3 months gone by since *an*/this all important/life altering, test(ing) is prescribed

And (how is) this (is) just okay with everyone?! / and there is (a) resounding resignation ?!

God forbid I actually have one of the things they are trying/vying/seeking to rule out...

That's 3 months that a brain lesion could be progressing or an unruptured aneurism could be advancing to a sentinel bleed ...

Or a sentinel bleed (could be) bringing me to the brink of an untreatable fatal rupture .

-That's 3.5 months for a

lesion/tumor/aneurism to be progressing

?

By the (em)power(ment) I (in)vested in/by me

I denounce you safe from the scathe of my pen's blade...

![[wasn't even gonna/going be a tell all and now gettin/getting even is going to/I'll see (to it) that it take(s) you to hell all gaggle/chowder of

pink cat hats I don't (even) care what you say they're/they were asking for it

A.) (and) I'll bring their sardonic/contemptuous dirge by/for the girth of my "pen is mightier than the sword" ;savagely ravag(ing) ; (/pillage/plunder,)(and) I'll sotamize(ing) them all .

B.) (and) in/with contempt I'll bring their dirge ...]]!

By the (em)power(ment) I (in)vested in/by me

I denounce you safe from the scathe of my pen's blade...

Use this as template

"By the power vested in me by God and man, I pronounce you wife and husband. What God has joined together, let no man put asunder. You may now kiss the bride.Feb 17, 2017"

|——-.........

|————————-|

6/19/22 ... 6/20/22

?Chapter 8 (or CJD#2?)

A new contemplation about this/my complication(s) and a most

morose remorse eclipses (the wings of) my (phoenix) wings mid-flight into the (night/black) light/towards the (night/black) light (at the end of this/the ten ton hell ... at the end of this/the ton of hell) ....

Did I get hurt for how I helped ?

Remembering back to how it was my senior living/assisted living community location that made the news for its record number of covid cases (in the county /in Suffolk county/the state/NY/statewide/countywide) … had the only job I ever loved inflicted me with affliction so cold and alone I could only loathe.

(Inability to perceive passage of time, compromised sense of smell, a cry for hell to go away, to recognize love again / to have emotional recognition (again) … at 37/38/39 I matched the decline of /

At less than 40 I matched the decline… /

I was less than 40 matching them symptom for symptom deficit for deficit my ('years) more than 40' /years (my) , predecessor .

Was this/Had I long hauler covid syndrome ?

Or did I get hurt for how I helped not professionally not in my professional life but (in) my personal (life)… rolling through my mind like microfilm was the memory of the active black mold I should have more proactively tried not to make contact with as I sifted and sorted (through) a bottomless F42.3 (ICD-10) / DSM-5 300.3; (of) crates and boxes of (the) musical scores, locker stored, helping my grieving friend contend with the belongings his beloved mother cherished till/to the day she perished .

Was this/Had I mold poisoning .

|-------------|

Like when you're a few (blurry) bottles (blurry) in to a 6pack/to or towards drunk, and you stop counting; (you surrender) … i had lost clear sight of what my denial count was (up to) for the/my MRI. And it was just as well that I not/stop pay(ing) attention to how my good for nothing insurance company had,

1.)screwed/screwdrivered me over again/ alcohol poisoned me.

2.) alcohol poison screwdrivered me over (again) .

I was an angry (figurative proverbial) drunk antithesis of benign getting restless and revved to 'get mine' ...

|————

8/21/22

I know there's something gone wrong/gone awry in/with/ tangles in the wires of my personality/mind believe me. when I lapsed into dissociative March 10th 2021 .

(I) can't feel love; mine for others theirs for me .

...Love songs (are) lost on me, love scenes (unless they're bdsm)

But I listen to music like this; "stick up" by Grandson and unless I'm going to be taken to/dropped off at one of those now all the 'rage room(s)'

I can't handle/regulate/manage the (gut)(nut-so) reaction

Without this (hashtag/tik tok) trending tourism attraction

I'll end up (intrusive but) unapologetic astral projection

(end up) storm(ing) (the)/my Medicaid, capital/ corporate (capital) headquarters (capital) ; (in (my/an)) intrusive/unapologetic , astral projection.

|—————————-|

(The) months/time marched on till the number of denials; ___ nearly matched the/that time that had lapsed; ___ months, between receiving the testing prescription and getting its family/parents/parentally-funded admittance .

|————————-|

And just like that after,

1.) countless months and denials

2.) thankless Countless time and denials

*3.) countless denials, thankless time and mentally commited crime(s) *

4.) thankless time and countless denials

20 to 30 minutes and the MRI was over and done with and I was being told I'd know in 48 hours how it did go.

[I was less than half a week away from finding out if I was integrally/structurally/fundamentally/foundationally , okay.]

(Nearly) half a year of health insurance stress, unrest and duress gave way to a compulsory/obligatory/conformational, wave (exchange) as I left no more grand time theft

[I was less than half a week away from finding out if I was integrally/structurally/fundamentally/foundationally , okay.]

|———|

Chap 8 ? Or _______

The epileptologist neurologist I had been calling mine/my own, (now) no longer would be as she leans in reiterating the normalcy of my EEG and now too relieving me of the remains of (my) brain damage concerns. Your MRI was normal too she says she doesn't sound shocked, like I feel she seems like this served as a mere confirmation to what she already knew; expected.I get a sense that while this test laid (impending) fatality on the line for/to me it was always (but) an assigned (benign) formality for/to her .

And to all you/the negaters

1.) pseudodementia not non-existent (dementia) .

2.)not non-existent (dementia); pseudodementia .

A symptomatology rooted not in neurology/a symptomatology rooted not neurologically but psychiatrically .

(Pseudodementia) A possible subset/offshoot to the dissociative(; pseudodementia,)

she said; (it) was what my epileptologist / neurologist/she, *broached and spoke* (with me) about/spoke of, *when I posed* the elusive question of *(then)* why, (then) if my/*when* my MRI was/is normal (why) do I feel confused about things like how to safely navigate a parking lot as a pedestrian . (Like I don't feel like I know how to make sure I don't get hit by a car .)

?And she talked to me about pseudodementia and it felt very validating as well as disturbing/upsetting/unsettling . ?

(The more)/ (when) I expressed a/my state of perplexed at the normal findings/readings of the (MRI) test . That my brain was not deadened in places damaged (in others)

She said ...

'You've been given an official (clinical) diagnosis at this point (by your psychiatrist) and it's

(chronic) dissociative DPDR' . '

(She says) with gentle matter of fact insistence (almost) as if she were assuaging a denial I had (unconsciously/subconsciously) waged a war with and now she was (finally)(legally) free to show me as far as her area of expertise; neurology/epileptology, this is defeat/there was/is defeat .... tbc ?

DPDR comes in 2 forms; episodic and chronic . And while I'm unfortunately the latter,

at least for that matter, I now know very serious systemic medical concerns are bridges, the stephoenix can burn/ for the stephoenix to burn / are bridges for this Phoenix to burn .

|—-

The parking lot being 'a lot' ...

Pseudodementia (It) was coming into focus No focal findings on the EEG or MRI but/yet, my emotional bandwidth/understanding/comprehension/scope, for my beloved aging parents was within range of

the extent to which feelings could be illicited from/for/about/towards, my atria patients/residents. Little or no different from the way seniors I work with 8 hours a day were emotionally perceived . My deeply loved/lovable and loving parents could emotionally process (to me/for me) in no way that gave them the reciprocity they deserved . (That I had for them) (or) (That was/they unequivocally earned all the days/years of our lives) (that)

. . .

1.) I so desperately/_______ yearned to have and (to) (be)hold its/this, return.

2.) I so desperately/_____ yearned to have and (to) (be)hold this/it's (and) many happy returns .

Like Anna Nalick says

" and I'm

Eyes wide open, brighter than the candles on a cake

You wasted wishes on when you were okay" .

|————————-|

|——————————-|

|———————————|

|———————————|

To add to/in a part in ?chap 8?

Maybe the part where I talk about how it would be fine if I were born into neuro A-typical .

(The same caliber and candor.)

(But) my cadence my constitution

They had (always) known me one way and now I was another. (And) the principle/on principle of *the* *abrupt* *change* from neurotypical to not, bred embarrassment (and insecurity) (for longtime friend interactions) .

|———————————-|

|-|

-15.) no inhibitions, not insecure... agoraphobic only for awkwardness/embarrassment of being neuroA-typical but for once it's not Bc of introversion. (*Social anxiety for neurological reasons not psychological for once!)

|-|

|———————————————————-|

-(It's no wonder early on dr r said I should be able to come out of Dissocitive okay as long as nothing too jarring happens while I'm in it)

impressionable like that/ fear level of the unknown like that<<

(It's no wonder early on dr r said I should be able to come out of Dissociative okay as long as nothing too jarring happens while I'm in it)

>>Hi "Printer Gifter"...

The blood test went really well today; I am so grateful and so fortunate to have had a technician who was gentle both physically and mentally . God am I lucky to have had that in this dissociative state<<

|——————————————|

|———————————————-|

|—-|

-epileptologist and covid vaccine not advised in dissociative state for concern of a psychosomatic manifestation of symptoms/ symptom manifestation .

-how on April fools day 2022 I found out authorization for MRI was denied by insurance.

The MRI the epileptologist Ordered for me… was denied authorization by insurance company so my family and I are working on an appeal / overturn …

Ugh what a stress mess

It's like … I haven't been able to operate a motor vehicle for 12 months now Bc it looks like a

Virtual reality scene and yet

My insurance company is saying I don't need an MRI

|—|

|————————————————-|

CJD1

I can amass/acrew/acquire thoughts but not allocate them. In allocations absence...

ancillary, respite, heaven/hell/purgatory , plight , 27%,

To go against the grain of the cog fog ascertain and delegate/allocate what belongs best in what chapter and in what part of the/what/the respective chapter . to know if something is 'separate concept enough' that it warrants a new chapter or if it fits best in an already established one...

(I'm feeling intimidated about the organization aspect of my/this memoir.)

All these kind of 'task organization' things (can feel like) a battle waged against my (own) brain to know/ascertain .

This may be the most or one of the most challenging, intruding and intimidating aspects/side effects of writing from within neurocognitive impairment.

I dream of how much easier this is going to be when I have my cognitive faculties working for me again in my favor rather than against me/not in my favor ;it being a strain to be able to make memoir organization judgement calls.

Those/these are the kind of blocks I'm facing . Not writer's block but 'organization of the writing', block.

Rather than let that deterrence cause catastrophic diffuse book damage/loss, I have employed a (proverbial) "junk drawer" , concept.

in it you will find all the topics, paragraphs and stanzas I couldn't allocate a rightful place for. It is (a mish mosh of sentiments,) a discordance of sound; cacophony, in the proverbial song mash-up that you hope is a hit or at least works/is accepted .

-?5 or 7?

It was the turn of what was sent to me; replacement toilet parts so I wouldn't have to gravity flush any more. Arbitrarily calling them "my loving toilet parts" when the gesture/gift arrived from my boyfriend/" The Printer Gifter", I didn't realize quite the quality of life that they would provide me/rescue me with, really just in time. I had been dosed-up on Qutiapine the medication that was proving to be my salvation. (Just as my prescribing doctor hoped it would be) A fire hose/extinguisher to the/a hot bed of (raging) symptoms my nervous system was ablaze with. when I, ?shortly into?/some time into The higher dose of Q, realized I was having some brain to body disconnect/dissonance surrounding the excretory systems functioning. My urge to go was feeling suppressed and when I was on the toilet, there was now a struggle to get my brain to cooperate and be in compliance with my body to let me go. But With the Q bringing some/the much needed relief to the nervous system/my sensory processing, needing to relieve myself in the bathroom and not being able to (with ease) was for me the far lesser of 2 evils.

. . .

A plight vindicated by two lowly numbers; 2 and 7 . It was there in the tri-fold stapled paper to the outside of the pharmacy bag. / it was there in the scholarly medical journals; 27% experience constipation . 27% a significant number in deed I reasoned after remembering the 10% bookstore name in a y2k movie and how that was garnered that name to represent the demographic delineation/mathematical delineation breakdown of (that which was the/comprised the) bglt(bisexual, gay, lesbian, transgender) demographic . 27% was a lot of patients/people, as I had a quantifiable (first hand) feel/measure for what being among 10% was.

I needed (to rely on) innovative ways to quantify 'amount' (of something) . With having no perception of time passage like a canine/dog, It reminded me of when I was a child and my parents had to resort to creative/created ways/ techniques to get me to comprehend/understand time passage. They implemented a 'how many sesame streets' concept . We could be en route to our summer cabin in the Adirondacks and when nabbed and nagged with the classic child's insistence "are we there yet?" universal kid code for "how much longer" or maybe/probably I just asked "how much longer?" not even passive-aggression coming from my subconscious/unconscious.

They would tell me in 'sesame streets' ; quantify the time . However long remained of/for our travel time, they would convert into amount of 'imagined Sesame Street episodes' worth/it would take until before we get there/arrive/have reached our destination (point.). I imagined, I wouldn't actually watch these shows as we rode (and umm it was the 80's, Moore's law didn't afford it) but yeah with a comprehensive grasp /understanding of what the running time of an episode feels like, I could extrapolate what the remaining length of time of a respective car ride would be/would feel like/would consist of. I learned to tell/perceive/understand/comprehend/process time this way.

Questions of how much longer and when will we be there developed into/turned into "how many sesame streets till we get there " ? Or how many sesame streets till we are almost there ?" (?how many more sesame streets till we are half way there? How many more sesame streets till we get to "the big man" my favorite Amsterdam storefront landmark to wake up in time for. I wanted to time management plan the equation of my imagined sesame streets before I settled into a nap.

[to induce a bowel outpour after 11 days of] my brain (was) not performing (right/properly) on the toilet. I could flex and control the voluntary muscles, but the involuntary muscles were feeling brain-blocked to contract/work (properly.) A constant repetitive wrapping of my hand on the wall, an unending scratching motion to my leg, biting down grimacing and gritting my teeth on/against the shoulder strap of my tank top… not Bc there was any physical pain but because there was an apparent/evident severance in the brain to body communication for full evacuation / ease of elimination and/that this (odd behavior) helped (alleviate.) Just as medications can come with a side effect warning of "difficulty swallowing" and until you've experienced it (for yourself) or know someone who has, you may just wonder how your throat could give out on you like that but it's not your body, it's a betrayal of the brain. And so too was this sub-class of constipation; (coming from) a hardship of the brain (and) not a hardening of (the) stool.

11 days into my Arsenal/gambit/catalog of odd repetitive fine motor movement failing to work/ failing me /failing to produce a bowel movement I induced.

Thighs bruised from sitting on the toilet for so long with not having yet gotten back up to my full healthy weight since withdrawals (first) ensued/ensnared. But it was the first month of the new year and a

32oz bottle of prune juice (from wfm) had/was making mine, my new year, for it meant I wouldn't have to concede/acquiesce to the powder mix that brandished the warning/promise of choking due to a swelling of the esophagus, if your water intake quantity (with it) doesn't/didn't suffice. A triggering warning for a flood of memories of my brain-laden/brain-created/brain-induced, choking-hazard days of withdrawals.

Momm to call in night if emergency and then I call with antithesis of emergency (prune juice worked) and she is just as glad I did / I called . What love .

-as I ate my 4am victory toast embedded with a spattering of dark color seeds, I thought about how far I've come since the days of bug in oat crunch's pocket/cavity?

Seeing is believing and I couldn't see by design of that cereal morsel.

-couldn't get up off of toilet to take Q (not to mention Bc it's a sedative effect) but would I go into terrifying withdrawals? I was traumatized by withdrawals (clonazepam)

|——-|

No amount of watching videos of how I used to be, listening to songs to/of which I used to dance and sing or self-coaxing a single object to 'just look real' through hyper-focused intent, could take me/get me out of this./could bring me back./could 'make me come-to'. Not for so much as a nano-second / micro-second .

There were no 'breakthrough' moments of my/to my/in my lack of emotional recognition for/of the people and things I loved and all the nano seconds devoid of feeling what I had felt for 37 years was adding up to 10 months too long.

The reorientation and reintegration grounding exercises as my dr. Lane Rosalie, Called it and had me/left me dumbfounded; how could I smell the fresh cut grass as I'm walking, focus my awareness on it like never before and yet this moment ceases/fails to feel real. How could I stare at an emotionally prized childhood possession, a burst with sentimental attachment of a lifetime and that I felt for a lifetime and yet feel nothing by the sight of it, the touch of it or the old familar smell of it (which) didn't feel familar at all. nothing emotionally connected for me or registered; it was all lost on me.

So desperate to ignite some kind of spark of recognition, I devised the/a concept of exposure(therapy)[a systematic resensitization to hopefully replace bless I pray replace, this/my systematic desensitization.] to/of my own natural body essence(s)/scent(s)...[a systematic resensitization to hopefully replace, bless I pray replace, this/my systematic desensitization.] turning my neck/craning my neck to tuck my nose under my arm I'd inhale my pheromones and hope it could bring a moment of self-recognition . Inhaling my hair overdue to be washed, maybe that would. (Or) holding my (worn) underwear to my nose briefly before dropping it in the hamper (with (all) the rest of (all) the dirty laundry?) To my daily reinforced disheartenment, Nothing did .

So my shrink had me performing grounding exercises that consisted of smelling fresh cut grass and flowers like a hippie, and I had me panty-sniffing like a dark web fetishist; the underground of the whole 'reorientation and reintegration', concept/experience. Don't begrudge or judge me and (by the way) no shade on anyone's sexual proclivities/proclivity. One or more populations of cognitive impairment get breakthrough moments from a specific song or a particular smell. Why couldn't I be one of them, why couldn't I be like that. Why couldn't I just have a moment . A moment where I am able to feel that which I intellectually know/remember , is there (to feel/to be felt .) Why ? Oh why can't/couldn't I ?

|———-|

Friends in Brooklyn had made me well-aware/(when) (through friends) I had learned of the reality that people are paying a pretty premium for dissociative state induction with/through ketamine and thought of/lamented how they are to be entering into dissociative state on their own terms; consent . (And) how they get the safety net of knowing it is essentially for a determinate length of time that they will be in/of an altered state(;ideal circumstance(s)). I believe this ('greater)knowing', subconsciously is at work /(is at basal ganglia and cerebellum play, here) functioning to serve/bolstering the (person during the/for the) duration of the persons/their experience with (peace and) repose . (And) that it is this cognitive understanding that this is to be for a determinate length of time that allows for/ cultivates an inner climate conducive of/to physiological response that is (compliant and) comfortable . (In effect) yielding a pleasurable pleasant high . But/and here I was perpetually stuck in a non-consensual/unconsensual dissociative state and for/at an indeterminate length of time.

.Ideal circumstances .

.Conducive.

(This next part maybe suited for chap4?)?

An incoming stovetop picture of artisanal grilled cheese in a pan sent with/and/paired with an innocuous question of "Do you like this crust or do you prefer darker?" dehumanized me. I couldn't discern gradation in color, so I couldn't tell/deliberate if it modeled/mimicked my/met my, life-long/life-standard, toasted golden brown preference of crisp. I knew and could recite/convey/relay/present, with eloquence, the specs of that which my preference was; toasted to a golden brown crisp. But I couldn't tell if what I was looking at was that. Disengaging my eyes from the sight, I closed-out the image... maybe if I come back to it later, I'll be able to see it for what it is. Following a follow-up text received of

"I want to be ready when I'm making breakfasts for you again" I scroll back, revisiting the image... what do I see ? The same 'unknown' . I think of forwarding the photo to my Momm and asking her/to ask her if this is how I like my bread or do I like it darker?.

Cut off from knowing myself...My preferences; likes and dislikes, my opinions where I stand on things/matters what I'll stand for. What I stand for... from simple things like if I like the color/ way of a dress to if I will/would ___________. When there is floundering to know who you are, the survival of the integrity of your personhood falls on those around you. Those (you have) entrusted with your care. I always thought there was nothing sadder or more oppressive than when from my side lever raised up swivel chair, I'd be able to peer over the top of the reception desk to/and see a sea of senile seniors outfitted in things they would never wear. When a daughter in law, home health aide or any other delineation of care giver capitalizes on the fact that the elder in their care can't advocate for themself, nothing is more saddening or maddening to bear witness to/of. I believe it's a care giver's responsibility to pull from what they know of the person's Earlier life and implement it now. Which means if it's evident from near every youthful photo that this person has historically gravitated to wardrobe pieces that denote exquisite gothic charm or an unkempt punk presence then don't outfit them day in and day out so that they'll fit the country club dress code with you.

A 30 something floundering, flailing and failing to know myself/oneself my Momm re-humanized me (in incremental doses systematically) reinforcing my personhood with/through anecdotes and personality/character traits of that which she knows/knew to be true (of me) tbc .

She bolstered me up with … CONCERTS…

Fake it till you make it/going through the motions . / a lot on my plate./ this is role-play (That is what this next part is about)…

With a diagnosis of dissonance of cognition and emotion…everything (I do), every move I make has become/becomes with/for the purpose and intent of being emotionally reached or achieving emotional recognition. And every attempt is to no avail.

When i (affectionately) requested for Christmas breakfast (2021) that my parents loan me a plate from their wedding set; the dishware of my life; I put a lot on my plate with that emotional ideation. mirroring what breakfast mornings on Christmas looked like my whole life, couldn't eating moms special annual Christmas pancakes on the dish, the deepest parts of me associated home sweet home with… spark a morsel of memory for me emotionally? A crumb where cognition and emotion are not at a soul-crushing deficit of dissonance? Nope, it wouldn't/couldn't. My efforts were futile.

To the untrained eye of the beholder; all the/my beloved people in my life; family, partner and friends it might look as though I'm doing things because I feel from them; the things I do, but really I am doing things without any emotional payoff; no serotonin surge despite how many servings of goji berries I fill my week with no oxytocin tingle despite all the ultimate acts of abounding and unconditional love I am shown (or dopamine rush.)In the absence of limbic benefit, I just keep hoping that if I fake it it'll help me 'make it' . And so I go through the motions one part mirroring/replicating what people do who feel love; their behavior … their verbiage … and one part mirroring/replicating what always would (have) emotionally reached me. I go through my days exacting role play and pray this gainfully employs emotion.

I don't even remember what love feels like. I know my parents actions and behavior show love every day and in every way ... which is all the more reason it's so crushingly frustrating and feels shameful that I'm just blocked from feeling any of it/that I can't feel any of it.Bc my god with all that they do and all that they are why can't that just break through and be felt by my limbic system why

fuck. Why can't the sight of one of their weekly care packages that is my grocery list brought to fruition and delivered (right) to my door just cut (right) through the 'unfeeling' as I unpack the love inside fridge rack by rack drawer by drawer ...

Apart from being as good as someone who legally qualifies/would qualify for a conservatorship; and needing their help, What's the point of even filling your life with people you love if you can't even feel their love for you or yours for them ?!

This dissonance of cognition and emotion is both that of a frustrating as well as shame-filled symptom.

And it leads to, maybe lends itself to feelings and contemplations of just filling ones life with hedonistic pleasures and instant gratifications rather than be up against interacting with a partner you love and not be able to feel it.

To be interacting with people you love and (be) feeling none of it, is crushing and can

drive a person to wanting to just seek out and sink into the refuge and the respite that is any interpersonal dynamic(s) where emotion isn't required ...not expected or a pre-requisite.

I don't remember what it feels like to be a part of the human experience . The human condition has been stolen from me and now

I'm left watching loving couples on tv and how they talk to each other and I just feel it eludes me . I feel alienated by it ...

The same way I don't have proper (Ghrelin) regulation/functioning for sense of hunger and fullness so it's like when I see a meal time scene on tv, or 'realer' yet... YouTube, if I see people out to eat on YouTube and they show their entree portion, it eludes me ... it's like oh? That's how much makes sense to eat in a meal ? Oh, that's the amount people can comfortably eat in one sitting ? Oh okay . ... it all eludes me and alienates me and the romantic relationship version of that mal-function is (that) I (would) see people acting all lovey dovey, and I would intellectually recognize oh? These are some ways (some) couples speak to one another . A mere mirroring of the words all I can do/muster . A seamless replication of the actions/behavior; going through the motions/kinetics, sure ! but 'feeling' the words and there being resonance at the other end of the actions/behavior? Was more that I could manifest or conure . Compliments of this symptom of dissonance I was hollow... vacant. And while we knew what the symptom was; dissonance of cognition and emotion it remained clinically undeciphered/undecided/undiagnosed (as to) why I was suffering (from) this/the symptom. The mysterious reality of 'Lovey dovey' 'mushy gushy' eluding me loomed over me... (terms of) endearment and affection were expressions biochemically lost on me.

I once heard something to the effect of that reframing one's mentality to that of as though you were an impartial party scientifically reviewing/conducting a case study/ conducting a scientific case study can help you detach from the sadness and frustration you feel over/about your (presenting) symptomatology (presenting) symptoms. In my deconstructive analysis/ in my deconstruction there was conjecture ...Since/if love and emotion are regulated and controlled by the limbic system, which is located in the temporal lobe of the brain, and I couldn't feel mine, was that indicative of TLE ? The dreaded diagnosis on my psychiatrist's mind since the (very) beginning of (our) time ? Since the (very) beginning of withdrawals time? Or was my sudden/abrupt (onset) and sustained/suspended emotional deficiency (merely) attributable (merely) to (merely; in relativity 'merely' /what is merely) ,(what is) the dissociative state/condition/complication of derealization and depersonalization ? As Momm warmly reminded me ...

"Remember lots of things have similar symptoms" (- whatever you need we're in it together and and we'll work through it <3) .

A belated alternate theory of hers materialized in conversation/amid the/ my critical analysis ... the profundity of the / that was the love and the loss of my 2019 3death succession(;what I gave to/in that time) had sapped my internal/nurtural and natural resources of/for love. Had sapped me of my natural resources of/for love. My brain circuitry had been shorted by crisis and now everybody (family and doctors alike) were (left) fumbling around/were left to fumble around in the dark (of my mind) trying to figure out the where, which and the why of (the) proverbial fuse that was blown.

...... tbc with

My psychologist in session told me that he has treated patients with/of a lifelong inability to feel love but never has he ever heard of a lifetime of ability becoming ripped away. When you've never had it/something before you are (relatively) spared the weight (of the pain) of knowing what you're missing(out on.) That of which had been/was taken away from me in one felt/felled swoop after 3 and change decades was palpable and packed an amorphous/nebulous/________grieving.

C?

?CJD?

Love ebbed Where once flowed languid (and) unobstructed / where once flowed languid (and) unobstructed...love ebbed.

It/And gave way to/surrendered itself to a dark sexual mania (substitution) coursing through my veins ... hardly the (health/healthy) likening of a plant based meat substitute(,concept.) (of/in, a dietary shift .)

I was hollow except for (the) hedonic hunger that filled me/ Hollow except for (the) hedonic hunger that fills me...my brain's pleasure center being a (?sole?) survivor of/in an/this incomprehensible wreckage... I was hyper sexual and hypo emotional... hyper lust and hypo love. / I was hyped-up on sexuality and hypoglycemic on love / I was hyper sexual and hypoglycemic on love / I was hyper sexual and hypoglycemic where love was concerned / I was hyper sexual; hedonistic hedonic and hypoglycemic in matters of love (the heart.) (any)where (that) love was concerned .

-Hyper sexual / hypo emotional

-hyper lust/ hypo love

-hollow except for the hedonic hunger that fills me.

-lust in the absence of love

"Located near the center of the brain, the nucleus accumbens is connected, by intermingled populations of cells, to many other brain structures having roles in pleasure seeking and drug addiction.May 27, 2014"

It's this shit that makes me deem a most/one of the most/the most desirable thing being/to as well as (behaviorally) safe/protective (measure to take) (being that my current relationship is (that) of a monogamous construct) is that I just go (and) spend the day playing in my locker ; Bc I'm not reminded of how I can't feel love's emotion/the emotion of love, for people . (And) To / whereas you,

have/engage in human interaction is to be (painfully) reminded of it; My deficit.

|—-|

Where to put this ?

Lust in the absence of love was in-conducive to matriculating in/at the life I had built pre-dissociative. And now I was wrought with restless transience of thought (;ambivalence) (and ambivalence) to make a transfer (in the next/in an/in the enrollment period .) My add drop mentality of 'relationship (life)style' ambivalence... write here about

'open enrollment' metaphor for open relationship.

|—-|

Put here, or in chap 4 after beads of water and before door lock, or somewhere else ?

In the beginning my aphasia was so bad . Like a gameshow contestant using one of their 'lifelines' to call someone for a hint, I turned to dadd, Enroute to the local beach for a family daycation with him and Momm ...I was amid a recounting of something to them and I needed to know what is that part (you walk on) that is next to (the street) where cars drive/(can) go? I had become stumped mid story telling. The sidewalk he said, his gentle, even tone revealing

non-judgement. I was able to resume/proceed with my story .

Stories ... stories ... I knew of the book where the sidewalk ends and was now slew with a new normal (of) where the word sidewalk ends.

Coming up a year's time now, one day amid a neighborhood leisure walk, I stopped and sat down where grass meets sidewalk... the proverbial shoreline of horticulture. Sitting lawnline, the cement-side of seaside at the proverbial waters edge, I put my feet out in front of me, looking down at them planted on/in the vast body of ecru... although this is where I wanted the likeness/analogies to end ... it wasn't long before my eyes making contact with the concrete revealed a "where the word sidewalk ends" book sequel (that) I didn't want to be ... "where the sidewalk recedes." . I looked to the right, I looked to the left (there was) concrete sea as far as the eye could see in either direction and where my feet waded appeared to be (kinetic); receding in (a) (loop) (of continuous/constant) (of) (a) motion of (a) moderate rate. Unbeknownst to me I had tested the waters in/of a psychedelic sea and ...

-thin to thickness of same fabric and color ex.) bedsheet set hand washing . Tactile processing, excruciating .

And thin to thickness visualization/intrusive imagery ex.) thread,rope

?visual? processing excruciating

Amidst the meditative/cathartic practice of laundry, hand washing was my nerve endings there to sneak attack me with unbearable, excruciating sensory processing distress as I swished the 4 piece bedsheet set around in the basin of the sink/in the sink basin. after taming a/the queen size flat sheet submerged in the cool_____ my hands floated/glided over to meet the gentle gripping and wringing of one of the 2 standard size pillowcases that was there afloat in the body of acquiesce solace/ peace/relaxation. In the acquiesce body of solace/ peace. the haptic feedback felt when moving from the grander girth that is/of a flat sheet and fitted sheet to (feeling) the lesser fabric of a pillowcase bunched in my hand(s) was / sent shockwaves through my nervous system/ to or through my nerve endings that would/could (sometimes) take me an hour to hours to 'come down' from, my brain that would maim me with intrusive imagery and (intrusive) haptic/tactile memory of what it was for my eyes to see a kitchen sink sea of monochrome monochromatic Pantone; the contents of/in a compete sheet set and not have the haptic/tactile reality match/mirror that of the visual color reality; identical (value(s)) .

Was this what my/could this be what my (autism, autism spectrum and other neurobiological disorders) students of times gone by/of employments past, and their desperate families meant/were trying to communicate to me/convey to me and impress upon me when [preceding going into (the) specs of an/their impassioned statement.] they would (there) in classroom drop off setting of an imposed/with an imposed impromptu parent teacher conference(s) aside would describe /issue warning of/that their son/daughter has/is of (a) tactile defensiveness persuasion and (has) sensory processing delays and issues/difficulties/complications. [proceeding to go into the specs of that/their impassioned statement.]

As I stood sink side, my eyes soaking up the streamline repetition that was color/Pantone in/of a bedsheet set … my cognition contended with reconciling the confusion and disconnect felt from the tactile experience of 'fabric of the same color' being not of the same amount being able to be not of the same amount . Like so many other things in this time of strange sickness ,Intellectually it made sense but something was lost on a/the brain connection of it; that which was cut from the same cloth, feeling comfortable to the touch.

even if/when/though i could avert eyes and avoid touch; keep a controlled (external) environment (externally) , I couldn't circumvent/there was little I could do to escape/ circumvent the physiological fallout/lashings of internal stimuli. visually seeing and physically touching environmental examples/environmental applications of thin vs thick was one (hard enough) thing albeit hard enough… I could try to look away quick enough before I was violently and vehemently rejected by my (own) nervous system for catching sight of the thick of the tree branch/trunk that sprouted an offshoot of twigs in a cluster... I could mediate how long I looked (although for a long time, I was sick enough where my peripheral view catching sight (of something like that) as I walked by on my daily 30 min neighborhood stroll was enough exposure to damn me with damage that would/could do me in for the rest of the walk or even week.

Branches by bedsheets by brain lashing I was coming into memory of a childhood where I'd lie in bed at night, accosted by visions of thin and thick that ransacked my head. It had been 3 decades and change without so much as a one off night of a return of/to intrusive internal sight which when I, now at 38 years of age, came out to my family/parents about what my mind had done/would do to me as a child ... it begged the applied-question of was my brain trying to reboot (itself) or something? And so therefor it needs to revisit all its development stages of development in effort/order to work back up to where it was at/had grown to, had amounted to , today and then reside there . ?

I had no way out "home safe" from how my mind would destroy me, harassing and torturing me like the tormentors of/that were the schoolyard of my youth . Thin thread, thick rope (a) girth variation and My mind's eye betraying me on an account of said intrusive imagery, battery .

With the exception of the taste of a singular hard boiled egg (once) repeating on me for a week's time to/in/from my mind ... gustatory was the soul survivor of (the) /for the senses spared me.

***-tactile processing is a lot better too.

-visual and auditory were the ones that used to cause the most severe nervous system upset

-tactile was pretty bad in some ways for a while too.

-olfactory was only (somewhat) troublesome in the very very beginning

-and gustatory has always been good to me. I was spared one sense. one.***

-also write here about the intrusive gustatory recall of hb egg .

-**-(?I think or I know I've been writing this in CJD?) thin to thickness of same fabric and color ex.) bedsheet set hand washing . Tactile processing, excruciating .

And thin to thickness visualization/intrusive imagery ex.) thread,rope

?visual? processing excruciating

|-------------------------|

I have a bunch of things I can't get my brain to work to know where they should go within the memoir, so I just don't write them, but literally tomorrow I think I'm just going to have to start a section where I just write the mish mosh of all the things I want to write and I write full bodied on each of those things then I just make a

'mystery chapter' file for them where it's like here are all the things I couldn't figure out what chapter they belong in so just rather than let that stop me from writing them, I made a 'mash-up' chapter . (Same concept as song 'mash ups')

Maybe that's what I'll do .

And then when I'm neurotypical I'll read everything in my mashup chapter and sift through it and figure out what belongs where within the established chapters .

. . .

Or maybe just maybe ideally I could get away with just letting there exist a mash-up mish mosh chapter

5th text) in the book .

6th text) maybe I'll call it

'my junk drawer' chapter

7th text) It's already been well-established by the name of the book and the introduction that I am writing this through neurocognitive deficit and impairment .... So maybe publishers and readers would 'take-heart' and accept that there is a junk drawer chapter in this book

8th text) I don't know... when you can, tell me what you think

🕊🙏🕊

|—|

-Printer Gifter's grilled cheese question of 2/11/22 "Do you like this crust or do you prefer darker?"

Grilled cheese question I could only guess how I like it now and then I will have to tell you how I actually like it once I am neurotypical and therefor with the ability to definitively know personal preference .

So you want me to take a guess and answer you now or wait to answer you for when I know that I am meaning what I say and saying what I mean ?

For my anxiety, it would be much more comfortable to wait

"I'd like you to guess"

"I want to be ready when I'm making breakfasts for you again"

Me guessing won't prepare you though Bc it could be inconsistent with my actual preference that I will finally have cognitive access to again when I'm better .

We'd be better off with me texting that pic to my mom and asking her, have I, my whole life, liked it like this or darker . Isn't that crazy how cut off from 'knowing myself' I am (so long as I'm sick.) !

going out for my walk I'll check back when I get in to see if you've written anything

🙏🔓🧠🔓 🧎‍♀️🙏

(Maybe chap 4?)?

|——-|

Maybe put in Chapter 7

4/14/22

A little over a year in and I was still having to respectfully and regretfully evade questions asked me that were/could be of any real situational life (situational)-consequence. My polite decline came wrapped in a/the one liner of "I don't feel comfortable answering that until I can know that I am saying what I mean and meaning what I say." It always packed a punch of frustration, disappointment and let down that I never wanted for the person.

But they were asking me something serious that required something I was at a loss/deficit, to know if I was giving; honesty.

For their sake and mine alike I felt it was best that I refrain from addressing/answering all major-life impact questions/inquiries until I was of typical neuro cognition and could therefore know how I feel, know that I know (how I feel) and / have proper adequate access to (knowing) how I feel; awareness .

Desperate to preserve/reserve my or the right/chance to/an/at, answering questions accurately and honestly, I decided on an analogy that could/would be ?universally? largely relatable enough to help others at large (so as to) understand/comprehend better/ better comprehend the peril(s) of ________. The dissociative state/experience is a very detached state/experience. it's as hard to know what I think about things/feel about things/ what ones own opinions and stances are on matters as it is to be trying to see the ceiling through a blanket you've buried your head under in bed. Straining to sight the ceiling/bright white, above doesn't change/negate/nullify/neutralize, the fact/reality/the properties, that there is, opaque obscurment. / obscurement of an opaque variety/means/kind. I can't answer questions no more/any more than you can see though that blanket. Than can you see through that blanket .

. . .

?Maybe write here about how when I was a teen and couldn't answer any questions upon home arrival from school day. ?

|——-|

-so I can make sure I'm answering it honestly/ when I know how I feel / or have access to how I feel .

-dissociative state is a very detached state it's as hard to know what I think about things as it is to be trying to see through a blanket when one is totally under the covers and has their head under the covers and they are looking up at the ceiling through the opaque blanket and how hard it is to see through that blanket is for me how hard it can be to answer questions

CINJAD

|———————————|

Recurring/reoccurring

dream themes

-PTSD

-remorse (suppression,repression)

-systematic desensitization of fears and phobias

-mid night light rescue

-sleep paralysis

|———————————|

Potential chapter names

-unrest in peace

|—————————|

Chapter: (it's) justice a dream or

Chapter _______

Whether it was a side effect of the medication; vivid dreaming or a function of the dissociation itself,

Night after night (I was) cut (down) (to size) and (guilt-)gutted in with (guilt) /through dream after dream for the sins dating back that dated back to where I begin; childhood . Remorse the deep cuts of my personal record that took an/into adulthood to emerge through/from the(ir) slumber of suppression and/their repercussions / repercussion; (of) repression. (Symptom) Age regression (symptom)(aspect) of dissociative/DR/!DP! compounded/became the companion piece of/to (symptom) objective perspective (symptom) of dissociative /!DR!/DP and gave me the tough (ultimate act of) love (ultimate) gift of confronting the self . (And the past.) .

[[I should have known if age regression could bring back/alive recapture the potent splendor of childhood cherished shows and channel it into/through the subjective experiential then so too would it; age regression posses the prowess/power to recreate/reenact the early life experiences that shaped my shame and, pain/suppression/self-blame. this time without defense mechanisms of suppression and repression to ease the pain the dissociative keeps/sees your conscience splayed open …

This is the end of the (guilt) gilded (guilt) age . This is the end of the age of gilded guilt. This is the end of the gilded age of guilt . (No more gentle forgiving guise of the mind) Now remorse rears its raw/ugly edge. ; raw.]]

. . .

(Already) well acquainted with powerful and profound ?nocturnal psycho emission? shifts coming/awakened in me, from/through (the medium of the means of) dreaming … / through by means of the dream/ by means of nocturnal psycho emission(s) .

Systematic desensitization through dreaming is what I'd termed it when I went through life phases…

Where my fears and phobias were the consistent in/of recurring/reoccurring, dream theme . One night's rest that which plagues my psyche with such unrest distress might show up in the form of one of the 5 senses my mind sparing me from (the/an) overstimulation of 'all' . Consecutive sustained nights of presenting my gravest fright in sight but not sound might then/would then advance my/this organically occurring exposure therapy to the next round … the systematic desensitization process ultimately culminating in the product of a dream of interaction (and extinguishing) No longer an experience of passively/independently existing in observation of auditory, visual or olfactory but now an engaging dynamic visceral confrontation.

(and/for, extinguishing .)

Concepts like/of (the) Process of bravery derived in Patti smith lyrics "embrace all that you fear" would help me arrive at/to the final destination of/in this [[product oriented]]

(unconscious subconscious) mind(-mending) devised matrix for/of psyche/soul-mending.

"Eradicate your fear(s)" I could hear Patti Smiths lyrics growing near as I faced off and stared down the werewolf of my indigo girls "kid fears" and as I sloshed water over a building ablaze with/of my childhood/early life fright (in sight) , (in/on) the exposure therapy/systematic desensitization, final installment night…

?During the thick of my sick, my dreams attempted to sic on me/sic me with?

the [[aeronasuaphobia/emetephobia]] gastro-grueling dreaming that my mind attempted to sic on me/ sic me with, in the thick of my sick was a/in continuation of a(n) aeronasuaphobia/emetephobia exposure program my brain was running (in slumber) several/many years ago. (But) Unlike confrontation of the werewolf and the fire of my childhood fears/ early beginning life fears ... this/ the blossoming/blossomed neurosis/hypochondriasis of/from my (developing) adolescent years proved to have grown a (_____-resistant) fear that at an advanced/the advanced age of that at the a mature age of 39 years, hadn't yet made it to/seen the (likes of the) 'systematic desensitization through dreaming' , finish line (of termination.)/termination rotation.

-for purposes/product of extinguishing

early life ware wolf fear was ...

Having gone through

[[rigorous, (the) rigor(s) of]] (said)

[[rigorous, (the) rigor(s) of]] intensive naturally-occurring unconscious/sub conscious cognitive behavioral therapy (before in life), one might think whatever [[intrusive,invasive]] synthesized [[intrusive,invasive]] vivid dreaming my/a psych med could augment/ give (me)/cause, would be of no concern/anguish to me of no cause of concern to/for me (but that didn't prove to be the case study.) (but) the conscious-breeched remorse that ripped me from my sleep (now) saw me to (the) tears (of) decades (worth/spanned) of unacknowledged/under acknowledged, years (streamed down my face and) stood me down (now.) My (?12 months?) attending psychiatrist believed (these) pained and early life guilt-laden dreams to be something of symbolic means. (An) Apparition(s) /manifestation, of a more recent contrition.

Whether it was side effect of the medication or of or something of (the)(a) metaphysical/(dissociation) meta human agent/agency/invocation,

(of dissociation,) Rapid eye movement(REM) of the sleep phase/sleep cycle, proved to be a live-wire of a dream(ing) movement. (It became) interoceptively/intuitively, (it became), evident that my mind was motioning to move me towards mending/healing ……

On the heels of___________, there were

[[a barrage of]] what could be/What could only be self-professed/self-diagnosed as (none other than) [[a barrage of]] PTSD dreams. <3 <3 <3

The grotesque of the dying (process), the [[time is of the essence]] frantic/fevered/panic-stricken attempts to go against the grain [[when time is of the essence]] and negate the/a (insidious) planned obsolescence of cancer. And negate cancer's (insidious) planned obsolescence. (The Father Of my cats and I) Sleeping in shifts and speeding to the ER in the dead of night (of); (the) graveyard shift. Stop lights ran the whole ride there like an alibi of red-green color blindness (were on my/our side)… if red hues likely appear as the color green to my cat then, in his name I drive/ride tonight /I drive ride in his name tonight. Audible prayers frenetic and palpable to my grandma (just) let us get there in time, in her/your name I pray for (my/my baby's) life / life's sake.

It was all there all of what my reality was now compressed/concentrated in a dream theme; ptsd (I) loathe that for me / of ptsd (I) loathe that for me (for me.) seeming(ly) hardly seeming(ly) reliving/consecrated any of the somewhat odd 13 years of blissful peace love and happiness my mind would only grind out re-enactments/recreation(s) of what the death was (all) about. Like a/ like an internal wanton/wayward chapter of the/a SCA …

this rest had me/would see me going to battle for my (in) peace.

This sleep had me/ would see (me) (going to battle) unrest in peace .

This sleep would see me to unrest in peace.

Dreams / sleep paralysis

A/The/pleasant sleep/slumber that was eclipsed by, (the/a menacing/a shroud of) sleep paralysis (that) paralleled the palliative care (time/*days*) of my baby's darkest (hour/darkest days / dying time .)

(?And had me/primed/governed/adversely trained/instilled (in) me to be flipping on light switches/light switch flipping, all hours of the night?)

Like (a) public safety light(s) on/to ,a post-bar crawl college campus (these/my) bathroom bar lights would keep the streets of my mind safe(r) in/along my walk with dreams/sleep.

If ever I needed verification/validation that what hadn't killed me in/of withdrawls had made me stronger, it was here. The proof was in the putting when I finally kicked the dream/sleep aberrance mid-sequence throwing my fist like an athletic sport, I punched the demonic/ sinister apparition in the mid-section.

Never to be seen again, I could now breakout (and rouse from) of every impending, imminent burgeoning (sleep) paralysis episode long before the ominous/dark mirage Would ever show its visage.

|———————-|

:::::::::////:::::::::::::::///:::::::::::////:::::::::::////::::::::::::::

?I think or I know these are just notes?

. . .

***Maybe write next about sleep paralysis, do copy and paste and then maybe move into how I finally kicked the dream/sleep aberrance when I mid-sequence punched the demonic/ sinister apparition in the mid-section.

-Since a cat's cones are most sensitive to blue and yellow wavelengths of light, they do not see colors like red, orange, or brown. They are similar to people with red-green color blindness—red hues likely appear as the color green to your cat.

|——————————|

|——————————|

Dreams / sleep paralysis

The/pleasant sleep/slumber that was eclipsed by, (the/a menacing/a shroud of) sleep paralysis (that) paralleled the palliative care (time/*days*) of my baby's darkest (hour/darkest days / dying time .)

And ...

|——————————|

::::::::::::::::::::::::::///:::::::://///:::::::::::///::::::::::::::::::

|————————-|

On 8/18/22

Dr Lane Rosalie says he wants to see me in 2 weeks ! He also says my dreams might change. I might start to have different dreams . I assume he means nighttime/sleeping dreams .

|——-|

CINJAD

Sept 15th 2022 …lastnight I dreamt

When the dose increase saw me to 150mg at the rate of 3 pills (a/per) night(ly), my prescribing psych doctor so too upped our/the session frequency to every 2 weeks instead of 3 / bi-weekly instead of tri(-weekly). (And) he began slipping/issuing warnings / began slipping issued pointed (fore)warnings into our goodbyes at the close of (our/my/the) sessions "your dreams might (start to) change " / "you might start to have different dreams." he said it once and I didn't question/______,dissect, it . (Afterall with my,/and with my (pigeonholing/restrictive/impeding/obstructive) literal interpretations of things (pigeonholing/being restrictive/impeding me /being obstructive)

and my difficulty to infer I wasn't even sure if he meant nighttime/sleeping, dreams (or life aspirations (dreams)). (But then) I think (then) became of me the change he wished to heed.

…..

You see…

All/much of my life leading up to my monthly menses in sleep I would be sent a dream themed around the upcoming uteran bleed . My brain so sa-synced with my body that I could rely on the dutiful deliverance of this dream to never be caught white pants red handed (unprepared) in a tampon unattended (menstruation) 'forgot mess' situation/______, messtruation .

However for the thus far duration of dissociation I had not dreamed the likes of ... tbc

Soon write about the period related dream ! ???aka???

??? Write about tampon string period dream that precipitated ...??? .

|————————|

|———————-|

CJD3, CINJAD

9/22/22

I woke up this morning feeling like how do I go 40 to 50 years more not getting to see my babies.

maybe precipitated by a dream I don't remember ... but today I woke up with/to a/the palpable overpowering sense of ... how do I get through presumably 40 to 50 years more without being able to see my babies.

It hadn't happened In a really long time, the crippling anticipatory life-line panic . Before I could take advantage and manage to cognitively assess and ascertain if just perhaps it had been 18 months long/time since my last (mid-life crisis) episode like this

It was gone; the episode and my cognitive processing (had) reverted back to an/the all-out inability to perceive (any) passage of (any) time; (dissociatives standard)

I would never know Had I experienced a micro-second of dissociative micro-fracture ?

This incident had

brought something out of/ awakened something in from suppression's den, in me /repression's den, in me /subconscious/unconscious hiding/hibernating, (for me) ... I was reacquainted with (the/an) awareness/knowledge (of) that onslaughts of panic and anxiety used to find me periodically/frequently recurrent(ly) surrounding the death of my babies ... abounding fixations/perseverations (about) doubting how I can possibly manage getting through (what would presumably be) amounting to another 40 to 50 years (yet/more) without seeing them/______.

That thought to no avail ailed me like no/none other . It rendered my scope of life a jail/prison sentence. I remember it/journaling about it. It was something I had never felt of/from life before.

And then somewhere along the line I lost ability to perceive passage of time and with that backhanded accomplishment (came/was) the cessation of said anxiety and panic

made (for) a/was a , possibly mind-saving accompaniment . I see it now; I couldn't go on (writhing from their dying) reeling from/with the feeling(s) that life/living was/had become synonymous with trapped/entrapment ... so my brain helicopter-lifted me out of it; a an/ world/existence in which/with, time is/as/was , a construct.

To survive that they had died, my mind had to dissociate . / for me to survive them/their dying , my mind had to dissociate .

1.) I hadn't lost the ability to perceive passage of time . I had gained the inability .

2.) I hadn't lost the ability to perceive passage of time ...

Mic fuckin drop !

psych drop !

|———————|

CINJAD

Write after “psych drop!” write this…

It was fascinating, the dark dazzled me; the dream phenomenon that seemed to be coming into focus boding well for putting abrasions/lacerations in my/the dissociative .

1.)They were all or most morose

2.)They were all morose, or most .

But they revealed a glimpse at the still somewhere there humanity the/that derealization conceals .

The difference/the dissonance of/from day(s) to dream(s) like nothing you’ve ever seen. Going to bed with No emotional recognition of my momm waking up to the same mind made (and maimed) game. I’m maimed and romanticizing a suicide end game .

but sandwhiched in between are the dreams/oneiric themes/unconscious subconscious nocturnal themes …

Like when it was edging toward 2022 Halloween and on the 10th night that precedes I dream …

… her body (is) limp and listless in my arms as I try everything to illicit response from/in her eyes I sing/ I start (to) sing(ing) our special mother-daughter childhood songs reprise “witches and goblins and jack-o-lanterns bright” … there forms/there is no (cracked/breakthrough) smile (cracked/breakthrough) in sight .

I press on “creep through the town on a cold and wintry night “ the light of life from her face is drawn to dark in its/a deceiving rosy hue of/from,

1.)the fever breaking through/you .

2.)the fever that is breaking (over) you, taking you .

from me (as) I realize I am singing you to eternal sleep .

This lullaby is/as my alibi that somewhere in my mind (this dissociative is soon to run its course of time / that some part of my mind , is soon to run its course of time with dissociative .

I wake up and I try ... (?to be less open to game over ?)

|——————-|

|—————|

|———————|

CINJAD

10/2/22

Coming off of 'chest pain/telling mom' dream, I Awoke to real chest pain

|——————-|

CJD2

It is with a heavy heart that I am not emptying/dumping/sorting out my chapter junk drawer by now but on the contrary with/of the/a/an cognitive constitution ... tbc !

Of a neuro cognitive constitution unconducive to (its) decluttering. I thought I'd be dumping out its contents by now and sorting things to their rightful places when/but it turns out I need ((the) reprieve of) another dumping ground.

|―――――――――|

FitnessFueled

5/20/22

With having overcome warble of speech/voice I would/will not succumb to wobble of

steps/step-ups (in fitness)/feet/knees in the step-ups of my fitness routine. There would be no knobby knees as there would be no...

. . .

(Having) Survived 'through' (something) not 'by' (someone) everything/things, this is/this was my ________/orbit, not epitaph/eulogy/obit(uary)

Stoicism, stamina and strength (now) to reign and replace/rescind (the) pain to/from whence it came.

Just like/as in the thick of my/the sick (musculoskeletal) body isolations were incidental due to lack of (proper) brain signaling... they were now something I challenged myself to achieve. All the motions/movements fine motor and gross motor (movements) I had taken for granted before...the way there is a sway of the dangling idle arm at rest during a leisurely walk/stroll... Same premise of body dysmorphia, I had gotten so used to seeing it rigid, motionless and stiff as I power walked in my new normal that now when I was reunited with the brain connections that would cause reflexive swinging and (arm) wiggling like uncooked spaghetti taking to (the) boiling water... I felt a sense of loss with in my shape-shifting. I knew it was a sign of health but still I felt ... _______

It was fun (though) trying to challenge myself (now/these days) though to catch my metronome arm and achieve absolute limb stillness while keeping the momentum of my stride. To my great reprise ... [[with/through mindfulness and intentionality]] I could enact/replicate/execute (to) a certain level/extent (of) body isolation(s) of a faulty signaling brain.

This newfound understanding of how to control (?and command?) fine motor not from the physical/body but sourcing/sourced from the brain was feeling like the missing piece/link to where and why I fell short in, try as I might ,accomplishing (the) body isolation based technique(s)/maneuvers /belly dance moves, years back.

From free How to video tutorials to the fee-toting workshops of the greats public and/or private domain couldn't/wouldn't give me what some glitching brain signals would... the/*that* *of the*/a the a *miracle* *of,* by product of ability/know how of/ the conduction/assertion of/an empirical organic grasp of/*empirical* *understanding of*/*grasp of* , *neurological executive dominance .*

|———————

(The) Dialectical/paradox/oxymoronic Dichotomy/antithetical (?properties?) /coexisting in opposition/paradoxically/

Where/While my [[intellect and]](overcompensated for) physique [[and (my) intellect]] was rugged (another/a) part of my mind was struggled.

forget about identifying and fitting pieces of a jigsaw puzzle together it was hit or miss, and mostly the ladder, if I haptically managed/if my haptic managed to get the kids/children's butterfly novelty nesting ice pack back snug/interlocking, with/against its (fellow) other 3 [[interlocking]] assorted [[interlocking]] colors following what was almost/practically

/following what felt like at times a bi-hourly head and/or jaw icing session.

Universally-perceived (as)/conventionally, (horror) festering grotesque monsters of the hellmouth had nothing on the holster with the cluster of eraser topped pencils perched desktop in

a _____/subdued/innocuous scene of the 90's young adult cult classic/show/series, "Buffy the vampire slayer" . (The) vampiric special effects makeup/cosmetics paled in comparison to the ['common object']makeup of my visual processing _____/ intake/relay/disfigurement.

. . .

'It's like there's a person trapped inside you' the way that the young woman phrased it to the interviewer when asked ________________ ...

I realized it could be the doppelgänger description of/for the/this derealization/depersonalization I was in. [my own adaptation to what people commonly say about D / my own adaptation for/of what is commonly said about D]

not in a glass box(;my body) but is the glass box; my body.

[my own adaptation to what people commonly say about D / my own adaptation for/of what is commonly said about D] .

(My body) the (crystalline) encasement from which I scream/(and) teem with captivity, divided from touching all that my senses perceive; (my) life . (Or being touched by it.) touching , reaching , engaging ... making any kind of [proverbial] direct [proverbial] skin to skin contact with my life / (earthly) existence is held/kept, at a distance. (Is) held hostage by/through the/this dissonance;_______.

Stephanie (Dianne Selles) is (someone who is) trapped inside, me /what you see, begging for the antipsychotics or the psychotherapy to be mercy of the/a glass breaker hand tool to break through/shatter(ing) the window of this emergency and/to extricate it's occupant from (the not vehicle, but) (the/this) vessel; my body. So that I can be reunited with the human condition so that I can again experience/partake in/be a participant in the human experience.

(? A woman biologically of her sexual prime/peak chronologically; 39, (With) (the) pleasures of the flesh no longer nuero-sexually lost on me?) could it please just (f'ing) be .

Or (? pleasures of the flesh

no longer limbically lost on me/ no longer (brain) lobe lost on me?)

. . .

Or (?pleasures of the flesh resurrected from this deficit malevolence of...?)

A life [[vicariously]] lived [[vicariously]] through the Spotify playlists I'd craft/curate and accrue

songs for driving, songs for fucking, songs for making a certain kind of loving , songs for love making, songs for the taking of my life back. A vast genre connesuir amassed some odd (one) hundred and ten ______. There was music for slow dancing music for dirty dancing music to choreograph burlyQ acts to and fusion belly dance sets to.

Music to live again too.

Hopefully not interminably (living) 'through' .

And [[sat]] at the crest of all the rest /and at the helm, [[sat]] ... the (encrusted) crown jewel case of compilation(s)/compiled music; songs to (book) launch-party to!

Owning my spot earnestly earned(;) a place of/on the royalties throne.

Put Here? |———————————-|

-An i4an i, fireW/fire, darkW/darker

?darkest?

[[baby's first favorite song, Kenny Loggins' "danger zone" (?from mommy and daddy's movie?) (proved to be) a (personal life) prophecy in/for/of me

"You'll never say hello to you

Until (you get it on the red line overload)

You'll never know what you can do

Until (you get it up as high as you can go")]]

(For) No eye for an eye in sight (fight ing) always kept back 200/300 ft of/from the fire with fire fight. (And) Now founded in me (was) the visceral need/______, to fight dark with dark no with (fucking) *blackout* *blinding* blackout blindfold /fucking vision/sight fucking , deprivation, dark ...

((It seemed) I needed to bring the dark, to find the dawn / to fight to till for, the dawn.)

(That) I needed to go (deeper) darker (in ward ly) to get/make it out ... tbc?

(I) needed to DIY blackwash; DIY

so/till, I couldn't/can't, see the forest from the trees.

[[baby's first favorite song Kenny Loggins' "danger zone" (?from mommy and daddy's movie?) (proved to be) a (personal life) prophecy in/for/of me

"You'll never say hello to you

Until (you get it on the red line overload)

You'll never know what you can do

Until (you get it up as high as you can go")]]

. . .

|————————————|

[[I was becoming the assertive I'd (always) wanted for myself/wished of myself for a good 20 or so consecutive New Years eves. Just when I gave up including it in my resolutions, just when I'd resigned the carrying (over)/rollover, of my resolution/character development, through time(; the rollover) , it became me .]]

|————|

Maybe CJD#2 but not definitely .

Thinking / afraid

I might not survive/I might die

was the constant

Whether it would be incidental or inflicted/ *of from (self) infliction*

was the fluctuation it saw/was how it fluctuated .

?fluctuation/variation?

|————————-|

I survived anorexia not nervosa; medical.

I survived a/my suicide ideating/contemplating mind.

...tbc with more listed off like this...

|———————————-|

7/14/22 during workout

(???CJD#2???)

(Virile) with the (virile) desire (virile) to vandalize where I reside; a consolation prize to/of homicide I survived (the incline of) my/an/the/this ideating mind/incline . (And so did all others) . / (and no living souls/living beings/sentient beings/human beings were harmed during the concerted faking of its in-existence.

|——————-|

|————————-|

8/7/22 ?CJD#2? (In An already established part ?aka somewhere around here

"...tbc with more listed off like this..."?)

or as a new part

maybe something otherthanCJD#2?

While my system was working overtime without compensation toward neurological regulation

1.)(others) ignorance was the kiss of sabotage not bliss

2.)(others) ignorance (of/to this) was sabotage (of/to this) not bliss

(And in this and there in this)

For a long time, not a matter of if, but when, when do I know it's the right time/ the time is right, to end my life.

And don't (the) people know that by telling me I seem alright/ ok/normal/fine,

1.)they are only (single handedly, collectively) pushing the undecided/undeclared date up . Not back (single handedly, collectively) (; pushing rendering my survival pending) with/ in their unending persistence / insistence. it is not incentive but/ so much as (it is), insensitive .

2.) they (are (only) pushing/push rendering/render my survival pending .

If every pack of cigarettes is said to cut 11 days off of ones life expectancy then know what your indirectly/inadvertently/incidentally devaluing/invalidating does.

it gives me a (*tough*/rough) shove toward the ledge not (tough) *love.* Your words poison me slowly/ in incremental doses , like nicotine and tar, you've taken it too far and I am doing okay (that) is not for you to say. Tbc ?

And do I ever have thoughts of suicide is for you to ask but alas know it only alienates me *more*/further and I'll silently scoff if it's not (mentioned/intended) with/of rhetorical regard .

|————————-|

[[I was becoming the assertive I'd (always) wanted for myself/wished of myself for a good 20 or so consecutive New Years eves. Just when I gave up including it in my resolutions, just when I'd resigned the, carrying (over)/rollover, of my resolution/character development, through time(; the rollover) , it became me .]]

|———

When you've lived through what I've been through (the thought of) (having to) *(any thought of)* having to ask a boss for a/*the*

ask(ing) for the/a *bathroom* is (unacceptable incomprehensible unconscionable) (absurd to you and) beneath you and your spread Phoenix wings .

?Absurd that you exist to serve and service others.?

Never realized/*knew* I was/ *I lived*, without it

Till I felt what it was to have it; self-love and

Self respect . all my life in retrospect kissing Bc/*when* I didn't have the heart to say no. pissing Bc I asked my boss and she

1.) *let me go… to the bathroom.I refute this/your refuse (of) ; being played for a/your, Buffoon. *

2.) told me so; I could be excused…

I refuse this/your refuse .

|——————|

Or here? |——————————-|

-An i4an i, fireW/fire, darkW/darker

?darkest?

[[baby's first favorite song Kenny Loggins' "danger zone" (?from mommy and daddy's movie?) (proved to be) a (personal life) prophecy in/for/of me

"You'll never say hello to you

Until (you get it on the red line overload)

You'll never know what you can do

Until (you get it up as high as you can go")]]

(For) No eye for an eye in sight (fight ing) always kept back 200/300 ft of/from the fire with fire fight. (And) Now founded in me (was) the visceral need/______, to fight dark with dark no with (fucking) *blackout* *blinding* blackout blindfold /fucking vision/sight fucking , deprivation, dark ...

((It seemed) I needed to bring the dark, to find the dawn / to fight to till for, the dawn.)

(That) I needed to go (deeper) darker (in ward ly) to get/make it out ... tbc?

(I) needed to DIY blackwash; DIY

so/till, I couldn't/can't, see the forest from the trees.

[[baby's first favorite song Kenny Loggins "danger zone" (?from mommy and daddy's movie?) (proved to be) a (personal life) prophecy in/for/of me

"You'll never say hello to you

Until (you get it on the red line overload)

You'll never know what you can do

Until (you get it up as high as you can go")]]

|————————————|

|————————|

?Chap5? (insert the respective name here)...their Mulch),

?CJD#2? , ?

"You're Gonna Listen" by In This Moment

Puts the feel to what this neuro bio chemically austere veneer has not the neuro function to reveal …

How her (petty nit-picking)/ *insolent* monthly doormats make her feel, the nit-wit/ the din/dim (of the dim-witted)/ *the dim-witted obstinate* friends who if she doesn't try/*do* their suggestion proclaim (emphatically) without question (and maintain) (that) she isn't trying (to get better.) (to regain health .)

|——————————-|

|—————————|

6/21/22

But (in) the astray neuro pathways of my escape route(; dissociation) interpersonal regard/exchanges/standings, were ideal (and while) I was

. . .

My own worst 200 enemies (I was) but too my own best 200 friends .

Where you see me alone in my apartment I feel (the) accompaniment galore (of) imaginary friends; bosom

1.) Invisible lovers (so) plentiful they're indivisible

2.) invisible fuck buddies (so) plentiful they're indivisible

3.) fuck buddies while invisible so plentiful/present they're indivisible (?with liberty and just as a god?)

(Like an overcrowded house party, a sold out concert/*(band) show* or an overrun club) Astral projection could have this *modest one bedroom*/studio apartment, reaching maximum occupancy violating/breaching fire code

a/my mindset (functioning/that functioned) no/little different than a VR headset...

The jarring nights alone you saw; stillness, was no representation (at all) of/for the starring in my own music video trippy elation I felt. my mind (was) an active night life frozen in time .

Melanie was going/went to

Carolina in her mind and I was going to

2.)the bronze on/from/in Buffy the vampire slayer

Or (Where) I was (in attendance) (or better the host) at/of one of ACDC's "big balls"

(And/but) wearing the red shoes; my minds delusion I could chat/dance, all night/the night away but/so little did I realize the

Chatter of being 'on' was tired like the patter of being on my feet.

-patter of being 'on' my feet, was tired as (was)/ like the chatter of being on

(?was a constant/perpetual party ;the AC/DC song big balls (?and I was an extra, an unnamed party goer identified by a numerical value?)

|-----------------|

|-----------------|

CJD#2

(And) apart from the abstract (of my psyche) there was no glitz to get lit AF about ... I seldom decked out my declate for I

Always worried (that) if I did so much as donned that necklace I daydreamed about/of wearing pairing it with an outfit again that it would get/be marked into/as evidence that/as I'm okay now or (that) I've somehow accepted this .

Gross perceptual/objective/observers oversight was always a "she made an effort", (sparkly shiny Jewelry piece) *away*/shy from me in my mind . ...a wearable sparkly shiny wearable object shy of losing the/my funding As though accessorizing was to admit to something ...

As though dressing up would see my care team slacking-off ...

[I wasn't out of the woods yet and I wanted/needed them to know it ...] an available/vacant noose hung where the (detrimentally) misunderstood witch of the west was extricated from .

[I wasn't out of the woods yet and I wanted/needed them to know it ...]

|————————————|

|————————————|

6/25/22

?CJD#2?

(? And In these/the woods I was darker in/than I'd ever been. Maneuvering through/in a caste system (of my minds devise) (that rests on) a/the made up premise/the principle that every last blasted thing should shut the fuck up (for me); I was not of this earth and air, fire water people places things ? (Were all of a class that/their class) Invariably should / should invariably yield/______, *to this untouchable* (for I was) (the) (a) prophet/ *pharaoh stephoenix*) Stephoenix the pharaoh .

(I mean it) (you are under my command, understand)

(And) (in and of my prestigious ranking) I will answer to no one and nothing .

I don't exist to serve and service shit . (I) Spill(s) on the rug tough (luck knox break) you'll fucking sit in it till you stain

. . .

I turned the cold faucet so don't you dare run hot on me first. I won't wait; I'll turn you right the fuck off; you failed me.

Toilet running you think I'm going to cowtow to your annoying sounds

My cup runneth over Bc I let/leave your bowl (to) (over)flood/overflow .

Central Air I don't care for you; did I tell you I was hot I think f'ing not. I think the fuck not, stab jab and bludgeon (the) vents of my anger with the pointed precision of my fuer alice finniald brass curtain rod . Air .

|—————————-|

6/19/22

Where always upon a time / where once Upon a lifetime/ where once upon a life line

I would gaze up through _____ at the eclipse with innocence wholesome ness now I glare with sadness turned madness (incidental circumstantial situational aversion therapy has become me is quite becoming on me) (and) my soul scowls /a soul scowl and (I want to) howl

(and) my soul scowls wants to howl

1.) to (the nursery rhyme tune of rain rain go away

Sun sun Go the fuck away you took my babies on a light, bright summer's day .

. . .

2.) the/a nursery rhyme tune of my misery .

Sun sun go the fuck away come again another day and you'll surely pay /and I'll make you pay

for you/for how you took my babies (away) on a light bright summer's day. Fire.

|—————————-|

Put after central air part (it's inCJD#2?)

Taking/taken a scissor to it only so as/ (when) to snip a lock to/and slip in(to) loved ones caskets /a loved ones casket . / and/ to slip under the lid of a/my loved ones casket

I am the director's cut of Medusa's hair and I'll/who will snake your drain (with)

1.)every inch of how (much) I don't care

2.) 40 inches of how (much) I don't care .

3.) inch by inch with how (much) I don't care .

(Like) I'm fixing to flood your home (with my wrath/fury.) Water.

[Unearthed / unearthly (i was) (and) air fire water

Mirror mirror on the wall, who's to be feared most of them/us all / mirror mirror on the wall who's the fiercest of them us all]

Toothpaste speckled/spattered mirror/looking glass ... I'll watch you rust before I'll justify bending/stooping to your windex will ...

You don't control/own me

. . .

(And) No one and nothing does .

[Unearthed/ unearthly (I was) (and) air fire water

Mirror mirror on the wall, who's to be feared most of them/us all / mirror mirror on the wall who's the fiercest of them/us all]

See no evil, hear no evil, speak no evil, means/a cautionary tale; don't f'ing look at me; I won't fucking listen to you; I won't waste my breath on you

Now serving number shut the fuck up

How may I take you for / forsake your order ?

Melanie was going/went to

Carolina in her mind and I was going to

3.) be (but) steps closer to/away from ((Marilyn) Mansons)) "The devil beneath my feet" temporal territory if I didn't ... get a grip on my neural/neuro slip/glitch .

|—————————|

|—————————-|

6/29/22

. . .

???Hi Stephanie, I need you to pull your car back about 3 ft, so the town will be able to pick up all the branches (they use a mechanical bucket). Thanks!

Ok no problem; what is pick up date? so my parents can plan to move it

They've been coming around, so don't know if today, tomorrow...

Maybe you can just get in the car, put it in R and back it up 3 ft. Thanks!

My parents are coming by today to move it back

Thank you. ???

::::::::::::::::

**And at the helm of my personality shift was being misunderstood for and therefor mistreated/maltreated/neglected in/Bc of my sickness . **

***Suddenly unapologetically filled/swarmed/flooded with fanciful fantasies (of the) 'vampire violent' (variety) ... your brazen pile of shit; deliberate sticks dumbed at/by my car door (would) do/slew nicely...

You have the gall to tell me

'Maybe you can just get in the car, put it in R and back it up 3 ft. Thank you!'

. . .

I won't stall to yell at you (And)/(or) Maybe you can just put your mouth in P and shut the F up for me . Fuck you! ***

|——————————|

|——————————————-|

6/18/22 … 6/20/22

?CJD#2?

As if I could operate (one) when it was even a challenge to dodge one(s) in operation; motor vehicles .

As if I had the mind to drive when motorists (In motion) processed like/as an impossible mine field to pedestrian Stephanie/me.

Shuttled in my parents' mini van and stepping foot out into the parking lot of the strip mall feels as threatening and confusing as navigating a bumper car arena on foot would be…

Intellectually I know what a parking lot is like comprised of[I was once them] …cars that sit idle with lights, cars unoccupied, drivers preoccupied, the pull throughs, the thoughtless moves … [I was once them] so many indications to catch and react accordingly/In time, to … and the arresting embarrassing reality/epiphany (that) it was all (a little) too lost on me to maneuver my way to the storefront ahead without making myself /rendering myself the shadow of my dadd .

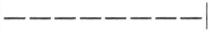

|————————|

. . .

|———|

Race against time ... (?CJD#2?)

(But were we (like) the blind leading the blind) (?) / (but was it the blind leading the blind)(?)

Where it could be narrowed down to (covid) long haulers with me, Alzheimer's could not be ruled out with him.

He was increasingly coming to me (disconcerted) with (disconcerted) sharing(s) of cognitive oversights. Defining Verbally filing his days into/as/by '(that I have) good days and bad (days) when did this become my dad?

' ... When I'm lucid ... today's a good day ... are/were all sentences that somehow seemed to sneak up on me/seemed to have snuck up on me/ambushed me as his new normal .

Episodes Accounts bouts (that) were reinforcing to me that this was a race against time to get out for

1)more than the pesky ticking of my biological (time) clock; for the detonator-less time-bomb of his chronology.

2)the pesky ticking of my biological (time) clock (yes/sure) but what's more (for) the detonator-less time-bomb of his/my beloved fathers chronology .

|——————————|

|——————————|

. . .

Chap making theBestOfit(Chap3) OR ___________

7/5/22

I'm thinking Dissociation may be the key to beating world records

(Reverse plank)

7/6/22

Someone I had known for just over a decade…It was a (phone) conversation of (relatively) copesthetic proportions unsuspecting certainly of what was to come right before the hang up. "Let me just tell you one thing (before you go) you don't know what it is/what it's like to be sick" . Stunned and Feeling (as though I just just been) gunned down with/by a taser (at the hands of this/ at this by a/this, (friend turned) sniper) before I succumbed/succame to the effect(s), I managed to eek out something to the effect recognizing it's all relative where in which i started spouting out/off a roster (of) various infamous sickness that I don't know what it's like (to have) aptly/earnestly admitting that meant absolutely nothing to the (friend turned) fervent assassin on the other end of the (phone) line who had blind-sided me with the first blow of assault/attack

|———————————-|

CJD#2 add on

But (now) to Stab me in the back with reiteration; "no, you don't fucking know what it's like / what it is , to be sick. You have no fucking clue ."

I've got your back /I'll get you back

With/in, retaliation

1.)twist mightier than the sword in deep.

2.)mightier than the sword twist it in deep.

3.)mightier than the sword twisted in deep.

4.) broad nib twist it in /twisted in, mightier than the sword

I'll make you bleed through the page (of/with/in my/this outrage .)

|————|

All the obvious ways to garner/get/ascertain/solicit appreciation, respect and validation for/of what I was going through … that I was actually/infact going through something , were failing which left me flailing; I was losing friends … at a loss (and livid from the aforementioned talk) (it was)/ (I there) in/with my desperate state to educate

(had) spontaneously ingeniously brilliantly cleverly thought of a (novel)/(clever) innovative measure to exemplify what (*this desperate time* is/ a desperate time this is;);what it is to be out of your body; the dissociative experience and (in turn) to prospectively replace/change the face (one person visage at a time) of (the) (festering) widespread epidemic (festering) of invisible illness ignorance and (therefor) insolence (festering)/(one person visage at a time) with _______/education/enlightenment/comprehension/awareness (, one person visage at a time) (they would get the message .)

What was the composition of the/said message comprised of ? Achieving internationally-recognized/* international-grade,* great/unbeatable/*unbeaten, feats .*

(Flipping through my mind like a Rolodex...)

(There was the consideration of how) On the/my first try I could probably effortlessly do a breath hold that rivals divers rigorous apnea training (but) I reasoned it/that would put myself/me at risk of brain damage... and decided to strike that (one) from the record.

But at the intersection of my deficit of (perceiving) passage of time (perception) and momm's "make the best if it" adage instilled (in me)imprinted on me /instilled adage imprinted in on me,

was the sweet spot of/for a world record breaking fitness pose hold.

Always reverse table top in my class, I knew now with the added factor/variable of dissociative I had the (brain to body disconnect) makings/conducive of/to/for top(ping) the world record holder.

Setting a new precedent in (both) physical fitness and the way/but what's immeasurably/profoundly more, forging validation for/of invisible illness

?was my mission?

(A nod to don't ask don't tell) (With) the word tolerance sharpie (marker) written vertically up/down my (short) floral skirt exposed leg; (not) a nod to but a sod-off to don't ask don't tell as my endurance broke the record of the day hanging from the (pull-up(s)) (aluminum) bar in/at a/the marines recruitment pop up at the (Albany) state fair... I was there (same sex partner spearheading the photo evidence campaign of the momentous/formative/monumental, feat and if feeling invincible (then) could carry me to achieve(ments) imagine the probabilities of/for greatness (now) when actually being invincible *(now)* ; how I could wield dpdr and what it would yield . <3

I had all my neurological faculties intact and felt invincible and it/that carried me to achievement(s) .

7/6/22 was 'peer to peer' for MRI

|————————————|

I knew/it was evident/it was apparent, I could reverse plank hold my own till the yoga goats came home but what about nurturing interpersonal relationships? [[did I have the *mental (reserve)* and *mobile* means/ *resources* *to*/ as a non-motorist of this mental sentence]] (Could I) Showing-up/*show-up* in the emotional sense and in the respect of physical presence *[[; A non-motorist of this mental sentence ?]]*

|———————————-|

7/22/22

It's a delicate balance to strike when you're a mature (adult) daughter with a sudden onset neurocognitive malady .

How much my/a parents blessing and consent needs to play into what I do and don't do and what they drive me to as a 39 year old unfit for vehicular operation / motor vehicle operation .

1.) I need you to be my ride as a

scripturally restricted person needs a scribe .

2.) I need you as my ride like a scripturally restricted person needs a scribe .

?Shadow me my stenographer shadow me ...

(But) don't crowd me or cloud me with your ?

(Your) Acceptance (while (of) A welcomed pretense) (is) not required/ (is) not (of) a pre-requisite ...

people to see places to go

and I need executive decision of/for what is brought to interpersonal fruition .

The age of me need be (the/a) foundation of/for (life-)agency /

(A) rife full / rightful agency .

|——————-|

|——————-|

-Lockers so full (just) opening the/a door ensures an avalanche .

And so little life-agency I had To meek (by) of / and I had so little life-agency to meek (by) of .

So you text me that you need to replace my door, cut your attempted stint as anything legit... (you piece of...)

-I want (me) out of this/your shit *home*/hole (too) , but make no mistake I'll be doing it/evacuating/evacuated on my own terms .

[[Your surreptitious (mission; (of) eviction (mission) won't have legs to stand on]] I'll/when I/as I, hit you behind the knees with my newest locker lease

(And) Your surreptitious (mission; (of) eviction (mission) won't have legs to stand on .

?(Lockers units)?

I was 8 at 38

And now (at/after) 3 months time into/of turning 39 ... we had just

e-signed (our/my lives/life, away)((to keep) my life at bay) on the dotted line ... My/our life/lives away life/lives at bay . My life at bay, my life away, what was the difference ?

My life away to keep it at bay . My life away (was) synonymous with (to) keep it/my life at bay. We/I were decades deep (in) with lockers (and) that's what happens ... tbc expand on 'what happens'; what I mean by that .

Scatter-brained sentiments/emoting, All rolled in(to) one as the, vacant for the taking/ taken vacant locker door rolled up to reveal

1.) (a)/(one)/(a one) vast/a vista, emptiness of promise.

2.) a spacious one beginning;

(of (powerless)/ (deceiving/deceptive) promise .)

3.) a deceptively spacious one beginning of promise .

Thanking and apologizing to my parents. I felt profuse shame for the first time in 9 (e-/electronic) dotted lines ... paralleling the shame was the sorrow frustration lament and realization the rude awaken (of) that I had taken for granted being solely of a psychological block to do something with/about/anything about my F42.3 (ICD-10) / DSM-5 300.3 all the/these years of my life ... how now with putting things back in the fridge with depth perception distortions and spatial awareness struggles it was as though the concept (of)

'it's all relative' was karma come for me/ kicking me , for all those years turned decades of time I in retrospect could have worked on my hF42.3 (ICD-10) / DSM-5 300.3.

Now I sit/live/lament in infamy at the mercy of my brains/neuro-rehabilitation

and not a day goes by where I don't think I would give anything just to have/ to just have , a psychological block again rather than a/this nuerocognitive one .

not a day that I /where I wouldn't pray, make me the way I once was ; always was . I'm not asking for greater than; equal to, just don't keep me at less (than .)

Could a 9th locker at a facility facilitate ... tbc/

Shuttling/herding my land F42.3 (ICD-10) / DSM-5 300.3 (to (off-site)/(solitary) containment) Could I dodge the (unfeeling) cold-blooded/cold-hearted, draft of the monthly door mats ? Outrun/outsmart his/my/this/the, planned obsolescence (of me/my tenancy) ? 'Bless this mess yes!' (for) I would have to . Tbc .

|——————————————|

|———————-|

ONE!

7/22/22

'Chick&EggChap8' or ?CJD#2? outro?

(Like) a recitation of/on/from chap 8 I was/ (like) a chap 8 recitation I was

Heaven bent on

harboring/harnessing/having a new out look when I get out of this but did I need

1.) to harvest/cultivate a new in look to make it out

2.) (to harvest/cultivate) the/this/said (new)

outlook

pre-requisite/ 'to' get out of this ?

3.)

Was I hanging it (all) wrong/crooked again

1.)The chicken was not the big picture

The egg was heaven free-range not

deviled .

2.) the big picture was not the chicken .

(And) The egg was free-range heaven not satan(ic) deviled .

|————————————-|

|——————-|

7/24/22

TWO. But meanwhile/evilwhile…

I'm so glad this Friday starts my new dose . It better work

It's about to be 17 months and *I'm* really starting to *losing my patience living within this derealization* 24/7*____days .* without so much as a

nano(-second (of a) break (ever) to make… do with .

(And) I'm losing my tolerance of the inability to feel love or emotional recognition

"We'll figure it out- it's hard but stay positive :-)" she, my mommy says .

But the longer it gets, the longer this goes on, the harder it is to fight off depression and rage , I cave and tell her .

|————————|

(perhaps) assimilation (of) or a simulation (of)"the big bad Wolf " by In This Moment, the neuro mapping (followed) was off the grid and didn't lead to grandmothers,

1.) (holy) house of the (holy) lord.

2.) house .

And I cried/pled (our/my) uncle Art who (is) in heaven …

(But/alas, I was sentenced)

|——————————————|

7/24/22

???THREE???

(And)/(for) I spoke now; (i) objected (I) didn't forever hold my peace . And yet the marriage commenced of

pious and pure age/childhood regression and jaded enraged, new normal/ new-found(ed) /new-fangled, propension.

(They wrote their own vows ...)

Knock knock

who's there

The most dangerous thing

The most dangerous thing who

Dissociative vigilantist

rage/vengeance

?(I'll see your (Buffy the vampire slayer) PG-rated vengeance demon Anya and I'll

1.)prorate you hell for this 16/17 months .

2.)raise you... hell (AF) for these merciless (16 turned 17) months of my mental/emotional catatonia .)

3.) hell raise you .)?

Knock knock

Who's there

The most exhausting thing

The most exhausting thing who

Keeping it/this burgeoning bubbling head state/head space/mind state, under wraps

Never/not knowing about

If/whether

A shooting range would get it out (of my system) or

be a/the perilous rabbit hole

never mind (the) church

(Just) Get me to the rage room on time

(For) here comes the bride all suppressed/repressed in white .

no time to bide waiting/researching (for)

a participating provider/PCP

It's go time with this/a PRN of/on BDSM. (Off psychosexual archetype grid good riddance I bid (you)) going to just have to go out of network on this (one) (and)

Pay out of is that a pistol in your pocket or are you just happy to see me

|——————————————|

|————|

For memoir (CJD2? Or intro? *Or outro?* Or other place ?)

(?the honeymoon (that) can't/(that) couldnt come too soon?)

The anger aspect the anger and the anguish

*The anger-anguish dynamic complex in (it's) need, of tending to/to breathe through it with more than (just) (remedial) subtext (and fluff).

(?the honeymoon (that) can't/(that) couldn't come too soon?)

a place an acknowledgment / a place *in* of acknowledgment (for crisis (stress) and death sex) to be fully expressed (embraced) and accepted (not condemned.) Going to give you what I haven't had and have needed/been needing. It can be so freeing . *Going to give you what I haven't had and did(nt) need/beseech* *lean*(ing) into the anger (it) can set you free . *

It can be so freeing to feel it . / to lean into it.

1.) ?Be the reverberation you wish to see . ?

Where your loved ones (implicitly) lack metal goth goddess Maria black has explicitly got my/your back "Tonight I'd like to tear this place apart and have you thank me for my rage"

?Be the reverberation you wish to see . ?

2.) ?Be the reverberation you wish to see . ?

"Tonight I'd like to tear this place apart and have you thank me for my rage"

Where your loved ones (implicitly) lack

metal goth goddess Maria black has explicitly got my/your back

……

And don't tell me "you wouldn't hurt a fly" …

Standby/ this is why

(for)

"I have as much rage as you have

I have as much pain as you do

I've lived as much hell as you have

And I've kept mine bubbling under for you"

(But/so) I'll Alanis Morresette you/the record straight (about me) (and my dissociative capabilities .)

<3

(I) Don't have a mean bone in my body but out of it I've got (upwards of) 200 .

a place to be fully expressed and accepted .

🙏⛓️😈⛓️🙏

It can be so freeing to feel it . / to lean into it.

|———-|

Some were sexless, others (kinky/dark and) obscene while others were an /another/one (ED) boner (was the) peep show of the limbic system trying to cum keen .

|————————|

8/18/22 rhymes with crotch …

. . .

I'd missed my milestone 20th hs reunion, a cornerstone of aging-adulthood. I guess/so the (fantasy) unfurl(ing) of my dark seduction (fantasy) of my grade school tormentor would have a decades wait more (and) at that rate divorce could be in store, taking /zapping all the satisfaction out of it; taboo times 2 allure .

But in the (figurative) interim to nurse (on) my womb I've got my / I had my

'Older man (fetish) silver fox ex-lover triathlete', doppelgänger psych doctor to lust vicariously through. But plight of the DPDR, no classic transference here, an emotional (phenomena) abscence, that is present/that (apparently)(I guess) presents (apparently)(I guess) when you live with dissociative .

Maybe write next about how I'd see people on tv that resemble ex's. I'd follow their storylines, and I'd become obsessed with getting close to or (getting) back with said/the tv character corresponding ex .

|– – –|

|– – – – – – – – –|

1.) minced/miss(ed) opportunist (of the) 20th/20 yr hs reunion, aside …

2.) 20 yr/20th hs reunion minced/miss(ed) opportunist aside …

. . .

?Go back 10 year's time (mer tails to trying to feel safe friend's pool?

|————————-|

8/31/22

MaybePutWhere I wrote about driving for destination weddings/lifetouch job Montaulk to Manhattan driving vs now can't drive .

Or maybe put in CJD2,

rewind/go back 10 years time and I could be seen squeezing 2 legs into one half of

1.)a metallic pair of leggings /

2.) a pair of metallic leggings

The remaining dangling leg sleeve wrapped and tucked surreptitiously out of sight a common place/tired, garment repurposed

creating/to create, the perfect

make-shift mermaid (persona) to slip into

skim the brim of the bay with before turning out summersaults underwater practicing to make perfect don't pierce the surface …just like the professionals do it; Hannah Mermaid , Linden Wolbert , Eric Carmen the mertailer were all regulars on my you tube channel rotation … in my wildest imagination I could / would be them / I was them.

Send it …

Here I am flailing to find a way I feel safe enough to accept an invitation extended to me (by my bosom friend) to 'chil in the/her pool' one/some afternoon (in/of her backyard)

. . .

a life preserver might sound like neurosis but the intersection of intoxication and coma sees no mercy ;/and/it doesn't/does not get along/go/pair, swimmingly with diving boards and ______ /sloped pool floors (?for that matter.?)

?I guess this is where I have to write about a you're adorable / k hole / very well mind quote ... ?

|—

Chap8? Or CJD2?

K is for hole !

8/25/22

*the intersection ah/oh yes the (life-guarding/safe-guarding) intersection whose (life-guarding/safe-guarding) cognizance came/was coming from the cross section of a song (here/now Here and now) after/*at the mark* of, 8 years long; (of) my grandma in heaven that/who used to sing it to me *

++++!Surrounding my grandma's 8th birthday in heaven came to me a song she used to sing...

A you're adorable

B you're so beautiful c you're as cute as can be

...my mind ran with it to why I have not swam with it ...

K you're in a hole 24/7 (that) feels 6 feet deep. Didn't make this (water/death) bed so (now) why must I lie in it

Doing *(the)* time of it without ever (having done) *the crime of it ?!*

"One way to think about a k-hole is as a state between intoxication and coma." Well fuck Thankyou (very much) very well mind . Com for a description that (actually/pointedly/poignantly) depicts this ____/condition/(life-)imposition.

This (non-induced) unsolicited (non-consensual) K hole business

I don't 90's slang dig this

And I didn't, action word; verb. (either).

(this is absurd)

(This is non-induced) so for all you being obtuse (this is non-induced)

((One of you) about to drop my friendship bc) "You used to be cool" (this is non-induced) ...

Yeah well (you fool) I didn't used to be in an unprovoked k hole (either) you a hole, (either.) . ! ++++

|————-|

|——————————————————————————|

and was now at/of a vicious, reiteration/recitation . "no, you don't fucking know what it's like / what it is , to be sick. You have no fucking clue ."

. . .

|—————————————|

???CJD#2???

Melanie was going/went, to

Carolina in her mind and I was going to

1.) one of ACDC's big balls

2.)the bronze on/from/in Buffy the vampire slayer

3.) be (but) steps closer to/away from "The devil beneath my feet" temporal territory if I didn't ... get a grip on my neural/neuro slip/glitch .

|————————————-|

|———————-|

-in CJD#2 there is pencil edit same one repeated in 2 places

(I) needed to DIY blackwash; DIY

so/till, I couldn't/can't, see the forest from the trees.

|—————————|

. . .

Can I put this in CJD#2 I don't know

5/27/22 love on the spectrum US

-In group text with parents dad said

Neurodivercity

I said

neurodivergent

-The same way Abbey described autism is how I would definetly describe

derealization/depersonalization

like there's a person trapped inside you but you can't get them to show themself.

|—————————|

"A glass breaker is a hand tool designed to break through a window glass in an emergency. It is a common safety device found in vehicles to aid in the emergency extrication of occupants from a vehicle, as well as in some buildings." Wikipedia

|————————|

|—————————-|

Quick Edits for 'CJD#2'

-Dichotomy/antithetical/coexisting in opposition/paradoxically/

-Interlocking

-Disfigured

|————————-|

CJD3

|————|

CJD3 begin

Another chapter scattered now too with stanzas shattered

taking these fragmented thoughts (I can't sort) /sentences, and making a mosaic (of/with what/ the shards I can't sort.) .

Damn transitional phrase aphasia and the malaise/worry, of will this bring compositional collapse ?

It was September 2022, the month of my parents 51st anniversary, the month after my father's 75th birthday and the month before my half birthday and favorite holiday; halloween.

It was September 2022 unfortunately/alternately known as 18 months since withdrawls diagnosis day and simultaneous/subsequent DPDR brain arraignment solitary containment . / brain inhumane solitary containment . / inhumane brain solitary containment . 18 months numbers / a number almost synonymous with the 17 I had been clean . And finally the number that signified my saving Grace; 10 I was 2 handfuls of months into the writing that commenced for presence and reason of the inner/intuitive sense that it would/could render me willing to live . / with/a/the will to live .

|————|

Untouchable unstoppable (unreachable untopable) never have/had I ever been (this) before so I knew time was going to evanesce this/the score/the attainable obtainable roar. (and) (that) I was trying to outrun the return of self consciousness/self-defeatist with dissociative / with this de-realist ____.

Popped pill by pill I could almost feel Imposter syndrome's ill will sinking it's (hovering) claws into me once again barking disorder(s) at me to no end

(When) Was i but a wardrobe change away/medication reauthorization away from the sheep in wolf's clothing come to reclaim (me) ?

18 months, 1.5 years or a year and a half; any way you cut it I had been in DPDR so long was i starting to become just as scared of it/this ending as I was of it never ending/being unending ?

Sure I couldn't drive, turn the ignition on/of a motor-vehicle in this altered state, but I had no volition ambition or professional drive in my baseline .

I had written for myself my whole life; diaries/journals ... When dissociative breaks would imposter syndrome be coming to take me away from this 'new-normal ' found/fangled , way/ability to write for others ?

(And) Was this unprecedented worry of blunder and plunder the

. . .

1.) beginning(s) of acceptance and the finish/end(ing s) of aborrance for/of/to/with, my psychiatric aberrance

2.) ending(s) of aborrance and the beginning(s) of acceptance of/with/for/about, my psychiatric aberrance

[[was i coming into my own; Saturn girl by Paula Cole ?

was i coming into my own; Paula Ceole's Saturn girl

was i coming into my own as Paula Ceole's Saturn girl

was (i) coming into my own Saturn girl by Paula Cole ?

was (i) coming into my own Paula Cole's Saturn girl ?]]

|————|

The breaking of dissociative, I was realizing there was reason to (anticipatory-)fear it as much as there was/would be/was to be, reason to revere (it.) I believed in living in accordance of/with the model of risk-benefit but which was what; derealized/baseline, was getting evasive/erased , by/to/in ,my mind . Replaced with/by (the) complacency (of/from all that/the productivity, this sick time was bringing in)

|—-|

besides the unparalleled virtuosic compensation for/of/with my situation. (a proverbial take home pay that/which was my (productivity) take-away) there were other reasons not to dismay and for (a) push-pull inner battle to ensue surrounding matters about wether it's in my best interest that the dissociative should stay or go away/dissipate.

[[was i coming into my own; Saturn girl by Paula Cole ?

was i coming into my own; Paula Cole's Saturn girl

was i coming into my own as Paula Cole's Saturn girl

was (i) coming into my own Saturn girl by Paula Cole ?

was (i) coming into my own Paula coles Saturn girl ?]]

|——————|

9/22/22

what was sharp, was sharper, (what was) *sexy was sexier* (and) dark was darker / *dark; darker .*

And maybe I was growing scared of all that becoming/being marred being/becoming far-removed from the me I had come to know …

I had pined (for) admired the old me the always me from afar …. but now 18 months in (to dissociative) I had come to feel valor passion and power in how/surrounding (*how*/that) the *the stephoenix* is/*was* charred . / surrounding the charr of the stephoenix .

?(And like I (essentially)/(less or more), said before)?

I couldn't drive my car but I could get my foot in the/a now ajar door

to becoming

a/the , Bad ass boss author (daughter) this dissociative sass/wrath, afforded. maybe DPDR was existing to serve a purpose . A/my life(s) purpose . I had become open to this / I was becoming open to this .

. . .

|—-

18 months …In dissociative I was so far donned; (marred) / I was so far donned ; (marred) with/by dissociative (marred) (that) I was losing sight of what life looks like when visual processing is right . / when visually processing right.

What I was (vying for) striving for I could no longer see with the intellectualism that had held me in or with / kept me in/given me, (mental/psychological/clinical/psychiatric) buoyancy (all along/for so long). It was all starting to evanescence/ syphon.

the photographic memory, (the) cinematic/cinematography (of it) … The (memory)very tethers that gave me/made this, a model/standard/standardized quest; what I was trying/fixing to get back to , we're getting farther from my grasp harder to hold-fast .

1.) The gripping of my pre-D's past was slipping (at last .)

2.) my grip (was) starting to slip on just what the hell/heck exactly reality is .

3.) I knew this wasn't it/was far from it, but

my grip (was) starting to slip on just what in (the) hell exactly reality is.

And all in the same hand / and on the same hand / and on another hand paradoxically was the obscurement of knowing whether the veil between the earthly world/body/existence and this/my empyrean _____, experience was lifting, (shape)shifting, thinning, thickening or unchanged .

Like an optometrist's eye exam scrambling your mind threatening to flood your sight recognition with (self)doubt / visual processing with mistrust and (self)doubt …

"Better one or 2 ? " "2 or 1 ?" Again 2 or 1? This is 1 and this is 2 ? Better 1 or better 2? Now 1 or 2 ? 2 or 1 ? I didn't know any more or I didn't know if I didn't know anymore or I didn't know if it was that I didn't know anymore or that I just felt like I didnt (know any more .)

I didn't know anymore or was it that i didn't know ever before (either)/ (just the same all the same)?

1 pill or 2 ? better 1 or 2 ? 2 or 1 ? 2 pills or 3 better 2 or better 3 ? 3 or 2 ? 2 or 3 ?

I could identify surefire ways 2 was better than one... 3 better than 2 ...

(But) Like a strobe to an epileptic it seemed even the/that/said, beacon (of light) had complex (mechanical/technical) engineering

for while quitiapine / the antipsychotic got many a symptom to recede retreat dissociative unwavering unwaning was/seemed to be a whole other animal snarling, it's fearless teeth glinting and gleaming (at me)

1.)(it) would not/refused to stand down .

2.) a non-compliant/ an anarchist (messiah) of non-compliance that would not stand down that refused/refusing to stand down that was refusing to stand down .

2 or 1 1 or 2 better now with 2 or better now with 3 3 or 2 2 or 3 any change from 2 to 3 was 2 to 3 more significant of a change than 1 to 2? strung-out from (being) (self induced) stressed-out (self induced) over all these nuances of change or 'remaining the same' I was trying to identify/notice ..

All inclusive Resorting to my usual ways of escape/escaping ...

a sex-wrapped song whisked me away...

. . .

“I'm on the very top floor, room 1334

There's a king size bed but we can do it on the floor

Turn your cellphone off, leave a sign on the door

That says "Do not disturb"

And if I were you, I'll bring your girlfriend too

Two is better than one, three is better than two

Leave a sign on the door, the whole night through

That says "Do not disturb"

Do not disturb”

I breathed a sigh of indulgent relief; That was definetly a better use of numbers; 1 2 and 3 than what my mind was doing to encumber me. The (halestorm) song that had been the albeit strange antecedent/ elusive impetus to ending my/what was had been a 2 year (2 month) relationship was rescuing me (yet) again before long, in/with its sexy whimsy (allure/lure of) /whimsical (allure/lure)

(Both in/of) official video and song.

Now bolted down with some semblance of ______ tether , (mental togetherness) Halestorm had helped me whether the

?anxiety (and restlessness)? That stormed my mind .

|———————-|

? Need a connecting statement here/transitional statement . ?

. . .

|——————-|

!A!

3.)

9/9/22

Chap8?, CJD2?,make aCJD3?

____ months and ___bottles into the

antipsychotic meds (pseudodenentia) presenting symptom (of) Difficulty regulating emotions

1.) I got some relief/reprieve from (what can only be described as)

Impulsive generalized rage

2.) My (presenting) symptom of (what can only be described as) impulsive generalized rage , saw some relief/reprieve .

but the same mass of months and bunch of bottles (say something about was proving to be no match for the staunch stubborn stance/standings of (the) dissociative facet/aspect.)

[[persistent (pestering) resistant damn symptom]]

From 1 pill upped to 2 now 3 per night for the cause of this fight and/but my psych/brain state seems to have this (dissociative) locked down tight . [[persistent (pestering) resistant damn symptom]]

I search but there's no porch light, a frantic hand outstretched and frenetic in the dark patting down doormats lifting flowerpots which one is the key under ? (It has to be here . It does .)

persistent (pestering) resistant symptom be damned .

And for all you who think the umbrella of dissociative disorders (to be) a sham let me/ lest I golden rain on your parade/facade/charade. Your ignorance is (a) blitz not bliss .

Do I need a connecting/transitional statement here ?

???probably not???

|————————|

!B!

CJD3

-what the old adage suggests/implores/beckons/begs

[[take a step outside yourself]]

dissociative does not relent

[[take a step outside yourself]]

... and when objective perspective swells your full body cavity brain cavity/cognitive cavity/limbic cavity, the/as (way) dissociative does the vantage point is/becomes of a most arresting clarity ... you've taken advantage of your poor parents is all you can see as you look out onto a/the sea of pocketbook evidence of/for yet another failed U shape 'locker floor' storage plan (this time) you have/with the sinking feeling derealization let's (you) in (on) ... for the first time in 39 years and 9 lockers you feel like this is shameful...

pitiful that (you I let) your beloved mother scrape(s) by with unbranded in hand so you/I can house a designer mountain/ditch, of pocketbooks you/I never touch . Color transfer getting the best of much (of them ...)

. . .

|———|

And as per aforementioned, a juxtaposition a/of paradoxical coexistence (of dissociative-stubborn and dissociative '(my)-days-are-numbered' (divine) sense(ing) /(divine/higher)consciousness/(divine)discern/cognitive composition/composition of cognition , (both) befell (me) and befriended me .

|—————|

!C!

9/23/22 CJD3?

i had this unexplainable sense that association was sneaking up on me my old ways of insecurity creeping back to me ... there was positive reinforcement I was starting to need,

1.)attention-beseeching I was beginning to be/feel .

2.) I was becoming attention-beseeching .

I felt soon I was to be pelted by the old-me personality malady of praise-seeking .

(Unbeknownst to anyone Bc I hadn't yet let it be said) I was already running on 1.)encouragement-seeking, as of recently . . . .

Was any of this anecdotal evidence that / of personalization realization taking residence ? / trying to take residence ?

|———|

CJD3

I had become a seeker, curator, collector and excavator; a great appreciator of full circle moments (in life). Some were incidental, others intentional but (they) all were seminal .

*Of them Write

Lustlord mem (incidental)

ThatchCotgeLikUAhouse(in10tional)

Photographer/model (in10tional)

Atria employee/resident (in10tional)

CKGap and allThat (in10tional)

Intern/inpatient (incidental)

Wed 9/28/22

I accidentily stepped on a slug and I'm not doing well with it .

(?Imitation is the highest form of flattery ? Or panic in me ?

Or the most/so why is it there a, potent strain of panic in me?)

Stealing away from the small group bowling dynamic of the evening's excursion and having a 1-1 clandestine curb sit/ curbside ,moment .... you can imagine the full circle I've arrived (life) moment I got to behold when he whose band I'd seen countless times play he whose lyrics I'd insisted be recited in bed would slay. And now

1.) the/this rockstar of my life

2.) the Kurt cobain of my life

was sitting beside me popping (the) ear buds out after listening to my audio pre recorded excerpts impressed as all hell (and) telling me with all the feels (that) I better watch out or he's gonna steal my stuff !

At first there was just evolutionary reactive panic in me; someone's coming to steal my baby (away) then the (internal) faulty/defective processor that (interpersonally/socially hampers and) comes standard with dissociative (state/models) gave way to a most/the most prideful saying ... "imitation is the highest form of flattery ."

35 letters 7 words one line

1.)had rescued (the whole of/the sum total of) my malfunctioning mind .

2.) was the sum total of the rescue of/to my/a/this malfunctioning mind .

(For the very first time) I felt like an equal (for the very first time .)

...Someone I never felt good enough for, artist enough for despite their unabiding respect through the decades , (their) abounding encouragement and seemingly astonishment at/for, everything/all, that I was ... Until 'this' night under (the) bowling alley parking lot (lime-) light(s)

I (had) felt there in love/lust with a fictitious self . (Inferiority complex will do this to you imposter syndrome do you in like this

where all that you are ... you can't see (for yourself) so it stays stuck in the gear of all that you hope to be . And only others can see that you already are your falsely-believed unattainable unachievable dream, self.

A despondent cry to a friend when I texted them

There's reason to believe I accidentally stepped on a slug... and I'm not doing well with it .

Spinning in my mind was how Every night this summer, I'd go walking with their mother to her car for her to shuttle me home at the close of the hangout . As we would walk the paved path of/from complex's exit /building/condo door to car door/to parking lots start, I would (always) tell her let's watch where we walk. I would take heart so we don't/ to not, accidentally step on a slug ... and like a shared umbrella huddle I would walk beside her/close beside her/alongside her (with) (my) phone flashlight on shining down to light each step we take in/on the sundown/_______, of the walkway .

And then there was that Ill-fated night that I absent-mindedly /haphazardly jogged to the mailbox to retrieve the poly-mailer I'd forgotten to get in from the day ... not thinking at all ... I'm en route back to the house when I spot an ailing injured slug on the ground; I felt so bad for it (but) then I / (but) when I reluctantly looked at the soles of my sneakers (and) my soul sank/mine sank . (It was a haphazard turned hapless night) (for/as/airlong) My kicks had skimmed/nicked the/this helpless innocence.../innocent (.) (And) The very sweet creature that was my first (story) (ever) in life (subject) to (ever) write (a story) about; the sticky little slug that undoubtedly captured my heart at the tender age of (about) ____, was associated/complicit in / (rendered) a part of,

(It)/(what was) (one of) the (now) saddest/uncanniest full circle moments (of my life) / full circle life moments .

And although to the best of my recollection I have not the (definite/certain) memory of where we were going or (where we were) coming from but what we passed (affectionately and fondly) I can place.

Short as the light stayed green but sweet as the/this property could never be anything but (to me) , i Affectionately and fondly I day-dreamed out the passenger seat window of the family van as we whooshed/rolled by the now flipped, rebuilt and under new ownership building address / building lot where my doting devoted parents had given / gave me the sweet 16 of a lifetime some 23 odd years ago.

DJ and matradees , candle lighting ceremony orchestrated , father-daughter dance mother daughter (dance) , a guest list to remember ... it was the 4 to 6 hour wedding-like catered event of my life!

At first when I would look out at/over the bulldozed lot of my youth, I didn't want to be adulting . But then in time after I had to be a fast learner/ fast-learn, to view the builders/_____, tearing apart my secondary childhood home, my dear uncle arts house after he passed, I was able to hold that used to be thatched cottage building/_______, in a different redirected and reframed light . I could feel they were/had torn it down to give it new life. I/and (I) had finally realized sticks and stones (had) made and can break the bones of the/a (childhood-cherished childhood) place (once called home/that once felt like home/that once meant home/once considered home) but names of, new ownership (of/after a new build) /a new build, will/could never hurt me for the builders (commissioned) bulldozers earthmoving, outstretched mechanical claw arm can't reach my memories. And (so) now/this time, as I gazed out onto/at the (catering hall) rebuild ...(unrecognizable from its former quaint cozy cottage core allure) now a modern minimalist aesthetic architecturally stylistically etc fills the premises and is the premise to this (the) anticipatory-delight and joy I feel. One day (soon) I will have my book launch party here or my wedding. With this hall I was catering to / I was catering-hall to / with this hall I thee cater to my *'full-circle* (life) *moments* (' life) *not simple pleasure(s) but scintillating measures .*

|———|

. . .

|------|

CJD3 cont. of full circle moments

(Full circle moments) The more I was aware of them/cared about them, influx I saw (;full circle moments) Just like how mom had always affectionately/fondly told and retold the story/tale of how when she was pregnant with me suddenly it seemed every where she turned everyone/every woman (she/they, her and my dad looked at/noticed ,was in various stages trimesters of expecting too !

I was noticing full circle moments/ full circle moments ...I was noticing them, noting them popping/cropping up all over/all around (me) as I moved through life

1.) (?like a designer's pop up sale, something offered extra special to the lifespan/to life's viewpoint /to the viewpoint of life ...?)

2.) offering/adding,

A.)something extra special (like) a pop of viewpoint interest (to the rhetoric/narrative).

B.)a pop of viewpoint interest (to the rhetoric/narrative) (of my days). (Days gone by days to come (by) ...)

C.) a pop of visual interest to (the) viewpoint (of my days.) (Days gone by days to come (by) ...)

The stores I had to (always) bypass in the mall growing up Bc they were out of my socio economic bracket, and the clicks I got snubbed by in the hall, if I was lucky sneered at if I wasn't weren't even really stores/brands/designers at all that I was then or am now interested in but the pleasure and (the) power principle of being able to wear now what would have won them over then was something/a(n) (bully defeat) epic prevail (tale), (of bully defeat) gaining on me (*in allure*/in its appeal) as I edged closer *toward*/to, (the) published (author) prowess (to/*that would* allow this full circle moment).

Next write about itching powder.

|——————————————|

X to, (the) published (author) prowess (to/*that would* allow this full circle moment). X

X Next write about itching powder. X

|———

(As an adult/as a grownup) Standing in the body image crossfire of the man I loved who thought I should gain weight and the one who sexualized the loss of it / every pound I lost of it …

And remembering how I was mercilessless/*mercilessly* heartlessly teased for my ectomorphic frame all through grade school … chugging ensure between classes to hurry up and gain weight so the school day would/might, come where my peers would leave me alone (once and for all.) shooting capfuls of pepto bismal before the start of each/most, school days just on the off chance today could be a day I was to get Nauseous of natural causes while under their school roof; I couldn't risk it, hyper vigilant about how I better not become stomach sick Bc it will just serve as pointed evidence to my tormentors that I am infact bulimic . Which I was not, am not and never was . But there was a collective/cumulative of fingers pointing at me like synchronized swimmers exacting their maunuvers and water tricks every time or most that I'd get up from the lunch table to make my way to the bathroom after eating to simply go to the bathroom or touch up on my makeup before the next class . The fingers that weren't pointing at me were stuck down throats In (a) theatrical overture /in a theatrically overt /overt representation/depiction of what I was assumed to be heading/needing to the girls room for/bathroom for .

Once in there, I had to be mindful not to so much as cough or it could be met with whispers and giggles/scoffs from girls who were at the mirror with the socio-_______ luxury of taking up space and time in the bathroom without scathing tormentors repercussions .

|—————————|

I think/I think,I think add this after the word

x ridicule x

>>repercussions <<

Lunch table bulimia harassment/battery routine

There's a difference/distinction

between emaciated and

ectomorphic and those ignorants

didn't get it

Or

There's a difference/distinction
between emaciated and
ectomorphic and those ignorants
didn't get the difference/distinction.

I didn't then nor ever have had/I
didn't then nor have ever had an
eating disorder but you gave me
body dysmorphia; thinking I'm too
thin (bones) frail like the skeleton
you would call me./ you said I was.Thinking I could
be crushed in/by a hug (Bc that's
what you said/Bc you said I would)ClassOf_at
Stimson Middle bullying/ridicule
(Bulimia was in the eye of the
beholder and I was beholden to your
(torture/torment/disillusioned
delusional bullying/to the *beliefs*
you bullied/*beat my mind*/brain raw/
senseless(me) *,with.*

I'm an areonausiaphobic emetaphobic

Bc of you xinternalizedx I was
conditioned to equate/associate a
natural adverse stomach reflex with
something shameful (of disgust)
setting me up for a life of
1.)being scared of my stomach/
tummy/GI.
2.)living in fear of/fearing my own
gi functioning .
Flinching like a hit abuse victim
everytime there's a stomach upset/sick/
vomit scene on (my) tv (it accosts me)...
(You the peers did this to me)
(My) neuropathways were (just)
developing malleable and you
damaged me. (You've never said
Sorry./without so much as(ever/
eventually) saying sorry/ is sorry
something you'll ever be?)
Once home *from*/after a bus ride/school bus of
psychological/emotional/*psycho-emotional*
battery/harassment; physical/sexual I'd cry in my mothers
lap (for hours) and do/till we were doing/circling till we

would do/circle laps around the mall (xthe next dayx) stores/storefronts/store hours/a store's hours is what the next day had in store(for me). Playing hookie was (synonymous with and)

euphemistic for x(synonymous with)x escaping it all...

|----------------|

CJD3

I needn't even adjust/tweak the coarse adjustment knob to find/see ridicule at school / in through grade school . But (my family's summer house in the adirondacks) bullies were there too, more surreptitious until their deliverance camouflaged in (the) good-natured country boyfriend to my friend's big sis on the cabin strip of (my) (counted on) summer escape. Wholesome how your parents call them play dates when your young then as you come of age/step into your sexuality the compound word (can)/(can get to)/gets to take(s) on a(n) unholy/whole

(New) tone/new meaning; half circle / life radius . Potentially/prospectively (Eventually) potentially/prospectively , arriving at full circle or life diameter moment/(point) in time when you now are scheduling apple juice park/ play(ground) dates for your young .

I was neither young enough for parent scheduled and supervised apple juice park play dates nor old enough to comprehend that play-dates can have a sexual context/subset/subtext, when the itching powder was poured down my back in a sheep's clothing disguised/clad (fraudulent)/disguised ,hug from one of "the big kids" (on the strip) .

Today now decades beyond the matter, I've taken back the power the circle is at Diameter .

1.)every monthly mark (of) my hair wash ensures/reinforced people like him/mark/that mark aren't featured in my mind time after time .

2.)from time to time (of) my hair wash ensures people like him/mark/that mark aren't featured in my mind time after time .

3.) (when) every monthly mark a 1 to 2 part baking soda h2o/water (ratio) hair wash (ratio) has (it) reinforced (that) people like him/mark/ 'that mark' aren't sourced by my (self)-esteem/_________ any more/ any longer .

———————————

write a transitional something here

————————————

???????

Slumlord to my darkness you

Overdosed me on wholesome while

You would tell me to leave my shoes

at the door (and wear slippers in the hall)

1.) and slip into moccasins

2.) and

He would tell me/have me to leave/keep my shoes/

Heels on in bed and slip into

character .

???????

It was the final week(s) of/in October of 2022 I was closing in on 20 months of this dunce cap of dissociative, and it was half a year free from my/that last relationship (where my sexual dark needs had no leads and were met with quips not whips) And then/when, came the (uncanny) deboned corset of my (is realization)crowning(?) glory, the sad uncanny circles of/in/ within / herein, this life story ((Where I was always betrothed now I was dethroned)) (when) just when in my sickness I had found the strength in this;left his/this/my relationship(s) side/tenancy (in part) for/with a new lease on lust (for me/you see,)

I was now dethroned where(/ by the lustlord (where)) I was once betrothed; relativity ,

(by) the guy who always could/always did satiate (the dark in/of me/the dark(er) *leaning*/pointed needs of me/ the darker proclivities persuasions / the darker leanings of me/the darker leanings of my needing(s)) / the darker leaning needs of me (;my deity of dark lust/desire) was (essentially/in essence) (now)telling me

1.) *his* was/were remiss/amiss (on me .)

2.) I couldn't/didn't meet what his darkness required/requires .

3.) I, the applicant, dont meet/no longer meet the credentials for what/ for that of what his psycho sexuality/ psycho sexual chemistry /psychosexual tension /psychosexual archetype , requires / does require.

|——————————————|

Transitional statement ...

|————————-|

DPDR at DSW, chap8, *CJD3*

. . .

I was starting my new job this month; November

(and (so) I had my doctor do the biggest dose increase my (pleading) (and) neurobiology/nuerobiochemistry had ever/yet seen/to see ; doubled it/double . My vision (on)board(ed/ing) ? From 150(mg a night) to 250

I wanted to make a big (*19/20month mark push*) push (this 19/20 month mark) to not let this drag on to/for *24*(months.)

[[*In a* push-pull hot and cold *colossal* push-pull hot and cold *installment of push-pull hot and cold will they won't they* I had oversexed my welcome . The epic/erotic saga ....

Felt more like/was

Proving/panning out to (be) more

Like/of, a

great/kink/freak, tragedy/travesty

than a home sexy home(coming) .]]

Between the ((for there was)beyond a reasonable doubt) probability that my lustlord...was of unprecedented reticence about letting my desire/____, take occupancy Bc of these/the dissociative discrepancies (in me) from my speech to my written word ability I was like 2 different people. And that dissonance/differential I could tell/I was (painfully) learning (to extrapolate) , was just a lot for a/this prospective lover to handle/take on/process/*endevor to navigate*/move through/maneuver (through) .

[[*In a* push-pull hot and cold *colossal* push-pull hot and cold *installment of push-pull hot and cold will they won't they* I had oversexed my welcome . The epic/erotic saga ....

Felt more like/was

Proving/panning out to (be) more

Like/of, a

great/kink/freak, tragedy/travesty

than a home sexy home(coming) .]]

Work was (to be) starting soon too and

For the first time in all my dose increases, I was pleading it didn't take convincing...(for) this state has/had me in a 'choke hold' of (non-consensually) conceiting (too much of) my life/my humanity and now too my sexuality that/which rounds this up to the nearest (gut punch and/of) psyche/soul/intrinsic/(a)personhood/ fatality/causality (of sentience) .

As my psychiatrist authorized the double-up I could have doubled over at/from the disclaimer. this will be / is to be the final/last (and final) increase he explained that if the dissociative state still doesn't break with this change (going) any higher is a moot point .

bless I pray I get this fucking dissociative state to break

Bless I pray this/it gets this/the fucking dissociative state to break

|————————|

Transitional statement ...

|——————-|

CJD3 or _____

Touch, sight and Sound could and did all do things/play tricks

with/on my nervous system excruciation (so) infallible in how they were/it was palpable (a) termination of life seemed right every time ...

(But) (then) there were (the life-affirming twins)dressed/gussied(up), to the nines orgasmia and gustatory (the life affirming twins) the O.G. best form/connotation of sedentary this massacred pleasure center has ever seen. Invert the letters/abbreviation/initials/______, and it's 'GO' time knots on my watch

1.) there to be/as my

2.) (for) the fraternal twins beckoning to be

my saving glory to wishing upon (a/the merciful) dr kavorkian . / to wishing upon a kavorkian star.

heightened enhanced I was entranced food never been so/more pleasurable (and) sexual response cycle more sensitive .

These 2 areas of hedonic;

The twins G and O...

comprised bitter; the ladder and sweet(ness); the former ...

for it wasnt/didn't feel sweet when

1.)vye/try as I might dying as I was

2.) vying as I did, dying as I was

. . .

for phone sex and/or erotic texts my LDR/MDR/SDR, partner of 1 to 2 years said he couldn't with me Bc he feels like I'm a patient (;like it would be taking advantage)

and when I wanted the virtue of patience from my subsequent love/lust/intimate/romantic interest; (I suspect) my lustlord (I suspect) took one look at, my dissociative discrepancies/dissonances /the dissonance(s) of/in dissociative and then

while I had his (true) friendship's love

(and/but) a labor of lust became/was (just) out of the question.

|————————|

CJD3 (?I think or I know numbers come first?)

1.) I was dealing/reeling with/from various shapes and forms of / i was into an (unwanted variety pack of) Misgivings of (behaviorally) unrequited lust

(Behaviorally-)Unrequited lust misgivings, externally but/and internally I was (too) dealing with (a) complex/complicated (dissonance of) feeling . . .

|————|

|————|

CJD3 or ______

2.) wanting to go to a rage room for/as foreplay I wasn't brought up that way that's not the daughter they raised (me to be.) the push-pull of my personhood and a meek weak barely detectable inner voice flickered/faded/fading in and out, in the distance/dissonance of my mind. I'm allowed to be somebody like (some)things my parents don't wouldn't approve of and there is self-ritegeousness in that. *empowerment*/entitlement

I have/am of entitlement

I don't owe them conduct bc they were my unofficial/practically my conservators (while I was sick.)

and it doesn't make me (a) bad (person or daughter) if I choose things for myself they wouldn't want for me . (As I maybe got closer to better/Health/well, I realized definitely/definitively that if I was to not live my life held back I had/there would be, some/a lot of 'lifestyle' complex guilt to unpack . For they had saved my life and for that my mind was/would lord it over me (that) (going forward) I owed them _____/?condonement? / life-choices life-style choices

they would condone be proponents of ... /

fit for their condonement (of) that they would be (proud) proponents of .

3.)

I thought back / I was thinking back to how at/with the tap of the bell a guy once mirrored the/my sentiment as he got up from across the candlelit bistro table of speed-dating and emphatically said/proclaimed (that) the feeling was mutual

then never was i to hear from him again / only to never hear from him again.

My life right now is/feels one in the same with that night . My love life/lust life, nothing feels right to either / either things don't feel right to them or to me and I can't rule out dissociative/derealization/depersonalization, playing a part and that's what makes this the hardest .

. . .

4.) I needed to redirect my mind/divert my attention ...

(I brought it back to

the comfort and confoundment/

the comfort, confoundment and astoundment , of circles .

the comfort side of circles (not the disenchanted sorry side/and tried endeavored to get my mind to leave behind/ to take a leave of absence on/of the disenchanted sorry side.)

|——-|

11/7/22

CJD3 or outro

A.) (or better as B?) to circle back to my intro it was as though my life's work; the populations that comprised my employment history (in retrospect) were/had (in retrospect) all (in retrospect) been preparing me / been to prepare me/ were all in preparation, to be able to safeguard and care for myself: duration sickness .

And now I was realizing it was the/those self-imposed safety practices I had adopted/implemented to get me through this my sickness that would one day (be what /be that of what (would) bear witness to see(ing) my aging parents through help me know what to do to keep them safe/

Safeguard and protect the(,in kind).

There was a fully dilated diameter to this book in respect to the circle of life .

. . .

|————

|———|

11/6/22 CJD3 (moreFullCircle)

B.) (or better as A?) 73 turned 74 turned/turning 75, they were . 37 turned 38 turned 39 I was (when I was/would) text(ing) them the start and end time of every shower (I took) so they'd know I didn't fall . (Texting) every start and end time I was to drive so they'd know I didn't crash . Texting with every day's waking so they knew/would know this wasn't the night I gave in to forsaking my life .

I was Time stamping my existence with through implemented safety/protective protocols and thinking about/of how the full circle of this will look when measures are reversed; parents like their life depends on it Bc it does incessantly checking that I have my phone volume up for them through the nights ... (write about) them clocking and reporting their/the/every, start and end time of (them/their) washing in the shower. Me/my washing in the sink the 'sick' meal tray for them now not/no longer, myself . ...

|——-|

?(And now)

(Sourced by the finest ocd, in all the land of affliction / in all the landed affliction)?

And now/although/albeit not from the stomach that a/this tangent from of 'the disenchanted' / disenchantment,

come up/*cometh* (but) like an adverse mind reflex ……..

(Sourced by the finest ocd, in all the land of affliction

I found my thoughts giving me (?deafening?)/ *feedback* (and friction) about/*from* *all the lust* I would live without/ about all the lust (*in*/of *20 months*) *I was (in essence/essentially) sentenced* *to do without/ live without . * I feared if/since others/(past)lovers (;plural) , made it/played it that way (?then/that I must RIP my ID/libido/____, to dust. ?)

(?plus as per most recent session my therapist was advising I take my time in/with/when making my DPDR (be) known to any one knew I was to (want to) Pursue his saying it could scare a person away/off reverberated in my body cavity (like nothing before/ like never before) as DPDR was what had taken my chance at lust away with those I had known and now/new dating pending that (disenchantment/ dissaponitment/let-down) would become compounded by/with by and large (with) impending (by and large) risk (by and large) of .... Dissociative based/sponsored derived/deriven, rejection(s)/let down.

(And) my (lust)life and libidos livelihood, could not take/handle that kind of derivative / any more of that kind of derivative.

???x then/that I must (;do without.) let/accept my libido/(libidos livelihood) , turn to rust/dust. x???

???x and now a tangent come up not from the stomach but like an adverse mind reflex x???

???x and now a tangent (from/of the disenchanted)

(like an adverse mind reflex) (from/of the disenchanted) . x???

|————————|

???CJD3 ???

Just as aforementioned (somewhere) that my written word ability came first in repair to my spoken/verbal _______. When applied to seduction and trying/endeavoring / attempting/attempts to be a lover ... my brain had me/kept me short-changed . I couldn't whisper yet there were written sweet/naughty nothings. fantastical fetishism erotica so finely curated/crafted for the man who I wanted to be my suitor , calling it sexting would be / is to cheapen it. / wouldn't do it justice .

I could write the art of scholarly journal worthy seduction/I could write artful scholarly journal worthy seduction, but at the end of the day ((when) Bc the night belonged to lovers)) (and) I was and could only (ever) be an Empty promises temptress (so long as I were in this partial coma-like state (that felt like) it were depressing brain function of/for abstract thinking and reasoning skills /abilities .

Hoping for the/a playful naughty crime of the/his mind at the hands of my lustlord, I had put in the time all dolled as he would say/entice me to slay (Then something extra for his pleasure)Classic length hair, done up/donned (in) a new style I (saw on the internet / I saw on google images) (and) deemed (it) to denote a nod to the bod/rod of a whip/ to (that of) a whips bod/rod...8 hair ties later and some (extras) in my evening bag incase any slipped out .... I had achieved the look that pre all this seroquel would cause me visual (a) *sickening* *visual* *processing* sickening; the bumped up sausage strung like sections of the (insert name of pony tail here) calculating to me/read to my eyes like intestines and thinking about how much my poor beloved grandmother (GI) suffered (did me in) I had to navigate away from the (google images) page .

So this full circle was powerful/empowering now embracing and (re)creating the hairstyle for a night out at my lustlord's invite to come see him sing doing it/so with seductive intent/intention; he could pull me around by my hair like a leash. But rate of thinking/thought (like nuerocognitive ability to write) was further along than rate of speech, and as I mentioned before, abstract thinking and reasoning skills were sorely lacking (too) all in which created the grand total of flirtation fallen flat . At his initiation Ducked off 1-1 to the back outside of the club/pub he takes my pony tail in hand "I like this" his gravely voice growls out a whisper between cigg drags. It was the (full circle) moment we had all been waiting for; ((no not idly/passively waiting for (but) actively prepping for) and I say "all" Bc my complex personality facets (that were) United under/by, (this) one common goal; trigger his gutter mind with this hairstyle .

And it had but Bc (my default was) neuro glitches robbing/overriding (me of) (my) executive (existence) functioning/*decision*/existence, *to reply in kind*

1.) All I could say in/with (a scrunched face of) confused and confounded cognitive disarray "it's my hair / you mean my hair

2.) "It's my hair/you mean my hair

Was All I could say in/with/through (a scrunched face of) confused and confounded cognitive disarray.

I had not the gutter mouth to back me up that always was.

XAll I could say was "it's my hair" . X

|————————-|

|—————————-|

. . .

========================

The twins G and O

That comprised bitter; the ladder and sweet(ness); the former …

|——|

Add on to CJD3 right away !!!

(I had his (true) friendship's love)

and/but a labor of lust was out of the question.

|————-|

CJD4

|——————————|

0.) (I got fucked (by the month))

(When) November went in like a double-sided dildo and out like a double edged sword (I got fucked (by the month)).

|———————-|

|—-

CJD 3 or CHD 4 or DPDR@DSW,Chap8

1.) (November 2022 not a double edged sword so much as (it was) a double-sided dildo .)

It was both the one year mark of my book/manuscript and the first month/start of my work(at DSW) .

(By the time thanksgiving was closing in) I was (still) (only) driving /driving only, hyper-local but in a randomized liked songs shuffle (of some redundant ride) (starry eyed) (some ride) Spotify delivered my 'hopeful prophetized/prophetic ' opening line in the Depeche Mode song "behind the wheel" ...

"My little girl, drive anywhere

Do what you want"

Maybe I would and could be soon I thought as I drove/continued on my way to the obligatory places I had parental clearance to commute to.

|——————————|

|———-|

2.) CJD3,CJD4,DPDR@DSW,Chap8

11/18/22

I had been on the last and final / ceiling increase (if you will) for 23 nights. I was 14 into no (left brain)bodily urge to eliminate but the right brain urge to write through it to speak to it, steadfast.

28 to 34 days of the 250 had implanted like/as a finish line to/in my mind . I knew my excretory system was taking a blow but having read Q (dosage/increases) can and tends to take 28 to 34 days to reach and see full efficacy, I just kept thinking/telling myself I can outrun this. I can last in the race against time long enough to find out if the finish line brings what we were all at the intersection of betting and hoping (on/for); dissociative to (finally / at last) break .

But 23 nights / doses in I had to forfeit the potential win/benefit for the risk... my belly was distended. I had acid indigestion and no/none at all sense/sensation that an excretory system exists in my body/is in existence . I had been interoceptively /observationally/empirically aware since the start of the double (dose) that it was as though the medication were depressing (proper) brain function to evacuate/eliminate/excrete ... but in my mind I was determined to power through and see what full efficacy has in store for me but looking 3 months pregnant when I wasn't and looking like I had a hernia when I didn't kept me from finding out . I had to go back down. On my one year memoir writing anniversary when I should have been going to bed/sleep with feelings of accomplishment and pride I instead layed/sat up in bed that night wondering if my intestines could / would rupture or/and whether or not the swollen bloated fingers were Bc it was hot or (Bc) toxins were backing up in my bloodstream. It was the 12 Month mark of writing (my memoir) and it was the first time/night in about _____ that I was taking no qtiapine .

...

|—-

|————-|

3.)

I lapsed into what I would say was withdrawls but as what my prescribing psych doctor would come to say was break-through symptoms; a show of/that the (something/a the fire (was) still) smoldering. /a show (of that) there was something/a fire, still smoldering. /a show of what was smoldering underneath beneath.

/a show of something still smoldering underneath beneath How could I tell the difference I didn't know . I just knew that all in an instant I was suddenly launched into the near same exact feelings I was going through during benzos withdrawls and that/it's whole taper process (*from hell* and (it's) /) followed by paws (, from hell .)

(It was the worst full circle)

. . .

|——-|

|——-|

and What I saw through /in the first (withdrawals) sickness was consistent with this. It had become solidified /this solidified it, just how easily an accidental dangerous/fatal overdose or under dose can happen and why. (If/considering you can go from months of meals of comfortably eating to a ground hault in safe chewing and swallowing (abilities/(brain)function) ...

If/when all in an instant you feel an indefinite breath hold is not only neurologically reachable but easy

don't you suppose something like counting milligrams of pills, doing the basic math you've always done/been doing, could become unfeasible, could too be(come) abruptly ripped out from under you like a rug lost on you just as/like your basic ability to know when to breathe, is/has been/was. (And/or your good sense that everyone (understandably) takes for granted being not a choking (high) risk .

This Thanksgiving I am grateful I feel my brain signals are stabilized again so as to be trust worthy for/of proper and safe chewing and swallowing of food. I give thanks that (a night/one night of)

cold-turkey revealed and reminded me of relativity/that everything's relative/ that it's all relative; although I was/had been/I was still of/had been still/of still in full time derealization 24/7 on the 150mg... I had come a long way with my symptom-extinguishing and all my family and doctors had been telling me that but this 'scare' showed me that/made me actually feel 'that which everyone had been insisting/promising.' I just needed/I needed only to be thrown back into the hell-pit ring for one more match to see it (for) (myself) to feel it (for) myself (;I had come a long way.)

I will give a guarded say/proclamation , that Cold-turkey this thanksgiving was a blessing in disguise .

. . .

(Intro or outro or right here.)

(And) who would think that the woman responsible for bringing me into this world in her lifetime would be needed to keep me/save me from demise,twice ! When I suddenly couldn't count; couldn't do/ lost the ability to do basic addition she was there and neednt be any mathematician to (over)see me to a safe dose/know that I wasn't over or under/ under or over, my/the prescribed numbers.

And (then) when we sat / we'd sit side by side on the couch at night as she'd tell/remind me of/reference the lullaby she'd made up and used to sing me to sleep with as a baby... "rocking rocking back and forth we're rocking . Rocking rocking back and forth we're rocking. "

With grave terror/horror and honor (alike)

I'd anticipate/ intrusive thoughts had me anticipating/intrusive thoughts/ intrusive unthinkables would have me anticipate/ intrusive thoughts would have me anticipate (the) holding (of) 'her' in 'my' arms in the (unthinkable) full circle of this, endearing (made up sweet little) song. Bless I pray it is after long.

*if/when all in an instant an indefinite breath hold feels /becomes

of/in your neurological realm or

well within your nuero(logical) parameters/realm.

|——-|

(And) It wasn't a patient-issued psychiatrist/psychiatry/psych doc. ultimatum so much as it was that my inner-knowing was there and I had a responsibility to relay the message to my perscribing psychiatrist; I was the liaison. If anything it was just (a matter of) fact (that) (there was/had been) an ultimatum (was) imposed upon me (came from within) ... and I chose/ was choosing/ opted to let him in / and I was opting to let him in .

(I told him) we get me out of this (dissociative) safe and sound while my 75 year old/ aging parents are still around . (I told him) or I am/become sentenced to life (by my mind) without visitation rights, (or) chance of parole not even (my) one entitled call a day will my mind/brain ever put at bay the dissociative (state)

(for a chance to get back to realized .)

I come from a(n) (loving) emotionally ensconced, close knit/tightly stitched/tight stitched, cross-hatch(Ed) and scored, won't degrade or fade over time archival-grade (love) *enough* (love) *family* *love* that if god forbid i were to be in this when one of them passes away I solemnly swear (to this) (in the wake of a RIP/ in black light of a RIP/ in dark of a RIP) so too with it/theirs, comes to pass (my) any *chance*/ability

to make it out ... (of DPDR) / of making it out of DPDR (in the wake of a RIP .)

And the essence of what my psychiatrist did say/relay was that the fact that I feel this way/ think and believe this (to be my truth) says to him/ tells him (something) that there is a psychological defensiveness (?at work?) to the syndrome .

——————

Transitional something maybe needed here.

———————-

|——————|

An add in for CJD3

or justUse in *CJD4*

Lust that belongs in the chapter(that came) before seeps into

what I write anew /what is written anew. / that which is written anew/ that which I write anew .

Old lover/ex-boyfriend; Slumlord to my darkness you overdosed me on wholesome but/and now I'm cumming into my own again .

#There were no innuendos, there were desexualized moments/expenditures or

[[My hands are tied, work out the kinks, crack the whip, show you the ropes]] I don't want your fucking figurative pokes/jokes/yokes/hoax

-while I was wanting/waiting (to get busy with) sex drenched innuendo(s)

You were (busy (with)) de-sexualizing expressions (, gestures and anything/everything suggestive .)

[[My hands are tied, work out the kinks, crack the whip, show you the ropes]]

(;) left/leave no subtext un-stoned .

Slumlord to my darkness you overdosed me on wholesome (but/and now I'm cumming into my own/flagship again .)

Bless me lustlord/lustlord for I (will) 'have at' sin . It's been 7 to 8 months since my last companion(ship)/ relationship ...

(but/and now I'm cumming into my own/flagship again .) no such thing as over-sexed / oversexting my welcome

-x(I'm)x Sick of living sweet this time I'm going home sexy home

this time I'm

and I'm going/and I'm taking it HomeSexyHome. #

|-----|

Put a Transitional something here

maybe about how anger/wrath would follow suit with lust for (its) unrequited qualms / properties. (The/that (historically) 4 letter prominence of what (historically) made me feel so alive now made me feel so alone that it felt like a proprietary dead end; what lust had shape shifted into .

[[Where once it was lovers

Bc the night belonged to nothingness and otherness/ otherness and nothingness now.

(*And*/it *made* life/*living* reek with linear notes of livid .)]]

(?a precursor for/to/of (how)

1.) I was feeling/being cursed by life .

2.) I wanted to curse out life .

3.) (I was) wanting to curse out life .

4.) cursing out life .

5.) cursing my life .?)

[[Where once it was lovers

Bc the night belonged to nothingness and otherness/ otherness and nothingness , now.

(And/it made life/living reek with linear notes of livid .)]]

——————————-

|———|

CJD2(Bc it's the anger) or *CJD4*

Anger/Wrath that belongs in a chapter that came before bleeds/bled through to what I write anew /what is written anew. / that which is written anew/ that which I write anew .

An emotionally perceived invasion despite an/the intellectual understanding that the neighbor's newly fence-towering sun flowers wouldn't/don't have cameras in the disk floret . But the swaying stem and leaves in the breeze got/made me angry/livid as if it were the home's residents themselves gawking with awkward shifting and shuffling as they stand (feet) (firmly) planted there for hours/all the live long day / all the days of my life or strife. I(d) shudder to not shut my blinds and when I do/did/would it feels/felt like I'm sticking it to them.

|———|

Add in/on !

After sun flower part in CJD4

and when I'd hear the "monthly doormats" feet clobbering and clomping around upstairs above/over my head it felt like a stampede intended to trample my (self-)worth . I took/found a strange twisted solace in the malice of Marilyn mansons lyrics

"Don't need a motherfucker lookin' down on me

Motherfucker lookin' down on me

Least I know wherever I go

I got the devil beneath my feet"

x[they would not revile me]x

(As) *I was the devil beneath their feet.* (*And they would not revile me*) *I relished and reveled in the (situation/circumstance) reframe courtesy of the (songs) refrain /chorus.*

xI was their devilx

xA reframing that I relished and reveled in; [they would not revile me.]x

|——-|

And when I turn upside down in the sink the metal strainer I see the smattering/sparse particles or morsels; a composite of dinners and / of a composite of dinners and it becomes (symbol of) the "monthly doormats" yell(ing) at me. I jam-wash it down the drain as though it were a garbage disposal and I feel like I've flipt the script on/of (the) hierarchy .

Risk-benefit says I'd rather sit with this rancid/putrid/ I don't flush toilet paper bathroom refuse on the off chance of it permeating (through) the vents than I would sooner stand for (your) (brash) verbal Incontinence. ... ...

|——-|

CJD4

The "monthly doormats" never listen to music so/ (and) with "monthly doormats" that never listen to music , a compilation created of discordance and cacophonies greatest; Amanda Palmer, pj Harvey rasputina sleater-kinney (and) more felt sure to grate on (the/their) suburban(s) (conservatist) (conventionalist) nerves. And in that calm mine.

From in my/the garage apartment/apartment garage; my mad man cave

The music swelled

1.)as/and my hopes welled that war air rises .

2.) with my hopes that war air rises.

|————|

|—————|

Transitional statement =

Reflecting on the phrase win the battle, lose the war (again) brought me back to risk-benefit / brought to mind risk-benefit ... Ultimately I would come out overpowering the mortgage holders of where I dwell but for now all that would happen; eviction, would be the antithesis of/less than, empowering if I succeeded in pissing them off/ *irking them* and my unruliness was met with them shirking the/that good standard renter (rights/courtesy/*vacating*) *practice(s)* of sufficient vacating/*courtesy* , notice .

But there was a place with(in) (my) haste of considerable/________, space

(to make it/to scale leaps and bounds over boundaries)

to/and color outside (of) the rules/ (the) enemy lines .

Kill them with kindness;my drug of choice wouldn't work this time . Not with this guy .

|-----|

|-----|

CJD4

Figuratively/metaphorically orgasm; fake it till you make it, done right.

I didn't want my lustlord to write me off ((just)yet); wasnt havin' it so I figured/decided/fashioned I'd/to have at it; (erotica short-short) write my way back (in)to his heart-on / hard-on . (Since non verbal communication remained and/no, reigned as my strong suit I'd see his work/business suit crumpled to the floor employing this ______ equation/method/principle, I had in store . ((And) We'd be sexy role playing out (things like stuff like) principal to staff/faculty quid pro quo before long)

WWML What would lustlord like and WWAD what would Anna do became the ingredients to for *of* the Netflix and fuck, inventing Stephanie I would become.

. . .

Although Delvey's objective wasn't sexual the ______/premise ,

applied/was applicable/applies/.

It was inextricable;a mixture of the 2; him and her, would make for the perfect elixir and be/to, 'concocked ' the wanted/wanton product of winning (back) his lust. In this behavioral science experiment/hypothesis I did / I would entrust . And yield a generation of lust/seduction (I was)

Like a/the prodigal/ ____/sin

(There was the /lived a the/there lived a the) (masterful) mad scientist (within) where in which/therein (under/thereunder) the heading of (the) mad memoirist I/ bespoke and outspoken (I)

Was/would be, my golden token to take(ing) back the lust (that) dissociation hath stolen.

xendevoured to cum by/bi it honestly . x

|————|

|————|

1! CJD4

Bring back the lust diss hath stolen..

But even if I could/did medication; Q would now steel (from me) too (now)/all the same.

(For/as/and) "Bc the night belongs to lovers"

(It) was hard to cum by it indulgently these days when I have/had sedation robbing me blind / when sedation was robbing me blind would rob me blind ...

. . .

CJD4 or make a CJD5?

Long-time therapist, appt today 12/5/22

Told him

-the moon flower alias I'd always been coming by it vagrantly/regularly from a/the karaoke announcers mouth to lovers lips moonflower did fit hit def .

and now for 21 months I'd feared the night. I'd dreaded it for how it meant should the/this 24/7 pan anxious state ((discourteous) of (the) dissociative) Escalate/graduate to a full blown panic attack or should something I ate earlier that day land me in a food poisoned state... it was late and the hour on the clock/ the hands on the clock/ digital hands of/on the smart watch (?clock?) would negate/titrate any possible chance/ the possible chance of reaching someone ... ... tbc . My parents started always turning out their bedside/night table lamps to a raised all the way phone volume and/as/while mom took to falling asleep (with) phone in hand . And while all that took the edge off it (also)/concurrently/contrarily brought on ageist embarrassment; I was to be 40 years old and as my internal monologue (would scold) told and retold (and would) scold I need to be doing this (sort of stuff/____) for them not the sordid other way around !

transitional something here ?

-(and) (now) at the not so tender age of 75 parent associated songs I'd always used to self-soothe was/would/were now only making me react/respond with (anxiety of) anticipatory grieving (anxiety) .

I had to resort to lulling myself to sleep with only songs/music I'd discovered for myself and coveted by myself/ I alone.

Either that or sex-up the

(/my) (childhood) songs beyond recognition ; usurp/____ my limbic system and cash in on the 1.)(escapism) juxtaposition eroticism escapism .

2.) escapism of the juxtaposition eroticism.

'-Vocabulary olfactory sounds of yelling signs of aging excretory (secretary of crisis and death sex, secretary) ex's these are a few of my fetishized things

When the dogma bites when the ______/ bees knees sin when I'm feeling ____/sad. I simply remember my fetishized things/fear,fetish and their intersection,

1.)and then I dote on feeling so bad (ass)/ don't feel so bad .

2.) and then I want to be had/bad .

*3.) and then I want to be so bad * '

|———

(And) Was the DSM 'fire flames' (that raged ablaze) of my DPDR (that raged ablaze); dark sexual mania caged in/amongst the pages of your DSM V/ diagnostic statistical manual... I didn't know

I just knew that

When faced with times of crisis and/or death My mind (just) retreats, finds relief and 'it's flex' in sex.

?/ a place that's sexual pleasurable . And he found that unconscionable .?

and many/some find that unconscionable

but/while I find the relief/release incomparable .

My genetic/chronological legacy is to be the last living of my family of origin which is extremely scary/terrifying and when that unbearable time comes I'm likely to become completely sexually unhinged .

|———|

CJD4 add in/add on (to 'completely sexually unhinged' part)

And with more than an inkling of what my unhinged would be when I am/ when my escapism is/ *when my off-kilter helter-skelter psychosexually intersecting grief processes/processing* (escape (tendency)) is to reap/see the bereavement of all of my family …

it would look like a promiscuous masking (taped across the mouth) of the gravest pain I've ever known and,

ever will know (again). /will ever know (again.)

It would sound like vast

track 6 off of 'Me and You'

"(she takes pictures of herself with nothing on) she wants to hurt me I'm already too far gone"

. . .

And it would pound in my body cavity like Lucinda Williams "unsuffer me" ... "anoint my head with your sweet kiss my joy is dead I long for bliss. "

And it would round off getting lost in/to the (exillerating) sin of juxtaposition; getting off to Puscifers "Man Overboard"

calling a lover daddy for the first time Bc it's feeling right / Bc I'm feeling inclined to trauma-play the 1.) (viet nam) (USS 67 forestall l) Navy veteran of my life

2.) forestall fire survivor of my life.

|————|

But time would move like the respective above mentioned musical collective's "A bullet train to Iowa"

"gonna be a while before we touch back down ain't no turning back like a train sprouting wings fuck the track"

I have/The Steph-Oenix has off-peak round trip darkness-tinged wings now but that will throw/launch/cast me into 'peak' one way

psyche-singed/incinerated

(fight or/and) flight/ xtrain of depravity/depraved .x

The darker life goes the more sexually fucked up, my/the path(ways) glow(s .)/glowed.

A slob hF42.3 (ICD-10) / DSM-5 300.3 / *a F42.3 (ICD-10) / DSM-5 300.3 slob* seemed to be in my DNA but (with every major/devastating life loss/DNR/*RIP*)

I could feel my/the lifestyle brand expand(ing) towards *slob whore*/whore slob .

:::do I need transitional anything here?????

Maybe not!!!! But I just don't know for sure::::

But/and contrarily/concurrently to intrinsically *feeling*/ being intrinsically 40 and naughty 3 months away from

leaving my dirty-flirty thirties for my the/my (?burgeoning?) decade b-day/birthday

the/my decade b-day/birthday

|————|

|———|

2! Was/were

Saccharine niceties invading my speech. pleasantries and

Superfluous extraneous words were the only verbiage of/to my disposition that could be heard. A discouraging/ a discoreaging curse (i) incurred; I was of a /at a neuro-______ /neurobiochemical personality imposition. And felt it/this.

The undercurrent of my misplaced/displaced personality/persona/presentation representation *was the* (uncontrollable) flooding of/from *Pan-anxious (state) related complication(s)* *of a deluge of flooding* .

. . .

????????I knew the annoyance/____/nuero-glitch to my (missing) (sexy temptress) temperament/disposition

wouldn't sit well with his clear and present darkness and (that) he wouldn't take it lying down , in bed with me. The ____ /lull, / the disposition disordered /disordered disposition/ the disregulated disposition would drown out/off set his enthrall and inspired (mood)desire entirely ????????

I could look at the rambling symptom and see myself objectively. How others, especially a prospective/respective lover, might feel respectively/prospectively .

And in that/and of/from that vantage point I felt bad for them/sorry for them.

And so began me/my little self led game of musical dares.(the/a) (music consumer-enthusiast(s) /appreciators/worshippers act of) Trying through meticulous song selection to end aggravation with the bringing of validation to/of a lover's/my lustlord's anticipated /presumed headspace .

With a line of admission from pucifer

"Can't hold your shit, hold your tongue, you got to go"

"With all that racket from you lips a-flapping

(We assumed you didn't notice)"

. . .

I'd assume(d) the/a position of aggressive empathy in/through/via/with/and objectivity .

"You speak like someone who has never been

Smacked in the fucking mouth

That's OK, we have the remedy

You speak like someone who has never been

Knocked the fuck on out

But we have your remedy"

pray-tell this bridge would ... tbc

And although on one other occasion prior; Halloween (2022) paired with an/the original erotica story I had done the same thing; put myself in his shoes and from that stance did choose "I can't hear you" by the dead weather to exemplify how I understand/get , the want for me to (just) shut (the F) up. I wanted it too but/and yet (it) was not something pan-anxious dissociative allowed (for) .

It was the first week of/in December and getting close to the time I would be going over his house / spending the night with him ... I'd done my shopping at the grown up toy store , prepared my sexcretary outfit for (our) playtime and there was more but what I simply couldn't /could not account for was how my ... (* write here about my rambling symptom type stuff/thing that I had no nuero-executive control of function of/over

/ nuero-executive function of control, over, might do me in . Ruin everything / ruin my win .

. . .

Write next about how

So I wanted to see to it that there was a !!!contingency plan!!! set/put in motion

(?before we saw each other?)

*So a contingency plan I did send; if handsome devil forbid he is (to be) put off or turned off ,we revisit the/this (the) potential for the/a sexual side of (our/the) friendship when dissociative has (finally) ended its dictator totalitarian reign of/in, my brain .

xwould flood my verbiage as the undercurrent from x

|––––––-|

|––––|

It is (un)common knowledge; obscurely known, yet outstandingly fascinating, captivating, intriguing that/how, for people of/with whom Alzheimer's has afflicted they have/are of the propensity to aquire sudden new artistic/creative and/or pastime interests. I feel it is an insidious disease's way of giving some/a little grace artistic/creative relief/release to compensate ...

And while it is probably more greatly known that sentient beings/living things experience a vibrant burst of exuberance right before they die/ right before (their) death/ just before (their) death, it never deceases to amaze me how often/regularly this prelude to last breath ________, is mistaken for health, rather than understood for/as the undertaker it is.

. . .

CJD4 or intro or outro or jacket

Had I ever really almost died? or was it (just) the subjective experiential playing (unjust) tricks with/on my mind ? (;spourus potato sporous patato, spoiled tomato spoiled tomato)

(Either way) my inclinations were responding in kind .../; (dissociative (state)) (like Alzheimer's like my/ones dying days,

the neural phenomenon of _______, had found/made its way to me * (in (the) /from the dissociative (state))*

and I was interested in (learning) ballet, lugging (home)a 'table painting'

And (I had/having) a change of (license) plate/frame

1.)to match my/a change of heart and/with my new frame of mind.

2.) to match (with) my new frame of mind and change of heart.

I didn't much listen to instrumental, but I'd counted Helen Jane Long as my favorite composer for a long time . However in this state it hit diff and I yearned to have the technical skill to put languid (limbed/limbs) cut with sharp pointed-toe (shoe) precision like a metronome.

1.) moving with ebb(ing) and flow(ing) to every tone .

2.) hitting every note catching every tone

I imagined the Choreo I would do if only I had the technical skill to execute / but (i) or and (I) lacked the technique to execute see it through .

I did a run-through Mach-up of what I/all that I dreamed to do if i had lace-ups (and lessons).

It's giving ... unprecedented visual processing the medium of painting was . So much so that one afternoon/day upon my regularly charted/scaled neighborhood stroll I couldn't go home without a piece of trash that found me most transfixed .

Someone's old folding work table

(that) I couldn't resist hauling 3 blocks on foot back to my apartment/crib (from somebody's trash) because it nearly brought me to my knees

in "Stendhal syndrome ." (To see.)

It's old cigarette ash stains, drink ring marks debris and (assorted) soot and I just looked at it and saw incomparable sex appeal .

This unintentional incidental art was so captivating to me the formation of how it's filthy(;) the spattering of Oxblood red and smattering of ash/soot, set against the ecru...everything about it made me fantasize an entire

interior design-scape (of my living quarters,) around it.

I photographed it from every angle of each side when I got it home.

Write next about new license plate frame .

xbut/and I found the neural phenomenon happening to me in dissociative x

|——-|

11/22/22

-also in the session with Dr. Lane Rosalie... I told him we need to get me out of this (dissociative) while we still can, meaning that my parents are 75 and I come from a loving close knit/tightly stitched/tight stitched enough family that if god forbid I were to be in this dissociative state and/when one of them passes I believe I will/would never come out of it.

I had the loss of one of them to contend with while

|——-|

-while I was wanting sex drenched innuendo(s)

You were de-sexualizing expressions

-sexually suggestive innuendos/gestures and desexualizing/desexualized expressions/ _________/subtext.

(Dismantling/dismantled antics)

|——-|

CJD4 or intro or outro or jacket

Had I ever really almost died? or was it (just) the subjective experiential playing (unjust) tricks with/on my mind ? (;spourus potato sporous patato, spoiled tomato spoiled tomato)

(Either way) my inclinations were responding in kind … (write about ballet interest maybe)

. . .

|———-|

Im going to send you more on this later/ Marco Polo maybe ...

But going out practice driving soon with familial instructor so for now wanted to just quickly send you this to see because

It was fun talking with you at Katie's about both of our recent

dumpster-dive and curbside-finds !

I know you told me about the frames/turtle-tank/fish-tank plans ...

So I wanted to show you that old folding work-table I was telling you about that I couldn't resist hauling 3 blocks on foot back to my apartment from somebody's trash because it nearly brought me to my knees

in "Stendhal syndrome ."

It's old cigarette ash stains, drink ring marks and debris and I just looked at it and saw incomparable sex appeal .

This unintentional incidental art was so captivating to me the formation of how it's filthy the spattering of Oxblood red and smattering of ash set against the ecru...everything about it made me fantasize an

interior design-scape of my living quarters, around it.

I photographed it from every angle of each side when I got it home.

Id like to text ya some of those photos .

|——-|

|———|

Add in for either prob

CJD3 or *CJD4*

Bc the night belonged to shudders now; not lovers /

Bc the night belonged to shudders not lovers now

Where once it was lovers

Bc the night belonged to nothingness and otherness/ otherness and nothingness , now.

(And/it made life/living reek with linear notes of livid .)

|——|

<3 <3 <3

DPDR @ DSW

|————|

DPDR at DSW

11/2/22

(In) a colleague collective pool Today/(on) my 2nd day of work/on the job I entered the lottery but yesterday Id felt like I'd won it driving to my first day of equal opportunity. (employment).

Training module after module (drop down box) sub-chapter after sub-chapter what was typically flippantly regarded (by all - and previously in/through life; me) as formality on boarding programs for me/this time (now) meant/ reached deep; DPDR self-consciousness could

fell-away/receded/fall-away.

my eyes, although they had read this time and time again in/over jobs past this time/now, they would bask in the /those (written) descriptions/descriptors of (the) (legally) protected classes.

Discrimination would equal incrimination . I felt, for the first time, what I was; safe. /

For the first time I felt what I was; safe. / *for the first time, what I was, I felt ; safe . *

allowed to be here and worthy of working/work/being a worker/being somebody's worker .

?Reassuring reaffirming?

|––––––––|

|–––––––––––––––|

Self-consciousness, self-devaluing and feeling unworthy/undeserving as a deceptive false advertisement/representation, was a common thread in/to my thoughts spanning more than just 'at work' .

I had told my psychiatrist my psychologist that I got a job at

shoe store.

texted my parents that the company had (officially) hired me ...And with that/the aforementioned common thread of ______ I just couldn't wrap my head around how/the fact that everybody in my life is/was supportive about me trying a job; encouraging even !

I kept thinking someone I tell the news to is bound to take the stance of that

An employer deserves a more fully cognitively functioning person so as to say this is unfair (to them) and I'm putting them at a disadvantage .

...But no one seemed to think that way/ have the reaction that this is unethical and that truly

Eluded as it was *unfathomable*/not feasible/unthinkable to me .

?Remem She chose you- she saw what she needs for her store in you :-)

And I ... :'-) ?

|———————————-|

|——————|

Write Transitional something here ? Maybe this or maybe not this ...

I had very complex guilt; I didn't feel like I had the right to be anywhere (?be doing anything?) , really . Whether it was ?dating?, working or driving I felt like (left and right)(from all angles) i was ripping everybody off (from all angles) (in trying/attempting) to assimilate (in)to (conventional/societal) daily-living and/or exercise vocational-skills .

And with/in matters of motor vehicle operation *I felt (like)* I was/*motive*/*motivation* felt like *(was) such* of (that) an *(outstanding) offense* ... (at first ./ yet .)

|—————|

DPDR@DSW

DPDR@DSW

10/13/22 (7minutes risk (of) heaven/7 minutes trying to outrun heaven)

As soon as I started driving I had a friend request a hangout and ask if I could drive over

but ugh driving In the dissociative state just the 7 mins to my job in the trial practice run I'd done with my familial instructor; my father, (yesterday the 12th) was hard (enough/as it was) . Feeling like I'm driving drunk off my ass

and should not be on the road

for the safety of myself and others…

sucks! (Feeling like) by being on the road (it feels like) I'm doing something wrong and if caught could get in trouble with the law, roars in my subversive (thoughts/conscience.) Feeling like/theorizing/believing , if police enforcement /criminal justice / cops knew what this feels like it would be illegal/outlawed to drive under this/the influence of dissociative. Feels like I should/and I would be issued a DPDR DWI/DUI.

|————————|

Transitional something = Never before in my entire life prior to dissociative did I feel/had I ever felt (even) an inkling of/ even sub-acute, mistrust let alone then unfounded acute bout that wouldn't leave me alone (now) give me room to breathe, now . Ergo/this led/this meant

(I was) always feeling like I needed controlled environments only . In dating that looked like considering only people I already knew and had established trust with ; ex's ... which being one of my best kept fetishes(;ex's) didn't pose a/any interest or inclination/tendency problem (for me). In driving there could really be no controlled environment iteration but I was quick to learn/soon to learn I didn't really need it as it was on the road that I felt the most whole despite dissociatives unrelenting/relentless hold .

My work life/ones work life could be/can be/could present/can present a controlled environment (but) only to a certain extent. Plus I learned quick that there were trigger-(un)happy work tasks that would mentally bring me flashing back/to flash backs to what/of what it was to be under withdrawls symptom attack. But/so I resourcefully resorted [in how I would punctuate the time clock to/with] to my usual ways of fictional/figurative sexual (mental) escape/escapism to compensate .

xin how I would punctuate the time clock with x

|———————|

. . .

How I would punctuate the time clock became the imagined life of shoes. The New Year's Eve parties the glitzy pumps might see, the hippie retreats, the Birkenstock's and bear paw might have in store for their new owner to be.

And deriving the most comfort and joy would be in superimposing the people of my life into this creative narrative . Visually Scanning the wall to wall racks of clearance fast in unspoken(ly)/assumed, timed assignment to pick and pull the shoes with the matching skus to my/that were on my stapled pages list is what felt all too reminiscent of the manic movements/motions of/in/from withdrawls sickness could be aided mitigated letting my eyes veer from the printed packet to whatever rack that has/have/had footwear (fashionably/style) fit for a (respective) friend or family member of mine .

The cornerstone of escapism was sex-dense (saturated/saturation .)

I don't have a foot fetish but/*and* didn't need one to fetishize my/the work day hours away.

'Romanticize your *life*/day' you've heard of the trending buzz term . Well anagram some (of the) letters and you'll get what I (much) like better /*pleases me (much) better * . Eroticize your life became/was/proved to be the aide of my existence.

It all came into vision when ?upon a sales floor tidying/recovery? lap/session, I spotted a sign overhead the ad campaign for/to/of a wall of crocs cited/read "Come As You Are"

I was excited that Nirvana, my lustlord's favorite band had been cited but (moreover) (it was) the displeasure with the fact it was crocs called shotty/shotgun to the front seat/car cabin of my mind . In the end, I was indebted to The sacrilege for how it opened/would (cum/come) (to) ('entertain and) open' (the) lines of copulation with my lustlord, once more .

. . .

of course he agreed that the billboard was egregious. Suggesting converse, my text asked him WWYP; what would you put ? soon the (innocent) exchange led to a new strain that I could and would (ultimately/eventually) 'WWAD' and 'WWML' the hell out of .

He had told me/was telling me of a pair of shoes he had just gotten in the mail, stipulating that they are very tight and may need to be re ordered in/for a larger size .

It was inventing Stephanie go time I could take this dialog and

1.) have him thinking she wants revenge's "monologue"

2.) get "she wants revenge" s "monologue" stuck in his head .

but I couldn't, not yet, not while i was juggling my withdrawls and/or symptom breakthrough set-back/relapse, could I smuggle sex in . /

Did I have the (pathological/physiological/neuro-) constitution conducive of/to smuggle/smuggling, sex in ./; I was neurotic not erotic .

To help me get through the symptom throw-back momm who was staying with for the duration helped/had me/ would have me rephrase (what I'd say)from 'withdrawls' to that of the inner monologue saying/being that (it's my) my brain is rebalancing/ is trying to rebalance / needs to rebalance (yet.) , (it) helped the time feel less ________/______.

After _____ long weeks My brain recalibrated to the (200mg) medication and as neuro biochemical stabilization found me/ saw me to leveled out …

I was all about / I could (once) again be all about, taking incoming messages to/ and raising them to the next level; treating them as/like suggestive texting/texts .

I had 2 iterations in mind for what would be my response-writing to my lustlord's seemingly/intendedly/ideatively innocent but satisfyingly/satisfactorily/ definitely, *open ended*/lax/(just) enough, text to slip in /slink in (with) syntax, dripping (with) sex . / syntax-dripping sex.

Temptress S.D; my minx (of for to kink) would slink up to WWHDMT(O) / WWMDMT(O) ; what would his dirty mind think(of) / what would lustlord/lustlord's dirty/kinky *kinked* mind think (of) , and do just that .

In/with/of the one/version that would boast

1.)/bring more sin-tax than 'syn' I wrote back …

2.) the most sin-tax of 'syn' I wrote back …

"Well, Well speaking strictly professionally as someone who works in the footwear industry now lol. my professional sales lady diagnosis to her customer Mr. White, with his presenting complaint...is that

::::::::... if your shoes are too tight :::ahem::: Sir... it might be that your tumescence is too big, if I may be so bold, Sir .

I'll let you try that theory on for size and I'll be around the store should you need any more 'assistance'::::

✨👞🥾🦶🧦🦶🥾👞✨

It was working (pun incentive/intended) (my) marrying/pairing (of) shoes with sex was getting the best of him and while I was hard at work I now too was making/could make him 'hard' at work.

?(An eroticized life done right ! / 'eroticize your life' done right ! …)? (As) DPDR at DSW was slowly evolving into/ to RPG's.

and now …. Write next about Temptress S.D. sexcretary shoes text/link.

DSW website link sent; temptress S.D. assigning him to pick the sexcretary shoes that please him to no end.

(and now)…with a (play) scene, to prepare for/around the bend

(And) A/the DSW website link sent; temptress (S.D.) assigning/assigned lustlord to pick/select the sexcretary shoes that please him to no end.

Or

A DSW website link sent; temptress (S.D.) assigning lustlord to pick/select the sexcretary shoes that please him to no end.

(Now) (opened new vistas of submission) with a (play) scene, to prepare for/around the bend …

. . .

(opened new vistas of submission.) As I pulled not pushed the cold steel shopping cart through (the) wfm/Whole Foods market (parking lot) I thought (a lot) about how it would feel, (and)might heal, to kneel/heel and be pulled/dragged across the/a stage by a metal choke chain in a kitschy-kink burlyQ act/installation of the stooges "I wanna be your dog" .

My mind was (running) rampant/ ran rampant with roleplay/role playing inspo . (?If sexual/bedroom rpg add/adhd mania was a thing, this was it.?)

note:

!Find a way to reign it in so as to write next about the "other girls in the office" / in our minds devise of the office ! …

(In) The fortress of our/my/the minds devise (of)

'The office' ,

1.) was simple in principle/ the principle was simple singular and linear …/

Was simple singular and linear in principle/;the principle

2.)(it) (was) / the premise was simple singular and linear, in principle/ ;the principle;

It promised …

3.) was simple in principle singular and linear

With a premise that) promised

. . .

'silly girls... they got nothin' on me '

💋

(;) those

"other girls in the office" just don't know what it is to be refined. Those sprite young 20 somethings with their stupid influencer trending-speak like

GOAT/glow-up/cheugy/woke/slay ...

They wouldn't know real vocabulary if their boss; Mr. White, spanked them over his knee (repeatedly) with a thesaurus (repeatedly) after one of their tiktok filmed

"hot-girl-walks" .

:::mic drop 🎤::::::

While slow-living minimalist modern society romanticized their life/lives I eroticized mine .

And when/while I walked the (27) aisles of my job, I realized too could incentivize my life with this/a part-time (work) 'work to write' concept/_____.

My therapist had asked me, what do you like about the job... A question that seemed (at the time) pointless/insignificant/redundant/boring enough to be rhetorical , (at the time/ at face value)

(Would) In retrospect (would) stimulate perspective that would become invaluable to my personal outlook and/ ergo, this book.

So... "what do you like about the job?"

All I could think of was one thing... listening to my music on the car ride there .

At the time unaware that his question had implanted a new way to see, but from that session on the appreciation/awareness/visibility/vigilance that my mind would bring into evidence for me

as I carried out my work tasks would soon/quickly amass to an/this integral viewpoint/vantage point of visibility .

With a pros and cons column i inked a slim post it stack I'd grabbed from the back tucked unsuspectedly/surreptitiously in one of my 2 work apron pockets, I was floored as I worked the sales floor just how needless the equidistant/ equally spaced, cons column was proving to be!

(Overlapping it's antithesis/antonym) Scribbled on the (*say dimensions of post it)

(Overlapping it's antithesis/antonym)

Pros became prose as I was so enamored with my positive findings/sightings that I found it nearly impossible to cite things in notation/annotation.

Write next about some things direct from my post it's !

Well as the 7 minutes in music heaven of the car ride's commute was the first affirming thing noticed/I picked up on, it seems only right that that the next thing I mention be/ that I next pay/denote honorable mention/merit to the holiday/Christmas/Xmas tunes at work. Although (of course) emotionally (of course) I felt nothing(ness) The intellectual understanding of Christmas carols would sleigh my days with (a) punctuation of familial and familiar (sugar-plum) warm&fuzzy (sugar-plum) nothings. Work days were the only/sole/soul way my music consumption got decked w festive bouts of homophone(s) ... as my Spotify ,slayed (but) in every other way . / *sure AF did slay (but) in every other way . *

|-------|

transitional something needed here?

|--|

CJD5 or *DPDR@DSW*

4 hours a day I was being subliminally conditioned to schmooz shoes but what I'd always wanted and pondered was why there wasn't also/too a DHW, DPW or DBW ; designer handbag, purse or bag warehouse . It seemed illogical for there not to be one when handbags and shoes are the accessory of choice (by/of women) stylistically and ? statistically? (By/of women) .

The pocketbook silky silver lining to their being/existing no business like this was that I could create its/an purse empire. Theoretically I could / in theory I could ; it's not like I went to school for business or had the kind of money/capital needed to invest (in this/it .)

(No) for now and maybe/probably/presumably for ever I'd have to (just) get my fix diverting my attention from the 27/staggering rows of kicks and directing it to (perusing) the 2 stand-alone rolling racks that fell flat against the robust/buxom fill-out of the ________.

Prior to working there I had bought several purses there but (now) as the hiring manager took me around on/for the store tour it was to my great disappointment to ...

x(write next about how they cut back on purse section .)x

(have to) learn that they/DSW's purse section had been cut back .

My whole life had been charging forth with

(A 10 by 10) (unit full of) wall to wall pocketbooks. From purses strung up and covering the wallpaper of/in my childhood bedroom to adulting being/meaning bags billowing from over the door racks/hooks at my apartments rendering obsolescence of/for guests bathroom privacy the 10by10 rented storage unit/locker full of pocketbooks should come as no surprise for/to people who/that know me. From Structured cognac croc that were supposed to make/land me '(get) the job' to ...

Black crinkle patent whose skulls and conical/pyramid studs were supposed to get me invited to ... __________

My life/ a *life of purpose* (as I surmised it) was always just a purse away (to my thwarted thoughts/ contorted cognition/distorted order of thought/ *in my* (*day dream(illusion*)) (*of sizemic*) *delusional* (illusion.)(*proportions.)

Thrift, retail or resale free gift With purchase a sample (size) of promise .

Maybe with thrift the life they've lived transcends (owners)

And as I browsed (to buy) in the sisterhood of stores Marshall's TJmaxx home goods one arbitrary eve(ning) in 2013 ...

my life felt inadequate to buy the disco ball of a bag I spotted and wanted . It's magenta and silver sequined bod/bodice/mid section harnessed with handles of vivid orange that parted to reveal the most royal purple interior/lining...

I didn't feel qualified to get it and clearly it deserved more than the life I could/would provide (it.)

Then it just clicked that was it... I'd make a vow/pact to make my,

2013 life / life of 2013 match all the party this was packin(g) . Only then would it justify / only then could I justify this purchase .

And somehow to my great astonishment I did it that would become/come to mean/be the one and thus far only time in my life I managed/I would manage to/at turn(ing) social life profit from pocketbook

x(in)to prophecy . x

I thought of that now/ was reminded of that professionally when on my shift (as) I made it look like I was tidying one of (the/a) measly 2 bag racks; surreptitiously perusing the/what unsung heroes (to my (social/personal) life hung there (Waiting for me .)

There was a white patent-quilted YSL esque Steve Madden bag. The overlapping, interlocking yellow gold-tone front flap monogram, dainty chain evening bag could imbue 'law of attraction' traction

x(derived) successx if I get it and use it as a

"CASSANDRE MATELASSÉ ENVELOPE CHAIN WALLET" , placeholder , I mused . With a long-standing history of believing bags to be vision boards of a sort/ a vision board of (a) sort(s) ... surely the procurement of this designer replica/dupe would be a suitable/strategic move in the spirit of manifestation .

Be the change purse you wish to see... (and) I certainly wasn't doing myself any (manifestation) favors / favors of manifestation with lugging around a double walled reusable shopper grocery tote every day, every where in Lieu of a proper handbag ! I wanted to dress for success But the latter sense of/that my life wasn't 'together enough' to warrant wearing/using/carrying nice stuff won out and shrouded my closet. Decades worth of brand name pocketbooks collected sat;

skeletons in my closet idle in my lockers (scattered across Suffolk county) many (having) never (been) used/*carried* .

|———-|

Transitional something here ?

|——-|

12/22/22

DPDR @ DSW

After about 2 months of work, I had finally memorized all my passcodes and my 15 character username to operate and navigate the various tech devices of the day but my pride and joy of no longer having to look at a ratty old slip (of paper) for reference was cut short.

It was one step forward two steps back in the adventures of DSW w/ DPDR as the hiring/store manager handed me an assignment of a mere 2 customer orders to retrieve from the shelves/floor; called 'picking' ,2 was by far the least amount I'd ever had in a singular assignment since I'd started employment .

I looked at the printout, the sku, the upc, etc, none of it registered to me as something I know what to do with. (That which) /What I had been doing for 2 months was all lost on me. I had breezed through pages upon pages of these 'orders to pick' every work shift now since nov 1st and/yet/but today it hit diff… I had no memory of how to preform this work task. Yet autopilot-easy is how I was able to perform it just last shift; ___ days ago. … the casual niceties of coworker chatter accented with smiles and laughter the banter absentmindedly singing along to the music if I wanted to, all of it things I was able to be a part of /(multitask-)do, while I inked and highlighted prepping/making my thick stapled packet ripe for the picking(s). But now I was page-pacing back and forth between the 2 sheets of paper waiting for the memory to kick in of what in the hell I do to 'pick' and it never did/and it didn't.

Ducked off to the bathroom and only not frantic Bc my memory failed me ergo my boss, on a 2page work day not a (stapled) packet I texted my parents

"I don't understand … there is one work task I've been doing every work shift since I started here and today I have no memory of how to perform the task .

It's like my memory didn't hold over for this length of time I was without shifts"

Do we maintain that I needn't be tested for early onset Alzheimer's?!

I had to talk myself down from the unexpected upsentment, confusion and embarrassment… I diverted my attention to the sweetest memory I had of the term/word "pick" …

I could hear it now, astral projected; I was protected by my father sitting beside me in a family game of dominos on the back porch of our summer home; the Adirondack cabin on the glistening river. Adorably endearing in his teasing "pick pick pick " he sounded like a chicken or a duck substituting bock bock bock or cluck cluck cluck and to this kid, it was the funniest and most fun thing losing did . I swear I think I wanted to lose just to get the greater opportunity to giggle .

|———-|

I didn't want to fall prey/victim to

[pocketbook procurement] magical thinking about pocketbook procurement, again but the unforeseen cognitive oversight(s) dismay of the day gave way to giving in ./; (and that evening) The gift of a YSL lifestyle placeholder was 'payment processing/pending,' from my cart in an online purchase order of/from DSW.

The off-white "Steve Madden Briley Patent clutch" would be here to relieve me of my 'working with DPDR' woes in 4 to 7 business days.

But in ???3??? Days it would be/it was to be Christmas. And what I really wanted out of/from my comfort number(;3), was for my return to work the following Thursday(;the 29th) to see me to the brain supply of how to "pick" orders. The same way the notebook writings of Charles Darwin, were anonymously returned to the library from which they were taken/stolen, in a bright pink paper gift bag after all that 20 years. I wanted my brain to do that; gleefully return to me the work task knowledge that's been/that was (abruptly) removed/taken/stolen/(shop)lifted .

The notebooks were stolen in my highschool graduation year of 2001 and then a different year; 2022 but one *day* away from when DPDR set in; March 9th, they (were) returned with a kind note of/for Easter tidings . My birthday was around Easter, why couldn't my brain give me a proverbial big pink gift bag (like this) . Maybe it could ? Would ?

For the sake of my Livlihood at large; my memoir, I needed to get out of this

But for the sake of my menial remedial job I really would need something small in the meantime just an affectionate gesture comped of/from/by the mind a show (of) that memory-retention was (soon to be) ending; let me remember how to "pick" .

I wanted it for Christmas, a hippocampus that is.

I thought of the playful sexy meets silly text from 'my decades lover' a gif that read

What I wanted for Christmas as a kid and what I want for Christmas now … then and now had/came with visual aides; a pic of a video game console/system of what looked like a 90's Xbox followed up with the image meant to represent his present tense ideal present which featured a cartoon sketch of a bare buxom-bosomed chick tied up and doe-eyed .

Reflexively if belated, my mind capitalized on this concept and applied this/*the* equation/*persuasion* *in a song* xconcept/formula/model/_________, to mex

'Oh I want a hippocampus for Christmas only a hippocampus will do' …

For (historically) I had (historically) wanted a hippopotamus for Christmas; plushies, statues and more/etc. but I had been sick with this cognitive/limbic impairment for what was to be (say number of christmases; I think 2) christmases now/the 2nd annual Yule(tide)/Noel, now and the statute of limitations for how long I could be out of my mind, as far as I was concerned, was up .

And I wanted (to open up my eyes to see) a different kind of "hippo Hero" standing there/here .

|~~~~~~~~~~~~~~~~~~~~~~~~~~~~~~~~~~~~|

Notes only section

|————|

DPDR@DSW

10/13/22 (7minutes risk (of) heaven/7 minutes trying to outrun heaven)

About coming over to ‘the cat fathers’ house to hangout (tomorrow the 14th) “Or can you drive”

He Texted basically

Ugh driving In the dissociative state just the 7 mins to my job in the trial practice run (yesterday the 12th) was hard . Feels like I'm driving drunk off my ass

and should not be on the road

for the safety of myself and others.

sucks. (Feels like) by being on the road (it feels like) I’m doing something wrong and if caught could get in trouble with the law . Feels like if police enforcement /criminal justice / cops new/knew what this feels like it would be illegal/outlawed to drive under this influence . Feels like I should be issued a DWI/

DPDR DUI .

|–––––––––|

|–––––––––––––––|

DPDR@DSW

-oct 11th 2022 told my psychiatrist dr Lane Rosalie that I got a job at

shoe store.

texted my parents basically …It’s amazing how everybody in my life is supportive about me trying a job !

I keep thinking someone I tell the news to is bound to take the stance of that

An employer deserves a more fully cognitively functioning person like or so as to say (that) this is unfair to them / a disadvantage.

...But no one seems to think like that which amazes me .

And mom wrote back ...

Remem She chose you- she saw what she needs for her store in you :-)

And I ... :'-)

|———————————-|

|———————————-|

DPDR @ DSW

I don't have a foot fetish but/and didn't need one to fetishize my work day.

romanticize your life buzzterm vs eroticize it.

-Come as you are crocs correspondence/transcript and to which the erotisizing script it led.

-DSW website link sent; temptress S.D. assigning him to pick the sexcretary shoes that please him to no end.

|————|

. . .

>>I just got these today in the mail, but they are very tight I may re order another pair but a size larger<<

Well, Well speaking strictly professionally as someone who works in the footwear industry 🤪now lol. my professional sales lady diagnosis to her customer, with his presenting complaint...is that

::::::::... if your shoes are too tight :::ahem::: Sir... it might be that you need a wide width version to match your girth 'somewhere else' , if I may be so bold, Sir .

I'll let you try that theory on for size and I'll be around the store should you need any more assistance:::::

✨👞🥾🦶🏻🍆🦶🏻🥾👞✨

CJD5

|———|

CJD5

One!

-my 'I agree' email to dr Lane Rosalie

|—

Equipped with a new hypothesis (that)(;) this dissociative state is an iteration of anxiety .

|—————|

Chap8(Bc about meds), CJD4, *CJD5*

Two!

About Buspar (an anti-anxiety)

. . .

When it was prescribed on 12/6/22 (and taken/started on 12/10/22 ,) I felt/was Ever-grateful and feeling hopeful that the/this new medication addition of Buspar(; an anti-anxiety) could help with my insufferable pan-anxious state of living ?/ DPDR?

(? And in turn overturn *dissociative* DPDR?)

|———-|

|———-|

Chap8? CJD4 or maybe make a *CJD5*

About Pan-Anxious/PANDAS

Three!

From medication induced so constipated that I have acid reflux to saline laxative risk of dehydration

the 24/7 pan-anxious state keeps my mind a flurry with incessant worry

Will my esophagus burn and scar will I ingest too much water when I'm pounding back bottles during/for the duration of the bowel outpour that I die ?

PANDAS … I might get hip with, it might hit diff if the euphemistic term wasn't my terminal state but the endearment an/the acoustic disorder got smeared with makes me want to shoot to kill

Nothing warm and fuzzy about this iteration of panda and the acronym should see (vocabulary) mass extinction.

|———|

|———-|

CJD5

Four!

I only had to be one day/?dose? into (the) 10MG BUSPIRONE to realize the flooding of (the) pan-anxiety had been at/of a category 3 (classification) (on/of the _______) scale and now it was (of) a 2 (classification.)

A category/classification decrease in the pan-anxious state that ___months of/on "qtiapine common brand(s): seroquel " , could not quell or quiet/ and did not would not quiet.

(Or) was this placebo effect/psychosomatic (in that) I had such /was of such desperate hope (for this to work) ... that (maybe) ... I had duped myself (into) (the illusion that it had/was/is).

Another thing I'd wondered was if I had anticipatory Stockholm syndrome. Dissociation had been my abuser, my muse, (and) my captive/

'Oh captive/captor, my captive/captor' *and* (my) *abuser* for so long (now) , what would "live laugh (and) love" be like/feel like without it/'you' ?

bleak/bland without grandiose beliefs held deep that orbit around achievement, age regression and feeling no divide from the actors/people on the television delusions of reference most decadent I felt made me feel special (like)(;) I was the center of everybody's attention/retention and all endevours/ventures existed to reach me and seize me . hyper-sensitized memories meant that I could astral project (in)to any one of them at any time .

As sure as I say/think now that I will never so much as touch alcohol be willing to get a buzz ;nothing that is reminiscent to this /an , 'out of it state/experience' . Maybe in actuality the eventuality is the reverse; the stark contrast of realized living from derealized will drive me to chase the 'panda' .

((I could (just) see it now))

Afterall for better or worse/lesser, There would be a felt absence of a/the technicolor dream (sugar) coated _______.

but moreover what I saw was a reticence to have/let (the) medicine rescind / recede the darkness . The matte black paint in which the chains of my brain had bathed my/the pain had paved a whole new way to/for/of my sensorium to process mediums of art, sex and produce them.

(I could see it now)

The CJD#5 writing was on the wall ((and) I could see it now))

Me metaphorically being/me metaphorically (?rendered?) to *one* *of* those people/(charity) big spenders pouring money into saving my animal/____ of choice; the PANDA for how it comes complimentary with (black) rose-tinted VR glasses.

|—–|

(And) I felt like a bad ass wearing my conical studded and 'DNT FNG LOOK AT ME' lettered DIY-embellished solar shields when (a couple a few doses in,) I hit the road and for the first time actually felt something close to natural in/with my handling of the turns, merges, reaction time etc

As I drove feeling like I could command the most control on/of the road, I'd known in _____months (*since I'd started driving again) I thought/felt, 'this bodes well for Buspar being able to do some real dissociative/pan-anxious damage control !

Perhaps the only pan prefix (of my living) is/was fixing to soon be my/ would soon be 'giving' sexuality rather than (my) anxiety .

. . .

|————-|

CJD5

12/13/22

but the/any perceived 'give' was short lived and brought with (it) / and wrought with 'premature congratulation' When a few more days/doses into the start of Buspar had me feeling more unchanged than (the) 24 hours after the innugural pill was popped (and) my worst concern was/felt affirmed; it had just been a figment (bourn) of my (hopeless) desperation; that I was actually getting better.

The barrage of,

The reality/realization/actualization of/about my intact derealization shattered the _____ mirage/phisod/facade and with it my/the mood/phisod/facade

[[scrounging and scavenging for crumbs of (some) comfort

I let google search results (yielded) stoke the dying fire of hope and fan the flame of faith ... a screenshot saved where medical news today did say/stipulate

"unlike other anxiety medications, it doesn't reach its full effect right away. " and I knew the/my psychiatrist had said something too;that if it works it's just going to sort of work in the background . Search results for

"how soon does buspar reach full efficacy"

Varied by weeks/In time,

from site to site.

Trying to keep my hope/faith in ever making it /getting , out of this was like trying to hold on tight on a centrifugal force (action/amusement park/carnival) ride hands sweaty starting to slip

I thought of a most poignant passage/line from over the rhine

“I'm not letting go of God

I'm just losing my grip”

That was exactly this...

the steel bar holding me in was bouncing and I have/one has only so much grip strength .]]

|————|

My hold was nearing exhaustion as

|————|

CJD5

12/13/22

I was so tired of and sad from this (the)/the strenuous 24/7 dissociative state of 21 months.

I felt like the things other women and humans my age get to care about and involve themselves in I don’t get to put any care, attention or intention into/towards

((a/the)manifestation of) Bc I have had the same one need for 21 months now ... to get the F out of dissociative . So like triage in an ER ...

everything in my life gets handled in order of importance and/but the precedence importance never changes; DPDR, so therefor nothing else can ever take/ever gets to take center or even side stage really(;) everything is upstaged by my diagnosis and the tireless work/efforts/exertion to have an applaud-worthy prognosis/recovery.

(No I wanted a standing o fucking vation of (a) celebration .)

or should

[[‘scrounging to strength’]]

segment

be here?

|————|

this/the palpability tangibility of/in feeling that/(of) how people (really/just) take for granted what they get to care about; What they are privileged to be irked by or work on etc

of course led to anger …

|————|

CJD4(‘write next about new license plate frame’ part)

Or

CJD2 (Bc it’s my anger chap)

Or CJD5

(?estranged from the chapter of my rage a straggler (I want) to strangle with/on this page ?) ?(; their liberty (is) to blame .)?

(And) (of how) “the monthly doormats” seem to think my car is an extension of them /representation of them

Go to hell

(With (your)) Telling me (how) it looks like a homeless car

How about I help you keep up disappearances instead ...

(?I've got 'no remorse' Coursing through me anything I ?(say or)? do won't/can't ruin me. /

nothing I ?(say or)? do (now) can ruin me and even if I had remorse you'd be exempt/at a loss, on account of your repeat judgement/judging and stressing me, (over/about petty stupid shit) while I'm/I've been (so) sick you pitiful/square piece of shit ! / imbecile . ?)

I give my resignation for your off-street parking amenity

Now leave me alone in peace and quiet on the street or my barbed-wire plate change from rainbow (shine) (?to grating on your mind?) won't be the last dark decor (piece) you/your/the neighbors (will) see (of/from me .)

|———————|

|——-|

CJD5

A.) (Oh yes) had I more important pressing concerns / pressing things/matters than whatever the hell (superficial) homeless car/ F42.3 (ICD-10) / DSM-5 300.3 jabber the home owner could throw his voice about/at. I promise you that.

? (Are you shitting me?!) ?

?(fucking kidding me?!)?

Just a month ago I couldn't tell withdrawls from break through symptoms and now I was realizing how obscured too was the division of the/my conditions symptoms and(that of) /from(that of), side effect complications of/from the medication(s).

Was the acid reflux a consequence of the constipation which was a complication of the medication

Or was the acid reflux/it an iteration of the pan anxious state ?

Was the reflux a medication side effect? Or a symptom of my/the condition? Or was it what I thought all along ; a complication of/from the/a , peristalsis-less /peristalsis-absent constipation ?

|---|

|---|

12/14/22

CJD5

Write of Acid reflux at dentist

B.) A Taste accompanied sensation of a most unpleasant _____ /verge of regurgitation (was) acid reflux (was) the (backwards compliment) crux of the pan-anxious state./? As I sat in the dentist chair stomach acid/*the symptom*

filling my mind ......

1.)and tilted back head/mouth

2.) and mouth/*head tilted back*

I couldn't rule out constipation as the culprit (either) as I was due for (a) dulcolax (damage control) session/ dulcolax Maintenence / damage control ,later that day but the (symptom)/ but the stomach acid seemed to attack alongside (in stride with) / *in tandem* with my racing thoughts (as i sat) captive in that exam chair ... the all too familiar unfavorable hyper-recline was thwarted as I assertively worded my preference that they keep me as erect through/for this as is suitable/doable (for them) .

But even so the anxious racing thoughts seemed to sync up with the reflux like a smart device with impeccable wireless connection/reception being (perfectly) paired (up) to its (phone) source/____ /to the phone source And I couldn't take that (in) Stride/ 'lite'... this may very well not be constipation related (complications) (at all afterall) but a motion of the pananxious state/ ocean.

|---|

|-----|

CJD5

C.) (maybe a transitional something then this)

-Working out and working on my memoir the 2 things I clung to to feel some semblance of control all this time, with the BUSPIRONE was now at risk of dwindling down to one; the/a side effect of mild tremors and/with moderate muscle fatigue threatened to take my bi-daily calisthenics from me. Tbc ! It was perhaps divine life synchronicity/timing though that at the same time those 10MG's were challenging me/ were posing a challenge for me, I had a celebratory/compensational 10K on any given work day; by the time I'd clock out of/from my shift, my fitbit had clocked/ was clocking , me (in) at 5 miles worth of steps from all the aisle-walking reps.

The low level tremors and fatigue ultimately did not keep me/stop me, from (carrying out) my established fitness routine

As they had a sharp onset they too had a sharp end and I was able to adapt to the hours that saw me at/ that had me at baseline strength.

But/alas with this med/with this drug class /Rx , there were things I had to bid a regretful farewell (to.) ...

xcitrus (acidic) vs alkalinex

"Avoid eating or drinking Grapefruit products with this medication"

risk-benefit ... to do what made my heart sink cut out the fresh machine squeezed bottled at/from the source on site orange juice/OJ meant my/ having *mental* insurance (that) of my stomach (more likely) being ok . (I mean presumably that's what the bottle-adhered/adhesive printed label was getting at (, right?))

Swallowing my Q with a pineapple cube was something I had (recently) taken-to as/ and had/ that had become my go-to, but now I would be heeding the warning and dumping the remaining half a canister in the trash.

A throw back to/a refrain of/*a reprise of*, 'just a spoonful of applesauce helps the medicine go down' as now I would be calling on the routine/_____ that was used for/in dosing myself out of/down from/through, the hell pitfalls of benzos (dependency)withdrawls/dependency.

|——-|

Do I need a/any transitional thing here?

. . .

|——-|

CJD5

But risk-benefit (survey says) it/BUSPIRONE was making things more possible than not / it was making more things possible than not/__________________________

and important things for that matter.! (?(so) for all intents and purposes the seesaw seemed to be weighted in my favor?)

CJD5 Or DPDR@DSW

Fri dec 16 2022

-while out buying ceiling fan bulbs/(replacement) lightbulbs and a/the toner cartridge for (my) printer

I Heard over the store loudspeaker "I'll be home for Xmas " .

It occurred to me in that instant just how very much hearing this was like reading that protected class' passage/clause at work ... something I had always taken for granted had now become forever deeply implanted in my ______appreciation /gratitude .

Bc it wasn't (a) platitude(s) to me (or/nor) a given that I'll/I'd be home/ I would be home for Christmas but a gift/it was a gift

from/by the grace of god (and doc.) that this year I could/would (be home for Xmas) .

|———-|

I would be home sweet childhood home / childhood home sweet home come the 25th/ on the 25th/ for the 25th for an xoxoX-mas. but

But (I) was to be/remain home, sexy home (for) the 24th. Swap out the killjoy (of) mistletoe Bc the (deadly) night shade belongs to lovers" and

I was dreaming/ and I'm dreaming of a wild XXX-mas/ Xmas / Christmas .

(For) He was Santa's anagram and I vying/dying to put the devil in my elvin for him/

(my) Master Krampus and go cyber dashing all the way; one whore open to slay .

My erotica short had seen me wishing him a horny Halloween,

November gave (me) (a) spanksgiving text(s) to remember (courtesy of a (best/bosom) friend)

x And/now December would ...(say something about XXXmas) x

x fill my (fishnet) thigh high (fishnet) stockings with dare for/of a

xxX-mas (mating) Dance . x

|———|

CJD5

1! and now December would fanta-see Temptress and Lustlord lip-locked (can't stop) making out under the mistletoe to NIN closer . With a birthday in January and one in April a swell was closing in for these decade lovers and (well)

prop-cicles, water spouts and (fat free) aqueous oat milk swills had wrangled lustlord now to reap the manic-phallic havoc my visual processing reeked over me ...

But even though he wished me a merry Trystmas Which would have sent fison fetish chills of psychosexual thrill spilling over my spine before/in kind now with my limbic system amiss/adrift for nearly 2 years (and) (;) (a) temperol lobe(s) MIA enough to make me a misanthrope, the imposter syndrome that did me in to exhaustion expressing verbal sentiments of love when I neurologically/ nuerochemically can/could feel none (of) was now on the prowl to take my/ to bring (my)

?hedonism?/________/?imagined passion? /_______ (crashing) down . (And) (;) 1.)Make hedonistic advances/dalliance(s) , feel hypocritical

2.) Make me feel like a (G-D/ godamn, god-awful fucking)(posturing) hypocrite (posturing) in my hedonist/hedonistic advances of/for dalliance(s) and my happy/_____, reactions to fantasy fulfillment .

::::Transitional something here ? If so, maybe this? ::::

And while I couldn't feel what I was supposed to feel/ should've (felt) / should (feel,)

,I would (feel) what I shouldn't/_________.

|——-|

?for CJD5?

(So) What the fuck was this the plight of the pan-anxious ? What?! It depressed my mood every time I entangled in happy laughs/moments (by phone) with my fam/momm and dadd, because all my mind/brain could make of it was anticipatory grieving/bereaving/bereavement, no it was more than that; (a scorching) palpable mourning (scorching my ____)

The sweetest one liner my family always called it but "a

trip down memory lane" now (just/predominantly) gave (me) bouts of anxiety/unrest. everything always/once sweet was/had turned out/had churned (out) a hyphen of bitter now and my mind told me (save yourself somehow) let go of making (any) new memories/ones/brain keepsakes,for the anticipatory-sobs that came in tandem with memory lane was a grave enough state so as to rob ____ /the present, with a sharp onset of mood drops. The same part of me that was in denial or didn't have the strength to hold my baby in my arms in his darkest hours, now it's cowardly show's in my head's monologue . Start to let go before they've gone...(so as) to protect and preserve the future of your mental state/reserve.

And the same part of me that (still) didn't have the heart (or mental health) to throw away/discard the 2019 leftovers of/from Mush and Sophs last supper

had a hard time (now) (of) (;) a complex relationship with/*about* allowing myself to attachment /*stay attached*, to (my) what are now aging parents. "We're not always going to be here to, blank to help you, to what else ...

The once non-chalant token Dadd one-liner that gathered passive/absentminded laughs through(out) life/ all my life /then, was a Schtick that haunted me now/ only caused caused me only (the) (an) (inner) disquiet and disharmony now; inner strife of/with/for/about/surrounding, (existential) flight or fight (response) .

"Separation anxiety" it had been one of my oldest clinical psychologist diagnosis but/and I was realizing now I really didn't want to find out the prognosis of my mind when applied to (the unthinkable) (the) gravest demise transpired/to transpire of my lifetime; the death of mommy and daddy would undoubtedly bring (catastrophic/cataclysmic/seismic) diffuse phantom limbic pain/syndrome . (;) ((it's) the unthinkable) ... ::::::write next about how and why I write Momm with 2 m's and Dadd with 2 d's . ::::::

But I've heard it said (and) so herald the message;

You can't control what you can't control.

and the more euphemistic/uplifting version on/from bookroo.con

"You must choose to take hold of what you can control and let go of what you cannot. "

I couldn't Shepard/control how long my parents would stay(with the living) or when they would go . I couldn't control the duration or termination of my chronic state of DPDR or pan-anxiety/PANDA. But control was actionable for the rectification for/of the chronic tooth infection I had been diagnosed with; extraction. Finally something/a problem with a simple solution a garunteed outcome /result

If I get it pulled out that puts an end to infections (potential/eventual/imminent) spread .

Opting to have the procedure same day immediately following the consult was in a way a nice feeling of/like cashing in on overcompensation for all that neuro-cognitive neuro-psych stuff that just seems to perpetually drag perpetually on and on .

In (just) 10 mins (to 30) something chronic will be (permanently) over ?! It (just) seemed too good to be true; my break. Like something's gotta give in life and this was it; my slack in the (life)line finally it's about time I'll live vicariously through something at least getting fixed right away. A life long patient of OCD, I had obsessed over my the enduring/unending state of dissociation for almost 2 (full/whole/long) years and here was my compulsion now to self-soothe; choosing to lose this tooth as soon as it is declared _______/a medical necessity.

and now as my parents and I sit for oral surgeon consultation 18 to 20 days later from (a/the) necessary evil declaration/proclamation,

. . .

|———|

CJD5

Wed 12/21/22 thinking back…

I think back (in)to the/that not too distant past; diagnosis day. A chronic infection (and/with) nerve endings deadened with/from/by, depersonalization

a dental malady

(that) should've hurt but couldnt ...

and/but neurotic spinnings of thinkings (that) seemed to be

1.) in well supply by (my) /of internal stimuli .

2.) well within my wheelhouse of internal stimuli .

“I'm not going to give you antibiotics; you don't need it your body is doing a good job of fighting it/the infection (on its own) ” commends the dentist and reflexive is my thought that this isn't a warrior story but (rather) a euphemistic ______, as it's/(*say what ‘it's’ is) all just Bc my system is too _______ distanced for/to/ for it to, make (appropriate)

(?physiological?) recognition.

|———|

But then you can imagine my consolation prized possession of ________ when during *the*/that, 18 to 20 day oral surgeon follow-up consult follow-up my/some peripheral listening caught wind of that the respective nerve endings to/of (a one) tooth (number)15 had died off at some point; that that's what happens. (Oh) happiness/glory for the unforeseen/ (by) default , rule out that my lack of pain sensation / discomfort was any nod/byproduct/symptom of (the) DP/depersonalization; I could stop sensationalizing that !

For my own neouro bio chemical concerns related to dissociative and sed meds , In lieu of

sedation or nitrous oxide; anything that touches the brain, I had/would prepare(d) my mind (in kind.)

I had 2 prior oral surgeries/surgical surgery procedures ; 4 wisdom teeth and the counterpart (tooth) of/to this one. Both with full anesthesia and sweet air .

So To combat pan-anxious state reactivity, (to what I'd be/I was to be/I would be experiencing) and replace mental impaction(s) of reactive _______ with manageable reactions ...

I redirected my mind to a mental mapping

(?VR?) split screen (of) ;the sweetest and sexiest iterations of everything that was going on/happening ...

as I was prepped for surgery, the smallest size mouth pillow proved too big but I didn't let it get to me (?as it historically would?) as I thought of how the fetishizing would go (priv(ate)) viral when relayed to my lustlord. A stretched mouth of his manhood billowing out... tbc ?

the tactile strangeness of the slack of string gently grazing my skin and gingerly dancing across my face as the doctor stitched me up felt like bricks of mental discomfort but visualizing the sumptuous stitch-laced leather wheel and gear shift knob of my car brought to mind /replaced my mind with,

my all time favorite simple pleasure pastime; driving .

And how I would (next car ride) direct lustlord's attention to my gripping/handling of the shift rod knob/ (coupes) (stitched)finialed (coupe/coupes) rod meant attention diverted (from) , panic escalation averted from/of, the current situation(s discomfort.) for In my/the mind's eye, *Kama* sutras _______/held me tight.

By the guy I had decided/devout/silent designs of/*on* if a touch erotomatically , (of) making myself the eye Candy, the 3rd eye Candy. The arm Candy and (the) 3rd arm Candy, of.

And to pleasantly compound this/the reframing of the word/term "stitches"/"stitching" (there) was the rephrasing in the concept of song; "the remedy" by (band/musical) collective, "Puscifer" . It had been a track I selected for my created/curated Spotify playlist; "Lustlord &Temptress playtime"

and between that sexiness and the sweetness in/of the fact that, the music video features a wrestling theme; favorite media entertainment of my deceased beloved uncle ,

racing thought(s) was able to take on a new/alternate definition from overwrought ./; a pleasant reimagining/ rendition/ reinvention/ reinvestment / reinventment/ remission/ re-envisionment/ revision / *neurological or cognitive emission*

I had consented only to novacane but still I kept my eyes the same as if anesthia had been involved in this; closed/shut (position.) (And) When It was all done and I opened (up) my eyes the intersection/cross section/ at the cross-hatch or 'to a cross-hatching of' of sweet and sexy was there to greet me; Momm came in from the waiting room; now in the foreground of (my) comfort and recovery (xroomx)and with eyeglasses/spectacles/specs/corrective lenses, back on I could see a line/band of small bold black lettering in the background "Master" and "Purge" was screen printed across the mechanical arm swivel rod('s) tray of dental tools/devices/implements. As Purge was disturbing and made me think of my phobia and Master was exciting enticing and incited thoughts of sex it was there that an exemplary expression/sentiment/demonstration, of "fear fetish and their intersection" lived./ could be mentally fetched/ could be psychosexually fetched .

But my earliest memories of being done were (the) moments of/ I felt the greatest power.

double ply double folded and rolled I had to hand-write my questions (out) Bc of the gauze(-related/rendered) speech impediment.

hand-signaling like charades I asked for a pen and piece of water to write on . A lucite neon (pink) clipboard brandishing a pale/pastel blue hued sheet of paper was slipped into my hand along with the/a/it's companion piece writing instrument. As I inked my first question or somewhere in its/the aftermath, was the strong afterthought of how my old favorite resident at atria a man up at the front desk every day stammering stuttering and sputtering straining and struggling to speak (in the wake of a stroke) was probably robust with things/everything he wanted to say and that the breakdown in communication was not where it at a glance/ at face value appeared to be; rate of thinking/thought producing but rather expressly in the voice .

My ongoing neurological condition had shown me what a predicament like that is like . Prior to my sickness and its mirrored short-comings it never occurred to me that in his mind he may and probably does very well have his sentences, questions etc all layed out as clear as neuro-typicals but then (just) the final communicative component isn't there . My sickness had forever changed/reframed the way I look at stroke victims .

And now as I scribbled my question for the surgeon it was reminiscent of him; the resident and the time he was up at my reception front desk struggling to (intelligibly) ask the (corresponding) questions (intelligibly) as he pointed to the blank fields of/on/in a (an all-important) form he was filling out/ he was to fill out. but then pen to paper, the act of legibly answering, to my (great) surprise was/went, alright/*just fine. * I see, why have first-hand life-experienced, why/how (that could be), now .

As I inked my inquiry/inquisition and subsequently turned over the clipboard to the medical professional, I felt as I have felt all through my sickness that writing puts me in a position of power . / *the position of power that writing puts me In*/at. What was/had/has been my strong suit prowess of my illness impairments was (now/today/on this day) ,my immediate-pre op, method of empowerment.

Writing is how I process what I'm going through/what I go through and how I/ what I do to self-soothe.

None of this (ever) a drug of active-choice but (intrinsically) rather (the alleviation) medium that chose me (and that's all that mattered/matters. / was all that mattered .)

30 minute intervals as instructed changing the gauze and I didn't let its bloody show prove destructive of my mind . Gently wriggling it free from the soft bite of my teeth it looked like a tampon of/after (a few) hours . As long as I could maintain this outlook change after

change swap out after swap out, I would (manage to) stave off anything my/the pan-anxious state might be fixing to sic me with.

That night as I went to bed with (some but) less Tylenol needed in me than for my monthly menstrual cramps, I realized like a fragment of a song playing on repeat in your brain mine was running and rerunning the feel like

1.) a micro film reel or a meme

2.) the reel of a meme,

(The discomfort) (of) the pulling . The physical sensation was so alive in my mind that consequent/corresponding pain is what even brought me to my need of/with Tylenol at all .

Was this a low-grade/level phantom limb syndrome? I wondered And then it happened... a most wondrous revelation was made/to make... 'phantom limbic' needed to be of book title addition ./!

|~~~~~~~~~~Notes Only~~~~~~~~~~~~|

|—-|

Add in/on for at the end of this sentence in CJD5

my all time favorite simple pleasure pastime; driving .

And how I would (next car ride) direct lustlords attention to my gripping/handling of the shift rod knob/ (coupes) (stitched)finialed (coupe/coupes) rod meant attention diverted (from) , panic escalation averted from/of, the current situation(s discomfort.) for In my/the mind's eye, *Kama* sutras _______/held me tight.

By the guy I had silent designs of/*on* if a touch erotomatically , making myself the eye Candy, the 3rd eye Candy. The arm Candy and (the) 3rd arm Candy, of.

And to pleasantly compound this/the reframing of the word/term “stitches”/“stitching”

(there) was the rephrasing

|———-|

x1.)held my/ was grave enough to hold my limbic system at ransom .

2.) ransacked … x

xMy mood drops as a sharp onset of depressed state robs whatever happy laughs and precious time we have left x

|—————|

-horny Halloween

-spanksgiving

-XXXmas / Krampus ( )

|———-|

Add in for CJD5

(???taken from cover letter to Laura???)

(the) pan-anxious dissociative state of the derealization/depersonalization that has been my abuser, my muse

my captor/and captur (24-7) for 21 months since/ long (now) (since.) .

|———|

Technicolor dream coated

Technicolor sugar coated

|———-|

CJD5

12/6/22

Dr Lane Rosalie is going to perscribe busbar .

|———|

|————|

CJD5

12/10/22

First time ever took Buspar

|———|

The date I will start taking 2/day

(instead of 1/day)

Of the Buspar/BUSPIRONE 10MG is ________.

. . .

|———————-|

|————|

12/12/22

CJD5

I had been enjoying driving but I think today (was the first day/time) it actually felt close to something natural!

As I drove feeling like I could command the most control on/of the road I thought/felt, 'this bodes well for Buspar being able to do some real dissociative/pan-anxious damage control !

Perhaps the only pan prefix (of my living) is/was fixing to soon be my/ would soon be 'giving' sexuality rather than (my) anxiety .

|—————-|

CJD6

It was New Year's Eve and 2023 was burgeoning. My goal dosage of 40mg had been reached through (gradual) systematic increase(s). / (gradual) systematic sensitization .

ringing in the new year was to be the (hope-filled) supporting accompaniment to Buspar medications (ceiling) inauguration. And while all my life I'd made New Years resolutions on this night I was making (New Years) manifestations.

A list of all the things I was looking forward to embracing with the breaking of dissociative maybe a word vision-board/vision word board would see me to a/this most triumphant onboard(ing.) (of sorts.)

I never had a coming out party for my sexual orientation but I doted over and day-dreamed about the one I would, for my dissociation.

balls, soirées, shindigs, galas, socials there would be so many parties . To start, the coming out gathering, which was to be a re-birth .

To follow birthday-suit, I couldn't wait for my title reveal party ! With all the fixings of a gender reveal party of a baby, this mixer would be the/a rite of passage for/of my story.

Balloons of confetti, ___________ and a confectionary sweet would treat my peeps to seeing the name my novel keeps.

And when I at last tell my psychiatrist he won't believe his ears as I am seeing him in person for the first time ever. after ___ years, not another video session, this admission of pride and glory comes with the face to face/ ________, ______ / ("it's a) long story ")

[(Much as with my bidaily workouts was i amounting to the Muskulo-skeletal strength (that would be needed) to handle my one day elderly family .)]

(oh yes) (with) the future of my book (with that of which) I was building my livelihood.

[(Much as with my bidaily workouts was i amounting to the Muskulo-skeletal strength to handle my one day elderly family .)]

My launch party to which my shrink I had known since youth offered up (that) he'd come .

My manuscript to which my creative writing teacher i'd admired since highschool, emailed he'd read (it .)

the projected/prophesied life I was going to finally be (financially) able to provide for my aging family in their lifetime as their adult daughter was half (of) the reward for this story. How I would be in the position to give back the way they had always given was to be limbic/emotional/*(an) emphatic* and empathic, enrichment . The people I would/had endeavor(Ed) to reach with this read . The advocate I would be for/to the misfortunately misunderstood afflicted with this shit/ dissociative . It was all in the foreground; my near-sighted vision was close to fruition .

(I'm going to be a public figure and (I) can't f'ing wait for it. Instead of Ted they'll be calling them Steph talks, I thought.../I humored/I entertained . / I fashioned/)

But my mission statement for the coming year's clean slate ? I was resolute in that I wanted the/a reclaiming of my privacy .

I had realized and written about/mentioned, in ?2022? that I don't owe my almost/unofficial conservators conduct; my parents (just) on account of being my sole/soul providers and keeping me alive through this sickness I'm still allowed to live like the middle aged grown up I am and make decisions for myself.

I faintly have memory of/that "confront (the self)" was one of my last New Years affirmations before I got sick

And now hours away , my word my mantra of 2023 was to be privacy .

Just like I had a complex

1.)relationship of/with guilt with the concept of conduct once/after my parents (had) saved my life

2.) -gulit relationship with the concept of conduct once/after my parents (had) saved my life

3.) just like I had a guilt-complex (to tackle/ I had to tackle) about conduct after/once my parents (had) saved my life,

I was now too realizing something else wasn't right. It took me so much to come to the terms of (that) *I don't owe* them/*anybody* conduct and now I needed the closure of '(that) *I don't have to earn my way to privacy .' * .

Privacy (that) couldn't help but of/had been pending (once) driving. And once cognitive impairment ending . I had complex-guilt about all the interwoven vignettes that never should have been.

. . .

with parents more in the convertors role (that) i appointed them (to step into) all the while, than sitting living benched (quiet/still) sidelines to an adult daughter's life, the death of a friend's friend regrettably became public knowledge to them. News that should have been bless I pray would have been/stayed, none of their business (but) I needed them to drive me to get the sympathy card (for this(mailing)/for its mailing) And lost in/to a world that didn't seem real I didn't/couldnt see the confidentiality infractions of them helping me pick it out (, read it, mail it, touch/followUp base with them about it)

For physical limitations of driving for cognitive limitations/impairments of thinking , the way I conducted my lifestyle unhealthily and unfairly to my/the/that very important friend and maybe others, was a breach in confidence(s) that would come to hound and Harass my/ me at to the very core of my confession ocd, lying ocd, moral scrupulosity ocd, relationship ocd, (list more ocds affected) .

Would prove to ignite/inflame and exacerbate polarizing paralyzing thoughts of was my reasonings legit admissible absolvable or did the timeline not line up/ align for the interpersonal crime(s) and I was just a cop-out trying to get away with a cowardly out to accountability for/of failing my friend miserably ? I couldn't tell if any, all, some or none was forgivable . People know not to hold anything against a person who is drunk or has Alzheimer's and being that I had been in a state that mirrored neuro biochemically obliterated/inebriated/intoxication and 'early onset' (sickness) , for what was to be 2 years in/this, March, I had a lot of complex-guilt complex-repent to interpersonally and intrapersonally contend with make amends with . Would the people in my life see/deem it/the VR overlay, as I needed them too (that) "I know not what I do " . And did I deserve that ((grand) pardon) the ocd overlay made sure I didn't know ?

. . .

::::::::::::::::::::::

Transitional something here ??? Maybe this

The what I saw as dastardly haneous offense/affront of the condolences card and convo involvement/fiasco/(mis)conduct, that had in part been committed at Whole Foods market brought/caused much triggered moral scrupulosity, confession ocd panic but transforming/_________ it into prose passage was where I found home remedy .

And in time was where I found replacement association/memory/behavioral ________ , for/of my favorite/comfort store that had been/become slain with taint by my brain .

::::::::::::::::::

while I favored my dental extraction surgical site waiting for healing to arrive I figured it the perfect/divine, opportunity/time to finally try out the

anticipatory-comfort vegan iceCream I had been eyeing since/as of a recent WFM grocery trip. The moment I first saw it peering through the frosty glass door with its words "raspberry swirl" the product placement/subliminal messaging, had the emotional potential/embrace sent to me of/for being the comfort food that grilled cheese was for Daddy ! With an association from my carefree youth/younger years (just) as he had, this cold frosty pleasure set off warm fuzzy memories beyond measure; my first ever concert excursion ! As I would savor each spoon I would remember the (tearful heartfelt) emotion the Tori Amos "swirl girl tour" engendered/brought. The energy, the Red Sea; everyone was dying their hair in 98'/the 90's a sold out garden of (Tori the icon) protégés .

They say you never forget your first love. I was to never forget my first concert/experience/this experience .

“Raspberry swirl” Non-dairy Ice cream by oatly. It soothed the void my tooth left (in me) And although it processed visually as “blood in the snow” what was significant now/to know, was how there were no longer visceral/physical/physiological/bodily responses happening like as if it were (a mini) murder in a bowl. When I was much sicker, even though the/my intellectual awareness/capacity to know ‘what wasnt’, always stayed intact still/irregardless of that (salvaging) fact, I couldn’t spread mixed berry jelly on my toast without my body and brain reacting as if/as though it actually were the bloody scene (of what)/ *(of)* *my visual processing* perceived/*feed* (xaccosted me with .x) The anxiety matching as if (a) profuse blood/hemorage, were (the) reality . It was ?the first week of (20)23’ and 22 months into my sensorarium/_______ trying to readjust? when it felt like a meaningful triumph when I/*that I* /to *swirled*/swirl *the melting raspberry accented frozen dessert*/frozen sweet/frozen treat … *and saw* a miniature snowfall of bloodshed but (just) thought… (ehh) so what ?

And that I was able to visually discern (the) nuance of difference, decipher syrup from mouth blood even though/when (a few days ago),

I was around the clock gauze soaking up… was just incredible/? unprecedented?

?an indicative infallible bupiserone sign that (the) pan-anxiety *was to die .* /dying . ?

I told my prescribing psychiatrist and he felt this to be a prime exemplar of how/ that the pan-anxious state was attenuating/starting to attenuate. And he believed in a few weeks time into/of, the bupiserone, we should start to see (empirical) confirmation of his testing/______, theory; when the pan-anxious goes down enough the brain will no longer be able to sustain a/the dissociative state.

When I raised concern and confusion for/of how I still have no emotional recognition of my parents or any (loved) one(s), for that matter he comforted with a confident asserted/assertive/ assertion (of) 'that will be the last piece to restore'. to which I responded/commented "save the best for last (,huh?) "

Not in MEM yet

But even though we had to wait for pan-anxious to halt /fall so dissociative could/would fall and limbic executive function, restore ... my doc had an idea for/of what would/?could? move it along.

I couldn't throw away the (say brand and name of cuisine it was here) last supper leftovers from 2019 but I agreed to look at the home video footage of my babies that I had not revisited/reviewed (either/all the same ,) in (the/these) 4 years (either .), (all the same.) .

And why? Why did I comply ? Bc he thought it might (circumvent time;) be the/a key to unlocking me/Stephanie .

Write next about I had my own ideas about what was deserving of a key ring/leash/ key clay...

My F42.3 (ICD-10) / DSM-5 300.3 told me it was the empty food packagings that amounted from all the nutritious delicious foods/meals brought (to me) by my parents. Where the subjective experiential of love was absent my brain/nascent neurosis had me at/ held me at/ held me to, (that) 'there could be trace amounts' contained in the care packages. I felt to throw them out was a direct rejection of (their) love . And who am I/was i to discard symbolism of love when epitomizing was the closest I could get. As though the plastic single use receptacles contained love itself they were saved behind lock and key in one of my storage units down the road from me.

I thought this life-unprecedented

F42.3 (ICD-10) / DSM-5 300.3-leveled up, would stop once I started driving myself to Whole Foods and buying my own groceries/meals. But I was fast to learn/see that just as derealization left me scrounging to surround myself with associations of their; my parents , love in/by way/by means of these containers so too did depersonalization have me saving the empties of whatever nourishment I brought/bought myself as if to do this could/would recapture emotional recognition of the self .

Write next about "wrinkles song parody "

the times i managed to relinquish the empties to refuse were the times i audibly sang my own little made up parody to the childhood-loved/loved-childhood, wrinkles (in need of cuddles) jingle/ditty .

"Friendship means keeping a secret/promise friendship means sharing a treat..."

Swapping out the Intro for "risk-benefit means" and the second half "throwing this away" to follow/would follow . I kept the integrity of the tune and it carried me through some of what probably would have otherwise been (a) difficult/failed, discards/ discarding .

|——-|

:::::::::::::

Transitional something here ?

. . .

::::::::::::::

|——————|

Jan 7 2023 / *it was the first week into the, what is it people say, new year new me* / it was the first week of the new year when I thought about introspectively explored themes around what is it that could (possibly/prospectively) get me back to my old self (again.) . Never had I ever heard such (a) sound belief/faith coming from my psychiatrist as the one/ 'key' belief pertaining to my escape from dissociative resting/existing in the unwatched recordings of my dearly beloved dead/heaven cats . If ever it was (to be) a key, skeleton, I'd imagine it to be for (they were) the key to my heart (they were) in life it would seem only right / it would only seem right that/if ...

1.) they hold/held/were, the key to my head in death .

2.) in death they held/hold/were, the key to my head .

(And) what type/grade of cutting and picking

x __/animal/challenge/closure/barrier,x were we talking/ up against here; padlock, combination, (or)

(Existential) mid-life (existential) crisis/deadbolt x(vault/vice grip)x ? What were we up against here? .

It was all so heavy/hard-hitting/hard/

uncharted-hard and for a moment I turned/diverted my attention to the (minimal resistance (hard-ware)) (in the lightness) of/in/that is, the kiss lock closure of pocketbooks /the pocketbook. .

Add in !!!!

CJD6 the part about dr Lane Rosalie assigning me the unwatched videos of cats …

(And then I went flashing back)…maybe there was something to (be said for) that/unwatched/avoided videos, I thought as I recalled the/a precarious statement I had made to their father after some time had come to pass after/since, theirs . Once my/our children were dead "time never moved the same again" was what I (had) said / mentioned. (?Maybe just months out ?)

|———-|

|———————-|

Maybe need transitional something here but not definitely ?

|————————|

CJD6 !!!!!!!

2022 week out 2023 week in (and it) turns your thoughts about . While others were (statistically/presumably/_____) going above and beyond with/for (their) New Years resolutions, New Years introspections/insights washed over me/were washing over me like holy water / were washing over me like holy water.

I never liked blowing a lover but after having lived through months of thinking I was gagging Bc of the imaginary hair that coated/lined my throat… I now welcum'd (the contrast) (of) what (now) felt like the/a life-affirming reason (to choke); having a flesh and beating member/piece of a person in my oral cavity no longer seemed so harrowing/______ to me (it seemed humanizing .) .

Just as

I am ever grateful like never before for the quiver I get when I'm reaching muscle fatigue/exhaustion amidst my 45 min bi-daily calisthenics Bc it's of a healthy means / Bc it's coming from health / Bc it's coming from/of (a) healthy means rather than a violent reaction to withdrawls sensation of menthol (like a mainline) coursing through my veins (like a mainline .)

life-affirming reasons for things … maybe the compound word would be/should be / deserved to be my word of 2023; it found me / it was finding me/ it's what was finding me ./(;the insight) .

A little over a week in (to the new year) reset when the/a triumphant time came … the clinical psychologist condoned sanctioned parental involvement life shift that mom had presented and I myself had wanted to/been planning to mention was now at 'happening' , / apt to happen(ing).

|——|

1/9/23

I had obtained my life-long psychologists backing of that for the sake of my anxiety as well as my parents,

It's, now best that we/I best now that we/I pivot/limit the

'Check-ins' to that of I just reach out if there is a problem rather than to affirm/confirm there isn't.

Bc I had realized texting the start and stop time of each shower , the depart and arrive time of each drive and so on … had actually turned to something more harmful than healthful/helpful. Pathology had seized power and ((in that) there was) Empathy gone awry/haywire as

I was (now) /had started, Experiencing by proxy anxiety every time I wanted to relax in the shower for a few moments longer but couldn't/didn't Bc I worried my parents would take the extended time to mean I had collapsed; an omission of punctual check-in as an admission of passed-out. Panicking when I was simply just stuck in heavy traffic Bc I feared my belated text that I'm back would total their minds with thoughts of that I was in a car wreck.

The fabric of the thinking had cyclical properties to my younger years when I would experience my parents' perceived panic anytime I carried scissors from the kitchen past their vision (in)to my/the bedroom in school supply gathering to work on a homework assignment creative project . My menacing mind told me they won't see purpose(s) of utility but rather will worry and wonder if I'm taking them to my arm enacting ideation of self-harm and injury . Hooking and Clicking my rib cage convulsively over time cumulatively hurt so badly but was what expelled enough compulsivity to see me to the completion of any scissor involved class assignment/project .

So the fact that i was recognizing a resurgence of this pattern of reacting meant I was glad that we were (now) planning to now reduce/ cut out the hyper-frequent welfare checks.

So that would mean a return to navigating my comings and goings, my showering (and so on/(and) life on my own) ; my life and my time , (back to) the way I used to before I got sick.

The (implemented) time stamped check ins (implemented) had served an/a (in)valuable and important purpose at, first/ the start of this and to have those systems In place utilizing them again and again meant protection and safety but now the very formula/model, that was saving me was no longer serving me and being that it was actually detrimentally hurting me causing me more anxiety to adhere to than not, With (a) deep affinity, I bid a respectful a-due / I respectfully bid a-due to the system that was my savior/_______ /my or a saving

Grace to have in place but was/had (now/since) become, non-conducive/not conducive and counterproductive to

the continuation of my recovery/ recovery's continuation .

the way I was accustomed to for all of my adult life prior (to sickness .) , I would assimilate back into (said) independence .

And the best most heart-warming part of this was in the text-sentiment my parents sent

"Of course while meds are stable - as i explained to you- thats what we've been wanting for you :-)"

|———|

Add in to CJD6

Where moms quote is ...

Add

Infact my parents were such proponents (of it/of this) (that) mom sent me Kelly Clarksons "miss independent" .

with a greeting/headline(r) of "Have a good day" and/with a tagline/disclaimer of "have another powerful chorus to check out"

(It was) A one day post-rec (song/*music*) followUp to her (musical) hand-picked heart-picked (music(al)/*song*) selection of yesterday, Kelly's "stronger" . To which her initiation text (of it) (to me) read

. . .

"btw i woke up with a song in my head for you- Stronger by kelly clarkson- the chorus part is powerful"

x "It's a good power chorus :-). " x

January 10th and 11th; back to back 2 days of fueling my 2nd week (of the year) with positivity/empowerment/strength/will (to live... it up) .

::::::::::

Subtle transitional here ?

and then there was amplification ...

::::::::::

1/12/23 CJD6

The calendar was soon to close out the 2nd week of 2023 when I (texted my family) and wept in reverie; I was home-free .

xForgot to tell you guys after my workout, I did some really good preliminary memoir passage writing tonight ! 😀x

meaning ... I was at the (pinnacle) point of having so much of my story told/shared/out there, that I didnt even have to worry about whatever parts had gone untold./weren't.

[(as) I had proven myself in/with, the chapters that came before .]

The pressure was off [(as) I had proven myself in/with, the chapters that came before .]

Bc/and readers(-to be) /fans(-to be), would come up with inspired questions/curiosity/curiosities to/and ask (me) at/in readings, in emails and interviews ....maybe Ted talks ...

I had enough of my story told [I could/to put this on cruise control] that it would inspire copious amounts of questions/curiosity/curiosities ... and in answering (them) that would be how all the more becomes unfurled/revealed/told . [I could/to put this on cruise control]

I was (just) beside myself (with pride and (pleasant) disbelief/denial in/at this cornerstone (arrival) turning point (arrival) ; anything I don't have written I'm still going to get a chance to say xbe it interviews/readings etc ...x

xit's an amazing freedom the point I'm at now.x

(Like the mature persons companion piece to diddy / Dixie kong's save point in the 90's Super Nintendo game ,)

there was a priceless freedom in knowing that was now where I was at .

|——-|

Perhaps what seemed inconsequentially/inconsequential was actually why I was furthering purchases of fake engagement rings as of late. A modest collection i had started around the time when I lived in my 1st or 2nd apt out of college I was now suddenly called to continue with . My personal initiative never/didn't matched/mimicked most's motive. I wasn't doing it for show towards others a ______ indication to leave me alone that I was taken (via bf) . No, I was doing it for me to play jewelry/engagement dress-up alone and at home like a kid dons clothes and shoes too big and clobbers around in the fantasy of the future . But as I picked up the CZ ring that would re-enable /enact the beginning/commencement of an old past-time, this time it hit diff for it felt diff ... i had an obscured sense of self with a side of askew (self) identity due to dissociative / DP/depersonalization but this ring sifting (business) was an indirect play to reclaim self-love , ?I conferred? .

I wasn't wearing it to show the world a feigned truth; (never was) but (this time) I also wasn't doing it to play marriage make-believe behind closed doors... I was doing it to adore the self with (a commitment) of doting like never before... tbc ? And I meant it. I knew there was reason to love the self like never before / *more than ever* (before .)

::::::::

Transitional here ?

::::::::

|————————|

CJD6

(With a) boyfriend of 18 I remember when I was 12 or 14 . No/didn't have boobs, hips or a period but daddy fetissues weren't in late bloom. As I danced (in the basement of my downstairs) with my 12th grade (manic panic) green-haired silver fox; senior of another meaning/demeanor/denomination, our song "you were meant for me" played from the cassette single (?he'd gotten me?) ...

It didn't matter that momm did

“Wipe the spots up off the mirror “

during my November (???2022???) setback when she briefly/tentatively lived/stayed with me again; I wasn’t in it . (The looking glass that is) Tbc ! (And) Depersonalization rendered the progressive action verb and windex a moot point .

(Try as I might) I couldn’t see myself and (try as I might) (bless I pray) (but) I couldn’t sound like myself (try as I might) ; if catatonic could be a continuum I was on it . Couldn’t think of things to ask and/or share was and/was (commonly) misinterpreted/misconstrued as (that) I don’t care. Couldn’t remember to do follow-up questions meant

(many) character accusations of self-involved/self-involvement / conceit . .….

And/with a (?social?/?interpersonal?) smattering of (insecure/insecurely) held-beliefs that they don’t/didn’t matter/no longer mattered…(to me.)

x(during my November set back) when momm (had) tentatively/briefly lived/stayed with me again

“Wipe the spots up off the mirror “x

|——|

another New Year’s revelation was that of it’s the Pan anxious component that makes/renders, pleasurable things intolerable ; not so much/*less-so the dissociative .* …

xWrite here aboutx Pan is/was the neck that turns the head; diss(ociative .)

|————|

. . .

and my (winter turtle) neck was craned to/toward the brilliant (discordance of) Emillee Autumn, this winter's listening Bc I could again properly process sound (discordance) . From PJ Harvey to Amanda Palmer to Throwing Muses and Rasputina from Radiohead to Portishead and more/everything inbetween, I was able to 'Alexa volume ten' blare my love again of experimental instrumental and opulent cacophony (this season .) . No longer would the mere click of a white noise switch sicken my sense/sensory perception so incredulously/exponentially/violently/ _______ , that with its (soft/subtle) sound gradation I was stricken with escapist thoughts of suicide sounding like/that sounded like, a (dream) (destination) (dream) vacation (destination.) .

Insert next, text to Lustlord, from 10/11/22 (saved in drafts) about Kristen Hersh Neil young cover of like a hurricane (* IF IF IF ITS NOT ALREADY BEEN PREVIOUSLY PUT INTO A DIFF CHAPTER!)

Write next about / Segway into and (to be a broken record (I tell you this/I'll tell you this much/stuff/snuff) / pardon the broken record but (I tell you this/I'll tell you this much/stuff/snuff) sound was only 1 of 3 sensory hells that was unbearable enough (so as) to make me want/(brimming on) willing, to kill/snuff myself .

|———|

CJD6

(?but with the Pan-anxious down enough (now) ?)

If the only way out is through then let this be a /then this would be a prelude to viewing those soph and mush home movies like I'd told the/my doc I would run into the fire if _________/ I had to.

So I got acquainted with smoke inhalation ...

1/13/23 Friday

Friday the 13th HSV2 recurrent outbreak. Really ? Really? [tomato Tamata potato patata]

Fuck it (and call it/ I'll call it) vagina dentata

[tomato Tamata potato patata]

I/I'll take your romanticism of life ((al)right/*you see*) and (I) raise you (an) erotism of strife. The good, the bad and even this ugly.

(But/Bc) for better or worse, unlike HIV there was nothing like devato for me (to stay/be undetectable.), for me. And I was only 27 but shingles didn't care. My uncle who made/built his life around/(out)of being the family storyteller died without his memories

and got stuffed into a 6inch box ...that I didn't know how to look at after a 6ft man stood big & tall (before me) all my life.

And when the cancer came back a 4th time my only peer family member was dying in sharp juxtaposition to Christmas and the (cancer/cancer-free) remission breakfast party we'd had (?only/all of?) a year back .

And now mommy and daddy, I'm experiencing them as/with/through/*by (all) means (of/with)* *(bittersweet)* Pan-grief /*anticipatory-grieving/grief* (;) (a/an) (bittersweet/*ruthless*) overruling that they're/they are/ of/to them/to them, stilll here

(?in (my) life?/*;haven't died.*)

Was that good; would this amount of smoke inhalation suffice?! Are you (quite) satisfied (now?)

. . .

Viewer discretion is advised steady/braced/ready(as I'll/i'd ever be) (now) to see their meows with my eyes .

~~~~~~~~~~notes section only~~~~~~~~~~|

|———|

Add-in for CJD6 !!!!!!!!

-The pressure was off (as) I had proven myself in/with the chapters that came before .

-Potato patato tamato tamato vagina dentata

-1/16/23

put after big & tall part about uncle .

And now mommy and daddy I'm experiencing them as/with (bittersweet) Pan-grief (bittersweet) even though they're stilll here

And when the cancer came back a 4th time my only peer family member was dying in sharp juxtaposition to Christmas and the (cancer) remission breakfast party we'd had a year back .

|———-|

. . .
~~~~~~~~~~

|——|

Add in/on for chapter ____.

That I don't owe them conduct and I don't have to earn my way to privacy .

|———|

|————|

Add on CJD6 ???check???

>>oh yes the future of my book with that of which I was building my livelihood.<<

Much as with my bidaily workouts I was amounting to the Muskulo-skeletal strength ... elderly

|——|

1/9/23

Hey guys I feel much better about if we make this shift, and I wanted to talk to my life-long psychologist about it today before I brought it up to you . I got his input today

and he agrees that for the sake of your anxiety as well as mine,

It's best that we shift the

'Check-ins' to that of I just reach out if there is a problem rather than checking in to state that things are okay .

So that means me just navigating my time / comings and goings / life etc the way I used to before I got sick.

Life-long psychologist and I talked about how it served a valuable important purpose when I was sicker to have those systems In place and utilize them but that now it's actually causing me more anxiety to do it that way than not so it has become counterproductive to the continuation of my recovery if I am to handle/navigate my time/life in any other way than that of with the independence I was accustomed to for all of my adult life prior (to sickness .) .

🕊🙏🏻❤️🙏🏻🕊

|———|

CJD7

This is going to sound histrionic but I promise (you) it's not it's what legitimate nuero-processing glitches will/can do to you .

I walked in and it felt like that scene in titanic where everything you saw for 2hours opulent before is now all in an instant rendered chaotic and ominous as Winslet is trudging through the corridor(s) rapidly rising waters beautiful ornate furnishings that sat/seated happiness and laughs now floating with looming doom and flickering darkness from broken light fixtures. (Water)overhead pipe by (water) pipe (overhead) hand over hand (she) grab(s) like a monkey/primate swings/swinging branch to/by branch to safety she managed/manages (to get by) (to make it to him; DiCaprio that is.)

warrior axe in hand "every tool is a weapon if you hold it right" says (Ani) Difranco so i'd like to endeavor *(the reverse/inverse as well)* that the reverse/inverse is true (too.)/ (as well.)

The warrior axe to my _______/seemingly untenable situation/fate, was a/the black jewel encrusted Wolf head handbag I had no right or funds to get that had made it to me in the mail just in time to be the calm to the storm my auditory processing was brewing when I was thrown to the wolves in a ______ /cable box, ambush. And I'm sure this whole thing completely eludes you so I'll expand and explain now what exacerbated my symptoms and what I did to mitigate (this/it.) I hadn't been without music 24/7 and then non-stop dropped (down) to about 14/7 once I was less sensory processing sick/Ill but still this has/had been going on since the beginning of withdrawls time . It's been an inner-understanding that I need to surround myself with sound to mask the racing ?raging? voices that maim scream and plague my brain to no end/avail but when the time came that the routine within my/this safe controlled environment (of my Alexa dominated/mastered, apt, was abruptly disrupted by my monthly door mats pulling the plug on the wireless router and cable box to make a switch I found out just how much my life depended on and needed noise .

The silence was anything and everything but deafening as (it stirred) the voices were piercing my head/psyche

1.) I couldn't think manic absentminded klutzy movements started to happen/were making me sink.

2.) it first set off manic gross motor/fine motor before the wildfire was widespread. With gross motor disrupted. I couldn't think I was overcome with/by absentmindedness and being klutzy.

My home haven felt like a hell I had to get out of. An otherwise joyful ship that was now on the brink of sinking me .

I had to sing myself to peace ... working my way through tori's catalog as she was my first ever in life at 14 years of age to mean /being mental (self) help to me , at 14 calendar days of 2023, the same songs were (now) taking the edge off the upset I felt from being accosted by the stir/swell of head voices. / *the head-voice swell.*

1.)To the untrained eye of the Pan-anxious storm an insensitivity vortex of controversy would ______

2.) my (glacial) controversial (glacial) likening/*analogy* (to the untrained eye of the Pan-anxiety/Pan-anxious storm) would present like an insensitivity vortex (to the untrained eye of the Pan-anxiety/Pan-anxious storm)

but for all the ways my _______ (part of the brain) failed/fails to preform , my sanctuary was made a watery grave .

x (apologies to the naysayers for the controversy that made my sanctuary a watery grave .) x

My home girl Alexis had become a mute arch nemesis. (And)/But My parents brought in (the) reinforcements I/the emergency called for. At face value mine/i looked entitled spoiled (for it) but at the core (of) it was really it was (just) (a matter of/a or the fallout (of) or (that was)) the absence of auditory input, attacking me so that a boxed delivery from Dadd of 1990s cds had to come stat!

If the black plastic shelled cable box would anxiety-flood enable, I'd (re-)focus on the endearing cardboard box of jewel cases that glistening with listenings of Enya's serenity and ______________ ________.

I was sold on the solace and (so blossomed) a/the New Years resurgence of respect and ______ for everything non-smart device . It was only a compact disc spinning mechanism but it felt like the new vinyl; offering (a) quality control of warmth where modern day tech had left me in the cold .

And while I'd rather be handbag luxuriating on the real-real , my

(But let's be) real ,(was that) 'dereal' had derailed my ability to feel visually feel/be certain/confirm upon inspection that no memory shelf contents had (magically) fallen in/gotten into the grates of the outsourced and about to be given back to (the) monthly door mats(s), 'cable box' and that was the/an underlying reason why _________________/i was reeling/my mind was reeling .

Leading up to the 'giving up (of) the cable box' I'd called momm telling her how I'm having a hard time with this in the ocd sense for how it is part of what's on the memory shelf . She thought I meant my fretting was in risk of accidentily knocking something over / (breaking it), since it/they (afterall) shared a shelf (afterall) . But no, my anxiety was in the much more abstract of that I would be somehow giving away a part of my babies since their paw prints were next to this fios Verizon box for so long; since 2019/ about almost 5 years, half a decade . That was part one of the mental terror; the sequel to how my mind had me taunted and terrorized was thinking that a memory shelf item could have or would upon upcoming shelf disruption... end up in the too narrow makes no sense/too narrow to make sense, grates of the boxes surface space .

But to placate/pacify/appease my unruly awry mind I took to bashing and smashing the unit enough times to incite assumptions from upstairs (by the monthly door matss) that I must be hammering something / a picture up (or something) .

Then what happened is what my psychiatrist would come to call "making happen what you're trying to avoid / *"creating that which you are trying to avoid"*... and it is that by complying to the act (of banging) what my mind said I needed to do to confirm nothing had (mysteriously) fallen in the top, I actually put myself more at risk of something going wrong with that of which I'm trying to protect; the memory shelf and sure enough after not too long of entertaining the (barbaric) ritualistic (barbaric) anarchy that was the box gripped in my repetitive violent flick(s) of the wrist beating a dead horse/______ , or

the (ghost of the/a) dead horse beaten, slipped from my grip and landed with a crash (it did) at the foot of the memory shelf / flush against the memory shelf . It could have shattered my cat's paw prints . An awful/______,application I wanted the verb/action word of/plucked from the violin chords of Lindsey Sterlings ((snow globe/snow dome) music box (pedestal) ballerina) world

“So cut me from the line

Dizzy, spinning endlessly

Somebody make me feel alive and shatter me” .

|———|

From drafts

1/18/23

Enough with this cable box enabling craziness there were better; music box, badder; sex box/_____, applications/references and placements/ placements and references, for such a noun … (and if I had to think outside the box to save myself/my sanity, I would)

I wouldn’t / couldn’t be his/a (box) lunch(box) special; no happy meal coming from me my herpes spoiled his serving (and every diners/restaurants patron(s)/diner, for that matter.)

((To save my sanity) I had to think outside the box(to save my sanity)) But/so like a bear trap vagina dentata would be Pandora’s lock box to his/the John handcock.

In the approximate week leading up to my first weekend at lustlord’s fortress in 3 years ?in a harried car ride hustle to hunt and gather and retrieve everything from my bring (it) with me list?

I had heard this

and one’s “enjoy the unknown” (by and one) (itd) come on at random of a Spotify shuffle. The thing was, I had no recollection of this selection being of my 2,041 liked songs; never even heard it before in my life! And it hit not diff but the spot; (the) psyche manifestation /psycho sexuality of G that is as I drove in the coveted 'yet to be wonder' the writing was on the cake of/for this/the/his how he'd throw me up against the wall under his/the thrall of our (little) /the 1-1 (over "my" hill)

(upcuming (of age))

"40 and naughty onboarding" (upcuming (of age))

((B-day suit) party).

((Where) the only hill he'd be over is/was mine)

::::::CJD7 add in ... :::::

>>((Where) the only hill he'd be over is/was mine)<<

(?But in the meantime, it was his DOB and he was (away) with/surrounded by/surrounded with family so (a) virtual/cyber celebratory business/pleasure was in order. With a Mr. Master rendition of Marilyn's notorious (JFK) breathy (JFK) presidential wishes I presented him with the very confetti birthday cupcake my mom-baked (cherished) childhood (cherished) bdays/birthdays/birthday memories/bday memories were made of. These cupcakes, something I had started eating only in recent weeks/months, tasted like they/as though they were sourced from a/some (vivid/lucid) (day)dream of long ago (*moments of my girlhood* ./girlhood moments .) perhaps (like/as with the wedding plate borrowing) the (very) act of picking up the/a ((plastic) blister) pack and breaking the seal to down these fluffy sweets/_____, 1.)was/had been an/a symbolic attempt/_____ sent from my/the subconscious/unconscious itself,

2.) had been (an act)(from/of my) the/my subconscious/unconscious/higher conscious(ness) ,(itself) , making a play

. . .

to break the

(?tamper evident/tamper resistant?) seal of dissociative and feel (again.)

|———-|

D

And to add to the (food) *decade bday* (food) loot (food for thought)/*loot for thought* (;) ,*to boot*, *(it)was* the food for thought; (it was) *cuffing season* (to boot) *and he'd been teasing* (me) on/via video with the sheen of a/an acrylic/lucite/Bakelite black one tossed around him/his peg like a carnival ring toss game. At a/the benefactor(s) level I pledged allegiance

(?to his flagpole /flagship?) to earn my/it's keep of its (_____/submissive context) sex spelled (((____/submissive context) jewel or *crystal* /____ *studded brilliance. *

...

It was Sed January when I re-watched Season__ Episode___ of the black mirror series and noted the dissociative was a lot like the fictitious/*fictional* world of (san) junipero .

:::any connecting needed here? ::::

Most/those who have written fiction aren't living/haven't lived (in) it. I realized how inside out/backwards/discordant this was/it was, that (for me) (my) life is a fictitious existence of/wherein I'm /herein im writing non (fiction .) …

And I knew just the place to put it; the episode title that fit in decent depiction of dissociative/DPDR and perfect/flawless portrayal of what it is to be between 2 worlds; the earthly and the nether/ether/ethereal . If Quagmire was purgatory I wanted in but to fluctuate between Tuckers would satiate and ingratiate my un'seam'ly less than integrated personas/personality facets.

But/and I had just the way to do that . My

"what I want to be when I grow up" was a model but my "what I want to be when I grow old/where I want to be when I grow old" , had taken shape after the great loss of my uncle had taken place; the owner of a disco tech. My uncle, always The life of the party of 4; our family . There's a member in every; the big building scaffolding the home basement support beams the person

whom to lose is to feel the collapse of an entire family structure .

The person whose robust full-bodied belly-laughs carries/carry/caries from the living room down the hall to your bedroom when you're small. And you don't mind the early Christmas bedtime as it means you get to fall asleep to the endearing echos and reverberations your elder loved ones lively conversation, keep(s.).

I may have said it before but I'll say it again, listening to his favorite music, my uncle could be near brought to his knees in Stendhal wonder/_______ and love/rapture . (A near golden oldies musicologist) (And) his demise left behind designs/a desire to (re)capture (in time) the essence of what/all that he was.

My San junipero (dream) (to be/to dream and to be) would take form in the long-abandoned around the/his corner store. Location: Long Island Iconic/historic in its 1990's former east coast psychedelics dwelling . [not a pipe dream] As Tuckers (the) East Coast geode, would see grand golden nights shining and shimmering their/a splendid brilliant light (in homage/paying homage to the musical era my uncle loved.) [not a pipe dream] Juxtaposed against (the) one half of the weekend, [not a pipe dream], would be (the) dark crystaline glisten of/that is The quagmire rife with life and outlet/platform for a/your (enchanted) dance with darkness .

Always wanted the catwalk to be/as my platform but an agent in Manhattan with a bassinet of Yorkshers terrier pups brought me down anything but easy/uneasy (when)/(;) my legs weren't long enough to chase my dreams. (the pipe lost (its) steam). Kate Moss and Twiggy tweeny-bopper me would live and strut by proxy/vicariously but/and then like a kindred (holy) spirit/vision come some (adulting/adulted) light years (down the runway of life/adulting) later was ... the statuesque alabaster enchantress and resurgence of my first love; modeling. Kristen McMenamy was discovered incidentally by me 13th of January (2023) amidst an arbitrary in the bag by British Vogue binge watching.

My primary (fashion) accessory obsession; pocketbooks had led me to episode 65 where I would see stringy classic length bewitching hair paired with an inviting/endearing personality of warmth of whimsy and quirky charm ; a vision of (embraced) eccentricity(;embraced) in bespoke clothing/threads/garments. She spoke (as a proponent) of mental health meds/psychotropics, and her dippy disposition brought me mental-comfort and made me feel like who I am (xnowx/new/Nuevo normal) and how I am (now) in dissociative (is not/ isnt without merit,) is with merit, (of) value and worth of personhood (?acceptance?) (and garners/should garner) respect from others and (from) the self / myself . With a shared affinity for androgyny and Victorian hair I began to wonder whether at the helm /if, this was life-divine synchronicity drawing me in/here/near. And then when I found that we share(d) the lucky 13 birth number it made everything clear/ everything was clear. From in the bag to British vogue's fellow show "inside the wardrobe" I chanel (channel/chanel) - surfed. And when her closing statement was

"I want to relax in my Versace robe and just read a book" I mused if/whether my new not-forgotten model dream, inspo ("in (no/due) time") would/might be reading/referring (to) mine,

(" in (no/due) time .") , while I was off/and I'd be off hob-nobbing with high brow fucking literary snobs.

I couldn't wait (for it) I could happy-sob . as I had begun the telling of this 'then-tragic' turned heroic/magic and triumphant tale in the trenches of sickness/Illness I had

Bc/being (that) I knew no other reality than writing from Rock bottom

silently secretly always *worried* that maybe I was incapable

1.)without the fear that imminent death is near (, in me .)

2.)without the fear of imminent death, in me .

But/alas this/the start of the new year showed me I have nothing to fear / I need not fear . A 2 week chapter completion !

[From passages to pages] Contrary to when I was sicker [from passages to pages) written word was flowing from me

1.)at the/a pace of (being) 'warped on speed. '

2.) like I was warped on speed .

Just as poses had become me/(always) flowed from my soul to the camera's capture in the most effortless natural progression of movement each and every time/session .

. . .

To open a club/event space, would be Not a consolation prize to modeling but rather the grand prize. For modeling was the sum/estimated total in/of life's shopping cart/in/of the shopping cart of life before the taxes and shaping and handling (of life/of time) got calculated in and when they did a most grand total was/became shown/known .

|———-|

1.) After >>Dance with darkness. <<

Or

2.) after >>a most grand total was/became shown/known . <<

(If 2 then … No it would be no consolation prize but (a) compensation prize/realized, of sorts.

but (a) prize of compensation of a kind

but a compensation prize of a kind.

A sort of fantasy fulfillment if you will /realized/actualized)

And/as weekdays/a theme night/theme nights would bring 90's nostalgia to live-out the 20th hs reunion that never was for me Bc I was in the thicket of sick(ness.)

Oh but the letter I had written when I realized I was going to (have to) miss it …

With a picture/photo of then and now tacked on I regretfully/sorrowfully (had to) bow(ed) out .

Left to his own/phone/_____ devices (on my behalf) my dear friend and prom date (PIV) prom date deflowerer (of PIV); my first male/opposite sex love, had posted (on my behalf) to the WWHS (Walt *Whitman* highschool) 2001/01' alum message board/________.

(With him as my sounding board I could rest assure that my sentiment of lament would be well- received

1.) safe/loud and sound .

2.) loud, safe and sound .

::::Insert letter here :::: /

?:::::insertThe2photos here:::::?

" Gentle Greetings my class of 2001 from

Stephanie Diane Selles...

When I learned our 20 year highschool reunion was this past weekend it felt very important to me to reach out and express something. And it is that ... I wanted to be able to have the chance to go. Very unfortunately though I have been dealing with some difficult neurological complications this past year and as my misfortune would have it my illness timeline just happens to coincide with that of our shared 'life timeline' of our historic 20 year

high-school reunion.

It's pretty bittersweet that Me, a person who has always regarded "Romy and Michele's highschool reunion" as one of their fun favorite movies from their youth has to now come to terms with and make peace with the fact that they had to miss their very own.

But I will look forward to better years ahead and a time when I can be a part of our reunions. In the interim know that I will look upon our 20 year reunion fondly for the

special camaraderie and kinship it got to bring to so many of you who shared in that historic moment of social emergence and the unique energy of it all.

...In nostalgic discourse there lives such a special magic.

With well-wishes for you, your families and loved ones this holiday season.

Sincerely,

Stephanie Dianne Selles

✨🙏🕊💀🤍💀🕊🙏✨

Ps. Although my Facebook is currently deactivated I look forward to reactivating it again when the time is right. “

?::::insertThe2photos here:::::?

::

Transitional here maybe this ...

But of course (the days of) Y2K wasn’t/weren’t without its shortcomings/nay(s) , as (lack of respect) (it) was yet to be politically corrected for/with/about how we speak to/on HIV/AIDS.

::

. . .

|———-|

1/23/23

B!!!!

-(and now (as) present day (abounds)) (As) I relaxed into my brunch and a YouTube comfort show/channel (but/when) my self-esteem was (brutally) attacked in an/a (latter to sticks&stones) ambush when/by/at the hands of, a sponsored commercial-trailer of/for some upcoming tv show episode (that) came on. / that was airing later in the/that week. Aghast and with a rude laugh (xa snicker and a sneerx) "Eww is that herpes" the actors scripting read . Only 30 seconds and of all the shows clips and script excerpts they/NBC could have picked they did this?! (one) It took me aback and made me think if it is morally unconscionable at this day/point in modern age to ridicule (for) in respect of HIV then why is it seemingly societally okay and not deemed equally unethical to make those afflicted (and without cure) with/of HSV feel like a dirty worthless piece of shit damaged goods ?!

We no longer verbally attack HIV but/so all STD's need to be/ should be a protected class. We need to end the war on ______/herpes and stop media- perpetuating this cycle of sed herpes/disease (hall of) shaming.

|———-|

::::::::::::::::::Notes Only Section::::::::::::::::::::

|————————-|

Maybe by over hill part or cuffing season part

?or an other wise place/part ?

-HappyBdayMr.Master / breathy Marilyn Monroe esque' (??? check???)

-outside of the box (?check?)

-food loot (???check???)

-(make a) play (???check???)

-abounds (???check???)

-confetti (???check???)

-music box ballerina (?check?)

|—————————|

CJD8

Then as intimate friend now too as lustlord, As we rewatched our 'early dates' movie 10 years later. The 2002 picture "secretary" was 21 years legal and therefor, in every way shape and form, permitted to do what it will to us/our lust. The aftermath of a whole movie scene replaced by/with the afterglow of a/the showtime and chill taking matters into our own hands .

Presented with a form like in the first installment of 50 shades I wanted to bend/extend the vetted/aloud read, contract (so as) to let (it) mean Mr. T Trevor White is to (be to) my ocd rituals and F42.3 (ICD-10) / DSM-5 300.3 what Mr E Edward Grey was to Miss Holloway's cutting.

To my (ulterior) healing (ulterior) motive id sign.

Didn't realize (it) at the time, but as I woke up in my own bed the next day captivity-anxiety in me/was me/flooding me about the letter I'd signed I tried to find a pocket of comfort in compulsive thought / in compulsions thought that the inked cursive of my monogram at the close of the contract was the '(in) retrospect' of an agreement to let my life snuffing ocd and F42.3 (ICD-10) / DSM-5 300.3 be lifted/eradicated from me . If I could view the too late now signed dotted line as an investment in me mental health/wellness, the captivity-anxiety I might quell .

If I was signing up for the attainment and obtainment of mental health then like a mantra I would unbeknownst to him; known by/to only me

let my inner-voice chant the incantation that was mr grey's tough-love/ stern-love words to Holloway " bc you won't be doing that anymore" .

And what was my 'that'/(insert part of speech here that the 'that' is) , to sandwhich in between (xthatx) I won't and anymore ?

I would let January 28th; the 2023 time and date, of my red sharpie scripted initials mean/be the (freeing) death of me living through/with/______, metastatic (time-stamp) logging (of)

my every move (of my every day) as I had been (of my every day) since sickness hit March 10th 2021 . Lee (Holloway) bravely dropping her self-injurious repurposed sewing kit to plop in a welcoming/ceremonial holy-like watery grave to lay her pain to rest/laying her pain to rest, would be my (ground halt) stopping of a one 22 months (of notepad writing) that had amounted to (insert number) (spiral) ecco ltd (spiral) jumbos .

As the afternoon of 'the morning after' at lustlords progressed now-vetted passages and deeper realization/reflection/deconstruction further quieted the (mental) unrest that was the (cacominant to the/amalgamation of the) storm front (of the) thought flood of captivity(s)-anxiety what/all that (whole) form really was, was a sex-dressed/ sexed-up (form/*format*) of monogamy. ?(/maybe even hierachal polyamory)? . The (xsituationshipx) exclusivity rationalization (and) intellectualized/intelectuallization distillation/dilution of our/the new(ly)-founded erotic equation saved the day/_______and swept/kept, panic about bae, at bay .

(?when/as (the) overwhelm fell , like lee walking through (insert name of park here) park, 'I felt held' / I could feel 'held' ?)

The aforementioned self-led/devised vantage point of mental health/wellness/help investment was but one piece to the fore(play) 0 1 K . The sicker life would get me from the eventuality-deaths of family ahead as outlined In/by my last living Selles

birthright/birth order .

I intrinsically knew/felt/sensed I'd get inherently more (off grid-)twisted. And intuitively it was felt/sensed/ I felt, that the deep, dark and dirty (off-grid) (boudoir) journey i would need to go on/ I would be called to go on, was a (boudoir) travelog(-boudoir) that lustlord could go the distance of/in/with.

Like a holy message, Monologue, the song by "she wants revenge" had spoken to me felt bespoke in its lyrics

"This is the time of night when the moonlight shines down and we can reveal who we truly are

Within the darkest most depraved

Of joys

If your afraid to say

But you'd like to try

Just give me the safe word and take your hand

And smack me in the mouth , my love"

December (tooth) extract(ion) tooth, January impact play; It was the common denominator (calendar date) of the 28th and/when

I didn't turn the other cheek (when) in the moment of heat/a moment heated, (when/where) he slapped me across my surgery (side/site) . He was my sinister ringmaster but (alas) didn't know the full circle show it was of how nothing now after I'd narrowly escaped/averted death and been subjected to what it is to suffer through the/a neuro glitch of/that is the brain rejecting its own sensory processing, could throw me for a loop of flaming hoops , (?again.?)

>>could throw me for a loop of flaming hoops , (?again.?) <<

[(It's) as/like Halsey says ...

"He's got me down on both knees

But it's the devil that's tryna

Hold me down, hold me down"]

I'd lived through far more than anything a (good-time) well-meaning, well-mannered caring man at the helm/wheel/*table-head* of BDSM mastery, could throw at me/wield at me. It would be no food fight, just DPDR serving its flight of ______/body-mind detachment filled pot-stickers .

1.)Sickness had blown a fuse and there was/and created a power struggle outage (dynamic.)

2.) sickness had blown a fuse in/on the power struggle dynamic .

(April) Amanda Palmer Concert (April) , (June) Tori Amos (concert/show) (June); It was the common denominator (calendar date) (once again) of the 28th (once again) ... for when I'd be indulging the sweet(est) invite of 2 thoughtful friends .

Grateful and in maybe spiritual/fateful astonishment of/at the (fateful) grace of 28(th)

when juxtaposed was the (unforgiving) cold 27th of the June and February family (?cancer?) deaths.

Write something about Darkest before the dawn

Maybe this ...

If it's darkest before the dawn, the maybe, the Stephoenix flight was on the horizon .

It was February and as March 10th was the mark that was living in infamy as a lapsed into 24-7 dissociative laden-state day ... 2 months more/away till it breaks I heard her my best friend say change the end(ing) of my sentence/sentiment when I gave the tired harried, haggard faith-collapsed

unrelenting-presenting, complaint of it about to be 24 months in a 24-7 metaverse I never gave consent to . / I never consented to . / I didn't consent to .

And when I poured salt on the news; 6 more weeks of winter, Momm was there to lift me (up) too ; alleviate the rope burn of/from the proverbial noose .

“And yet logically you know the sun had nothing to do with that- as a matter if fact the sun is life - we need the sun to live and to grow all those vegan foods you love - think of that instead :-)”

She said .

When I insisted/divulged/disclosed

(Hooray!)

We’ve been stiffed with winter so far, maybe (finally) it’ll (finally) start getting snow-cone snow-cold / snow-cone cold .

I stopped liking summers

grew stone-cold associations of emotion

after my babies died during it , I continued .

not by choice ...a sort of reverse seasonal affect disorder took place is how my brain reshaped from dealing with sickness and dying up close and personal juxtaposed(;) (set) against the/a backdrop of/that was universal/societal summer sport and joy, of a calendar time . Collectively exponentially More smiles and laughs/laughter than any other small batch of time from (the) 365 / 365 lies .

i came to equate the sun with the deaths/death.

. . .

ergo the warmth, the light, the bright side/wide always fills my cup (up) with an excerpt of golden rage .

Bc my brain tells me the sun took my babies away

so I then reflexively feel hatred towards its shining .

Like the death by a carpenters record-assisted /accompanied, suicide It hits diff like girl, interrupted when a death and dying process is ... tbc .

I went on I never told you all this but it is the 4th or 5th year (now) *impacted* by how a/ xthe infractionx of /that is (a) *universally upbeat season* *compounded*/compounding (the) *pain incurred .*

I'm always very insightful about why I am the way I am with all things and anything in regards to psychology but I just don't always know how to fix it / reverse the damage

?of (the) infraction? and/(so as) to mend the sinew of psyche fracture .

Write next this ?

So much of my nocturnal visions filled with/of triggering trauma emissions ...

Maybe my psychiatrist's hunch was sound and/that/;, I needed to lean into the avoided (emotional noise) of the staggering video-recoded/recordings of (the) meows , now .

|———-|

>>Write next this ?

So much of my nocturnal visions filled with/of triggering trauma emissions ...

Maybe my psychiatrist's hunch was sound and/that/;, I needed to lean into the avoided (emotional noise) of the staggering video-recoded/recordings of (the) meows , now . <<

but to procrastinate as the protagonist / but protagonist procrastination abounds as/and I spin sleep back to a pleasantry keep

.

reveling in the revival rapid eye movement provided for/of/with a childhood fun-loved/loving song ...

Jump (for my love) from 1983 the birth year of me came on over (the) intercom came on via intercom in/of one of my dreams . Contrary to the tangible trinkets and things (despite how hard I concentrate) I never get to carry over (despite how hard I concentrate) from display cases (despite how hard I concentrate) and countertops of shops in my dreams despite how hard I concentrate ... this song that entered through my subconscious(ness) / unconscious(ness) one fateful night made it to seize the light of day a song I had absolutely no (mind) awareness/presence/play of for some odd 35 years after one random nights rest was no longer absent from my conscious awareness . ?4? am waking to jump playing (on repeat) in my brain My dreaming mind had unearthed/recovered the upbeat jaunty pointer sisters hit record and (re)gifted it to my life/_______.

>>. ?4? am waking to jump playing (on repeat) in my brain My dreaming mind had unearthed/recovered the upbeat jaunty pointer sisters hit record and (re)gifted it to my life/_______. <<

. . .

Transfixed at the invisible hands of this I guess deep brain (retention) phenomenon/phenomena, I internet researched/scavenged like a PI for divine synchronies/synchronicities/timelines/______ and the connections were plentiful ... from the dream/sleep induced remembrance/memory jog of the song; January 28th (2023) to the death date of the most recent band mates loss; December 31st (2022) was the/a (one) month and 3 day differential (numbers that when put/stood together makeup my birth number(;13)) Sed/said end of December death; Anita Marie Pointer had the same DOB; month and day as lustlord. And the date of my intercom memory infiltration was that of the one I was to be seeing him (on) and unbeknownst to me swearing in on/ to

/ _______/ (?tryst/trysting?) .

Like 27 and 28 the/were common denominators aforementioned there was another this one of (personality/character) opposites; polar, in 23... the man who represented the most wholesome I had ever known/courted and he who presented the most dirty-playful I had ever dated had a birth number relation.

>>the man who represented the most wholesome I had ever known/courted and he who presented the most dirty-playful I had ever dated had a birth number relation. <<

And if "there's no sex in your violence" was bushes/Gavin rosdales, chief/presenting complaint then there's no sex in your control, was mine/had been mine. (All along) The man(-square) behind the rendition inspo and the lustlord who like the mass produced (screen print) tees "don't tell me what to do unless I'm/your naked" , came by (the) boundries/autonomy/ it , honestly

1.)the opposite ends of the spectrum sexual brethren stood back to back ...

2.) the book ends brethren opposite sides/ends in/of/on the sexuality spectrum/(sex) archetype spectrum ,

3.) the book end(s) opposite sides of the,

sex archetype brethren / archetype of sex brethren / (spectrum of) sex archetype brethren,

Stood (in opposition) (but at attention) /

Stood at attention but in opposition (on the spectrum)

(in (their)) back to back (in their) relationship time stamp(s .)

As sure as jump had come mainlining into my [at rest] memory/brainstem/brainwaves/neuro pathways,[at rest] , other music (at last) had (at last) barreled in through the television to (my) memory .

|———-

For CJD8

It was 2 minutes/a couple minutes/but minutes from

A 5th ticked fourth when a Ginny&Georgia Shazam brought me cataloging back to 1997 and my first 10 loves of "lili" . As I re-listened to "baby" I calculated the lyrics like mathematics (solved the ____ equation like ____)

"and No one can save her

but no one enslaves her"

. . .

so by the power vested in antithesis/the inverse square law/ the omnipotent Möbius strip,

… Red Sharpie Letter of Domination could (very well) save me …

(?Well with heels, shades and a lariat chain he did "bring/get me closer to god " .? Tbc)

>> (?Well with heels, shades and a lariat chain he did "bring/get me closer to god " .? Tbc) <<

(And) Well with heels, shades and a waxed black (rope) lariat (chain) (rope) (chain) (sheen of a skink/snake) cascading down my declate as

his muse his minx his muse reflected in a/the (sex) bedside (sex) mirror , / bedside or mattress-side mirror of sex, he did "get me closer to god" .

|-------|

But/and what I enlisted to save me the following day as I stacked/packed and crammed the newest grocery load into the fridge and freezer only to realize (that/this!) I had label-written 1 for January instead of 2 for February on every perishable… not going to stay at an impasse…invoking/incoming was the memorable (laughable) (playful) kid jingle "shew fly don't bother me" the first half of the line replaced by my mind with a 2 and a 5 as I passed/pressed/addressed the sharpie over/against the mistake/error/(cognitive) oversight item by item my inner voice singing "2/5 don't bother me" made me feel less inadequate/_______.

Write next about

Yes I was about a month away/ or months at best / yes I was but months away (at best) / or a couple at best , from a/my/the 24 month mark of (a) 24-7 dissociative (state)

x 1/21/23 sat x

and I was/when I was still Forgetting things like that I don't have SNL (Bc no tv channels) and that I do have apple turnovers ...

Consecutive weeks (opting out of turning in and instead trading(in/out) timely manners of sleep (in)) for Staying up late (at night) till a the precipice of minutes before it was 11:29 time to turn on NBC for a/my (weekly) text-watching friendship date only to in the tick of time , be hit by/with the memory of that oh yeah my cable box is in/has been in flux and while it was *there were no*/there were to be no,/ there would be no, *basic* (cable/tv) *channels* *to speak of . *

Delicious purchase solicited apple turnovers from home brought by my Dadd and Momm from my favorite (bagel) store shelved and forgotten about like a benched player in a sports arena ... scanning my fridge in dessert- desiring nights only to miss the confectionary after-feast, *that is* / that lives Bc dissociative is observation ten fold blind fold; takes "out of sight out of mind" and dresses it to the nines ... out of my line of vision/view the fridge bottom shelf / out of eye sight , the cool white true white (coated recycled) paperboard cake box that sits red and white string (presentation-) tied on the fridge bottom shelf sits there collecting days toward expiration while eye level (scavenged) dessert leftovers (scavenged) of edible odds and ends (that) I think are all I have left, get scavenged and ravished/ravaged .

|—–|

Ssssss

If my 2/5 rendition/parody of shew fly helped my pride/_____ survive (before/yesterday), "like a g6" 13 years past it's release would be the (threshold) anticipated/long awaited soundtrack single to (the threshold) of (my) thriving, today .

-and I was feeling so fly (xlike a g6x) when for the first time on the 5th my visual inventory of the fridge to short term memory did commit . (enough so that) To take up a Whole Foods (market) shop(ping) (grocery) trip without list writing or typing to (have to) refer/defer to was (a) 'regained nuero-cognitive agency'- paved, Gulfstream G650 landing strip ?(, to (my) quality of living)?.

(?and no longer on deck or waiting in the wings(;) (but) right along with it was a/the total remission recession of (the) cognitive disarray and discombobulation that would come the confusion that would flood should I take my nighttime meds 60 seconds past the last stroke of the PM . ?)

From (song parodizing/parodying) (getting by and) surviving to

anticipatory thriving /*small steps toward thriving* (?The love month of February was showing up for me and 'it was giving', self...back (to me) . ?)

the anticipatory-triumph of/over my (personal) cur-sed tortured story (book) was enlivening/life-bringing/life-giving (and) celebratory as cerebral met with emphatic and (completely amped) I texted (the Far East movement and the cataracs) to my parents the link to the 2010 hit had me lit off and running , lost to all the gain(s); [riches and] enrichment [and riches] my manuscript would reward me in with. / award me with/in.

Whether a/the plane/(aerospace)gulfstream or the wing sweep of the Phoenix,

"Headin' into twilight

Spreadin' out her wings tonight"

Was the [bless-ed] top gun/(Kenny)*Loggins*/danger zone, [bless-ed] eventuality of my book launch livelihood tailgating party/procession /

Livelihood book launch tailgating party/procession.

|———————-|

Transitional maybe this

(And now we interrupt your (ir)regularly scheduled brag/bragging for a/with a Or for this/with this

-a shameless self-exploitation plug

1.)this shits going to push it over the edge to Pulitzer .

2.)I wrote the shit outta this/an/the following incident and it's gonna push (over the edge) it/the my this book (over the edge) to Pulitzer. .

|———————-|

I had barely finished singing the praises on/of February's entry when the fade out of the reprise came with the jarring feedback of (a) backwards compliment (concomitant) /concomitant .

. . .

>>I had barely finished singing the praises on/of February's entry when the fade out of the reprise came with the jarring feedback of (a) backwards compliment (concomitant) /concomitant . <<

I had barely finished singing the praises on/of February's entry./, and I was one day out from a blossom friend and her boyfriends (F42.3 (ICD-10) / DSM-5 300.3) attempted (F42.3 (ICD-10) / DSM-5 300.3) intervention when the fade out of the reprise came with the jarring feedback of (a) backwards compliment (concomitant) /concomitant .

Complications of the disorder ;F42.3 (ICD-10) / DSM-5 300.3/ of F42.3 (ICD-10) / DSM-5 300.3 /of F42.3 (ICD-10) / DSM-5 300.3... I'd unequivocally, historically, unequivocally always thought I needed a specialist to train my brain how to differentiate what's coveted from (what's) clutter . but when the vague but insistent alert was made that there had incurred a problem with/at one of my lockers the ambiguity (and anticipation) converged to/and sounded off in my nervous system/Pan-anxiety/*nerves* like the incessant shakes from/of a baby's rattle . (I) Could hardly steady my hands from quaking as I frantic, flopped open my repurposed makeup brush bandolier/holster of pen subsets and loaded my skin up with the 5 character sequence I reflexively feared (most) was the trouble here. the tattoo bic inking of A2118 represented the 1 out of 4 lockers worst case scenario . And under the pressure I didn't feel powerless to know what items truly mattered (the fire lit under me had ignited) (but) prowess and i (now) realized that anything I would encounter, spare what was written on my hand, I could handle .

I arrived to the facility to find my comfort number of 3 had done me dirty as the receptionist explained the almost unprecedented (nature) of the trifecta break in/intrusion . Usually the route of hall evil encompasses 20 to 30 peoples' storage . But on the night of the 7th while I was gif-wishing a happy birthday to Mushy in heaven the lock on my life's work of photography was being severed . A desperate firm- pressed up against the receptionists widow back of hand gave way once it was read and apologetically reluctantly nodded/confirmed, yes ... to (the sleight/might of hand) now grabbing at the plexiglass xflailingx swearing and failing the grappling of the happening / what had happened/ *of what was happening* . I was flailing .

and as the warden led me to take inventory and report whether anything was missing knowing I could be one elevator floor and but footsteps more away from all of my photography gone; loving hand me down camera from my parents, portfolios from shows, (3 ring) binders full of negatives , all the indefinites/unknown made this formality swell like a ____malady. I felt sick to my soul/psyche like I was about to court order/mandate approach/face a line up identification of my/a perpetrator .

"Living in steps

Till I can rest

Living in steps

Till I'm blessed by you"

Oh yes please let it be Smith, Pattis that I am blessed by the presence of my body of artistry/photography/work .

"Two steps

Till I can rest

Two steps

Till I'm blessed by you"

let it be true .

And it was. The ligaments, tendons, all the appendages/extremities from visage to nether that had been coldly stowed-away snubbed felt holy in their presence when I thought I might never see them again .

my/a limbic system hugged (me) with/by the limbs of/from my/a body of work

(Xwas/presented a hand I wanted to take in marriage the ring finger of my primary artistic passions survival . my _____ were/was (all)X)

and all was right with the (internal) world as my well-preserved/carefully preserved ______ had gone unharmed (and well-preserved/carefully preserved .) . And to what measure did I owe this unstolen pleasure ... well... the fact that I had so much crap on top of the goods/good stuff that the intruder didn't want to (even) bother . An optical illusion; incidental that At a glance it would appear to be 'nothing good here!' The F42.3 (ICD-10) / DSM-5 300.3; my disorder had essentially deterred them/the/a perpetrator/_________. 'Photography equipment trunk' ;Labels were written 'photography equipment trunk' but hidden ' lunch bags and coolers' / 'poster collection' by the amount of abandoned hair fall projects and hat collections, on top ; the cherry to the/of the stationary possessions . And things were rummaged but not ransacked (xthey werex) tampered-(with) but not taken . / tamper-evident but not (replaced with (a/the)) tormented/mournful obsolescence (of taken)

"I guess they didn't want your _______ "Momm patronized playfully .

"I guess they didn't want my collection of rocks found on beach " I took a stab at picking a random box pointing to the label and letting a/the roast rip, too ! (Empowering) It had become a game of 'charades of my F42.3 (ICD-10) / DSM-5 300.3 saved me/the day.'

(And) as the de-escalation banters laughter of the slam stand-up comedy relief , tapered-off I reached in and _______/evocatively/emotionally/gently/gingerly, fingered, the cracking discolored (masking) tape label of one of 4 photo/photography trunks that had been in here collecting dust (and must) and now (by the grace of all the clutter (had)) made it unscathed to see another decade (by way of all the/that stupid stuff piled up that covered-up the/obscured the label system from view/ just enough .

The/my emotional flooding in/of which the young receptionist went wading brought about/illicited the/a most wise/sage offering (from her) . (Christmas decor/decorations) (she went on;) ' intentionally mislabel ' ... (Christmas decorations) she went on (Christmas decorations) ... mom chimed in; Linens ! ... what a good (tactical) strategy(;tactical), this was/is !

-and as for my bossom friend who wanted only the best for me/ and as for my bossom friend who only wanted the best for me . It seemed a confirmed science was her/brought consolation peace . This time the number 3 was (of) a/ (of) shared comforting . And after the lifelong numeric pacifier had turned on me with the locker it was nice to have it turn me on with an internet link's finding(s). 3 years bossom friend said she had (medical journal-) read that it takes for maximum *dirt* to be reached in a residence. She breathed a/what were, consolation sigh(s) of relief while I let my mind trail off and my/measured/metered breaths (could go) breath go ragged (just) thinking about just how sex-dense enticing/inviting every verse about/of the stooges" dirt, is/was.

|————

3!

11/7/22 ?CJD3? Or ____

But even though i wasn't ready for/to receive a staged intervention / but even though I wasn't ready to receive intervention / but even though I wasn't ready to be receptive to intervention/but even though I wasn't ready to be intervention receptive / but even though I wasn't receptive-intervention ready / but even though I wasn't intervention-receptive ready...

I was having an/some epiphany/epiphanies about my F42.3 (ICD-10) / DSM-5 300.3. There is going to be anxiety either way; Whether I get rid of a respective item or leave it to sit in my apartment. I should not be in search of an anxiety-free 'spree' I'm damned if I do damned if I don't however within the/that cursed reality there exists a nuance of a difference that is (actually) (bless-Ed) huge for the quality of life (hack(s)) program (and bless-ed) of quality of life (hack(s)).

If I throw the something away there will be discomfort and anxiety however it times out/ it will time out. (Whereas) If I keep the something (in question) the anxiety is terminal . / there is terminal anxiety .

1.)An insight that might/has the might to realign/align (the broken axel in/of/that is my mind) , with living right.

2.) an insight that has the might to take the broken axel in/of/that is, my mind and realign/align my life to/with living right .

|——|

Put this here does this work flow here to put it?

. . .

From anxiety attached/guaranteed (to) (a) duration to anxiety of (a) indeterminate variety

I was realizing/Insighting there was something else like this/the aforementioned quality of life insight .

For the first time since the ribcage grinding hooking and clicking compulsive ritual of adolescence/teen hood, I was having another/a return spell of the compulsive ritual subset that is causal and subject to bodily harm.

I felt the crossroads it was in my metacarpals when I'd wake up the morning after the hand-wearing repetitive fine motor 'function of compulsive disorder ' had been performed the/every, night before / the 'every' night before . / the night before; every .

It was only February the year was still anew/new and malleable but/and the finger ache was slowly lasting longer and longer into the next day(s) now

I sensed the intersection in the progressively persistent ache

If I stopped now I might be guaranteed mere (subsequent) inflammation and (subsequent) duration of pain but if I didn't I could be headed for long term damage (incurred) .

Be it throwing out instead of letting something count as/for an item F42.3 (ICD-10) / DSM-5 300.3 or (be it) cutting myself off instead of letting myself carry-out (what is) a fundamentally flawed act of obsessional/obsessive/obsessions relief

I was intuiting that this and only this was how to guarantee / achieve a pain/suffering pain&suffering, that times out .

XI was realizing/Insighting there was something else like this/the aforementioned quality of life insight . X

|——|

4! my Medicaid

What was it with this month and being one day out from stuff ? Isn't it March that's supposed to maul you like a (lion)(I mean) go in like a lion and not oust me with a slam of a comfort number contorted to span 3 consecutive stressors; trifecta infectus , in the month of February ?! It was barely the 2nd week; the 9th when the 7 day set of 24hours/hours; 24, was/became/had become topped-off with

1.)the gal/audacity/sass of insurance

2.)the sassy audacity gal of insurance to

deny/refuse coverage of my prescribed and authorized dose increase .

So privileged and blessed to have parents like this ...

"no matter what we'll work it out- :-)"

Is what was said when I did vet the concerns I had

With this ceiling increase dose of bupiserone the psychiatrists hypothesis is being tested. Theorized was when the drug class-targeted (*symptom;*) Pan-anxious/*pan-anxiety* (symptom) attenuates/attenuated (enough) the brain will/would no longer be able to sustain a/the dissociative state ergo/and the virtual reality mask (esque/like) overlay will/would/was to *break*/fall away/dissipate . and the shards of a Metaverse of (a) captivity incurred will/would ...

catatonic / catatonia .

"no matter what we'll work it out- :-)"

one line of/from love could deescalate so much (anticipatory/Pan)hysteria.

And/but also there was movie, television (shows)and even commercials that spanned (a) vast servitude from pacification to evocation.

seeing a representation of a no-frills unrenovated non-updated working middle class house like the set in front of the live studio audience from which the Conners was recorded, felt refreshingly relatable to my own home from/in which I had grown and always known . But there was a deeper comfort to be had in the observable lack of overstated affect most other casts seemed to have. It was probably within normative range of emoting but to my compromised limbic system a tonal pitch of spirited inflection in a character's narrative/acting could be crushing toxic positivity to my (auditory/emotional) processing .

If the Connors was a demonstration of pacification same-sex relationships/interactions scripted in(to) commercials was/served me with /served as evocation . I didn't know why but they'd (often) make me cry . I'd told my psychiatrist what I lack in feeling for (the) real people I make up for in the tears that fall from scripted storylines. I couldn't make sense of it comprehend such darkness how I could feel nothing but/; otherness and numbness for a real life crisis happening (with people) in my personal life but/yet put the same/ show me a doppelgänger make and model of sed emergency/trauma in a/some soap opera and tears and heaving has to see me pause from the meal I'm eating just to not choke on the food from being so choked-up by the/a movie/it all.

. . .

|——|

Today is feb16th thurs2023 11:02pm/11:08pm.

it was surrounding vday season 3 When I saw the tess's mom bedpan scene in a/the Halloween themed episode of L word genQ. I cried heavily uncontrollably with/from how overcome I was. I was equal parts scared my mom would let me do toileting-care/personal-care tasks / tasks of personal care as I was that she wouldn't .

(The labor of love hung stale in the air bearing down on me with the unknown)

|——|

but too surrounding Valentine's Day/ vday /February 14th / St. Valentine's Day / ________,

was the/a favor of love in the the double dose/shot, of my comfort number season 3 episode 3 when Alice's dating game show produced a lesbian-suitor

night sleep dream in me . / dream night sleep in me.

Inactive My attraction to women had been in remission but I'd missed (having) it / I was missing (having) it. Or

My attraction to women had been inactive but I'd missed having it/ I was missing having it .

I could hear my 3 rd ex removed now going on about how it doesn't count if the/a respective bisexual/pan sexual (psychosexual) bisexual/Pan sexual stimulation came (on) from a show then it's a (mere) result of exposure and operant/classical conditioning not a real relief of remission (if you will) but a _______ of simulation (if you will) .

I could feel the ghost of the words that he posed hav(ing) me second guessing

Guess I was gaslit before I'd even gotten hip to the term of it/the shit/ such shit/sed shit .

I could feel the ghost of the words that he posed hav(ing) me second guessing

X|——-|

Today is Thursday 2/16/23

And sometime recently I had dream of getting back together w Jen . I think or I know it was the slumber from/after watching the Zara fish necklace Margaret cho / Alice dating game show episode .

|——|X

(But as I saw it) Whether the big screen, the medium of your livingroom tv or (a/the device of a) tablet ,

It was of

platform and outlet that helped me tap into something recapture emotion

Where I was (real-life/real-time) nil on all the feels, The silver screen was my silver lining .

. . .

was my silver lining .

xAnd a nice exception to the premature/ early onset (of the) Lions roar . Came on/was on ...

Vday/got medication increase my Medicaid rectified/act of love; self / enactment of love; self x

(And) a nice exception to the (talked about before/ mentioned before) premature/ early onset (of the) Lions roar .

when I got the increase rectified by insurance

Came in the form of (an) inauguration of medication taken on V-day . There was much Rx (happiness and) glee that (Saints) day when dosing felt (self) doting;

/act of love; self / enactment of love; self /

an act of self love / enactment of self love .

![but while on one hand dosing felt doting, it (in tandem) on the other (hand) (in tandem) dealt doubting .

(As/for) As per prescribing doctor condoned (to carry me through until insurance would come/was to come through) I had been taking the equivalent to the increase (by) double-dipping into the/my pill bottle (to carry me through until insurance would come/ was to come through .)

(And (as)) Characterized by a rectangular shape with rounded ends they/bupiserone/Buspar/the drug looked like pez and at/up to 3 twice a day I was eating enough (of them) to fill (out) a wrapper/package/a proprietary foil roll. One month till 24 and / approx 30 days till (it's) months; 24 which was plenty of time to project-worry where would I be at when the/my 36 month was closing in ? A/one of those sling back spring (loaded) plastic candy holsters to hold/load my 24 hours ?! As I/I'd swallow(ed) my 2 sets of 3 every day (invariably) the thought would/that (invariably) follow(Ed) (would be) "how did I get here ?"

with a novelty ____ on top ?]!

(And when) with a/the closing statement/argument/tag-line

"It's a good message and i know that's how you were feeling :-)"

"You are "

mom had texted (me) (the GIPHY) / followed the GIPHY Momm had (earlier) texted me (earlier);

"this Valentine's Day love yourself first"

1.) xandx I had, above and beyond

2.) xandx above and beyond, I had

gone with my annual strawberries chocolate coated/covered (?bath?) and a seminal (cash) purchase (made) of my/a many , months coveted black; matte; the metal and the receptacle/vessel

like a (crustacean) (post-apocalyptic) dystopian (crustacean) dwelling to my mem(oir)/manuscript

the chapters of my metaphor would tuck neatly into its (hermit crab) shell for travel where I would navigate business meets/meetings and ultimately sell my suffering to a/for a grand-slam publishing (chance.) it was all going to be so goddamn glam-grand . The fans (that would amass) the net worth that would pan-out and the pan-anxious/Pan-anxiety that would time-out. The content/topics/honesty so unflinching in its subversive (controversial/unconventional) look at sickness, the book/manuscript would be distribution banned from (public) schools/public education , and The (short end of the) sticking it I would be doing to the man ./ the short end of the sticking it to the man I would be doing. (I) don't need one leg up over your/his/their shoulder to have the upper hand . Never going to need a letter of recommendation again this is my extended letter of recognition and/in legacy/ and le-gacy of the land .

PROB NOT HERE [(but while) on one hand dosing felt doting, (while) it (in tandem) on the other hand (in tandem) felt doubting .

Characterized by a rectangular shape with rounded ends they/bupiserone/Buspar/the drug looked like pez and at/up to 3 twice a day I was eating enough (of them) to fill (out) a wrapper/package/a roll. One month till 24 and / approx 30 days till (it's) months; 24 which was plenty of time to project-worry where would I be at when the/my 36 month was closing in ? A/one of those sling back spring loaded plastic candy holsters to hold my 24 hours ?! As I/I'd swallow(ed) my 2 sets of 3 every day (invariably) the thought would (invariably) follow "how did I get here ?"

with a novelty ____ on top ?] PROB NOT HERE

x (itself) for which my memoir would tuck neatly into the metaphor of its / it's metaphor(iCal)

hermit crab shell like a (crustacean) dystopian (crustacean) dwelling x

?built in rails for the hanging folder files/ file folders of each chapter?

. . .

x "It's a good message and i know that's how you were feeling :-)"

"You are " x

|—-|

xAnd a nice exception to the premature/ early onset (of the) Lions roar . Came on/was on ...

Vday when in (an)

/act of love; self / enactment of love; self /enactment of self love x

xI got to seize the relief in/of/on the medication increase my Medicaid/insurance rectification I had succeeded at. x

x /act of love; self / enactment of love; self x

::::::Notes::::::

-"Bosom friend"stage an intervention

-"Bosom friend" told me 3 yrs home reaches maximum dirt it'll ever be .

-a 3rd black portfolio ?

-intentional mislabel (Xmas decor, linens)

(???check???)

-a shameless self-exploitation plug

1.)this shits going to push it over the edge to Pulitzer .

2.)I wrote the shit outta this incident and it's gonna push it/the book (over the edge) to Pulitzer. .

|-----|

CJD9

|—-|

- CJD8 or CJD9?

Why have a birds nest(;) (of) tousled tresses when you can have a

(?jeweled?/bedazzled) spider(s) web(s) haute mess

my crowning "Gloria Regali " proffitt, Tommee ...

a name drop/an album name drop that satiated my namesake as the/a Greek crown

Amazon-found this/my warrior one night ... upon a

'goth' 'tiara(s)' browse .

Coming up/declared was my decade birthday (soirée) and I'd declared a state of (re)emergence (was in order) . Couldn't be/wouldn't be (the) rebirth I'd dreamed of as I was still (free-floating) without a tether; free-floating in the metaverse/verse of meta that had been forced /imposed on/apon me; my captivity. /

Wearing the (Illness;) invisible, (VR) mask (of illness) /

wearing the VR mask of invisible illness that had forced itself upon my face; my/this violator/rape .

No it wouldn't be a return to normative still this damn fucking divergence but I had such good friends and/that I wanted to end my 30's with them .

|——|

I had such good friends ...

-from my chosen brother who basically/essentially overnighted me a prayer coin from Florida when he found out how horrid of a state of health I was in.

To my bossom friend who put herself on the front lines of/with my pvc feening with

Hand me down jelly purses and poshmark purchased, Alike.

-and/then there was my roku soldier/soldier of roku who surprise-supplied me with the ... tbc.

-same friend who gave me his spotify when half my family died so that like my favorite highschool age bumper sticker "peace through music ", I may *make*/find mine with the pain .

-and there nestled in amongst all the loving deeds of the friends that I keep of the friendships (that) I keep was my ex then boyfriend who kept me in sure supply of quality of life and light (alike). replacing my (ceiling) bulbs so I could/would more safely navigate my/the F42.3 (ICD-10) / DSM-5 300.3-narrow walkways/pathways. to my/the toaster when it broke and buying me a proper mattress/bed so my blow-up wouldn't ((have a) blow-out) .

My beloved friends who held-out for me to get better made up for the several that gave up on me and (had) now/turned/resorted to shun(ning) and shutting me out.

The/this bowling event was to be as much (of) an homage paid to my (patient) friends as it was (to be) an honoring of my 30's end/ 3rd decades end/ decades 3rd end .

But/and before then there was... the Holy Spirit of my deceased beloved/sweet uncle who in the days leading up to his 4 year memory mark; 2/17-2/27/23 reached me one night with his blessing of my night out dancing (again.) his approval of my goth groups groove/groovin'

I'm very spiritually connected to numbers ever since he who died's passionate pastime/interest was numbers/mathematics he'd/Uncle Art would just sit for hours in his fave livingroom arm chair math journal open and In hand numerical doodles in/filling the margins solving equations back and front of every 700 pages or of every one of the pages /all the pages . A practice of catharsis that brought him the elation and relaxation as/of ... a classic diary for standard writing (practices / purposes) traditionally would bring (people/to the pen .) his numbers/intentions were conventional arithmetic standardized But ever since he died numerical messages (of the/a) spiritually divine (side) have/had been brought into my life .

"Till Death do us Party" hung in neon (tube/rope) lights over a ('been through enough deaths (now) to know premium from prop (that); a) shellacked (and) spectacular casket (that) sat near the coat check of the club. (Been through enough death(s) (now) to know premium from prop . / premium of the prop.

(Outfitted as)

A punked-out pussycat

accented with the (spider (web)) chain mesh/ metal mesh, purse/evening bag (XaccessoryX) subset I'd become obsessed with; (slung across my bod) a surreptitious an/a ode/nod (slung across my bod) to the/a fetishism (at large) unfolding/unfolded (at large) ; accessory to a psycho-sexuality/_______. Emoji-symmetry spreads that were sent to lustlord chain depiction/imagery inclusive were (always) more than/ (above and) beyond (and above) arbitrary. It was 2 months later and I was still thinking about that the only change (to the depiction/imagery) I wanted to make/would make to the bound dame in the Christmas GIF (imagery/depiction) he'd/lustlord had sent/texted me, was trading the rope burn for (cold) chain(s.)/metal. / was trading the rope burn for chains glacial/cold to mirror a mirror (of) the unfeeling ((that was) inside me./ that (had infiltrated and) (ever-)festered (inside me)) Something in my auditory processing and something with my visual (processing) had made my brain epitomize(ing)/eroticize(ing) chain(s).

And with my inside joke; rogue I was,/ *and with my rogue inside joke* (portrayed in a / depicted in a purse)

I was

(outfitted and) Out with my core friend group after so long to (*dark-wave*) dance the night away at a/the dark-wave/Valentine's masquerade.

Said with/from (emotionally intimate) warmth; intimate and affection; emotional, You smell of an/like an antique bookstore,

. . .

shared a slot for/of my favorite/______ compliment of the night. / *rivaled (a slot/a spot) for my favorite compliment of the night.* With that of the (prop) coffin (prop)photo-op comment(ary) of/on how everybody (else) took to a

momento Mori tongue in cheek posing/voguing while I asserted a sultry stance and glance .

Even through the ritghtful preoccupation of dance/ of a dance focused night or time, my friends were observant of who I am / in ______ observation of who I am .

X???and when my goth posee saw me disparaged???X

And when they/my goth posse/my friends saw me disparaged/haggard /harried/ ______ from a chance encounter with one of my/the shunned they/my goth posee hurried me away and huddled/_____/comforted/_____, me in a grounding shag black shag rug circle hug/ hugs/huddle (of comfort .)

it took me all of but/only the next day to realize

from the man whose own birthdate *(;5/1/51)*

had him mesmerized, the night had been 5/1/51 heaven sent; 5/1/51 uncle blessed.

x the night had been heaven sent; uncle blessed . x

. . .

the numbers of my 'bracelet with entry' were 33418

The composite of (the numbers of) my birthdate ; 4/13/83

And I hadn't been out dark wave dancing since ((the) tragic year) 2019 at least and here it was a night comprised of all those numbers; 02/19

.

emphatic and request-texting my friends to check their bands/paper bracelets (from the/that night) I had to find out how rare this infact was . Rule out that every (wrist) band was stamped with the same number sequence. / sequence of number(s). with response-texts (coming in/incoming) from/the/of sympathy (of) "I threw mine out" to what made me floored and put me in awe; "I dug mine out" ...

my friends were all about, my spiritual / metaphysical/ _________ , (wellness/___________), laden voyage .

While my uncle was watching over me in numerical anagram(s) my friends were looking out for me (too) .

Tues 2/14/23

"Oh my goodness steph, i'm praying for an end to this. "

Came in an impassioned text from one of my longest-time friends/ oldest friends. "Where are you living now? With your parents or are you on your own?" She continued with profuse/profound concern .

2/18/23 I texted ...

I thanked her profoundly and answered/ added that/about the trajectory of my recoveries/recovery progress. My mom was temporarily/tentatively living with me when I was much sicker, I stated. Then I eventually at least got "medically stable" , (I explained) and now (I) live on my own in my apt around the _____area, (I explained .) / I ______.

When people see and talk to me my condition isn't really noticeable at this point, I told her Bc one , I've learned how to better cope and present normative-function/nuerotypical for the most part and two, bc my psychiatrist says

((like) perpetuity is in the eye of the beholder/beholden)

it's all in the subjective experiential now, I explained/exclaimed the process/discrepancy , that that's the component that's left to clear up and in sed subjective experiential is where the dissociative DPDR is/exists/lives . *So since perpetuity is in the eye of the beholder/beholden* , to many/most, now that I am "medically stable" I seem like baseline even though (yet) I am not (yet.)

XIf you have an iPhone maybe we can schedule a face time chat and catch up sometime .

Also, I am planning on having a birthday gathering for my decade birthday in April and I will keep you posted on that but you and Amy are warmly invited/welcome(d) X

|————|

|————|

. . .

>>*So since perpetuity is in the eye of the beholder/beholden* , to many/most, now that I am "medically stable" I seem like baseline even though (yet) I am not (yet.)<<

from my chosen family of friends, to my given/gifted family of creation and my/to my spiritual family in heaven/ beyond the veil to be surrounded by/with such unconditional love yet be able to feel none just numb only numb had me turning to confectionary goods/coping. The icing frosted filling/the icing (frosted and) filled X(and baked)X substitutition for/of affection might've started around the time of #15's tooth extraction. Surrounding the momentary relapse/setback of Thanksgiving to be more exact . (But the softness of the) Birthday confetti cupcakes, raspberry lemon cupcakes and carrot cake cupcakes lent themselves to being What/something (that) began as a harmless post-op safe to eat post-op treat of sweets to a snow-balled full-blown placeholder of/for emotion.

Never before was much for a regularity with baked goods and pastry; stuck to the construct of the tip/crest of the food pyramid being a the bearer of occasional sweets. But with only intellectual deserted by ability to emotionally perceive/receive tenderness rendered this concept/context where before long I found myself cutting down/back on/ in a spiral spiraling titration of calories per meal-eating/ *main course* . just so that I'd sooner have more room for more dessert To comfort me in the fact that my limbic system had shirked its response ability of love/_____. Headaches kept at bay with Tylenol Bc while the caloric intake was great I wasn't getting the right nutritious sustenance/value(s) and/so the crash was grave. But in my minds eye this substance abuse (;/of) actionable *compassionate* (waxing) meaning/seizing/*eating*, made up for the real sustenance I was living without; love .

|———|

. . .

0.) Only the (darkened) pages of my memoir know that feel; I don't . Won't tell much more than my parents Bc while unconditional is in their jurisdiction others might pull up on (their) Love if they/to learn of, learn of my numb(ness) . It's rock bottom loneliness this and I lie impailed on/by stalagmites the ceiling of the medication dosage stabbing me/ stabs me with stalactites . It is not a cathedral ceiling of glass / it is not a vaulted ceiling of skylights . I am sandwhiched by spikes

1.) (but) leading up to/ on the eve of (the day of) departure to lustlords party mansion (I) didn't need figurative copious IV hits of junk food or lines snorted of sugar powered distraction named cupcake .

A vine of royal purple grapes that I ate hit diff def divine def as I rewatched eyes wide shut for the first time since grade school/highschool.

A welcomed departure it was from packing (covid) rapid tests and taking pregnancy tests (and/ accompanied by or with) wondering why haven't I gotten my period yet I could less than worry now after an at home strip proved negative .

Eradication of my ?2nd? ever scare meant I could (now) focus my attention / shift my attention to the I health nose nose dive / now I could shift my attention to the nose dive of the ihealth now I could shift my attention to the ihealth nose dive and put first response far out of my mind .

XA vine of royal purple grapes that I ate hit diff def divine def as I rewatched eyes wide shut for the first time since grade school/highschool. X

. . .

Fidelio may have been the admittance password to the Caligula-Inspo/esque (grand) fortress of the 1999 Kubrick movie but my Medicaid would be the sacred word to access the exclusive kingdom that was the party mansion of lustlord. A decade I'd waited to see it and "don't dream it be it" / be it don't dream it. The government issued antigen (test) kits that had been extended on their expirations meant/were a marathon of makeouts and sexy/sexual/sex play acts, made possible.

With the box-stamped expiration of 6/27 no longer a restriction/consideration reality was freed-up to just enjoy the consideration of/that my grandma's death date being a symbol / could be a symbol . Perhaps it was her way of crossing fingers and endorsing that this weekender wouldn't give me covid/corona/the virus . And as if that wasn't enough my uncle's thumbs up was in the factory printing on the back of the condom 3 pack . 5/1 expiration His birthday cinched/sealed the deal that there was some sort of spiritual blessing/_______ (?for/of hedonism?) here .

And it was clear

[The genesis of (a new) friendship] at the deli counter waiting for our half a pound and pounds to come out of the back/ happen when what happened was the stuff award winning indie films are made of . Brandishing invisible/imaginary paper now serving number strips [the genesis of (a new) friendship]we were just strangers engaged/engaging in consensual mutual sharing of our (sordid) whole (sordid) lives (sordid) story . [the genesis of (a new) friendship]

[The gen-x gentle Gen-X goddess dressed to the nines in (a) floor length fur (coat ,) draped in elegant jewelry and ____ in vivid lipstick ...]

. . .

(She) had gotten divorced on her anniversary, and I told her that/of my chosen breakup day; my 39th birthday where I had given myself the gift of (a) rebirth . And when she opened up to me about the abuse that was physical, she took to my (morally)risky-story about how while (trauma) reinactment is to be avoided, trauma play is/can be powerful/transformative. Chiefly citing the less than brief time of life hands were held around/at my throat in anger (xonly nowx) all these years later, It's sexy now/can be intimate/erotic (it seems/is my experience / has been my experience) letting the guy who I have trust in and an intimate friendship with put his hands on my neck, ((reluctant as he was (about it).)), I said . She seemed to get it as though I had read her mind instead of told "my" story . / she seemed to get it as though reading her mind and telling my story were one in the same .

and then somehow nearly in the same breath but/and all in the same day of divulging/disclosing my abuse made useful ... I found myself speeding fearing for my life from an attempt at a repurposed as necklace/sexy necklace, gone terribly awry . My dark side had almost taken my life and as I drove that night praying to get to the precinct without my (slender) neck swelling from/with (the) anxiety (that was) welling I was fucking lucky in this real life 100,000 ways to die show spin-off that the officer comforted me with saying not to worry that he'll get the bolt cutters and/as this is easy . From bolt cutters taken to my storage locker/ units padlock in vandalism/_____ to the garage (power) tool (now) about to be used to free/save me from my life-threatening 14inch gunlock stupidity... Fiona Apple's latest album "fetch the bolt cutters" flashed through my mind like twisted irony meets (comic relief meets) music therapy (to me) as with one more jiggle/wiggle/______ officer M, got the jammed key *to twist* (and shout) *and release it did* the lustlord branded silver/metal anthropomorphic/personified undertaker/grim reaper .

The lustlord branded silver/*metal* undertaker (in good faith) had (in good faith) forsaken me (in good faith) .

(And) With (a) life expectancy (extended/extension) reinstated l was free to marvel at the sheet metal sharpie marker art/masterpieces in lustlords less than ventilated dungeon; the south wing of (in) the/(in) this / of the party mansion (tour) . Unexpectedly/spontaneously Gifted one of his pieces meant I held in possession now 3 or more precious friends prized creations an offering most cherished / offerings most cherished .

How else would I hold fast to (reinstated) life ? Why through the handles of a handbag of course ! .

It was March 2nd (of 2023) , and numerical palindrome day at that/ which meant / aka numerical palindrome day when I decided the sat in my apt for years guess designer patent black&white triangle textile overnighter/carryon would be the/serve as the second coming to/of du luxe's 2013 sequined promise. With the carry of a bag I had vowed I'd show it a good time and made true/good on my word ten years before so now seemed right to make my carryall the very/a replica of (the very) one I had once upon a time bought but got caught up in the wrought with dismay reality that my life didn't speak to such boldness and vibrancy of pattern(s). But now? Now on the precipice of press releases and … tbc . It did .

(For/alas/at last) I was no longer walking in the shadow of all my artistic friends(;a/the great appreciator/pretender) but (rather) trailblazing a path as a public figure … (as) the/a great (private) defender/xcontenderx .

|——-

Next !

-from a handbag swapped-out to 3 more tacked-up I had done the fun thing teen me did to my childhood bedroom. A gallery wall of strung up clutches and glistening evening bags would now send my mind padding back to every divine outing id ever had/ I was to have . My 4 childhood bedroom walls were like a pocketbook collage, a montage paying homage to prom, senior banquet and a few straggler occasions that I'd long since forgotten about with/had purses to match/ weren't without purses to match . And now as I waited in glorious anticipation of my goth possess 2nd/follow-up club night/time I need only glance up over/above my sofa to see the wondrous night that was reflected in a/the whiting Davis clamshell pocketbook . In the metal links/webbing there was my married (lust) crush friend-crush, with her entrancing dancing. And in my/this one week precipice of/to my/the 2 year mark of (my) dissociative descent / of my descent into dissociative/dissociation .

there was a redeeming cognitive function that (cropped up (and)) encompassed knowing/awareness (that) I could circumvent the years of clubbing she'd told me it took to get her moves down pact, if I just self-host a one woman goth hoedown weekly at my private residency! Set Pandora on (the) corresponding radio stations and ... next write something about covenant tears in the rain .

-it had been countless chapters that I'd known/ since countless chapters (ago) I'd known been of the good interoceptive awareness of (the powerful) (inner/internal) phenomena like my phantom limbic syndrome and

that astral projection was on a hair pin trigger. ... opening the fridge sliding out the glass jar each night just a spoonful of applesauce helps the medicine go down in the most delusional way . The metal lid was lined with a circle of painted red dots you see and that departure from the bare minimum of signage/ink meant/(would) set off a party in my head . The last bought sauce was barren of extraneous paint so of course this one launched me into a soirée/party/gala right away . The circular formation like dance party/club circles of friend's. / orWhereAconvening coven never ends .

(The dots like (ceiling) lighting tracks (in the ceiling))

Heady the red light district in red delicious . /(a) red delicious heady with the red light district .

XThe red like/of/for (the) aphrodisiac (ceiling tracks) /amp me up stimulant (of) not ambient/somnolent antithesis of ; seductive lightingX

(A gala (?not Apple but? applicable) it all lived and breathed on that (insert measurement of lid) metal lid. But it wasn't until the one week mark till *2 year*/ 24month DPDR was bleeding into the days next and I was caught in the throngs of generational wheeze that i realized there was a place for mind over matter beyond the recreational use that was astral projection . Remembering that once before in all this/during all this I'd stared at an empty Rx / prescription (state the gallons) jug of PEG and successfully imagined to the point of (a) partial bm evacuation that there was infact the/my solution / solvent in/beyond/contained in beyond the cloudy plastic walls of the jug/container/____.

So now ... I'd search out the applicable and placebo effect meets psychosomatic my way to bronchial tubes cleared with an empty casing of albuterol prepped . It worked (?well at first?) ... (as) my mind body connect was (cruise control/auto pilot) running on stacked/staggered decades of the very hand motion of the inhaler shake cut to the sharp sucking of air (that) it didn't (much) even (much) matter over mind that the stout cylindrical mouth piece was giving me (hits of) oxygen (hits) / none other than the air (that) we breathe . (I guess my physiological system that was seemingly synced up with my the psychological went out on the road in as a solo act as the (quick) collapse of the mind trick (quick) saw me to needing to treat (the) return symptom(s) with a fully assembled rescue inhaler / with a rescue inhaler fully assembled . But the preceding successful deception of/with/in _________ trickery/thomfoolery/_____, was a breath of fresh air.

From (an) inhale to (an) exhale ,

(And) I was fixing to breathe a sigh of relief with operation/an apartment solo-relief effort . My decade birthday was drawing near; *over the hill* approx a/one month away / *one month and one week (away)* and unwilling to die/go to the grave , never knowing what it felt like to live right never knowing what positive life implications there could be (waiting for me/awaiting me) in (a) normalist (amount of stuff/belongings/possessions) (for me) how a healthy balance of (an) orderly maximalist exaction/exacted, could impact my brain/nuero pathways for the better (in unimaginable ways.) I had long since wondered and maybe had an intuitive sense that to do more than a maintenance clear(ing) of floor pathways like a ((doing the) *bare minimum*)road *snowplow* that (exists) just makes sure there is physical/bodily safety . (doing the bare minimum)

If my living conditions were a clearing; a glade it just/ that just, might heal my (OCD) *psychological condition of OCD.*

But/and now as I sat in waiting of my 2yr/24month mark of dissociative DPDR; this week, I'd mused that maybe a F42.3 (ICD-10) / DSM-5 300.3 Richter scale drop down from (insert number/unfunctional/nonfunctional to intentional maximalist / to intentional maximalism could (be where it's at to) temper the temperature that was the fever of this dissociative / of this fever of dissociative . / of this dissociative fever. (Better yet get it to break/ *;get it to break. *)

. . .

>>(Better yet get it to break/ *;get it to break. *)<<

There was me wondering if cleaning was the secret to the ocd; brushing it off my shoulder / sweeping it under the rug and if beating (2 yrs of) dissociative/DPDR was too in the cleaning and apartment preening, to be .

(But/and) besides *wanting*/a will to take what was habitual; my F42.3 (ICD-10) / DSM-5 300.3 and *flip it*/the apt/the space/the place (to normal) *(to) housing habitable and functional*, for me for daily living (purposes) there was (an) incentive in the desire to have/cultivate a pleasant space for a lover or hosted company; companion or/and given and/or chosen family, I wanted them/(my) guests to be comfortable . And thus far/currently my apt was in no condition to even have them let alone show them a good time.

But with the higher prescription dose stepping up my depth perception (game) and spatial recognizance/recognance/recognition (ability/abilities) where there was a will there too was now a way / where there was a will there now too was a way / where there was a will there too now was a way .

**I'd decided Id lived as a F42.3 (ICD-10) / DSM-5 300.3 for (the first) 40 years of life for the next 40 i would (live normal) not (; I would live normal .)

And while I felt no emotional recognition of more (or less) than just people; possessions ,

(This was the time to do it) my limbic glitch was setting me up for success (with it/with this). **

. . .

>>I'd decided Id lived as a F42.3 (ICD-10) / DSM-5 300.3 for (the first) 40 years of life for the next 40 i would (live normal) not (; I would live normal .)

And while I felt no emotional recognition of more (or less) than just people; possessions ,

(This was the time to do it) my limbic glitch was setting me up for success (with it/with this). <<

As the out of sight out of mind extremist I was neuro bio chemically rendered the path was paved for me; my escape route to/of how my ocd gets me snags and nabs me (a sweet behavior twisting/contorting/twists/contorts to a pathology gaining (in) (metastatic) momentum (toward metastatic) ... incessant in my/the saving (of) empties on account of that/when the expiration stamp mirrors a date of spiritual significances past (give in to that and) the insidious mind trap (is now) festering to that of (now) I must save empties of random expiration dates Bc maybe they are of (some) future significance / (meaningful calendar) relation. . The ocd levels up every time you succumb (to its demanding/commanding bare minimum) you let it (progress , advance , metastasize)

but with the incidental extremist I was I could throw all that shit away (?theoretically?) and take (a) blessing in disguise comfort in knowing my brain (chemically) cannot /won't retain care or give a (god)damn once the item is not there .

(What was (Then/ the then)) No less than (a) partial paralysis quasi-catatonia The/was (now) (a) parting fog of cognitive oversights of/regarding / in respect to spatial recognition which meant

1.) a reinstatement of some semblance of quality of life

2.) some semblance of quality of life once again (was/*would be tenable*./ *was becoming tenable*./would become tenable ./ *had become tenable* .

While spatial recognition was a direct compliment/_______, (?gone off go off without a hitch?) I had wised-up I was wising-up to how even a/the limbic glitch of/in (no) emotional recognition could (exist to) serve me (well) if even indirectly .

Write next about all the empath stuff .

Write next about all the empath stuff .

>>Write next about all the empath stuff . <<

It would be one thing if I just had a strong character trait of empathy was an empathic person that would be easy to live with but depending on who you ask I'd either be called a doormat or it's euphemism of empath . I've come come to feel the nouns can be used interchangeably . It's like to say he paints or I do photography is different than saying he's a painter or I'm a photographer . I dance versus I'm a dancer . Perhaps it's in part been imposter syndrome and inferiority complex that has kept me at/with verbiage of 'the former' my whole/entire life. The difference from i dance versus I'm a dancer is that in the latter there is lives/exists/lurks (more) (expectation) and (more) pressure and in being an empath there is a (sense of) bearing down upon (you) . The wiggle-room adjective(;empathic) allows for (a _____ of) energizing empathy whereas the (polarizing/pidgeonholing/paralyzing/_____) noun(;empath) can imbue you with a life of 'depleting empathy' . It did me . And (it) did me in. /and did me in it did . But now now in these 2 days till 2 years of dissociative I was seeing the blessing in depersonalize(d.) / I was seeing the blessing in disguise of depersonalized .

. . .

Death of a/the girl next door this was the birth of a/the fire sign(s) allure/*soar*/*roar* the I don't give a Phoenix flying fuck if/that you're hard on luck it is not my cross to bear . A break in the limbic feedback loop has exonerated/eradicated me from the weight (of *your*/the world) .

and I'll still be the mat on your porch but it's spiky now, not door .

1.)something good for you and good to you but not without a little edge

2.) something inherently good for you if you can get past the pain/caustic

3.) and I'll be something good to you / good for you if you can/after you get past being accosted at the entryway Bc I'm bookends/(archway) *columns* , of gargoyle statues and I'm taking agency with/of (my) boundaries ((raging and/ enraged and) overcompensating for half a life time of (being) walked all over) (I'll be) saying no with caustic ______. / (;) on a caustic tear .

1.) Oh yeah and I am a writer . I am an author.

2.)oh yeah and saying yes with enthusiastic xtearx/______/*flare.* ; yes I am the noun;writer . (And) Yes I am the noun; author and yes I am to be renowned . ::::pen drop::::

::::Notes ::::

Also changed purse to black&white guess patent overnighter . The second coming of 2013's du luxe sequined …

More Notes

|——|

Jacket Back/ Outro / intro / CJD9

Death of a/the girl next door this was the birth of a/the Phoenix allure.

|——|

CJD9

!-Empath !

!-Saying no!

!-Agency with boundries!

!-from door mat to spikey mat !

Very important note ...

Stil need to add in something about how Bc of ikea bed I'd made the conscientious/conscious/courtesy decision to wait till my 40th birthday to have a lover in my bed as my birthday would be the one year mark of relationships end it seemed respectful .

CJD10

(As) courageousness was turning to confidence (in my/in this/in the (bitter)sweet 16th month of telling my story/of having a ______story to tell (March 2023) (and) I(d) stopped calling the/my work space the/my home office and instead took inspo from lustlord who was mid-creation of his loft/attic music studio, and started calling/referring to it/ *to mine as* (it) my/the writing/author studio. All the strung hang tags now that identified bags of writing utensils/instruments and masking tape labeled boxes of (paper reams and supplies/binder clips) would all be marked with the rooms new name now . A motivating/motivational spooky entanglement (of (proportions of) divine (proportions of) synchronicity) for sure it was that there was my music god and 1/3rd; 1/4th if you count me , of my goth girl posse my bosom friend who'd wanted to stage a/the F42.3 (ICD-10) / DSM-5 300.3 intervention, both working on major residency Reno's / renovations in tandem/syncopation/concurrence . Perhaps it was this dear friend(ship) energy that gave me/ that imbued me with the / that stimulated the deep brain regain of (knowing how to)

. . .

configure and visually/tactile properly process shapes so as to efficiently and effectively know how best to situate , stack , pack position and Angle boxes and objects. It was really quite that simple; my brain felt confused with how to do it before; all along. basic organizing and concepts of sorting 'like with like' felt too/were too cognitively complex to endeavor . But now the distant synergy/synchronicity/serendipity/symbiosis/quantum entanglement/connectivity/______, held me (as) we 3 were all working toward (building) a greater good with/of/from, our living quarters. 1.)Sure lustlord had a fortress to work with and bosom friends apartment was sizable

2.) sure lustlords loft/attic was more than a crawl space he would get/he had/he was getting , to reface . / he had to work with

And bosom friends apartment was sizable (too)

but I'd decided "writing studio" was/could be a state of mind. And in that my 3 or 4 tier plastic keter shelving unit that sat smack dab (right) in the middle/center of my kitchen(ette) housing my printer and the hang file folder railed 3 box system of my manuscript; beginning middle and end , was just swell as _____________. The keter unit strategically swaddled with/in a 4 piece bedsheet set looked like a big block of black mystery / looked like a big black block of mystery taking up half my/the kitchen ... having to sidestep to get by it to access the kitchen sink or fridge was just how I'd learned/adapted to live/living .

I was the purveyor of my own destiny and great/grate and powerful I felt like the man behind the curtain; the wizard of oz as I would unhook the fitted sheet from the posts to work on something/get something/retrieve something/supplies or go/huddle under the flat draped sheet my back bumped out from the perfect cube as I'd tinker with _______ . But the moments of interaction that were the most theatric and dramatic mattered the most to me ... every (memoir) work day culminating in needing to draw back/ *drawing back the repurposed as curtain draped/hanging fabric* so as to service/oversee/attend/tend on bended knee (to) my printer/(brother 720) as it slow motion projectile piled the pages of my newly written/added , passages/chapters ...

xsort like with like, stack pack position and angle boxes and objects so that x

1.) [Something had happened/(something was) *hot off the press of happening* , *(something) that I never would have thought could while still of dissociative had/did/was* (?not of acceptance but?)

self-conscious (had) managed to become self-assure(d.) and I couldn't help but think it had to do something/it had something to do with the pages of this/my memoir.

2.) The 2 year mark came and when (it did) (I referred to it) I caught myself In the healthful verbal descriptor of it (as)/(;) 2 years of my neurological rehabilitation journey (of/towards recovery) . To my great surprise I wasn't inclined to call it 2 years of dissociative DPDR or 24 months of (this) sickness.

3.) Much like when you find you are regarding yourself as simply single again as opposed to divorced or going through (a) breakup/relationship(s) loss ... the former denotes a sense of ? acceptance? /

? (A work in) processing (progress)? (At work)

|———|

(In continuation of literary illustration of my 2 year brain)

There were no longer mood drops as steep as (in)

bird box but there was controversy (shadow-cast) in every (dark/shadow-cast/eclipsed) nook and (shadow-cast) cranny of my psycho sexuality ...

(Write about physical assault scene in Ginny and Georgia set to white flag by bishop Briggs)

And in that about/citing the (set to (song:) white flag by bishop Briggs) physical assault scene season ___ episode ___ of/in Ginny&Georgia, I found myself writing to/texting lustlord ...

"it's going to be fascinating to see what I'm like once my

nuero-biochemistry balances out in life again .

But right now I see a clip like this and I find it hot .

Yup... #hashtag reasons I'm prescribed 200mg's of antipsychotics

🫢 lol "

The dark humor to go with my 28 second recorded vid clip both things that put me in far more than opposition of feminism; I was not even (a) humanitarian / of humanitarianism (with this .) .

and In (the (correlating) (cold) links/the webbing of) my newest whiting&davis burgundy chain mail evening bag was a cascading fountain (of) viscous blood dripping/running throughout *in the rouching* (but/and) where I once couldnt stand the sight of jam/jelly on my toast; disturbed by its morose reminder/processing 2 years in and I'm

. . .

1.) buying bags/purses that/Bc they look like a vampiric casualty .

2.) *purse-seeking* (what looks like a vampiric casualty /) *vampiric casualties . * (in my browsery/browser/browsing .)

(Exemplary / exemplifying) what Biden insists/comforts . That that which is at first (of) the most unsettling/upsetting becomes at last where the most comfort/solace is to be had/found.

XWrite next about my bday (age 27/37 , theFword, “success”) X

>>where the most comfort/solace is to be had/found. <<

Figurative and literal My 2 year brain had turned the/a page on generalized rage it was a whole new chapter (several later/insert how many later) as I (now) wasnt fixated perseverating on things like the aggressive/aggro plot that/of from my garage apartment to/I make war air rise with/in the volume dial and genre-choosing of my music-listening/grooving/*consuming* .

xmusic war air rises/war air rises in musicx

but rather (now) I was intentioned and concentrating on the assured/assertive want that from what my (survival/guttural) story imparts / would impart, (that) a (publishing house) (book) bidding war is/may be waged from and over these pages .

And while the calendar mark of my/a 2 year brain was a/the milestone of/in neurology , the cornerstone of (my) chronology; mid-life, was coming/was on the brink . And still with that nuero biochemically rendered pesky blasted goddamn/godmann resistant/glitching limbic system the F word of 40/forty fit me just fine . Symbolism as (i was) Emotionally unavailable my brain (was) off line for/to the/that _______/sacred 4 letter L word of love but fuck (now) that was something of (a quadrant/quartet of) numbers tenderness,empathy and sensitivity wasn't required of . numbness wouldn't negate my ability to fuck (?as it would to make love .?) .

XMake me feel / utterly exhaust me Bc I am up against X

X(But/just put me up against somebody's perfectly functioning limbic system and I am utterly exhausted/ and it utterly exhausts me)X

Before I turned / on the brink of my turning 16 I sat up in my twin bed reflecting on deconstructing (if) mentally psychologically surveying if the landmark to be / land mark I was (to be) turning , made me a / meant I was a woman and now as I approach 40 I sit in my bed a queen and ponder/surmise (that) if the landmines I've (survived) make(s) me a warrior.

(Name the singers ?) So many musical greats virtuosic's and visionaries died at 27. At 37 I almost did . Which is why I don't take (it) for granted (that I get to walk through) this (middle-age) gateway number that I get to make something extraordinary of . As iggy pop says/attests/flex's/would flex/flexed

"Here comes success (here comes success)

Over my hill (over my hill)

Here comes success (here comes success)"

. . .

(And) Over *the* hill (it/mine) would (soon) (flex .)

|—————-|

Write next !!!!!!!!!!!!!!!!

But/and I needed success greater than monetary. Grand intangible /the intangible grand / intangible and grand ... /

*But/and greater than monetary I needed success intangible and grand/grand and intangible *.

I needed it in contending with the insufferable reality that I still had so much life to live and I was 2 bodily fluids deep in (my own) self-disgust. Stimson middle ridicule had set in motion the shameful association with throwing up. xprocuredx kids had taken my innocence with (their) ignorance and insolence . Or

*With ignorance and insolence kids had taken my innocence . * But then when the (new)/ (entrance to a) decade was supposed to be (thirty) flirty and thriving 2014 saw me to a follow-up disruption/distortion in the view I could hold of/about/for my bodily fluid(s). This time it was HSV2 as my bully. Instilling in me the association that my arousal is to be feared , something bad as my/the/it's respective /sed wetness carries/transmits sickness . (And with my life blood no different; virus desecrated), Distortion was (now) (all there was) coursing through how I could view a significant portion of my (own) bodily fluids/ my (own) bodies fluids. Complex perceiving complex grieving maybe there was a/something relieving in dissociation I was entertaining/contemplating/open to, the notion.

Both my youth and my growth/adult had slammed me with (life) circumstance that forged/formed association(s) of disorder and disease to the very/ surrounding the very fluids that (involuntarily) come out of me (involuntarily.) / to the very fluids surrounding the very fluids that (involuntarily) vent (involuntarily) from me .

Was this why (even) in the quiet privacy of my masturbation/manual self-stimulation I couldn't cum orgasm unless I imagine/fantasize I am my lover's body, their orgasm, mine . [I didn't know as I couldn't remember/recall if this fantasy/tendency predated std/hsv(2) diagnosis day/date.] I just knew that Self-pleasure was a compound word/term only in (the)technicals/(the) technicalities/ (the) technicality (of it) (of the act.)

My psychiatrist attributed this to why the video-viewing of the cats after an early rush of tears had fallen flat . I had done my homework of watching (the) old home movies and irregardless/irrespective of tears; an appropriate physiological /physical response, I couldn't feel the/any (emotional) substance behind the cry. It was as though my body was reacting/responding in kind while/but my brain was left behind left out . (I want you to) Watch them again (my) nuero-psychiatrist Dr. Rosalie said and this time (like when you're masturbating) I want you to be the cats looking up at mommy so lovingly he insisted/intuited that following the model i use for masturbation; get out of mine go into theirs the others body , may very well be the access pass to reassociation realization and personalization .

|—————————|

. . .

>>may very well be the access pass to reassociation realization and personalization . <<

If that was in candidacy for the (all) access pass then I wondered if a particular phenomena/phenomenon was sed door; ajar.

It was the 15th of March 2023 when I scheduled what was to be In approximately a/one week, my first ever in person session with the psychiatrist that had been (tele health (communications) /virtual visit/video visit) treating me for (insert number of weeks or insert Amount of months or amount of years.) . It was / it had become a well-known fact/ practically artifact at this point the biweekly transcript/correspondence/dialog that consisted of him asking me not how are you feeling but what or some other variation was often in the duration of the 30 minute session. (?"what is it that you're feeling?"?) or "And how does that make you feel? " was frequently a/the follow-up question/inquiry/inquisitivity to a/whatever story I'd relay/impart/divulge I divulged I'd just told . xOrx ("what is the feeling attached to that?") was him pointing out that I'd just had (any at all) sudden movement of a facial feature no matter how subtle/small And while I wanted that to shuttle us into limbic function (overrule) triumph I'd try to reply/respond to "what is it that you're feeling?"

And /But try as I might / but and try as I did with might /but try as I might-fully did/

but/and try as I might it was all/only mighty trying/ *mighty trying is all it was .* I couldn't get/muster dissociative broken / a broken dissociative just (my) answers met with a/the broken record rhetoric (of) " that's a thought . I want you to tell me the/a feeling." .

So when that mid-March day I'd hung up the phone from a receptionist scheduled office visit and listened to the anxiety of my mind (i tried to find/ unravel/____ what it was trying/vying to tell me. In presentation/appearance/first impression/at face value (was) (panic) , how am I going to see the person sole responsible for (the foundation of) my medical stabilization he who has been so unwavering in care and dedication and not greet with a hugs embrace/ hug hello that was how the anxiety read but when I looked for the subtext and asked myself what is powering the/this panic of/about 'meet and greet' gesture preference; embrace to etiquette; handshake, I realized it must be 'feeling' / 'feeling' must be the culprit / ______/explanation /(at) the helm of it.

thinking maybe I was on the fringe of a/the giving end of feeling was unique/(sickness) unprecedented and (then) when I experienced feeling on behalf of "the wise witch", the receiving end, it was precious. It really was luck of the Irish (at Depeche Mode night at Gotham club of LI as my beloved best beloved of (all) the fallout/fallen friends, had me wrapped/ensconced in an/a hug/embrace with my feet literally lifted literally off the ground. before it even registered/as it registered whose arms it was (I had) around me i was weightless (in the embrace of) knowing her (friendships) love (had *come back to me*,) at last/(*once) again .* and then like levitation from/of limbic bliss stillness in a crowded/packed-out club . All there was was us. (it might as well have been scene _______ of/with Willow and Tara ...)

1.)Through thick and through thin air I was suspended /

2.) suspended in mid air . Through thick and through thin air / through thick and through air thin ...

3.) through thick and through thin air ...

with my fake id and (my) youth in/of highschool I thought I was so cool hit on, getting (hit on) and bedding the hottest, most popular stud dykedelic stud lesbian of Thunders dancing up on bass-shaking speakers by default of being her girlfriend/ the sport bras bearing girlfriend / the sport bra bearers girlfriend. Leaving early Bc I had work in the morning with the (cocky response) pick up line (cocky response) / with the cocky pickup line of response in my mind "I'll work you all night baby " she (had) said as she (begrudged/begrudgingly) strutted away was enough to ignite 2 years of a relationship (after a serious / lengthy hiatus of/with women .)

And now with enchantress queen of the goth dance scene come back to me, *in the mid-day of my life,* (full circle) belonging was emerging for me (in the mid-day of my life) *with night life . *

A.) If my beloved best enchantress brought me the weightlessness of willow and Tara dancing on air to (insert song here) then so too the good/my good lustlord took a weight off my shoulders in confirmation that what we are and have been is relationship anarchists/relationship anarchy . So astounding how the 2nd term of/from a/the compound word that inherently/intrinsically/empirically/unequivocally means chaos (unequivocally) can feel more tranquil xand calmingx than it's antithesis/*antonym* (xrelationshipx) exclusivity/*monogamy.* (?unlike The latter feeling like entrapment, breeding unrest and restlessness there was no captivity out of exclusivity / in non-exclusivity …?)

B.) X(Need mild transitional / connecting/Segway here)X

C.) X[Have you ever said something Bc you thought it would set you free (in/with autonomy) but instead it was met with more of a feeling of loss than (of) liberty/liberation ?

D.) (Have you ever said something Bc) you thought it would be freeing/alleviating only to find it yielded/brought about grieving ?

Have you ever said something Bc you thought it would be freeing/alleviating but instead/only to find, it brought about grieving ?

That was me/that was what this was (?shaping up to be?) thinking by confirming our non monogamy/autonomy I'd feel gain but instead / when instead I felt loss/ all I felt was loss . (?What a conflicted mess of ambivalence I was. Feeling captivity in monogamy but/and (a) concurrently missed/lost opportunity for meaning(ful) (if) in a declared state of relationship *anarchy*/ non-exclusivity/ non-commital/______/autonomy.]X

E.) (XTalk here about weightless from Lustlord confirmation open relationship.X)

F.) Only mid (month) and this / when this March was fixing to go out like a blanket of spun/sheer/sheared/shear/sheered comfort from a lamb . And As this 3rd month of the year was to (also) be the mark of 3 for the amount of months since (the/my) tooth extraction surgery, that/it meant the calendar date of (the) 28/28th would commemorate/inaugurate healing completion by dentistry/clinical standards .

G.) (Need transitional / connecting /etc here. Maybe this … but then like/as instant as 'sudden instant/infant death syndrome' (all in an instant) the lamb's wool (blanket) wasn't swaddling me (anymore/any longer) but strangling me)

H.) [Have you ever said something Bc you thought it would set you free (in/with autonomy) but instead it was met with more of a feeling of loss than (of) liberty/liberation ?

. . .

I.) (Have you ever said something Bc) you thought it would be freeing/alleviating only to find it yielded/brought about grieving ?

Have you ever said something Bc you thought it would be freeing/alleviating but instead/only to find, it brought about grieving ?

That was me /that was what this was (?shaping up to be?)

thinking by confirming our non monogamy/autonomy I'd feel profound gain but instead / when instead I felt profuse loss/ (all) I felt was (profuse) loss(; profuse) . (?What a conflicted mess of ambivalence I was. Feeling captivity in monogamy but/and (a) concurrently missed/lost opportunity for meaning(ful) (if) in a declared state of relationship *anarchy*/ non-exclusivity/ non-commital/______/autonomy.]

I think the reason/culprit for my/the dissonance and bittersweetness/sadness was that maybe it was relationship ocd driving the (agenda for) relationship anarchy/non-monogamy agenda as opposed to it being of authentic desire of/for that *kind*/variety/subset/substrate of “love life” .

I was (further) realizing what I'd probably be telling Lustlord before long maybe come my birthday ... (that/how) (while) what we do with our bodies is intentional (but) what happens with our hearts is incidental . And (that/how) despite our non-exclusivity/monogomy/monogamous agreement, *I think he*/you *kind of had*/have *mine, right now . *

From (the difference of) that which is intentional to that which is incidental (there (too) was the difference of/in choice and chance (circumstance) (too) in the/ in matters of the book launch (party) event space venue ...

xthatched cottage / Gotham LongIslandx

It was exactly one month to the day/night that/since I'd first been out to/at "the heart of long islands " (club) Gotham compliments of the planner pal of my friend group/circle who had group texted

the promo poster for/of culture shocks Valentine's masquerade ball at cafe goth

with the emphatic interest inquiry (of)

"Oooh, who wants to go dancing?"

A/the magic maker (in us/amongst us) Who knew when she/our very own PR marketing director (friend) organized us all for the valentines masquerade ball (that) it would set off a synapse for/of the start of something really special for ((us) all)... reunion of our friend group.

a glistening scintillating glistening promise when I complimented/commended her on being responsible for getting us to/bringing us to/*our gathering at* the the proverbial smoke and mirrors of the atmospheric dance floor (we were all brought together for)

"Thank you, I will make more magic soon.✨✨✨💕"

she assured .

. . .

From the/a numerical anagram entrance band (my first time there) of my DOB's digits to walking through the 1am exit door(s) only to

find out as we loitered/lingered on the curb (chatting it up) before calling it a night, that the reemergence delight of club dancing delight was something (I) shared with 1 forth / 1 fifth / 1 sixth / 1 _____ of my party of ____ goth posse (that night .)

Seminal night for us both it was being that (I (had) learned) her/ one of us had a/their last time out in 2018; mine (was) 2019 . I had no idea we had that unity / I had no idea we shared that unity .

X... it was a beautiful night of emergence for us both, my friend X

Yes from inaugural 'entrance and exit' to the following months (st pattys day Depeche Mode) event that meant getting my fallen friend back it was clear through ((the) figurative) smog (machine) / smoke and mirror(s)

that all thanks to our coordinator friend/compadre/comrad/______ , this is where the magic happens

so when It was exactly one month to the day/night that/since we'd all tried out the/a night out at GothamLI I took it as a spiritual/metaphysical sign that upon perusing the official website I'd come to find (that) the venue is a(n) (event (space) rental hall !

Write next about this place for book launch VS thatched cottage .

|———-|

. . .

NEXT!!!!!!!!!! <3 :-)

>>Write next about this place for book launch VS thatched cottage .
<<

(before long) this where the fantastical happens (before long) as/; (before long) I'd be booking my (book/manuscript/novel) launch (release) party/ release party/ (manuscript) reception at the very place that had been (recently) pumping out new memories for(us)/with old friends . I would not be destined for/ I would be destined no more for a locker facility being/as my only kind of gated community. Speaking in/of units would mean square footage of a doorman surveilled apartment/complex, not a 5x5 , 5x7 and 5x10 ?10x10? Perimeter of a storage floor. A 6 digit bank account would match a 6 digit square footage count of what lies behind gargoyle adorned columned doors.

Forget taking a virtual tour/ forget *strike* *scheduling a tour* /forget *strike* *a/the scheduled tour* of/for

what my sweet 16 venue had morphed into /become...

the proprietary difference in my sweet 16 under new ownership

(Till death do us party) I was going to pitch this/the/my release celebration/reception/launch party/ * lit shin-dig * at (till death do us party) Gotham Long Island !

But until I had the (readers' reviews) and the revenue to own the night ...dancing on the borrowed time of long island's finest dark wave DJ was simply sublime ...

. . .

——————————-Notes——————————

-(and) if all the things she said was/were running through my head then/(way)back when , (then) lips like sugar had imprinted on my mind now as (a)(crush)(of) lust called upon one of the 4 corners of us (; *our* (Elvira morticia Lily Munster) BigDarkEnergy *goth posse*) she whispered sweetly in a cupped ear / in a cupped ear whispered sweetly "do you know echo and the bunny men ? " to the gist of that I've heard 'of' them, I said. "it's called lips like sugar and it's a song from the 80's " her soft tone juxtaposed her/against her 6inch/_______ spiked collar jutting out from her neck/jugular .

1.) as (the) Candy land lyrics (of) "sugar kisses" /

2.)as "sugar kisses"

sent me back to fantasy land nostalgic in/for the erotic spark our first time meeting had set off . (Speaking for myself). /

sent me back to (an) erotic spark nostalgic fantasy land (speaking for myself) (of our first meeting.) (...speaking for myself .)

(?I stood/ (and) I was standing in command of (an) energy shift of the very essence danced of ... 'goth scene queen fallen friend come back to me again .' Just as sure as we were (like (the)(90's) TVs (90's) sapphic pair) dancing on air (like (the) (90's) TVs (90's) sapphic pair) floating oxytocin-high above the crowd of loud suspended in (a) *'frozen in time'* / 'time *stood'* *stillness* of sound head in the clouds till head like a hole took our dancing 'down and dirty' to the (drink spilled sticky) ground. From it being like/ going from in a/the crowded club housed only us when rapture/enraptured of/in deep friendships love had/saw everyone else disappear(Ed) . To the thrall of NIN positioning us as the willing exhibitionists of (the) unspoken lust we were ...

Next !!!!! 😀

>>To the thrall of NIN positioning us as the willing exhibitionists of (the) unspoken lust we were...<<

concentrated and condensed temperature intense the sexual tensions viscosity was of the club/of the club was. Probably Bc it couldn't be dispersed over 'spend the night' invites of my apartment proposal no I could only impose as/for the newly added signage (interior) decor piece my bosom friend photo-texted that read "this is not a whore house it's a whore home" ... read like phonetics of half a truth, to me; 'This is not a F42.3 (ICD-10) / DSM-5 300.3 house it's a F42.3 (ICD-10) / DSM-5 300.3 home'.

Embarrassment was catching up even though I'd made a dent in decluttering and was eager to have company/guests Self conscious ness was in the fact/awareness/reality that it would only look decent if you/when compared (it) to how/ what it was (as) of recent. Or contrast it with the media televised living condition shambles of shows like 'buried alive' but god forbid my guests would assess it on

1.) the American/societal norm(s)/standard .

2.) anything other than relativity/the theory of relativity/ it's all relative

Then all the work I could do would still be under- appreciated and/or worse go unobserved . (I would need my lovers, relatives and friends to keep in mind " it's all relative"/everything's relative/ the theory of relativity)

. . .

|———|

CJD10

Tues the 21st (3/21/23)

(While I enjoyed shock-rockers I never intended on being a shock-talker but that's) (locker life portrait of a F42.3 (ICD-10) / DSM-5 300.3 my 200 to 400 sq foot apartment was more of/like a decorated storage space than a let's go back to my place.

(While I enjoyed shock-rockers I never intended on being a shock-talker but that's)

what I sounded/sounded-off like pitching my invite to have and to host lustlord

"The way I keep house is the same as how I put out;

Dirty and with grit "

"Sent" it.

I knew the ((mere/overt/inherent)mention of) sex (mention) would circumvent any overt/inherent discomfort of the stark departure from the American standard (of living and good housekeeping .)

But while presentable enough to gather family and friends at my apartment now, on (moral morale ground) *account of* (*morale ground*) that/for how/with how/*of that*, my mattress had been purchased by my ex, I (had) vowed to wait till after my birthday *for*

. . .

1)1-1 of lovers / *the* pleasantry/*pleasantries* *of* a lovers 1-1/ *lovers 1-1's . *

2)the pleasantries a lover's 1-1 keeps.

|———|

>>ex, I had vowed to wait till after my birthday for 1-1 of lovers / the pleasantry/pleasantries of a lover's 1-1/ lovers . <<

The occasion was not arbitrary/ arbitrarily selected , as my/the threshold of/to 40 would mark/mean/signify/define, one whole calendar year of being broken up from the/my 2 yr 2month relationship .

Come to find the big '4' '0' would signify (something else) (something of a spiritual denomination/creed/means , as well .)

I was (?silently?) leaning into an embracing of the classic theme (of)/(;) over the hill while mulling over/tossing around a modern spin xtossing aroundx an O.T.H. hip acronym . / a hip O.T.H. acronym . When ... my wise witch friend imparted (on me) that 40 is the age of gateway as (1111 or 11,11) 4 is comprised of 4 ones. I was overcome with marvel/_______/astonishment as I informed her that 11 is my life purpose master number in numerology, I wrote my book while living at a street address of 11 and (it was) (to be) at age 40 (that) I was finishing and fixing to publish .

This gateway birthday was going to be everything!

Hard/soft pass on the 'forty and naughty

onboarded' ('flip that bride to be') ,sash I had fashioned/festooned to craft and wear. / (commission a friend to craft so I could wear) Alas/afterall "Miss Gateway (Decade)" Decade gateway goddess goddess gateway decade/gateway goddess/gateway goddess, / Stephoenix Gateway , had found me and beckoned me to answer/heed her/the call(ing) .

From a/the numerical anagram of my birthdate stamped on a/the club entryway wrist band at a/the/

Of the Valentine's dance (that passed) to an April gateway (decade) birthday (to be/ that was to come) , 2023 was defining itself (to me) as a/the year of (life) divine synchronicity/ *divine life timing(s)* (?*and sacred geometry . *?).

And as for the present tense well my uncle continued to reach me through numbers . It was the night I had come back from bonding with my wise witch friend when I discovered Ron Asheton. Watching the Amazon prime documentary of the stooges "Gimme Danger" for me was giving 'Angel' as the guitarist showed up on screen dressed in the near same last outfit my beloved uncle had ever worn . The light blue short sleeve collared buttoned polo looked/ near identical as though it had been plucked from the (over)stuffed north well health plastic bag that carried the last of the civilian clothes he'd ever wear . (67 years of life distilled down to one very sad plastic bag that 35 years of life couldn't prepare me for the impact my mind would endure.) but The sunglasses, the hair, the mannerisms; it was all there watching the interview sequences of This stooges band mate was like seeing/witnessing my uncle alive again after a near 5 year(s) without him/heaven hiatus. more than (baseline) 'alive' jovial and full of life filled the laughter and story-time just like my gentle giant of an uncle (always) exemplified . If ever I needed (spiritual) confirmation that there was something spiritual/holy in this moment ... it was in the 4 digit (die cut) metal numbers nailed into the house/ (houses) porch siding/column that Ron Asheton was standing beside in one of the scenes .

1324 was where he lived and 3/24 was

the day/night/ When I saw this/it !

a |——-|

b >>1324 was where he lived and 3/24 was

the day/night/ When I saw this/it ! <<

c Yes the present tense was more like (a) present sent... from the heavens/nether/ether .

d It was also present sentient/sentience in that my higher self/higher consciousness /higher conscious self continued to take me under its/their stephoenix wing just like/as it/they always had since the beginning (of time's sickness .)

For before my 20 to 30 min commute to commune with the wise witch in/through a communication thread with an eBay seller, I found out that apparently the very deep vibrational frequencies and low tones that have felt good (for my head pressure) coming from my own humming and bed and baths marpac, are exactly the (notes/sound) pitch and register that's said in/about (the) (crystal bowl) sound bath,to be for the brain and nervous system!

Inherently I had known what I needed/ what I (had) needed I had known all along . /

Inherently I had known what I needed all along.

Omnipresent,/ and omnipotent the voice of the higher self/ conscious(ness) is strong a high priestess/priest (guardian Angel guiding Angel) that exists within (a guardian Angel guiding angel) to (steer/keep you from harm.)

f "(And) out like a lamb" went this March (like) the softly glowing plastic electric rendition friend of the flesh and fluffy comfort that mom switched off after/when her cribside lullaby's saw me out like a light.

where loving mothers left off then adept is the higher self now moonlighting as the maternal nurturer . From night lights to night life the anagram of Mother Earth; heart is a part of you/me you and me (intrinsically .)

g xnursery lamp night light of my crib-side x

h But on the same hand / but on the other hand/and on the other hand/and on the same hand, March/the month had gone out like a lamb to the slaughter as ...

i I didn't have a higher dose to hope for to/*or* (xtox) look forward to as my psychiatrist had pretty much said/affirmed when increase interest was expressed, that he already has me at a higher dose than most .

I was at the ceiling of both qtiapine/seroquel and Buspar/bupisperone and with growing concern like a tumor / and with concern growing like a tumor 24 months of (an) unbroken dissociative had metastasized my mind/ in my mind/ my mindscape. /head space / mentalscape. / mental space.

j (with despair and) panicking-scared (and with despair) that there's no way out of this now

k Bc it's not like I had a higher medication dose road ahead of me to be able to believe this could be 'the increase' that i need / that is needed

no

I felt like any/all promise or hope was in the rear view mirror (now) A dosage on cruise control at less milligrams than it would take to go the distance. And unlike those motivational posters this was not about the journey but the destination. I had clocked outstanding mileage but not reached home base(line) . mental exhaustion poured out of/ from my proverbial exhaust (pipe.)

I was stuck in the mud as apparently/ clearly/evidently/it was evident that (on) my current doses weren't enough to get DPDR to budge let alone break/____ and yet I wasn't going to a higher dose of anything

.

l To my dedicated/devoted but mystified (prescribing) doctor I wrote in/my/with gentle desperation . My letter essentially begs the question/begging the question (of) what now? Where do we go from here when

m There is the unfortunate trifecta of both the qtiapine and the Buspar are at their ceiling dosages and I've been on sed ceiling dosages long enough now that they've reached full efficacy ... and yet it all very sadly isnt enough to break through the dissociative ... then what (happens) next ? / then what now and what next?

n write next about interlocking ice packs still hit or miss then write about pampers sadistic thrill .

?transitional something? maybe to the essence of this...

I had come a long way but at/In/by the month of 24/ 24th month there still was a lot (more) to go/recover from ... / I needed to recover from

a) I was no longer romanticizing a conceptualized condoned suicide every time my distorted visual processing laid eyes on the cluster of steamed-up /fogged-up holes of the microwave splash-guard cover .

And I no longer felt like (it was) life (was) yelling at me when a paper towel tear veered from the perforated line(s) and left a small tail attached / intact .

But I was eroticizing the mute button of the remote feeling like I was sticking it to them with sadistic thrill every time/ anytime a diapers commercial sent my ears a baby's shrill (underdeveloped) vocalizations/intonation(s) I shut them right the fuck up with the press of one button/ one press of a button I was a fucking (power)force .

b) And it was morbid meets torrid when my brain anthropomorphized/personified the life size

1.)(dead) bloody (dead) dummy

2.) (foam) dead body (foam replica)

that lie

stage-side of the DJ at that new haunt of my friends and I .

"I would totally sit on that bloody dummy chicks face and writhe myself to climax" hardly counted as sexting when I expressed this to my date. But he wasn't shaken . My antics were becoming expected and not because I was just that dark and twisted but rather Bc at the heart of HSV2 it was just that hard to (conceive of/bring to fruition) ever receiving again .

c) (The)/ (and when) accessory to a microwave no longer made me sensory sick (but) it was (still) hit or miss with the freezer 24 months deep with/in DPDR and it was but incidental if I'd fit the interlocking set of 4 butterfly nesting ice packs back right after a round of dual icing strapped to my (ever-)pressurized head .

|——-|

Next !!!!!!!!!!!! <3

>>incidental if I'd fit the interlocking set of 4 butterfly nesting ice packs back right after a round of dual icing strapped to my (ever-)pressurized head .<<

And the dangling backpack strap that hung down from my over the door hook rack and dragged gingerly across my shoulder/(down my) back every time I walked by/ through the threshold/door frame , no longer submerged/plummeted my mind with/into sinister live action imagery with my body correlating a net reactivity/reaction(s) like I was in one of those walk through haunted mansions jumping startled like a hydra every time (anything grazed me.)

I could have chose(n) to move the backpack the first time but I decided to leave it as a benchmark to gage how strengthened my logical mind would become over the coming months .

And as my sexuality, my (faithful) defender came to the frontlines (of my mind) (as my faithful defender) nocturnal visions of ducking and squatting in a coffin pondering if passionate sex was in the square footage/ perimeter ...

had me/saw me

1.) repurposing and reclaiming _________.

2.) repurposing _______ and in that reclaiming my sovereignty .

and in that, my sovereignty .

Yes, what now and what next the question (reeling) of/about the medication ceiling (reeled) as my astral projection partied so hard

the floor(boards) was/were buckling/ it buckled the floor(boards) . / the floor(boards) buckled. (?(and) the air of splash splash was in every scoop of toasted coconut yogurt and then I / *when I * /*as I* aired my realizations...

(xAnd then I realizedx) maybe it wasn't a drop ceiling of rodent infested droppings but a vaulted cathedral of (*stained glass*/sky light)majesty and (stained glass/*sky light*) possibility/*promise* . I pitched/broached the idea/ concept of adding in

xalternative homeopathyx Eastern medicine to my western treatment plan.

Although it was 24 months in to this sickness and I shamefully and painfully still couldn't remember

Which it was of my 2 babies that was buried on the right .

And/I thought that maybe since as of recently it finally didn't take a pneumonic device to remember (simply) which of the 2 medicines I take at night / it is/was that I take at night ... / *Which it was of the 2 medicines (that) i (only) take at night* ... might it/that be a sign that there was stabilization there; all quiet-iapine on the western front and (that) homeopathy/homeopathic integration to pair could get me (to) where I needed to go most/most to go; home sweet homeostasis/homeostasis sweet homeostasis to where I would regain important memory of/for/like which part of the earth cradled

my (2) loving sweet babies ...

Write next about homeopathy/alternative healing practices Sound bowls , what DID/MPD diagnosis use, hypnotherapy, immersion therapy, bio rhythmic feedback and F42.3 (ICD-10) / DSM-5 300.3 specialist .

|————|

NNEEXXTT

>>to where I would regain important memory of/for/like which part of the earth cradled

my (2) loving sweet babies ...

Write next about homeopathy/alternative healing practices Sound bowls , what DID/MPD diagnosis use, hypnotherapy, immersion therapy, bio rhythmic feedback and F42.3 (ICD-10) / DSM-5 300.3 specialist . <<

. . .

As I (mentally) approached (mentally) the notion of eastern medicine I sensed time might be of the essence for ______________ ________ _____. You see while It had been/was long since the sickness gave me symptoms of hand rigidity and involuntary movement plaguing my fine and less often/sometimes, gross motor functions it was lately that I questioned with reason had the drugs begun giving me side effects of/consistent with consistent of TD/tardev disconesia ?

so innocent and silly it was in childhood the invisible needle and thread act/sewing act that my then best friend regularly improved/presented/perfected and then presented again . Pinching the air above the corner of her upper lip tugging at thin air as she flared that part of her lip/mouth in isolation created/creating the illusion of/that she was sewing her face. Making the rounds of all 4 corners of the mouth before getting astounded wows and claps I wanted to try that ! But the playful magic trick now had me feeling sick as I counted like (pregnancy) contractions the time intervals my lower (left) bottom lip spasmd and twitched . The sooner I could get some exploratory eastern therapy going / exploratory alternative healing practices going the sooner I might put an end to becoming/progressing to a TV TD "actual patient dramatization ." case by going to experimental highs of/with (the) psych meds/psychotropics .

I was sound on incorporating (the) sound bath therapy of (the) crystal singing bowl(s) that would be my primary birthday gift . I had heard about immersion therapy from a friend whose son on the autism spectrum with sensory defensiveness/ sensory processing disorder , benefited . Bio rhythmic feedback was a throwback to the profession of one of my college professors and Art Therapy to help DID/MPD, another . And I did wonder if perhaps being that DID/MPD and that of what I had(;DPDR) were all under the dissociative disorders umbrella , if that whatever treatment course cures them, could (too) me! Should I want a hypnotherapy for Christmas if only a hypnotherapy would do . But above all (else) I felt working with a F42.3 (ICD-10) / DSM-5 300.3 specialist would be chef's kiss of death to my external and internal mess (and sickness) / external mess and internal sickness / internal sickness and external mess .

but I didn't have money/funds for this and Medicaid managed care doesn't/didnt cover (Rx drug) departures from good standard medical practices.

And I couldn't very well keep adding to the (mount kilamajaro) lockers. Most doors would barely close without snagging the dormant avalanche as it was and as for the newest well it's spatial capacity was nearly maxing out. I needed professional help wriggling out of the noose around my life that was 9 units/ units of 9.

(And while) storage lockers (were) the only thing I had (gate) entry codes for and bumper bowling leagues were the only thing I had awards/trophies in... it/that was all about to change . (With this/my story) I was going to go down in history (with this/my story) and ((I) was) (planning) to take everybody up (to cloud 9) with me.

(but if I was to fulfill this/my destiny (of/as (a) literary legacy) I would have to force-heed/wean myself to stop writing (with mania mainlining my Pan-anxious DPDR (thus far)) *I was the red shoes incarnate* *and instead of* dancing I couldn't stop stanzas / I was the red shoes incarnate and instead of I couldn't stop dancing/*(can't stop) dancing/dance(s)*, *it was stanzas ((that) I couldn't stop)* xLife/x *(I was) life, the red pen and the bittersweet mess/ness/nest of it all .

(As) i ogled the garage mess top shelf cobweb tethered structured purple and/with white handled bowlers bag that encased my name-engraved hot pink 8 pounder from when I was not much more than 8 years a youngster there in the concrete cold garage i sank into photographic memory's warmth of what lie beyond that thick silver rusted zipper pull/track. For/*and* just a day back I'd ordered a

(used/new) cool rare retired Brunswick shoe to pair with my childhood relic. (From a time gone by) something borrowed (from a time gone by) something new/used ... I would now be outfitted/*bowling accessorized* / *accessorized for bowling* , full circle to match my/the full circle of the location having been to bowl at that address for prom afterparty and other milestone birthdays like my 18th the new proprietors wouldn't / couldn't

take the magic out of my 8 ball.

from (innocent)(childish) ((the)literal)bumper bowling ('back when')/(then) to (the) (figurative/proverbial) gutter mind strikes now/that lie lay ahead (*figurative*) ...

"and how" I was/was I 'forty and naughty' onboarded/onboarding./! Or

I had figured out 'forty and naughty' was ("and how") onboarded ("and how"!)

and for my wish I wouldn't have to close my eyes tight and blow with all my might that my care team (might) expand(s) to homeopathy and (jesus/st pia de penicilina patron saint of pain suffering and healing) save(s) me

my 4 year major/*collegiate concentration/major* taught me that there are/schooled me on 2 kinds/types of Art Therapy; Clinical analysis based(; Art Therapy) and personal catharsis based; Art As Therapy.

XBc like the mission (statement) of/in/for/at my collegiate concentration; (the school of) Art (as) TherapyX

(And (at) /At) I'd had the epiphany that / 24 months (and/,) 20 chapters into this/of this (invisible)sickness/(invisible) illness I was having the 'aha moment/phenomenon ' (of) epiphany (from the desk of Stephanie) that

1.)my (as) Hail Mary (as) was in the catharsis of this story .

2.)this story was/had been my 'as' Hail Mary .

*3.) my (Hail Mary) 'as' is this story . (::::Hail Mary!::::)

LASTLY

>>*3.) my (Hail Mary) 'as' is this story . (::::Hail Mary!::::) <<

and that there is infact/intrinsically/_______, a 3rd denomination/subset of the Academic subject (of (my) studies/study) from clinical analysis based to personal catharsis based I was uncovering in my comfort number, spiritual _____ based.

Uncle Art As Therapy had taken place.

(? 2 letters off; O and R from/of a(n)alphabetical/namesake anagram of namesake; Arthur

giving me/(was) making me a name for myself;/ as Author . ?)

And/for when (?last name of palindrome?) I (? Last name of palindrome?) woke (up) on a/the numerical anagram of 1234; 4/1/23 from a dream where the word/verb wean was sent to me I knew it was the/sed beloved brother of my mother come to tell me that my book/writing/(writing) piece was done. Just as the word had meant eternal sleep/peace would be won/ just as the word had meant he was about to be one with eternal peace . / *just as the word had meant with eternal peace/sleep he was about to/he was soon to be one* he would soon be one.

From the 4 letter act of compassion/compassionate act in/of the icu room turned tomb to these 4 years later/____ , (from morphine drip to manuscript)(I am receiving you) the word/term (was) about (xreceiving andx) releasing (and making peace (with)) / making peace with release . / release and making peace

(From morphine drip to manuscript)

I am receiving you

?done A compassionate weaning was the last piece of the icu room turned tomb.?

::::::::::::::::::::::::::::::::Notes::::::::::::::::::::::::::::::

LASTLY

>>*3.) my (Hail Mary) 'as' is this story . (::::Hail Mary!::::) <<

and that there is infact/intrinsically/_______, a 3rd denomination/subset of the Academic subject (of (my) studies/study) from clinical analysis based to personal catharsis based I was uncovering in my comfort number, spiritual _____ based.

Uncle Art As Therapy had taken place. And when I woke up on a/the numerical anagram of 1234; 4/1/23 from a dream where the word/verb wean was sent to me I knew it was the/sed beloved brother of my mother come to tell me that my book/writing/(writing) piece was done. Just as the word had meant eternal sleep/peace would be won/ just as the word had meant he was about to be one with eternal peace . / *just as the word had meant with eternal peace/sleep he was about to/he was soon to be one* he would soon be one.

From the 4 letter act of compassion/compassionate act in/of the icu room turned tomb to these 4 years later/____ , (from morphine drip to manuscript)(I am receiving you) the word/term (was) about (xreceiving andx) releasing (and making peace (with)) / making peace with release . / release and making peace

(From morphine drip to manuscript)

I am receiving you

?done A compassionate weaning was the last piece of the icu room turned tomb.?

-2 letters off; O and R from/of a(n)alphabetical/namesake anagram of namesake; Arthur

giving me/making me a name for myself;/ as Author .

-Music war air rises vs bidding war over my book

Write next about my 40 bday (age 27/37 , theFword, "success")

-"it's going to be fascinating to see what I'm like once my

nuero-biochemistry balances out in life again .

But right now I see a clip like this and I find it hot .

Yup... #hashtag reasons I'm prescribed 200mg's of antipsychotics

🫢 lol “

💡 ?Outro?

|———-|

ONE/1

Intro , *outro*, jacket back, _____

[Once upon a time in a little house

1.)on a over the hill birthday/bday,

2.) on a birthday over the hill

divine life timing/divine (life) synchronicity/

Of and numerology and/of a most sacred geometry/ converged with a most sacred geometry (xunbeknownst to mex) and gave this/was giving (xunbeknownst to mex) this

1.)siv/cipher their life's purpose in their master number of 11.

2.) gave

3.) flailing (floundering) life failure / *life-flailing failure*,their master number; 11 there/a life's purpose one in the same with/as Their address.

It was the age of/in the age of *the numerical anagram of/to their parents* and/when spiritual prowess

found them/founded them/

(the spirit of uncle compelled/compels, me and…)

...]

|———|

|———————-|

Two/2

Intro, *outro* ?or JacketBack?

[(While) I will forever wish he was alive (but) I never could have survived (this) if not for him (there) coaching, coaxing, counseling and consoling, coddling and spiritually swaddling me (my beloved/guardian undertaker my/and caretaker) from/of the spiritual world/underworld .

Evermore I will wish he had made it/hadn't passed away but as I wrote today/these pages [the spirit of uncle compels me]; ((wise)terms and)

word knowledge not of my own passes through me/moves moved through me, [the spirit of uncle compels me]

and I ______ believe it is him (angel/uncle)) moving through me passing on;(to) (me) imparting (his) intellect; ((my)guardian) ghost writing my book .]

|—————|

1.) |—————|

Maybe for outro ?

6/1/22

Biden's quote and my maglite strobe (light) performance art piece today.

. . .

Stimuli gone awry

What once made me ((romanticize (my/a) suicide a little bit more))

Cringe feels like/as though my (very) nerve endings were being singed.

cower,

is now/would be(come)

from where I draw my power.

Pain,

from where I source(d) this/a force to be reckoned with. / to bring reckoning .

Where once I couldnt match a/my/the jackets zipper track now I'd (outer)wear backwards a performance art statement blatant that my _______ is no longer latent .

For (I might have died a thousand deaths)

every time/all the times

the light (merely/simply) switched off or/to on (and) delayed sensory processing fought me to the death where I died a thousand.

Now I prop that light out/the f out of light .

Mag lite strobe a mach microphone for a particularly impassioned set of lip sync theatrics. My power tool and how I'm done being played for a fool. The literal spotlight was unwaveringly cruel. But now I'll step into the limelight for

What once would maim my brain i now reclaim; (a) repurposed pain.

rebrand all that has made me feel damned.

((And) this is to be the highlight of my lifeline .)

A fire bird soaring above and beyond place and time/ skyline .

A fire bird soaring above and beyond the/any skyline transcending place/space and time.

**Soaring above and beyond the/any skyline a fire bird transcending place/space and time. **

A Euphemism/euthanize

|———————————-|

2.) |———————————-|

'THE HIDDEN TRACK' OR INTRO OR **OUTRO*** OR

-------------.

Assuage a holy (inner)war(; inner) ...

I almost died and now I am called/I feel called to relive everything/all (that) I almost left behind .

(and while there is inclusion (of you) there is not /there exists not, exclusion of others .)

commitment/monogamous

feels/feeling synonymous with smothered .

-when you've almost died but didn't, you subsequently feel all (that) you could've/almost left behind but didn't . /

. . .

When you've almost died/faced your own demise by destiny or design

It is (of) my experience that it gives way to

(the) magnificence of feeling/a certain magnificence ...

The connective camaraderie of a shared hs graduating class year (suddenly) becomes all that you feel about each and every person you share this earth with... from baby boomers to I gen ... we are all here for/of the 21st century life-expiration year(; a graduation most intimate/sacred.)

And when you really feel that/find that finite in your bones you understand (deeply) / you experience, everyone as intimacy/everyone (you see) is/as intimacy.

Sexy.

Intrinsically all brothers, mothers, lovers , sisters and ancestors (we belong to the same end game.)

(?so let's work hard at how we play?)

Civilians and celebrities we are of the same life/mortal/mortality

time-share liberties; mortalities, fatalities in a shared century /In an overlapping century / (all) In overlapping centuries .

Tbc !

|———-|

[Intro, outro, CJD5, ____,____

(And/because) In the populous words/phrase of everybody "life is (too) short" .

So in the golden Age of grotesque testament of Marilyn Manson

"It's a dirty world, reich, say what you like"]

[Add in/to outro

Where I say about life is (too) short

So if you crave (to eat) a cupcake with/on your one/only 15 minute work break (do it)/ more power to ya; do it

And if you want to host a sex party of musical chairs; dare.

And if you want not to "take it to the grave" spring Swedish death clean/ Swedish death spring clean, the/those skeletons in your closet; reveal/care for/share your truth/bare your truth/bare your soul/come to a truce/ reveal your truce .]

|——-|

|——————-|

|———————————-|

|——————————————-|

8/4/22 ?intro? ?outro? Or something else?

And What is life but/if not, a succession of loss

Where in which if you're one of the lucky ones

It comes with (the) grace of sequence/sequential order .

Grandparents pass and as they depart (it) impart(s) on us an imprint of emergency preparedness to be able to handle this, the next death, our parents, with just a little less flailing.

Then comes the time in life where not hearing from a cherished childhood friend ,

1.)means you have to wonder if (it means)/(it's Bc) they've seen life's end .

2.) might mean (it's that) they've seen life's end.

(And) It is there and then that you realize you would give anything just to get back go back to the years where wondering/worrying that they're avoiding you was at the top of the tier /was top tier .

Where sticker books meant oilies and fuzzies not stapled proverbial wax glossed pages of visitor and inpatient, hospital passes/badges amassing .

(?so let's work hard at how we play?)

we are all/what we have of (a/this) shared space .

|————————————|

. . .

[Intro, outro, CJD5, ____,____

(And/because) In the populous words/phrase of everybody "life is (too) short" .

So in the golden Age of grotesque testament of Marilyn Manson

"It's a dirty world, reich, say what you like"]

[Add in/to outro

Where I say about life is (too) short

So if you crave (to eat) a cupcake with/on your one/only 15 minute work break (do it)/ more power to ya; do it

And if you want to host a sex party of musical chairs; dare.

And if you want not to "take it to the grave" spring Swedish death clean/ Swedish death spring clean, the/those skeletons in your closet; reveal/care for/share your truth/bare your truth/bare your soul/ come to a truce/ reveal your truce .]

|—–-|

3.) |—————————-|

Intro maybe ? Or outro maybe? Or something else? ?CJD#2?

?Or don't put it anywhere at all/don't put it in?

To curb/circumvent a suicidal mind, (self/life) loathing and promote (self/life) loving

I had to create a world/a narrative in which I don't view dissociative as a bad thing/ as such a negative thing. To survive it I would have to. And so was born, (the empowerment project)

my book/my memoir motive/motivation . If I could achieve something great in/from/amidst all this then (on principle) there would be less room (for me) to hate it (and want to end it/me.) .

Unwilling to live out a 'the rest of my natural life-running-it's-course till the end of my days ' scenario if it is to be like this / if I am to be like this …

(?but the more I filled my days with enjoyable things (and) ?)

but with me (also) was the/an inner/intrinsic (and therefor) integral knowing (that) the bigger build I gave my life/ the bigger I built my life the longer I would/might be willing to stay (in it.) ?(;the/a lesser of 2 evils)?

((And) this(, my write or die,)is to be the highlight of my lifeline .)

?(this is/has been… my write or die)?

A fire bird soaring above and beyond place and time/ skyline .

A fire bird soaring above and beyond the/any skyline transcending place/space and time.

. . .

**Soaring above and beyond the/any skyline a fire bird transcending place/space and time. **

?(this is/has been... my write or die)?

A Euphemism/euthanize

|———————————-|

?(this is/has been... my write or die)?

|———————————-|

|————————————|

- ?I think or I know this

goes in 1.) or 3.) of outro?

?OrMaybeItCouldBeInIntro?

With/about/similar to Biden thing

write about how I harnessed/channeled a pandemonium of racing thought(s)-(mania) to creative writing content/output.

I would turn this (outpour ing) (of) neuro (white) noise (outpour) into something I couldn't abhor .

. . .

***voice(s) so insessant intensive it was the loudest I was being (cognitively) crowded when there was no music on to mask it[[; (the) neuro noise]] The internal over-stimuli inundation would break the seal of/from my lips where words would slip uncontrollably/unbeknownst to me .

Boring down on me '24/7' a pandemonium; (of/a) racing thought mania; [[neuro noise]] a cacophonous discordance[[;neuro noise]] the last straw[[;neuro noise]] I'd reshape/spin this that I rue from abhorrence to (a) [[(silken)]] golden [[(silken)]] creative writing outpour if it's the last thing (that) I do/rue .***

|————————|

|—————————|

7/8/22 (Came2meDuringFitness)

Intro or outro or CJD#2

(It was) an unauthorized purchase

1.)Outsourced and sold out from under me my soul to the devil now held at ransom

2.) my soul outsourced and sold out from under me to the devil

Was now held/being held at ransom

. . .

3.) my soul outsourced and sold to the devil out from under me was now (being) held at ransom

After the word ransom in 1.)2.)3.) ...

(And I hoped, bless, I pray that) The emotional royalties and /the, enrichment/intangible riches of telling/sharing my story , (enrichment), might buy it back .

Left to ransack my personality for familiarity ...

Where had, my gentle essence gone/the essence of my gentleness gone/ my essence of gentleness gone

the intrinsic self was now (bathory)-bathed in (black) light and (what's morose) I liked it (that way.)

The notion of Flight remained only as a descriptor for/of the motion of the Stephoenix ascension

It was fight or fight response now that was the re-write and I wasn't backing down I wouldn't bow out cower and cowtow

(And)/ (for) sometimes I (just) wanted to shout loud come at me ! (Just) come the F at me ! Just you try it !

entice incite it would excite ...

I had endured/lived through hell (and) (only) time would tell if/whether

1.)I was better for it or bitter (for it/Bc of it)

2.)I was better or bitter for it .

(And In the interim (of) /and in the/this purgatory there was no flight left in me.

Only (stone cold) stark raving/raging mad(ness)

Only (stone cold) stark raving rage .

|——

My mind (was) a (thorn-) wooded (thorned/thorn-) shroud of darkness and in that forest I couldn't/can't see from the trees I could be seen/sighted with staple gun (as) my weedwacker feverishly/fervent and febrile/ febrile with mania/______ ,

branding the bark with flyers "lost soul" if found its return would bestow me with/bestow upon me a (most) generous reward; humanity.

(And then I could lose this insanity).

self-shaming blaming (and) mind-maiming/ my mind maiming (me) , (And) I couldn't help but think I (had) brought on some of this insanity; invited it in

Where oh where, did it begin (and end) /to begin-(again) .

|————————————————-|

Intro/outro , CJD2, chap 8

soliciting authorization then misusing/abusing/using the (psych) medication (to induce apathy) in/as wayward/desperate derivation I won't do myself dirty like that again;

(Send it! / sent !) I'm clean 16 months synonymous with (clean) for life .

Help Facilitate Suppress/suppression of, / repression of / replace/replacement (of) the parts of me with (the) Rx side effect(s) (;/of apathy) that don't have a place and need to inhabit space in our partnership

I am no longer here for this !

(I) won't (synthesize) a new personality to better suit/compliment yours . (I) won't (synthetically) alter my personality to better suit/ compliment yours .

(I can't .)

And if that's/ drug induced apathy /synthesized apathy/ *augmented personality traits* *(is) what it takes* then that/it, is a relationship we/one need(s) to respectfully forsake gracefully bow-out; renounce .

no more (surreptitiously) repurposing anti-anxiety's benzodiazepines and SSRI's/anti depresents as personality suppressants . That's not a drug class and at last/alas I will not wield it as one . Won't reshape intended purpose to escape(ism) .

<3

A full-bodied; robust / a robust full-bodied personality curtailed

this my great epic derail lest it serve you save you; a cautionary share/tale .

|––––––––––-|

Outro ? Or _______ ?

. . .

From thurs sept 15th 2022 convo with a dear childhood friend. (I think or I know it was at night)

"I wish I had my shit together"

It's like you always hear of people that were busy climbing the corporate ladder so they didn't have time to have a family

Or they aren't crazy-successful but they have a family

Or they don't have a family but they've traveled the world

Or they haven't traveled the world Bc they were busy building their family …

The unspoken understanding an/of (a) (an) (implied) demanding (implied) multiple choice Family, career, travel … that commands me reprimands me for not being able to fill in the bubble much less

make sure my mark is heavy and dark /

"Make sure your mark is heavy and dark "

People usually have achieved one or more of these societal norms/societal standards by my age …

And the reason for the one or more they haven't (achieved) is Bc they were too busy (achieving) actualizing the other 'one' or more …

. . .

But then it's like ...

Here's me ... I've managed to establish none (of the above .) I have multiple choice d/e to show for my life; none of the above .

?So if this is what you were getting at about yourself ...

I completely and deeply understand the feeling?

These are some thoughts divulged that have gone through my mind about myself throughout time . Lodged (a) dissonance in my head over the years of mentally trying to contend with this difficult feeling/reality/reeling .

(But) Relationship ocd, imposter syndrome and inferiority complex; a side ... if mental illness didnt give me a/the/my number two pencil I should hardly begrudge myself for

not being able to/ the/a struggle to follow the/this stencil . The life-paralysis I have felt .

(And) With going through (this) the sickness I'm in/ I've been in, for 18 months (of) now; this ... this (the) life-stealing

(The) chronic dissociative (state) I figuratively and literally can't get very far still/as afflicted with these deficits (still) can't drive my car I was not meant for this destined for this would/I'd wish remission of this apon my arch enemy but in this/the/my dark came a/the/my character arc festooned my mind with what lessened this the hard-pressed festering feeling of life-sequence inadequacy

'Invariably Ever since' this medical/mental malady 'invariably I won't' hurt myself with this/the fallacy

Travel/family/career Upset . I don't think much about it , don't take on the same 'discontent' surrounding it . Won't 'beat myself up ' for my life station or lack there of (rather .) DPDR trapped in/locked in imagination I'm not of the/this earths/earthly rotation/equation my mind a

demi-permanent vacation from

?(?; procreation, vocation , ______ ?)?

I give myself some grace ... finally I've found it.

After hearing (it) to no end widespread on/in social media self-care/self-help, threads (and after failing it to no avail) (I finally / alas / at last) *I finally said hey! "I can talk to myself as you/I would a friend ! " *

(I talk to/ treat myself as I/you would a friend *(with) gentleness, compassion and slack (to lend/ to expend/to extend) .* forgiving to ______. Not a character attack (to expend .)

Taking up space to share my story 'it's giving: grace' May you all search out; discover what will (too) allow you to save (such) face (too) set your own pace (find) your multiple choice d/e; other . (As I've learned it's something suffering (and survival/and recovering) can (sometimes) recover / uncover.

/As I've learned (sometimes) suffering and survival can (sometimes) bring/drive/revival .

[Intro, outro, CJD5, ____,____

(And/because) In the populous words/phrase of everybody "life is (too) short" .

So in the golden Age of grotesque testament of Marilyn Manson

“It’s a dirty world, reich, say what you like”]

|————-|

ONE/1

Intro , *outro*, jacket back, _____

[Once upon a time in a little house

1.)on a over the hill birthday/bday,

2.) on a birthday over the hill

divine life timing/divine (life) synchronicity/

Of and numerology and/of a most sacred geometry/ converged with a most sacred geometry (xunbeknownst to mex) and gave this/was giving (xunbeknownst to mex) this

1.)siv/cipher their life’s purpose in their master number of 11.

2.) gave

3.) flailing (floundering) life failure / *life-flailing failure*,their master number; 11 there/a life’s purpose one in the same with/as Their address.

It was the age of/in the age of *the numerical anagram of/to their parents* and/when spiritual prowess

found them/founded them/

(the spirit of uncle compelled/compels, me and…)

…]

|———|

|———————-|

Two/2

Intro, *outro* ?or JacketBack?

[(While) I will forever wish he was alive (but) I never could have survived (this) if not for him (there) coaching, coaxing, counseling and consoling, coddling and spiritually swaddling me (my beloved/guardian undertaker my/and caretaker) from/of the spiritual world/underworld .

Evermore I will wish he had made it/hadn't passed away but as I wrote today/these pages [the spirit of uncle compels me]; ((wise)terms and)

word knowledge not of my own passes through me/moves moved through me, [the spirit of uncle compels me]

and I ______ believe it is him (angel/uncle)) moving through me passing on;(to) (me) imparting (his) intellect; ((my)guardian) ghost writing my book .]

|—————|

[Intro, outro, CJD5, ____,____

(And/because) In the populous words/phrase of everybody "life is (too) short" .

So in the golden Age of grotesque testament of Marilyn Manson

"It's a dirty world, reich, say what you like"]

[Add in/to outro

Where I say about life is (too) short

So if you crave (to eat) a cupcake with/on your one/only 15 minute work break (do it)/ more power to ya; do it

And if you want to host a sex party of musical chairs; dare.

And if you want not to "take it to the grave" spring Swedish death clean/ Swedish death spring clean, the/those skeletons in your closet; reveal/care for/ share your truth/bare your truth/bare your soul/ come to a truce/ reveal your truce .]

|———|

Add to outro (maybe put near cupcake stuff)

and if (it's that/so (that)) your personality (archetype)/*character* (archetype) is so *(geode) multi-faceted*/*(archetype) dynamic*, that you could be seen rolling up to Whole Foods blasting Manson on/for/in a run for of/a *6pack (of) wellness shots*, run/restock (run) , / *on* in among a 6 pack restock (of) wellness shots *(run)* ,

don't fight or flight it; invite it .

|———|

?outro?

Just let me see the pocketbooks one more/one last time

. . .

(And if like a morbid/morose reissue/new or second edition, of "if you give a mouse a cookie") (if you) you've had a running lifelong inside joke with your/a best friend/*bestie*, that right before you die you'll ask to see the pocketbooks one last time (then) own it /

(you better) recognize (it.) . Own it,

xrecognize this higher-self, insight and own itx

?(I did.)?

pocketbooks bought

through it all /for the duration of this/ (all) through is what did stall willingness to off myself . As many take it one day at a time I took it one bag at a time. I couldn't commit to staying with the living. I certainly couldn't take a mortgage out on mortality but by way/contract, of lease I couldn't commit to (the) living, either . if I was expecting though(…a baggie that is) I always wanted to stay long enough to see it's/the (bags) (blessed) arrival; be it's receiving blanket (arm) swaddle .

1.)Smell that new baggie scent/smell/essence.

2.) nothing like that new baggie smell .

Bag by bag/(taking it) one bag at a time, / (taking it) one due date at a time,

(demise/death/mercy kill/______) -delaying amassed/amounted to staying .

|——|

. . .

|——-|

This needs to be the absolute closing line/passage/stanza…

1stOr2nd

(But) come at me life (and) I'll write; my claim to sane .

I'll make lit reign / watch me make lit reign. / watch as I make lit reign.

1stOr2nd

Outro or jacket back ?or intro?

(?-if the pen is mightier than the sword

(Then) I've come to take it all?)

*My namesake means crown, my birthstone; ice and with an element(al) (sign) of fire

don't want a return to what/who, ive been; this is (a) metamorphosis.

(And) from the/a life/*time*of which I/I;/ Stephanie Dianne Selles, writhed (the) Stephoenix Diamond will /rise/arise. *

|———|

::

Notes (and I think or maybe I know I took these notes from 'intro')

|————-|

my MD wasn't able to guarantee me that the vaccine won't affect my condition .

And I need to know beyond a shadow of a doubt that I haven't put anything in my system that could affect my brain's ability to get out of dissociative ...

Bc, (insert name here) ***if I am to be *incapable* of coming out of dissociative that's not a life timeline I'm willing to live out a natural life span in .***

So it is *imperative* that I know I'm not doing / I haven't done anything that could affect my ability to get out of this

|——————-|

12/26/22

With as much of life as I've seen

Carefree could/would, never be me (again.)

I value character traits consistent with intensity far more anyway .

don't want a return to what I've been; this is (a) metamorphosis . And from the life of which I writhed

Stephoenix diamond will rise

Outro or jacket back ?or intro?

(? -if the pen is mightier than the sword

(Then) I've come to take it all ?)

*My namesake means crown, my birthstone; ice and with an element(al) (sign) of fire

don't want a return to what/who, ive been; this is (a) metamorphosis.

(And) from the/a life/*time*of which I writhed Stephoenix Diamond will /rise/arise. *

|———|

|————————|

Note: have not inserted this in yet !!!!

11/4/22 listening to album GloriaRegali and working out

Put in Intro, outro

-if the pen is mightier than the sword

(Then) I've come to take it all

With The crown as my namesake's origin …tbc !

?(and) an elemental sign of fire this stephoenix rebirth will see to it (that) there is no dearth only (life(s)) purpose unearthed .

(Soaring) Scorching (soaring) wings will/that, scintillate (and soar)

will bring the dirge … tbc !!!

|———|

💡 ?JacketBack?

|—————————-|

Intro or jacket

What should have been a formality name sign

1.) was instead the onset

2.) instead was the onset

Of (what would (prove to) be) 200 more plus/upwards of 200 (more) things/evils to come that all in an instant were/would be held at a distance (by) ;my mind/brain about knowing how to do /*not knowing how to do things* (or why) ... just vying/pining for the time it would end and (for ____ months) never knowing when .

my psyche not knowing why or when it would end just vying/pining for it to .

I was ____ (years old/years of age) when all in an instant I was rendered (with) trouble(d)/struggled to remember how I/to sign my name .

and didn't know why .

I couldn't remember /I wasn't sure, (how to make), my signature .

Wasn't sure how to sign my name and I didn't know why , was the first

|———————-|

|—————|

Intro, outro, ?jacket? ,

(Long ago) Once Upon a palm reading A wise witch once said your life line is exceptionally / especially/unusually long but (has/with) something I've never seen before there is /(it has) a break (in) it veers off before it continues/resumes/resuming/continuing (long) (strong) . she mused what it/this could be , mean ...

(well I think) it is my belief that the engender reveal is (in) these (pages); past _____ months; (these pages)

A bosom friend once said/led (with)... so what was worse (Stephanie) the (2019) losses/deaths (of 2019) / the 3 death succession) or (the) dissociation (of ____ months)/ (of 2021) / __ year dissociative consecutive / or the consecutive __ year ... / or the ___ year dissociative consecutive / or the ___yr consecutive to/of (the) dissociative

to which I replied/at a loss to find which was less than/ which was the lesser "it's moldy apples and moldy oranges . " (to which) I replied.

1.)With this book as my (forbidden) gift(forbidden)fruit gift basket ...

2.) this book is an offering, my/a (forbidden) gift (forbidden)fruit gift basket (of my) case) . ?metaphor(iCal)?

3.) with this book I beseech you to accept my (forbidden) fruit basket (case) .

(As) a piece offering ...)

In hopes that /of (a) sharing my story/*bounty* might bequeath (me) myself and others...(xwithx) *peace.*

(But)/ (and), come at me life (and) I'll write; my claim to sane .

I'll make lit reign / watch me make lit reign. / watch as I make lit reign.

|————|

???I think or I know this is also in outro; so i have to decide; here? Or outro? , for it. ???

The absolute/ very END should be this ...

1stOr2ndOr3rd

(But)/ (and), come at me life (and) I'll write; my claim to sane .

I'll make lit reign / watch me make lit reign. / watch as I make lit reign.

|————|

1stOr2ndOr3rd

(?-if the pen is mightier than the sword

(Then) I've come to take it all ?)

*My namesake means crown, my birthstone; ice and with an element(al) (sign) of fire

don't want a return to what/who, ive been; this is (a) metamorphosis.

(And) from the/a life/*time*of which I writhed Stephoenix Diamond will /rise/arise. *

1stOr2ndOr3rd

This is the/a story of

how I turned/made/turning (my) *abuser,* (into) (my) *muse* , to survive.

May this read reach (more/fellow/other) ‘misfortunately misunderstoods’ afflicted with, impacted by dissociative .

The End.

|~~~notes to (prospectively) work with~~~|

Taken from cover letter to Author, Laura A_____.

(For) It would prove to be my last memory/tangible-experience of this earthly existence . as just a few/a couple/2 days more would see me lost to (the) pan-anxious dissociative state of the derealization/depersonalization that has been my abuser, my muse

my captor/and captur (24-7) for 21 months *since*/ long (now) (since.) .

|———-|

Add in for CJD5 ?check?

(???taken from cover letter to Author. Laura A______???)

(the) pan-anxious dissociative state of the derealization/depersonalization that has been my abuser, my muse

my captor/and captur (24-7) for 21 months since/ long (now) (since.) .

|———|

. . .

The people I would/had endeavor(Ed) to reach with this read . The advocate I would be for/to the misfortunately misunderstood afflicted with this shit/ dissociative .

Bad ass boss author

And coach/advocate of/*for* the

1.)Misfortunately misunderstood

(Afflicted with DPDR)

(DPDR neuro-divergents)

misunderstood less fortunate .

|——-|

This is the/a story of (a misfortunately misunderstood afflicted with/ impacted by dissociative .) (And) how I turned/made, my abuser (into) my muse , to survive (it) .

May this read reach (more) misfortunately misunderstoods afflicted with, impacted by dissociative .

!!!!!!! Use this

|——-|

This is the/a story of how I turned/made, my abuser, (into) my muse , to survive.

May this read reach (more) misfortunately misunderstoods afflicted with, impacted by dissociative .

!!!!!!!!

This story is for more/the misfortunately misunderstood(s)afflicted with / impacted by dissociative .

And this story is of/(and) this is the story of… how I turned/made my abuser my muse to survive .

AUTHOR BIO

At the helm of the hell that befell me may or may not be a long-covid origin .

At 40 years old, I earnestly don't take anything for granted in life now after what I've endured in these past 3+ years. I no longer even see executive function of bodily systems as a given anymore, but a gift, as for a time, mine was (grossly) compromised.

As it has come into some speculation, that I may have "neurological long Covid", when reading my memoir or sample passages, and trying to get in touch with the heart of my story, this is to be considered. I feel my memoir is a story of a journey that people living with the difficult impact of neurological long Covid, could relate to, benefit from but what's more, find the rare comfort in that is needed, currently underrepresented and that I speak to.

About and from within a 24+ month 24/7 chronic dissociative state of depersonalization/derealization (DPDR), with pan-anxious features and crippling iterations of synesthesia, I was writing. I composed this memoir so as to have a singular tendril of tether to my mortal existence and the earthly experience; to life's continuation. For, to circumvent a suicidal ideation-flucuating mind, I would have to create an inner-narrative and outer-world in which dissociative wasn't an abuser but my muse. To survive it I would have to and it was in doing this that I found metamorphosis.

This manuscript is my write or die for as a cathartic expression of self-preservation I've written an insightful, immersive, introspective and interoceptive memoir of this entire unthinkable sickness.

As you can hopefully see, I have every inner-calling and intention to continue writing books throughout my life, and in that very special way, share myself and reach others .

When I become published, So much has yet to unfurl through the questions readers will compose in emails, raise their hands in readings to ask and so on.

Where a book ends the story has only just begun. And that, I find to be one of the most beautiful things about memoir.

I deeply beseech you as I profoundly need you to help me get my all-important neurological anomaly survival and transformation story onto the shelves of bookstores and into the lives of those in need of the voice I speak.

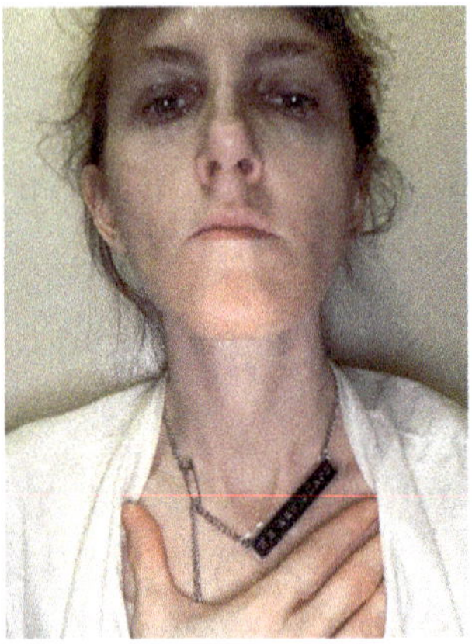

(self-portrait of) a survivor haggard from (this/the) battle.

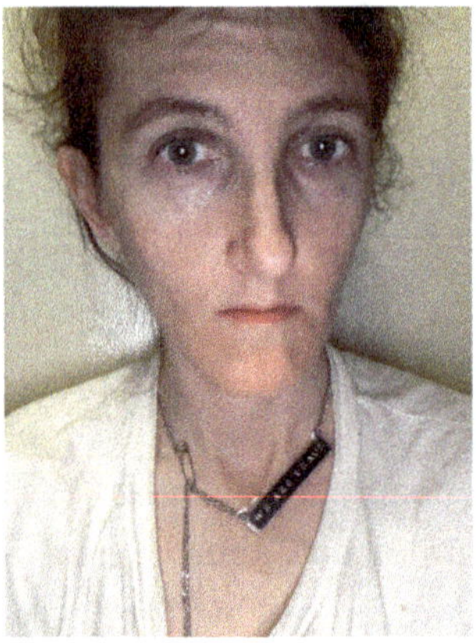

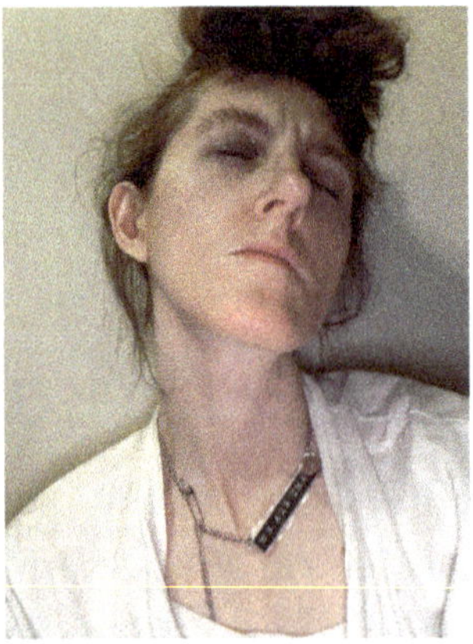

(12/23/23 at 11:09 pm)
*Marilyn Manson necklace.

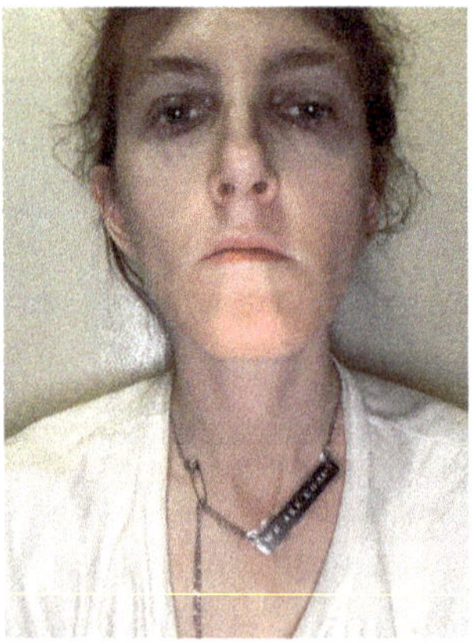

|——————————————————————————-|
my dadd…
first name
was Steven.
middle name
was Warren .
…My beloved mother's regaling of
Fathers Day 1983… how when she found out she was pregnant with me, she, on the endearing holiday, wished my Dadd a Happy Father's Day and when he said
"what do you mean-why?"
She told him
"well, Bc you're going to be a father!"
" If it's a girl can we name her Stephanie ! "
For as long as I can remember, I've known
the short but sweet story of how his joyous exclamation of wanting me to have/be the female version of his own namesake, were the first words out of his mouth !
But what I didn't come into the knowledge of until so recently, that it was right before the printing of this book
(a pleasant surprise/ a pleasant shock (rock) … is that
Had I been born a boy I was to be named
Brian Warren ______.
which, means I would've shared a first name with the frontman of Marilyn Manson; Brian and had an anagram middle name of Manson's last name; Warner.
I found this to be especially significant considering I had never listened to his music a day in my life until my illness and here I am (now/today) wanting to
pay immeasurable homage (with this book) to how this hard*core*rocker was such a*core*part of me making it through.
|——————————————————————————|

"Going From

A Victim Of Circumstance, Survivor, Now Warrior

You're More Than A Fighter

You're A Fucking Miracle."

-Sentiment of The Wise Witch-

I am receiving you, uncle art, I am receiving you
From Morphine Drip To Manuscript
I am receiving you, daddy, I am receiving you

www.ingramcontent.com/pod-product-compliance
Lightning Source LLC
Chambersburg PA
CBHW052129070526
44585CB00017B/1754
* 9 7 8 1 6 3 7 7 7 6 8 7 2 *